Computer Innovations in Marketing

Contributors

Roman R. Andrus	Robert A. Hammond
Joel N. Axelrod	Leslie M. Harris
Jonathan Bayliss	Thomas C. Jones
Louis Cohen	Evelyn Konrad
E. J. Sandon Cox	Philip Kotler
Robert D. Dahle	A. R. Solomon
Herbert W. Davis	Arthur B. Toan, Jr.
Emanuel H. Demby	Allan Vesley
Franz Edelman	Art Youmans, Jr.
John W. Garofalo	Lawrence F. Young
Peter J. Gray	Tom Teng-pin Yu

Computer Innovations in Marketing

Evelyn Konrad and Others

American Management Association, Inc.

International standard book number: 0–8144–5211–6
Library of Congress catalog card number: 70–113877

FIRST PRINTING

Preface

IN TODAY'S BUSINESS WORLD, which is changing dramatically behind its institutional facade, the concept of "the computer in marketing" is on the brink of becoming archaic. Indeed, the fact that the "computer in marketing" description is threatening to become dated long before literally thousands of marketing applications for the computer have been categorized—let alone discussed, analyzed, and digested—may in itself be a measure of the vast impact that the computer has already had on the economic process during this decade.

The reason the computer in marketing concept has undergone such a rapid transition from the embryonic stage to obsolescence is rather complicated. The hard-to-grasp progress of computer capabilities and systems has already begun to blur the traditional and institutionalized functional divisions within U.S. management. It is not a radical prediction to forecast that the 1970s will witness an organizational shake-up in the corporate establishment that is predicated on blurring the unnatural lines drawn among the production, financial, and marketing functions through a more encompassing view of the total management decision-making process.

There's a dichotomy implicit in this prediction due to the simple fact that present-day management has barely scratched the surface of the enormous potential of computer applications to the marketing function as it is currently defined. Furthermore, management's education in this area is severely handicapped by the staggering abundance of data that pours uncontrolled and un-sifted over executives' desks.

Nor is the problem one of management lethargy, if attendance at diverse seminars, registrations for diverse computer courses, sale of books dealing with centralized or tangential topics in the field, and frantic clipping of and interest in business and trade press articles are any barometer of the near-universal eagerness to learn. One of the problems may well be the continuing communications gap between the computer world and the business establish-ment—a gap transcending jargon and education and unfortunately caused by the different qualifications for professionalism in either world.

Simply stated, this means that today's management executive has no problem in finding information about computers in marketing or in any other function. However, this information tends to fall into one of three categories that make the knowledge difficult, if not impossible, to apply, not only to the previously unperceived problems that lend themselves to computer solu-tions but even to the everyday problems he faces in his daily business opera-tions. Thus the information avalanche concerning computerization can be grouped as:

- Generalized management guidelines are all too often so couched in truisms and platitudes that they do not serve any enlightening pur-pose.
- Technicians' data about computer hardware have the same relevance to problem solving as the typewriter had to literature.
- Mathematics-based systems analyses speak to the heart of the opera-tions research community but leave the top management decision-maker cowed but unhelped.

Yet the challenge to the managements of today's corporate giants is more urgent and immediate than may seem apparent on the surface if the leaders in today's industries are to maintain their edge against the expected onslaught of more flexible and less institutionalized teams of managers coming up from the interdisciplinary education of the graduate business school community in the United States or from the less institutionalized industries that have grown up since post-World War II both in the United States and abroad. If the threat seems negligible to today's business establishment, it is only because of the false security generated by knowledge that the great capital accumula-tions necessary to become a factor in most industries today are hard to come by without the momentum of an ongoing business. However, as the U.S.

economy continues to move rapidly toward a service rather than a predominantly manufacturing economy, inventiveness and methodology may speed the rise of a new breed of entrepreneurs.

During the 1960s, entrepreneurial energies propelled into the limelight principally new names in existing industries and in technologically based new industries. The 1970s may bring into the foreground a combined entrepreneurial and managerial talent challenging existing industries not because of the obsolescence of the technology in these industries but rather because of the obsolescence of their business methodology and decision-making process. The past two decades have witnessed the birth and growth of such technologically based industries—aerospace, to mention just one. The 1950s and 1960s have seen challenges to the entrenched food industry from technological innovations (such as frozen foods in boilable pouches) to the marketing innovations of bakery-goods-priced Sara Lee and Pepperidge Farm products.

In service industries, the malaise of the sluggish and entrenched insurance industry has found temporary solace in shotgun marriages with the younger and more consumer-oriented mutual funds industry. But to date, the basic premises of these industries have been unchallenged.

It is feasible and even likely that the new entrepreneur of the 1970s with a managerial understanding of the computer may be able to harness its vast, untapped capabilities to pose completely fresh challenges to the existing manufacturing and service industry establishments, unhampered by the functional and organizational rigidities that retard the contributions that the computer's technology could make even today.

If there is a moral in this encompassing indictment of current management decision making, it is simply that knowledge of the impact of the computer on the marketing function to date is necessary not only to marketing management across industries but to financial management, production management, and top corporate management. The scope of the marketing function, even as it is defined within today's institutionalized organizations, is very broad. The time, cost, and risk factors implicit in major computer applications are so encompassing that the most modest and seemingly isolated computer applications to individualized marketing functions are usually felt in management decision-making areas that are separated only on organization charts.

The burden of understanding falls just as heavily on the once-isolated, ivory-tower community of computer technicians, systems specialists, operations research experts, and the army of new professionals spawned by the computer technology who were previously restricted to disciplines apparently unrelated to management decision-making responsibilities. Unless these men fully comprehend the range of perceived or upcoming problems in management decision making, their potential contribution to the business establishment will be doomed to remain unfunded and unsupported by corporate management and may well be relegated to the turgid pages of learned journals for academic appreciation by their own peers.

No single book can solve the communications and education problems implicit in this discussion. This book has a far more limited purpose: It has only three objectives.

It discusses some of the ways in which different companies and industries are now using computer applications to solve a diversity of major and minor marketing problems. It attempts to view these applications critically in terms of their effect on individual companies and sometimes on a specific industry or on the total marketing function. It seeks to encourage meaningful dialogue between managers whose problems require solutions and computer professionals who can help implement these solutions.

If this book accomplishes this final objective, it may make a worthwhile contribution. If it fulfills the first two, then the author is, of course, indebted to the knowledgeable contributors from industry and the academic world who have taken the time to share their experience and thoughts through the chapters they have contributed to this book.

In addition, the research, correspondence, and painstaking follow-through required to bring these very diverse authors together in this book would have been impossible without the continuing help and assistance of Ann Zeleny.

Evelyn Konrad

Contents

Part Three

Marketing Research and New Product Development

Part Four

Pricing

Part Five

Advertising and Promotion

PART ONE

Management and the Computer

1

An Appraisal
of the Computer in Marketing

Evelyn Konrad

ON THE SURFACE, an appraisal of the impact of the computer in marketing bears some similarity to an appraisal of the audience in a movie theater. A theater can be judged to be half-full or half-empty, depending upon the perspective of the perceiver.

By the same token, the impact of the computer on the marketing function can be judged to be considerable if one takes into account the multiple manipulations of data which EDP makes possible and performable. Computer impact on marketing management decision making has been somewhat less considerable from many other viewpoints for a number of reasons. Before analyzing the individual areas where significant computer applications to marketing problems have been developed, it is important to discuss both the intrinsic and the exogenous limitations of computer-based answers to marketing problems today and perhaps in the future.

Marketing Problems

Compared with the use of data processing in finance (where billing and paying is an obvious EDP function) and in production, the use of data processing in marketing is voluminous and widespread. Since marketing relies on tons of research data—sales reports, market surveys, shelf counts, advertising ratings, to cite just a handful—there are obvious opportunities for churning these facts and figures into a multiplicity of combinations.

As often as not, this electronic manipulation of information can yield more valuable analytic tools and better bases for decisions than the previously undigested or raw data would. On the other hand, the excessive analysis of figures, when based on doubtful research techniques and questionable methodologies, can just as dangerously distort and overemphasize by endowing a shoddy input with a reliability that it does not merit.

These data-processing problems are more acute in the marketing function than they might be in production or processing, for example. The data used in the production or manufacturing process are the result of scientific measurements and therefore may have, at times, greater intrinsic validity and reliability than the data produced by some behavioral science research which provides insights into the marketing process.

This danger is intrinsic to marketing research. For example, sophisticated sampling and statistical techniques alone do not guarantee a valuable and meaningful research product. There are, within marketing research, too many additional opportunities for doubtful techniques that can distort the facts rather than enlighten the management commissioning the study. Questions that lead the respondent or introduce a diversity of biases can produce as mathematically precise a tabulation as another marketing research study employing far more prejudice-free techniques.

It is easy enough to say that these problems of interpretation and judgment concerning the reliability, validity, and meaningfulness of a marketing research study have always been with us. However, there is little question that EDP has been something of a mixed blessing in this area. Simply because it is now possible to combine and submit to complex statistical analyses a broad variety of figures and findings, it becomes all the more tempting to throw everything into the hopper on the mistaken assumption that precise figures from shoddy research, when combined with other statistical information in the purifying process of EDP, will somehow assume a value that they did not have on their own.

The problem of computer usage in marketing becomes infinitely more acute when operations research techniques are used as aids in marketing decision making. By definition, operations research is the use of mathematical and scientific methods to solve problems of systems or organizations through better analysis of the interaction of the various parts.

Unfortunately, this noble objective collides head-on with some formidable obstacles within the marketing process. How, for example, do you quantify the impact of one particular television commercial as compared with another, putting aside those more easily measurable variables such as size and demographics of the audience reached? In other words, how do you measure the effectiveness of the creative content of the message? Let us complicate this question a little more. How do you quantify the difference in impact between a televised message and one that reaches the consumer simply through sound on radio or only through sight in print?

Without repeating ad nauseam the age-old puzzler concerning advertising effectiveness, how do you equate mathematically the sales calls of three or more different salesmen, disregarding the measurable variables such as the length of the confrontation and the specific sales points made?

At the point of sale, how do you quantify with mathematical accuracy the shelf environment of one product as compared with the shelf neighborhood of another, leaving aside measurable variables such as the traffic before each shelf and the turnover frequency of the neighboring products?

Without adding to the multitude of examples in the marketing process that currently defy mathematical measurement, it becomes obvious that a large number of very critical marketing variables differ in quality rather than in quantity. Therefore, if and when operations research techniques are used as decision-making aids in marketing, they must on the whole ignore some of these creative or qualitative factors. They should concentrate instead on the many remaining and vital variables that lend themselves more easily and obviously to restatement in mathematical terms.

Mathematical Techniques

It may be appropriate to digress for a minute to add that qualitative and judgmental factors can be intelligently translated into usable mathematical terms when the decision maker or user of the information fully understands the purpose and limitations of these techniques. Thus the media strategists make an implicit judgment about the value of demographic subgroups in the target audience in comparison to other subgroups, and this judgment can be and often is translated into personalized probabilities or weightings.

By the same token, other qualitative or creative variables could be programmed into a variety of models by translating management judgments concerning their value into weightings combined on some reasonable basis of track record and experience.

This brief digression simply serves as devil's advocate to those who claim that the multitude of qualitative judgmental variables within the marketing process transcends the intelligent use of mathematics. The point is they do not rule out the use of mathematical symbols and models. They do, however, make the use of these techniques less obvious and more difficult. Perhaps it might serve as a word to the wise that such operations research exercises that do attempt to figure in the qualitative and judgmental criteria are not foolproof. But they are not worthless either.

The key virtues are probably threefold:

- They make it possible to combine qualitative and quantitative variables within one single model or within one systematic view of the process.
- In this combined form, this representation of the problem and alternative solutions can now be viewed by a larger group of experts or professionals than might otherwise have been called in to discuss this broad representation of the process or problem.
- And perhaps most importantly, the machinable model automatically and by definition edits out the personalities and idiosyncrasies of the individuals who express their judgments so that these judgments can be applied free from interpersonal relationships and communications obstacles.

It seems indicated that the existence of so many qualitative and judgmental variables in marketing does not constitute an insurmountable obstacle to the use of operations research techniques. Why then are they still used relatively less than they are in finance or production? A key reason is the paucity of theory in marketing contrasted with the financial and production function.

This lack of theory means, in effect, that even the most sophisticated marketing man must constantly rediscover fire and the use of the wheel in tackling his problems. He knows that advertising, promotion, publicity, point-of-sale material, and packaging are all part and parcel of the effort required to predispose the consumer toward his product. But how much of each and what kind of effort in these diverse areas remains, on the whole, a judgmental decision based on experience and intuition rather than on a theory relating these various factors into some kind of mathematical function.

It is not surprising, therefore, that operations research techniques have made inroads mostly in those areas of marketing decision making that bear a resemblance at the formulation or decision stage to other better-understood functions. For example, there are a number of models relevant to new product introduction. Since the basic decision concerning a new product introduction has more than a distant kinship to such investment decisions as purchase of a major asset or acquisition of a new company, it is obvious that this area of marketing inherits a considerable amount of theory from financial decision-making processes. Recently, however, a number of different new product decision models have been developed, and these have been designed as planning and sales forecasting tools. This application of operations research techniques is a refinement and extension of marketing planning models. If these owe a debt to other disciplines, it is not to such practical areas as production and finance but to a combination of behavioral sciences, statistics, and mathematics.

Systems Analysis in Marketing

Perhaps the status of systems analysis in marketing can best be summarized by quoting Stanley F. Stasch, associate professor of marketing at Northwestern University School of Business. Says Professor Stasch:

> Why has marketing fallen behind the other business areas in applying quantitative techniques and the computer to problem solving? This lag can be attributed to three factors:
>
> (1) Behavioral phenomena are difficult to quantify and hence difficult to computerize. It is to be expected that marketing problems with strong behavioral aspects will not be computerized until they have been quantified, and this development must await further behavioral research.
>
> (2) Of the large quantities of marketing data available, only small amounts have been collected and not all of that in an organized manner. Any second or third generation computer can store millions of memory bits. But what is overlooked by most industrial marketers—and by many

of their bosses—is that those bits do not come prepacked in the computer. They have to be gathered painstakingly by the computer user, and this is where most users fall short.

(3) Marketing people have not taken the initiative in closing the communications gap between themselves and computer personnel. If the computer—and appropriate quantitative techniques—are to be applied to decision areas in marketing, the nature and structure of those problem areas must be explained in detail to the computer specialists. The marketing decision maker must be able to communicate the following to the computer specialists and quantitative analysts:

- (a) The details of the specific problem.
- (b) The theoretical structure of the marketing phenomenon, at least as the marketing manager understands it.
- (c) The alternative decision choices associated with the problem.
- (d) The specific information and its form required by the decision maker.
- (e) The source, form, and frequency of availability of raw data to be used in the decision-making process.

Only when the quantitative analysts and computer specialists have been given all of this information will it be possible for them to apply their skills to the problem.

Guided by a list of management's problems and the information needed by management for solving those problems, data collection can be organized within the framework of an information system. The task of identifying the specific information needed by the decision maker can be facilitated if managers will first organize their thinking according to the five points just mentioned. In so doing, they will have thought through thoroughly all facets of their problems; they will understand their information needs; and they will then be in a position to communicate effectively with nonmarketing computer specialists.

Of the three reasons given for marketing's poor record of computer usage, only the first represents a situation which cannot be influenced by management; and a systems approach can be very helpful in dealing with the remaining two. If managers could adequately describe their problems and the information requirements associated with those problems, they would be in a position both to organize their data collection activity and to communicate with nonmarketing computer specialists. These simple steps would rectify the second and third causes of marketing's poor record of successful computer applications.*

Professor Stasch's appraisal can be considered either pessimistic or realistic depending, again, on the reader's perspective. The following three chapters attempt to provide a very specific charting of the amount and caliber of computer applications to marketing current within industry today.

* "Systems Analysis for Controlling and Improving Marketing Performance," *Journal of Marketing,* April 1969, pp. 12–19.

2

Operations Research and
Model Building in Marketing*

Philip Kotler

Early operations research breakthroughs on problems of production, inventories, and physical distribution did not surprise marketing practitioners, because these business problems appeared to have a clear quantitative nature. Then operations research began to be applied to marketing problems in the late 1950s, dealing with such topics as advertising budgeting, sales force assignment, and pricing strategy. By the early 1960s, some highly original marketing decision models had been developed. The published literature grew to include a bibliography listing over 200 marketing articles of a mathematical nature and several collections of readings. A number of journals such as *Management Science, Journal of Marketing Research,* and the *Journal of Advertising Research* increasingly featured sophisticated mathematical marketing articles.

One of the first companies to lay money on the line for extensive research

* From a more extended treatment of this subject in *Handbook of Modern Marketing,* edited by Victor P. Buell and published by the McGraw–Hill Book Company in 1970. Reproduced by special permission of the publishers and author.

into improved marketing decision models was Du Pont. The company put over $1 million in the hands of a specific group of company operations researchers to discover and quantify how advertising works.[1] Other Du Pont operations researchers made some early applications of modern decision theory to problems in product pricing and new product introduction.

Also making early appearances in marketing operations research were such companies as Scott Paper, which conducted sophisticated field advertising experiments; Monsanto, which developed a large number of computer programs to help its executives analyze a variety of marketing problems;[2] General Electric, which has worked for many years on the construction of simulators of specific markets; and Ford, which is carrying out advanced marketing systems analysis through simulation.

These companies have since been joined in the pursuit of new answers to old marketing riddles by such companies as Pillsbury, Union Carbide, Lever Brothers, Anheuser-Busch, and Westinghouse Electric. Advertising agencies such as Batten, Barton, Durstine & Osborn and Young & Rubicam have reported the development of sophisticated models in the areas of media selection and new product development.

A variety of other indicators exist to show the ferment in this field. An increasing number of universities are sponsoring special short summer sessions on marketing operations research. Business response has exceeded expectations and usually the programs have to turn down qualified applicants for lack of space. Marketing teachers themselves are going back to school to learn about these new mathematical techniques and their practical applications.

In still another development, The Diebold Group, Inc. sent out in 1966 an elaborate questionnaire to companies and schools doing marketing operations research in order to find out what was being done. Their summary report indicates among other things that the marketing areas of greatest application (in descending order) seem to be internal profit analysis, market analysis, competitive strategy, sales effort effectiveness, and pricing. Similarly the most promising techniques (also in descending order) appear to be simulation, modeling, Monte Carlo methods, linear programming, and critical path analysis.

The mathematical methods cited above are the defining characteristics

---

[1] "A Profit Yardstick for Advertising," *Business Week,* November 22, 1958.

[2] William A. Clark, "Monsanto Chemical Company: A Total Systems Approach to Marketing," in *Total Systems,* edited by Alan D. Meacham and Van B. Thompson (Detroit: American Data Processing, Inc., 1962), pp. 130–142.

of operations research in the minds of many researchers. There is no doubt that important new mathematical tools have been and are being developed, and they are critical to the progress of operations research. The tools go by names unfamiliar to businessmen, but they are fairly easy to understand in principle.

Problem Analysis Procedure

Another perspective on the nature of operations research is suggested by the steps through which the operations researchers go in analyzing a problem. These steps are:[3]

1. Defining the real problem.
2. Collecting data on the factors affecting results.
3. Analyzing the data.
4. Establishing a realistic criterion for measuring results.
5. Developing a model (usually but not always a mathematical one).
6. Testing the model on sample problems to make sure that it represents the system correctly.
7. Developing working tools, based on the model, to achieve the desired results.
8. Integrating the new methods into company operations.

These steps can be made more meaningful by describing a real example. The top management of a large brewery was concerned about its procedures for developing marketing budgets for the company's sales territories. Territory budgets were largely determined by recent sales and the degree of pressure and influence of the territory sales managers. Management recognized that territory sales did not necessarily indicate where additional marketing funds would do the most good. It wanted to find a better system for determining the marketing budget for each sales territory.

1. Defining the problem. Management's doubts began when it discovered that a leading competitor was spending less on advertising and distribution per dollar of sales and achieving better sales growth and profits. These were symptoms that the company's territorial division of the budget and the strategy employed were probably not optimal. A problem exists whenever there

[3] "The ABC's of Operations Research," *Dun's Review and Modern Industry*, September 1963, Part II, pp. 105 ff.

is a difference between a current situation and a desired one. Here it consisted of top management's belief that a better set of procedures could be developed to allocate marketing dollars to sales territories.

2. and 3. Collecting and analyzing data. The problem was turned over to the company's operations research department, which decided as a first step to determine the actual procedures being used by marketing management to set up territory budgets, including the information that management collected, the formal criteria used, and the role of personal influence. After many interviews, the operations research team was able to develop an elaborate logical flow diagram of the budgeting process. In addition, the team investigated the company's historical data on company sales and market share, competitors' advertising and sales promotion expenditures by territory, consumer brand preferences, and company and competitors' distribution coverage by territory.

4. Establishing a realistic criterion for measuring results. The operations research team needed a criterion for comparing various alternative ways of allocating the marketing budget. They decided to use a five-year horizon and estimate the impact of different allocation procedures on total discounted profit over the period.

5. Developing a model. The team developed a computer model that imitated the present procedures used by management to develop budgets for the various sales territories. This model predicted actual management allocations with a fair degree of accuracy. The team also developed an alternative model that based allocations to sales territories on a mathematical decision rule. The decision rule came about as a solution to a set of demand and cost equations for each territory. A territory demand equation provided a prediction of the territory's sales as a function of the amounts spent on advertising, sales promotion, and sales force. Having equations for predicting sales and also territory cost equations, the researchers were able to develop territory profit equations and then find a decision rule for allocating the marketing budget optimally over the territories.

6. Testing the model on sample problems. The mathematical model was tested against the company's present model on actual and hypothetical data and appeared to produce superior sales and profit results. The mathematical model helped reduce the mean sales forecasting error by a substantial amount.

7. Developing working tools. The mathematical model required periodic data on company and competitive expenditures and sales, as well as intervening measures of consumer brand preferences. Among other things, the company had to subscribe to certain standard marketing research services. In addition, the model called for varying allocations away from their normal levels in a small sample of matched territories in order to get a reading on the sensitivity of sales to alternative levels of marketing expenditures.

8. *Integrating the new methods into company operations.* The mathematical model now had to be converted into a system for planning and controlling territorial marketing expenditures. The final system is shown in abbreviated form in Exhibit 2–1. Time t signified the time when marketing

Exhibit 2-1
System for Territorial Planning and Control

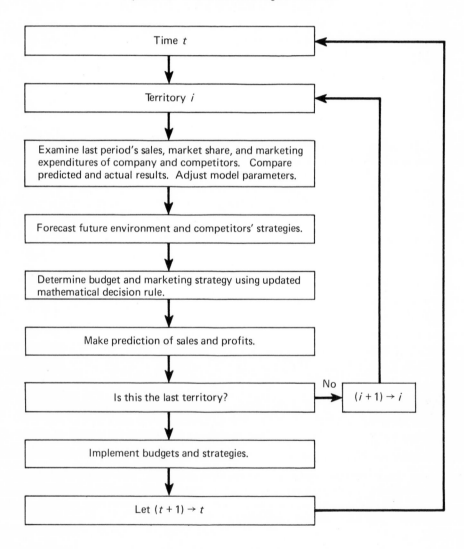

management had to determine the marketing budget for each territory. They first considered territory i and its last period's sales, market share, and marketing expenditures of the company and competitors. Marketing management compared these results to previous predictions and adjusted the mathematical model where called for. Marketing management then forecasted the future environment and competitors' strategies. These became inputs into a mathematical decision rule that produced a recommended budget and strategy for the territory along with predicted levels of sales and profits. The same procedure was repeated for each territory. After all territory budgets and strategies were determined, they were implemented. The whole process was repeated in the next period.

A system such as this is not static and is expected to undergo continuous improvement over time with use.

SPECIFIC APPLICATIONS[4]

The most viable marketing operations research models have been developed in the areas of (1) new products, (2) pricing, (3) physical distribution, (4) advertising, and (5) sales force management. Some leading models will be described in each area.

New Products

Two different types of evaluation take place in the course of considering a new product. The first, a compatibility evaluation, usually comes before the second, a profit evaluation.

Compatibility evaluation questions whether the product proposal is possible and desirable, considering the various company objectives and resources. A good product proposal, for example, may have to be stopped or dropped if the company cannot gain access to the needed distribution channels or lacks the financial resources or if the proposal is incompatible with the company image. Many factors have to be looked at in this connection. The major device for formally considering and weighing these factors was suggested over a decade ago and has been modified several times since then. It consists of listing the important company and marketing factors, assigning weights to

[4] This section is adapted from Philip Kotler, "Operations Research in Marketing," *Harvard Business Review*, January–February 1967, pp. 30–44.

reflect their relative importance, and scoring each factor according to the degree to which it is a favorable factor in the total picture. By multiplying the factor scores by the factor weights a single number is derived which reflects the desirability of developing the product.

If a firm finds it can logically undertake development of a new product in terms of company objectives and resources, it must determine whether it would in fact be worthwhile to do so. The question is answered by a profit evaluation.

The earliest profit evaluation model proposed a straightforward break-even analysis of a new product proposal in terms of its total expected sales and costs. Sometimes the payout period was made the deciding factor. More recent models have introduced additional factors, such as product life cycle considerations, cash flow discounting, sales effect of marketing mix variations, explicit consideration of uncertainty, and so forth. Here are a few of the more recent models.

Future earnings discounting method. One of the early refinements of profit evaluation was the future earnings discounting method outlined by Solomon Disman at Abbott Laboratories.[5] This approach is used in a number of companies. Instead of estimating whether the company could expect to sell enough in a reasonably short time to break even, Disman makes a direct calculation of the present value of the project. This involves estimating probable revenues and costs each year from the time of product introduction to some number of years later, the period known as the planning horizon. The expected income stream is discounted at the company's opportunity cost of capital to yield the expected present value (V) of the product proposal at the date of its commercial introduction.

Disman also recommends that this present value be scaled down by the subjective probability (P) of the company's actually achieving technical and commercial success. He calls the result the proposal's maximum economic justification ($MEJ = PV$), which represents the maximum amount the company is willing to invest in developing the new product. The proposal's MEJ is compared to the estimated development cost (I). A go-decision is indicated whenever $MEJ > I$. If several product proposals were being compared and not all could be developed, their relative attractiveness would be indicated by the ratio MEJ/I.

The DEMON model. A different approach to profit evaluation has been

[5] Solomon Disman, "Selecting R&D Projects for Profit," *Chemical Engineering,* December 24, 1962, pp. 87–90.

developed by BBDO and is known by the name of DEMON (*D*ecision *M*apping via *O*ptimum Go-No Networks).[6] The model is set up to indicate whether to go national (Go), drop the product (No), or collect further information on the product's chance of success (On). The decision is made on the basis of which alternative promises the highest expected return. If the answer is *On,* the model indicates which particular marketing research study is the best to carry out—that is, best in the sense that it would probably do the most to reduce the uncertainty clouding the Go-No alternatives. After this study is made, the results lead to a revision in the proposed marketing strategy, and a new evaluation is then made of the Go-No-On alternatives.

This approach requires that top management state its constraints regarding the planning period, payout period, minimal acceptable profits, profits required to go national, marketing research budget, and the degree of confidence needed. Furthermore, management must state its marketing program for introducing the product. The proposed advertising, sales promotion, distribution, and pricing plans are critical in making an estimate of product sales. Given demand, costs, and management objectives and constraints, the model leads to an estimate of the probable return and risk of the commercialization decision and indicates the desirable action.

The model has been used by a number of BBDO's client companies. One large drug firm found that DEMON recommended a radically different marketing strategy from the intuitive approach to back a new product. The company proceeded to implement the DEMON strategy in one set of matched territories and the intuitive strategy in another. The DEMON strategy was reported to have produced better profits.

The SPRINTER model. A complex simulation model developed by Glen L. Urban has all the characteristics of previous models plus one additional factor too often omitted: product interdependence.[7] When a new product is related on the demand or cost side to other company products, the deciding factor should not be the new product's absolute profits but the differential profits on the whole product line with and without the new product. The estimated profit for the new product must be adjusted downward if it reduces the profits on the company's other products.

Urban's model, which is called SPRINTER (*S*pecification of *Pro*fits with

[6] David B. Learner, "DEMON New Product Planning: A Case History," in *New Directions in Marketing,* ed. Frederick E. Webster, Jr. (Chicago: American Marketing Association, 1965).

[7] Glen L. Urban, "A New Product Analysis and Decision Model," *Management Science,* April 1968, pp. B-490-519.

*In*teraction under *T*rial and *E*rror *R*esponse), specifically incorporates executive estimates of demand and cost interrelationships between the new product and the other products in the line. The model was tested on a new product in a large chemical company with such good results that the company is implementing SPRINTER on a large scale.

Pricing Models

Though there is much talk about the growing role of nonprice factors in the marketing process, pricing remains a very complex issue for many firms. Pricing is a problem when a new product is being introduced, when a price change is contemplated in the face of uncertain customer and competitor reactions, and when a company must react to a competitor who has just changed his price. Pricing is also a problem in industries when companies submit sealed bids for jobs. And it is a problem when the company's product line is characterized by substantial demand and cost interdependencies.

In each of these areas, work is progressing in the development of useful mathematical models. Two examples can be cited.

The price modification decision. An increasing number of companies are using Bayesian decision theory for formal analyses of the likely response of customers and competitors to a contemplated price change. The Bayesian approach calls for executives to carefully define the company's objective(s), possible alternatives, major events affecting each alternative, and probabilities of these events. These data allow a calculation to be made of the expected value of each alternative along with the value of gathering more information before acting. Paul E. Green has described a specific application by one large chemical manufacturer.[8] The company had been selling a plastic substance to industrial users for several years and had captured 40 percent of that market. Top management became concerned as to whether its current price of $1 per pound could be maintained much longer because of a developing oversupply. Management saw that the solution to its problem lay in penetrating a certain market segment which was closely held by a substitute plastic product produced by six companies. Therefore, it was decided to evaluate the following four alternatives: maintaining the price at $1 or reducing the price to 93 cents, 85 cents, and 80 cents, respectively.

[8] Paul E. Green, "Bayesian Decision Theory in Pricing Strategy," *Journal of Marketing,* January 1963, pp. 5–14.

Among the chief uncertainties top management considered were the following:

- How much penetration in the key segment would take place without a price reduction?
- How would the six companies producing the substitute plastic react to each possible price reduction?
- How much penetration in the key segment would take place for every possible price reaction by the suppliers of the substitute plastic?
- How much would penetration into the key segment speed up penetration in other segments?
- If the key segment was not penetrated, what would be the probability that the company's competitors would initiate price reductions soon?
- What would be the impact of a price reduction on the decision of existing competitors to expand their capacity or of potential competitors to enter the industry?

The data-gathering phase consisted mainly of asking key sales personnel to place subjective probabilities on the various possible states of the key uncertainties.

The next step was to estimate the likely payoffs of different courses of action. A decision tree analysis revealed that there were over 400 possible outcomes. For this reason, the estimation of expected payoffs was programmed on a computer. The results indicated that in all cases a price reduction had a higher expected payoff than status quo pricing; in fact, a price reduction to 80 cents had the highest expected payoff.

Finally, in order to check the sensitivity of these results to the original assumptions, the results were recomputed for alternative assumptions on the rate of market growth and on the appropriate cost of capital. It was found that the ranking of the strategies was unaffected by the change in the assumptions.

The bidding decision. The theory of competitive bidding has received considerable refinement in the hands of applied mathematicians. The objective of a company in a bidding situation is to get the contract, and this means setting a lower price than the competition. The lower the company sets its bid, the lower its potential profits but the higher its probability of getting the contract award. As is readily apparent, the chief hurdle is that of estimating the probability of getting the contract at various bidding levels. This requires estimating the bids of various competitors.

A large drug supply company has developed a method of deriving estimates through a statistical analysis of the recent bidding history. While the company's final bid is based on a consideration of many factors, the formal analysis has proved increasingly useful in clarifying the implications of alternative bidding tactics.

Physical Distribution Decisions

A number of developments have renewed management's interest in the logistics problem and led managers to wonder whether they are overlooking many opportunities not only for cost saving but also for improved demand creation. Among these factors are the rising costs of physical distribution, the importance of service as a competitive marketing weapon, and the characteristic lack of coordination of company physical distribution decisions.

The warehouse location decision. Since the early application of linear programming to the problem of finding the best shipping schedule, the technique has been extended to solve the total system problem of the best warehouse locations, inventory levels, and transportation methods. However, the total system problem is so complex that linear programming is usable only at the price of a great many simplifications. Some investigators have preferred to take the route of modeling the physical distribution problem in all its complexity and trying to find a satisfactory solution through the technique of simulation.

One of the most widely used simulation programs, developed by Harvey N. Shycon and Richard M. Maffei, is capable of simulating a system of up to 40 warehouses, 4,000 customers, and 10 factories.[9] Another program, developed by Alfred A. Kuehn and Michael J. Hamburger and employed by a number of large companies, uses a technique midway between mathematical programming and simulation called heuristic programming.[10]

In this application, the physical distribution system is modeled flexibly, and certain arbitrary but plausible rules (called heuristics) are introduced to lead to quick and satisfactory solutions. Still another simulation was reported by a General Electric subsidiary with $50 million in sales.[11] GE found through simulation that it could save $2.9 million a year by some specific

[9] Harvey N. Shycon and Richard M. Maffei, "Simulation: Tool for Better Distribution," *Harvard Business Review,* November–December 1960, pp. 65–75.

[10] Alfred A. Kuehn and Michael J. Hamburger, "A Heuristic Program for Locating Warehouses," *Management Science,* July 1963, pp. 643–666.

[11] "The Case for 90 Percent Satisfaction," *Business Week,* January 14, 1961, pp. 82–85.

changes in its physical distribution system. Altogether, the value of mathematical analysis in the physical distribution area has been established almost beyond a doubt.

Advertising Decisions

A number of thorny problems confront companies in connection with the wise use of advertising monies. They would like to have better ways to analyze whether they are spending too little or too much on advertising; whether they are timing their advertising expenditures optimally through the year; whether their agency is choosing the best media; and so forth. Some of the recent mathematical work has shed light on these and some other important problems in advertising.

The spending level decision. One of the earliest and still most interesting spending level studies on advertising was developed by M. L. Vidale and H. B. Wolfe at Arthur D. Little, Inc.[12] These men worked with a number of cases on file and formulated a mathematical model for the effect of advertising on sales. The effect, they discovered, depends heavily on four factors:

1. The level of advertising expenditure.
2. The response constant, which shows how many dollars of sales would be generated per dollar of advertising at a zero sales level.
3. The market saturation level.
4. The sales decay constant, or percentage decline in sales per period that would take place in the absence of advertising.

These factors are related in an equation, and the job facing any particular company is to estimate the parameters (that is, response constant, saturation level, and sales decay constant) for its brand. Given the parameters, the company can solve the equation for the level of advertising necessary to achieve a particular level of sales or profits. The equation shows that the company wishing to achieve a higher level of sales must spend more on advertising (a) the higher the ratio of the decay constant to the response constant, (b) the higher the absolute level of sales, and (c) the closer sales are to the saturation level.

More elaborate models of the advertising–sales relationship have been

---

[12] M. L. Vidale and H. B. Wolfe, "An Operations-Research Study of Sales Response to Advertising," *Operations Research*, June 1957, pp. 370–381.

developed since then. A model by Alfred A. Kuehn deserves special mention in this connection because it was tested against some actual industry situations and incorporates a more complete set of marketing factors.[13] In Kuehn's model, company sales are a function of:

- The percentage of customers with brand loyalty and the rate of decay in this brand loyalty.
- The percentage of customers not committed to this firm or its main competitors.
- The size and rate of growth of the total market.
- The relative influence of price and distribution in the marketing process.
- The relative influence of the interaction of product characteristics and advertising in the marketing process.
- The relative share and effectiveness of this company's advertising expenditure.

Given the variables and the information required as inputs to this model, it is possible to derive a theoretically optimal advertising expenditure level.

The advertising timing decision. Kuehn's model also permits a determination to be made of the optimal timing pattern of advertising expenditures through the year. Given seasonal sales movements, Kuehn shows that the appropriate timing pattern depends on many factors, two important ones of which are the degree of advertising carryover and the amount of habitual brand choice. Thus, under specific assumptions, the only time such expenditures should be varied to coincide in phasing and amplitude with seasonal sales movements is when advertising has no carryover effect and when buyers have no habitual behavior. (If either of these conditions is violated, advertising expenditures should peak before sales peak.) Accordingly, the greater the amount of the advertising carryover effect, the greater the lead time should be; and the smaller the amount of habitual purchasing behavior, the more the advertising curve should vary in amplitude than the sales curve. These and other conclusions were drawn from his elaborate model of the advertising influence process.[14]

A somewhat different approach to the timing question has been devel-

---

[13] Alfred A. Kuehn, "A Model for Budgeting Advertising," in Frank M. Bass, *et al.,* eds., *Mathematical Models and Methods in Marketing* (Homewood, Ill.: Richard D. Irwin, Inc., 1961), pp. 302–353.

[14] Alfred A. Kuehn, "How Advertising Performance Depends on Other Marketing Factors," *Journal of Advertising Research,* March 1962, pp. 2–10.

oped by Jay Forrester of M.I.T. His technique, called industrial dynamics, involves modeling the company and its environment as a closed-loop information feedback system.[15] Through the company flow men, material, machines, orders, and information at varying rates guided by decisions on objectives and current information as to their degree of attainment. In one of his company applications, Forrester showed how the poor timing of advertising expenditures was responsible for accentuating production and inventory fluctuations.[16] This stemmed from the fact that advertising has a lagged impact on customer behavior; customer buying decisions at retail have a lagged impact on factory sales; and factory sales have a lagged impact on production scheduling and new advertising scheduling. By setting up a simulation of the process of information and decision delays, Forrester is able to investigate systematically the effect of different timing patterns of advertising expenditures on production and inventory stability.

The media selection decision. A third area of advertising decision making that has benefited from advanced mathematical analysis is media selection. On October 1, 1962, *Advertising Age* carried the headline, "Y&R, BBDO Unleash Media Computerization," and later BBDO sponsored full-page newspaper and magazine advertisements reading "Linear Programming showed one BBDO client how to get $1.67 worth of effective advertising for every dollar in his budget."

The model developed at BBDO uses a linear programming approach. The problem is stated as one of selecting the media mix which would maximize the number of effective exposures subject to (a) the size of the total advertising budget, (b) minimum and maximum usage rates of various media, and (c) specified exposure rates to different market segments.

In the meantime, the Young & Rubicam agency has developed a different approach that it has dubbed the high assay model. This model, although it is also an optimizing type, is designed to get around the simplifications—such as assuming constant effects of repeated exposures, constant media costs, no allowance for audience overlaps among media, and no indication of the best scheduling for the chosen media—necessitated by a linear programming statement of the problem. (Some of these simplifications are remediable through more complex programming statements of the problem.) The Y&R model uses a sequential rather than a simultaneous decision process. The basic idea is to start with the media available in the first week and select

[15] Jay Forrester, *Industrial Dynamics* (Cambridge, Mass.: The M.I.T. Press, 1961).
[16] Jay W. Forrester, "Advertising: A Problem in Industrial Dynamics," *Harvard Business Review,* March–April 1959, pp. 100–110.

the single "best buy." After this selection is made, all the remaining media choices are reevaluated to take into account duplication and potential media discounts. Then, if the achieved exposure for the week is below the optimal rate, a second selection is made for the same week. The optimal rate is a complex function of several marketing and media variables. The cycling process continues until the optimal exposure rate for the week is reached, at which point new media choices are considered for the following week. The cycling process is continued until the entire budget is spent.

A simulation model has been developed by The Simulmatics Corporation that does not profess to find the "best" media plan but rather to estimate the exposure value of any given plan. The model consists of a sample universe of 2,944 make-believe media users representing a cross-section of the U.S. population by sex, age, type of community, employment status, and education. Each individual's media choices are determined probabilistically as a function of his social-economic characteristics and location in one of 98 U.S. communities. A particular client media schedule is exposed to all the persons in this hypothetical population. As the simulation of the year's schedule progresses, the computer tabulates the number and types of people being exposed. Summary graphs and tables are automatically prepared at the end of the hypothetical year's run, and they supply a multidimensional picture of the schedule's probable impact. The advertiser examines these tabulations and then decides whether the audience profile and the reach and frequency characteristics of the proposed media schedule are satisfactory. Simulation complements the two previous models in that it is a means of developing the dynamic reach and frequency characteristics of a given schedule over 52 weeks.

Sales Force Decisions

In spite of the great cost and importance of personal selling in the marketing mix, surprisingly little operations research has been reported in this area. Much more analysis has been conducted of the optimal use of advertising funds, which in many ways is a less tangible problem than the optimal use of sales resources. Nevertheless, the few studies that have been conducted have significance for sales force management.

The salesman routing decision. A problem which has received a great amount of attention from operations researchers is salesman routing. Suppose a salesman must make calls in n cities. This means that there are n factorial possible routes. Specifically, given 5 cities, there are 120 possible routes; 10 cities, over 3 million possible routes. The problem is to find the one route through these cities that minimizes either the total travel time or travel cost. A number of different models have been developed. The real challenge is to find a program which can solve the large *n* case without requiring too much computer time or cost. Research is being conducted in this area both in companies and in universities.

The sales manpower requirements decision. Markov process analysis has been used by a large insurance company to aid in the analysis of its sales force manpower needs.[17] Each year the company loses a fraction of its sales force through resignation, retirement, and death. The exiting salesmen have different levels of experience, education, and ability. The company has to hire new men to replace those who leave and additional men to meet the company's growth requirements. Top management's problem is to estimate future manpower needs by class of service and age in the light of the turnover characteristics and planned sales growth.

The first step is to calculate survival rates for agents in various service and age classes. These estimated rates are then used in a Markov analysis to project future characteristics of the sales force if no new men are hired. Different alternative recruitment patterns are analyzed for their effect on the composition of the future sales force and probable level of sales. For a given sales target, the operations researchers are able to recommend to top management the minimum number and types of agents to recruit each year.

The optimal number of calls decision. The best level and allocation of sales effort depend on the correct assessment of customer response to variations in the number of sales calls. There are at least two published descriptions of attempts to derive the sales response curve empirically. One relies on a multiple regression performed on past data; the other depends on a planned experiment to generate information about the relationship.

The first investigation was made by the Operations Research Group at Case Institute for the General Electric Company.[18] Customers were sorted into classes on the basis of similar characteristics. The accounts in each class were sorted again into subclasses on the basis of the call time spent with each customer. Then the average dollar volume was computed for each subclass.

---

[17] Joe Midler, "A Simulation Model of Sales Force Development with Application to Manpower Replacement, Sales Forecasting, and Corporate Growth," an unpublished paper, 1961.

[18] Clark Waid, Donald F. Clark, and Russell L. Ackoff, "Allocation of Sales Effort in the Lamp Division of the General Electric Company," *Operations Research,* December 1956, pp. 629–647.

Finally, a curve was drawn through the scatter of points to show the relation-ship between average dollar volume and sales-call time.

The scatter for each class of account lay in a basically positive direction but unfortunately was too diffused to permit the fitting of a statistically sig-nificant curve. The operations researchers, after trying other approaches that fared no better, concluded that the lack of a clear relationship could be ex-plained by one of three hypotheses:

1. Uniform sales response curves do not exist for similar accounts.
2. Uniform response curves exist but are difficult to measure because of imperfections in the classification of accounts and basic data.
3. Uniform response curves exist, but the data in this study revealed only the upper plateaus of the curves.

The researchers rejected the first hypothesis because it would remove the major justification for call norms and would go against intuition. They re-jected the second hypothesis because experienced salesmen reported that they thought the classification of accounts was quite discriminating. This left the third hypothesis, which they tentatively accepted but could not prove. It implied that salesmen typically spent more time with accounts than was nec-essary. On the basis of this hypothesis, the research group recommended that the number of calls be cut back. They strongly felt that some diversion of calls from present accounts to new accounts was warranted and would also result in a substantial net increase in business. This recommendation was fol-lowed, and company sales remained high.

In a different effort, John F. Magee described an experiment where sales-men were asked to vary their call pattern in a particular way to determine what effect this would have on sales.[19] His experiment called for first sorting accounts into major classes. Each account class was then randomly split into three sets. The respective salesmen were asked to spend less than five hours a month with accounts in the first set, five to nine hours a month with the second set, and a minimum of ten hours a month with the third set for a speci-fied period of time. The results indicated that call time had a definite effect on sales volume, with the most profitable call norm in this particular situation appearing to be five to nine hours a month.

[19] John F. Magee, "Determining the Optimum Allocation of Expenditures for Promo-tional Effort with Operations Research Methods," in Frank M. Bass, ed., *The Frontiers of Marketing Thought and Science,* (Chicago: American Marketing Association, 1958), pp. 140–156. Also see Arthur A. Brown, Frank T. Hulswit, and John D. Kettelle, "A Study of Sales Operations," *Operations Research,* June 1956, pp. 296–308.

CURRENT TRENDS
IN MARKETING OPERATIONS RESEARCH

The area of marketing operations research is in continuous ferment. From this vantage point in time, at least six trends appear to describe the future direction of model building in marketing. These trends relate to problem definition, types of models, and data collection.

Problem Definition

Researchers are showing an increasing interest in analyzing marketing problems at a microbehavioral level and then aggregating the results up to total sales and marketing expenditures. This is in contrast to the time when they were satisfied to fit aggregate sales to various aggregate marketing categories.

There is increasing recognition that narrow statements of any problem may lead to optimization of one company activity at the expense of other activities, and this has encouraged wider problem definition. For example, it is hard to settle on the best advertising level without simultaneously determining the best price and sales force size. Various marketing instruments must maintain some balance in their levels. And marketing optimization itself must be considered in relation to production and financial polices. To determine the best level of an off-season discount to encourage early sales, it is necessary to consider simultaneously inventory, employment, and overtime levels.

Models and Techniques

There is a growing recognition that models and systems must be designed with particular users in mind. The models must be oriented around the problems and information of real product managers, sales managers, and advertising managers. The models must appear realistic in their assumptions and plausible in their results.

Researchers are showing a growing interest in decision models whose parameters are tied to a program of systematic field experimentation that provides for their updating each period. These models recognize that parameters of marketing response undergo continuous change and must be tracked through systematic measurement procedures.

There is a growing interest in field and laboratory experimentation and increasing sophistication in questionnaire design and scaling instruments.

Although researchers are enjoying increasing amounts of hard data, they are not willing to restrict their variables to only those that can be measured with hard data. This would doom their models to remaining very simple. Researchers are increasingly turning to the executives themselves for estimates of missing parameters and probability distributions, incorporating these in the models, and covering the risks of doing this through the route of sensitivity analysis.

INTRODUCING MARKETING OPERATIONS RESEARCH INTO THE COMPANY

An increasing number of companies will take a close look at their marketing problems through the eyes of operations research. This is inevitable because marketing budgets are among the largest and fastest-growing company budgets. Marketing accounts for approximately 40 cents of every retail dollar and 30 percent of the gainfully employed persons in the United States.[20] Competition continues to grow keener, customers more discriminating, and products less secure. Company prosperity requires the best possible judgment about marketing expenditures and strategy.

The company turning to marketing operations research for the first time faces several questions. Who should be hired to do marketing operations research and where should he be placed in the company? What influence will management attitudes have on the results? What marketing problems should be tackled first?

Operations Research Personnel

Large companies are likely to have an operations research department that undertakes scientific studies of company problems in the area of production scheduling, inventory control, and physical distribution. Typically their personnel have not worked on marketing problems, and this is a proper

[20] Reavis Cox, *Distribution in a High-Level Economy* (Englewood Cliffs, N.J.: Prentice-Hall, Inc., 1965), pp. 149, 155.

cause for concern. Operations researchers have a tendency to be technique-centered, and they tend to force familiar tools onto marketing problems and in the process often oversimplify the problem. They may come up with a good answer to a wrong statement of the problem because of their concern with mathematical solvability. They can avoid many pitfalls by reviewing the now extensive literature on marketing operations research.

The best arrangement is for one of the company's operations researchers to specialize in this area and read the relevant literature. In time his experience with several marketing problems in the company will make him very effective. As an alternative, the large company can directly hire a person who has specialized in marketing operations research.

The marketing operations researcher can be located either in the operations research department or in the marketing research department. There is no evidence as to which is the better arrangement; the answer depends much on circumstance. But it is clear that his effectiveness requires that he be in frequent contact with line and staff marketing personnel so that he senses their problems, their types of information, and their current procedures for problem solving. At the same time, marketing personnel will grow more familiar with him and the operations research approach.

The small company usually does not have the option of employing a full-time operations researcher, let alone a specialist in marketing operations research. Yet there is every reason to believe that the small company would benefit as much as the large company from the scientific study of its marketing problems. The small company's recourse is to hire a marketing operations research consultant. The consultant will be effective to the extent that he enjoys a long-term relationship with the company, is familiar with company personnel and procedures, and is given a sufficient incentive to spend a lot of time thinking about the company's problems.

Top Management Support and Understanding

It is a truism that no important new management idea will go far unless it has top management support. Marketing operations research is particularly vulnerable to suspicion by the rank-and-file because mathematics seems alien to marketing problems and poses a serious language barrier. For marketing operations research to succeed, it needs the cooperation and understanding of marketing managers who will be asked for data and ideas. For their cooperation to be positive, it is necessary for top management to establish at the beginning that marketing operations research is a high-priority activity and must be supported by all managers.

Some top managements have enthusiastically recognized that their companies are in the computer age and that nothing less than a crash program of in-house management education would prepare management to take up the challenge of the computer. This happened in Pillsbury when the president, Robert Keith, recognized the great potential of the new decision-making techniques and personally sponsored and participated in a several-day company seminar on decision theory, mathematical models, statistical techniques, and computers. This seminar was repeated at several levels of management and Pillsbury's management is now very conversant with the language, capabilities, and limitations of operations research in marketing.

Problem Selection

Marketing operations research also gains respect in a company to the extent that it achieves early successes. It is therefore important to select appropriate problems. Three types of marketing situations generally pose a good opportunity for marketing operations research.

Evaluation of nonrecurrent major policy changes. When a company faces a major marketing decision, such as a shift from one type of marketing channel to another or a price reduction in an oligopoly situation, the thinking of management can be considerably aided by simple decision tree analysis or simulation models, both of which are easy for management to understand.

Improvement of marketing systems and procedures. Most companies can benefit from studies of their current procedures for sales forecasting, quota setting, and marketing budget allocation. Studies of the current procedures yield clues as to alternative decision procedures that would lead to important gains in performance.

Developing better information and analytical facilities. Operations researchers can render a service by installing time sharing equipment and showing marketing managers how to call in various useful stored computer programs. General Electric has developed a new product decision model in which the computer types questions, one at a time, concerning the information it needs. The executive types in the estimates as requested and in short order gets back an estimate of expected return on the new product. At M.I.T., one interrogative computer program has been developed for testing different automobile dealer locations in a large city and another for developing media schedules.

Executives get very involved with time sharing as soon as they try it, and this helps considerably in whetting their appetite for computer methods in marketing. The problem, if any, is that they may become too enthusiastic about accepting the computer printouts. The point must be driven home to each executive that the computer models are tools to aid judgment, not replace it. The executive must understand the basics of each model he uses, or else he is liable to make serious mistakes.

*   *   *

Operations research is largely the application of scientific method to the study of business problems. Its distinguishing characteristic is the effort to express business problems in a mathematical form amenable to either optimal solution or, at least, experimental solution. The operations researcher approaches each new problem by defining it carefully, collecting and analyzing pertinent data, establishing a realistic criterion for measuring results, developing a model (usually mathematical) and testing it on sample data, and then implementing the solution into a workable system for use by management.

The increasing application of operations research in the marketing area promises to make a substantial contribution toward the analysis and solution of classic marketing problems faced by the firm. Although still in its infancy, marketing operations research has already produced useful insights and procedures in the areas of media selection, new product strategy, and physical distribution and is on its way to producing useful results in the areas of total advertising expenditures, budget allocation to products and territories, and sales force assignments and call policies. This chapter reviewed the major achievements of marketing operations research in specific marketing areas and summarized several strong trends in current work: deeper problem definition, wider problem definition, practice-oriented models, adaptive models, improved measurement techniques, and the use of subjective data. Companies that develop an interest in marketing operations research should develop or hire a specialist in this area, give him top management support, and sponsor in-house seminars designed to explain the new decision-making techniques to its executives. In the meantime, the marketing operations researcher should select marketing problems and techniques that promise to yield early and tangible payoffs to the firm and that are also easily communicated to the ultimate decision makers.

3

How Marketers
Use the Computer Today

Evelyn Konrad

Within the past two years, Fibreboard Corporation has been using input/output theory for a planning model (a representation of a problem or solution), and the firm has developed a data bank for its new marketing potential model.

To help provide input for its marketing model, the Western Pacific Railroad developed a marketing model back in June 1966 using freight commodity statistics.

Corning Glass Works' marketing planning group has been deeply involved in computer applications since the mid-1960s using sales forecasting, prospecting, and marketing potential models along with its more established uses of PERT and customer services models.

The Occidental Life Insurance Company of California uses computer applications for (1) market appraisal and production analysis by type of customer; (2) sales and census runs, such as sales and census data correlation for sales forecasting; (3) expediting communication; and (4) evaluating agent performance. And these are but a handful of this firm's marketing applications.

Isolated examples? Not at all. Indeed, the impact of computer technology and mathematical sciences on the marketing function has been profound and far-reaching, albeit not always as dramatically measurable as the cases cited.

It is ironic but true that some of the least glamorous capabilities of the computer—the sheer data processing abilities—and their applications to the marketing function have probably had greatest economic impact in terms of marketing efficiency and changes within industries, all of which, in the aggregate, may well have contributed to the growth and health of the U.S. economy. This fact may come into focus when one considers the impact of electronic data processing on credit checks and clearances as just one specific marketing application, with its broad ramifications in banking, retailing, and gasoline distribution, for example.

On the other hand, the more glamorous, sophisticated, and mathematically based the application, the more likely it is to be another temporarily unique application with one forward-looking company which has managed to spring ahead of its competitors within the industry.

To take the guesswork out of the eternal puzzle—how many major companies actually do have computerized marketing applications?—a survey research project was undertaken in 1968.

Industrial Marketing collaborated in this effort, sending a four-page questionnaire to the "vice-president of marketing" of each of 775 companies in the *Dun & Bradstreet Reference Book of Corporate Managements 1968*. This directory lists approximately 1,500 large companies in the United States. The survey sample was chosen by taking the name of every other company. The results of this research study appeared as a major article in the November 1968 issue of *Industrial Marketing*.

It may be an indication of the fascination that computers hold for U.S. marketing management that more than 225 key executives sent in replies. However, a handful of respondents claimed to have no marketing applications and were therefore not included in the final tabulation.

Exhibits 3–1 through 3–5 are based on 122 completed questionnaires from a cross-section of general business categories (manufacturers, utilities, railroads, banks, and insurance companies among others). The companies polled and those responding rank high according to any criterion of size within their business categories. Although they are not necessarily the specific leaders in sales or assets, they are among the leaders.

The findings, therefore, cannot be projected to apply to U.S. industry.

They are, rather, an interesting indication of computer usage among the cross-section of leaders. Here are some of the findings.

An overwhelming number of respondents claimed that their most meaningful applications were with customer or territorial analysis or sales analysis and control. (See Exhibit 3–1.) This finding, however, once again is more a reflection of the industries in which the responding companies operate than a conclusion applicable to U.S. industry as a whole.

New product planning, for example, ranked lowest as a meaningful application according to these respondents. Other research conducted by the authors indicates that this function would rank very high if the study had been conducted among an equal number of consumer goods companies. Exhibit 3–1 indicates what the marketing managements of the companies polled in this study considered their most meaningful applications.

By far the greatest appeal of the computer in marketing management continues to be its application as a more or less scientific crystal ball. This conclusion emerges from analysis of the 122* respondent companies' answers to the question, "In the past year, what specific marketing problems have you sought to solve or investigate with computer applications?"

The three categories that got the overwhelming nod as active, ongoing computer applications were those programs dedicated to (1) sales forecasting, (2) customer services, (3) prediction of market potentials for products or services.

While dramatic computer applications to marketing consumer products may get more frequent attention in the general press, some equally and sometimes more sophisticated use of mathematical models for computers is going on behind the scenes among industrial companies. Application of input/output theory is simply one area in which some industrial marketers have led the way. Simulation, a process of random sampling of a multitude of possible alternative solutions to a problem that are based on historical experiences, has also long been recognized among industrial marketers.

Bernard Berger, manager of corporate system analysis of United Nuclear Corporation, said: "Our mode of marketing analysis should allow simulations to be conducted based on assumed probabilities of order awards, so that product quantities and sales dollars can be related to specific time periods in the future."

Less glamorous but equally critical applications such as sales analysis, reporting, and control were reported by 40 of the 122 respondents. Inventory

* This is the number of respondents replying to all questions and, therefore, represents the total reflected in most tabulations.

Exhibit 3-1
Most Meaningful Applications for the Computer in Marketing

Category	Percent of Companies*
Customer or territorial analysis or segmentation; prospect analysis or segmentation.	23
Sales reporting, analysis, control, either by product, customer or salesman, territory, or whatever; the orientation is primarily that of the sales manager.	21
Customer service applications; these were typically order processing, invoice/shipping label preparation, shipment tracing, order follow-up, and so forth.	14
Inventory or production control, oriented toward better order response and customer service.	13
Sales forecasting; these seemed generally to be the more traditional type, as opposed to the models mentioned below.	12
Predictive models. (In context, these seemed generally complex mathematical models, as opposed to the sort of time-series projections of past data used in typical sales forecasts or industry forecasts.)	8
Proposal preparation; bidding assistance. (These applications were reported by both insurance companies and large construction/ engineering type of companies. A total of four respondents gave answers in this category.)	4
Distribution and logistics studies, warehouse and outlet location, and others.	2
New product planning; only one respondent here, but a most interesting application involving PERT for coordinating the various phases of new product manufacture, promotion, introduction, and so forth.	1

*Based on a total of 90 respondents.

management, on the other hand, was cited by a very small minority. Since other studies have revealed that inventory control has become computerized in an increasing number of companies throughout U.S. industry, the infrequent mention of it in this study may well be due to the fact that a large number of companies consider this function not part of marketing but of the production process.

It is more surprising that only 10 percent of the respondent companies are using computers for advertising budget determination. It is likely that this figure reflects the composition of the companies polled for this study—a heavily industrial group of companies and very few leaders from among the top 100 national advertisers using mass media.

Although there is no basis for a statistical correlation, it is interesting to observe that a comparable questionnaire study designed by Evelyn Konrad in 1962 and sponsored by a computer service company at the time showed that, as long ago as 1962, 10 major companies advertising their products through 21 key advertising agencies were determining their advertising appropriations (budgets with a combined total of more than $200 million in 1960) with the aid of computers. The remarkably low response relative to the total sample in this current study reflects the nature of the companies polled rather than a disenchantment with computer capabilities in this area.

On the contrary, other studies have indicated that some of the most interesting and sophisticated computer applications exist today in areas of budget determination, market forecasting, and marketing planning. It is not surprising, of course, that these applications and experimentations tend to occur most frequently among consumer goods giants, where profit and loss statements directly reflect the efficacy of their marketing process. (See Exhibit 3–2.)

It is apparent, therefore, that if the 122 companies whose answers were tabulated had been not industrial companies and utilities but rather consumer goods manufacturers, the answers to this particular study might have been significantly different.

Within the context of the industries polled, these are some of the particular problems cited by marketing managements in developing their own specialized applications:

- Educating and involving the noncomputer people for whom the programs were being developed and setting up meaningful communications between these "users" and EDP personnel.
- Getting particular information from salesmen, customers, industry, or government. (This problem has ranked equally high in other

studies conducted within marketing managements of consumer goods industries.)

▪ Gaining managerial support or project priorities. (This particular problem may be more acute among industrial marketers and public utilities where the marketing function may be neither as high in the corporate hierarchy nor considered as directly related to corporate health and profits as it is in consumer goods industries.)

▪ Defining the problem and objectives sufficiently precisely for translation into mathematical terms for use by a computer. (This difficulty was cited by 50 percent of the respondents.) Of course, this particular difficulty is equally challenging in consumer goods industries. It has been cited as the single biggest obstacle to harnessing computer applications to marketing problems.

Marketing functions are still getting, on the whole, a fast shuffle where access to computer technology is concerned. This fact becomes apparent if time on the company computer is any indication.

When one considers that all but the most routine data-processing chores do require time-consuming access to computers for experimentation from

Exhibit 3-2
Computer Applications of Total Respondents Compared with
Manufacturers and Utilities

Category	Percent Overall (N = 122)	Percent Manufacturers (N = 52)	Percent Utilities (N = 24)
Predictive tool for market potential for existing or new products and services	51	48	67
Sales forecasting	66	70	50
Customer services	57	53	46
Advertising budget determination	13	8	4
Other: order processing	4	4	4
Other: sales analysis, reporting, control	40	37	29
Other: inventory management	6	6	0
Other: miscellaneous	25	21	42

Exhibit 3-3
How 116 of 122 Companies
Allocate Computer Time

	Percent
Production	20
Accounting functions	50
Financial and long-range planning	7
Miscellaneous other functions	5
Marketing	18

alternate programs to debugging, then the significance of Exhibit 3–3 becomes apparent. The overall response of the 122 companies tabulated showed that marketing tended to have 18 percent (mean percentage allocated) of the companies' own computer time.

It is interesting to note that utilities (telephone, gas, and electric companies) allocate far smaller portions of their computer time to marketing. Perhaps this is not surprising when one considers that utilities are normally not faced with the same competitive situations as other industries. (See Exhibit 3–4.)

Significant, too, is the fact that the great data processing demands of big industry—payrolls and accounting functions in particular—quite naturally take up the lion's share of computer time. It is equally likely that this is a function that swells the percentage of computer time dedicated to so-called accounting functions among public utilities, all of which share the burdensome chore of regularly billing their individual customers.

Of the 122 companies whose responses were tabulated, 113 have full-time computer programming systems analysts on staff. Indeed, seven companies reported more than 100 such professionals in their own computer operations. However, over 70 percent of these respondents have only a handful (between one and five) on full-time assignments to marketing applications.

Other parts of the study have shown that most firms with particularly sophisticated marketing operations tend to call in independent software

Exhibit 3-4
How 23 Utility Companies
Allocate Computer Time

	Percent
Production	11
Accounting	73
Corporate-financial	9
Marketing	6
Other	1

companies or teams of academicians when they attempt to develop computer-able mathematical models to shed new light on the marketing function. (See Exhibit 3–5.) Staff programmers and systems analysts tend to be used for ongoing rather than experimental programs on the whole.

This conclusion also holds true in the way companies use outside computer service companies for their marketing functions. (See Exhibit 3–5.) They tend to farm out the atypical or the specialized runs such as consumer surveys or specific cross-tabulations of research studies—the special runs that would disrupt the day-by-day functions of data processing department programs.

But a significant minority of companies mentioned that they use computer service companies because they have inadequate access to their own computer facilities either because of physical distance from them or because marketing still had lower priorities. The latter reason reflects once again the history of the computer and its firm foundation in accounting functions, primarily, and production, secondarily. And marketing, perhaps because many of its multidisciplinary applications are more difficult to harness into rigorous mathematical context, still has to prove to top corporate management that the satisfaction of its computer requirements will have a bearing on the profit and loss statement.

Communication between the computer expert and the marketing professional continues to be a problem. The extent of this problem emerges from

Exhibit 3-5

Time Used for Marketing Assignments by Those Who Buy Outside Computer Time

Percent of time	0–10	11–25	26–50	51–75	76–100
Percent of companies attributing this percentage	47	16	0	11	26

Reasons for buying outside services for marketing applications

Category Description	Percent in each category (multiple responses permitted)
Capacity problems—manpower, peak loads, larger-than-usual programs, and others	36
One-time or specialized runs, that is, consumer surveys, cross-tabulations, and others	38
Use time-share terminals for flexibility, fast turn-around	21
Inadequate access to own company's computer facilities, either physical distance or low priorities	12
Own system not yet ready or just starting to use EDP for marketing	7

the responding companies' stated reasons for using their own programmers rather than outside programmers for marketing functions. The key reasons cited by over 60 percent of those using their own programmers were:

- Our own programmers know the company needs.
- Our men have specialized knowledge.
- Staff programmers are more flexible than outsiders.
- Sheer availability and economics are important.

However, the more sophisticated the applications that were being attempted, the more obvious it became that specialized outside help tended to be drawn upon—at least in the model-building stage, if not right through the programming.

4

How to Use the Computer in Marketing

Art Youmans, Jr.

THIS CHAPTER EVALUATES current uses of the computer in four major areas: (1) corporate planning, (2) analyzing markets, (3) the sales function, and (4) the merchandise-clerical function.

Some interesting findings about the *Fortune 500's* use of the computer in corporate planning, analyzing markets, the sales function, and the merchandise-clerical function emerged from a 1968 study of 100 companies from the *Fortune 500* list. These findings are shown in Exhibit 4–1.

Sound planning requires complete and accurate data and a management team capable of utilizing these data in an optimum manner.

With the advent of the computer as a planning tool, industrial companies have revised their traditional planning techniques. Descriptions of some of these new planning techniques follow.

PERT (*Program Evaluation and Review Technique*)

PERT is a network technique for making optimum use of manpower, equipment, and time in the accomplishment of a complex project, such as

41

Exhibit 4-1
Random-Sample Study

CORPORATE PLANNING Activity	Percent of Firms Using EDP
Improving information flow between departments, divisions, and units	74.4
Planning short-range strategy	44.9
Critical path method techniques	44.9
Program evaluation and review techniques	35.9
Planning long-range strategy	33.3
Setting market growth objectives	28.2
Setting profitability objectives	25.6

ANALYZING MARKETS Activity	Percent of Firms Using EDP
Marketing research	69.2
Market segmentation	38.5
Mathematical model decision making	34.6
Location of new markets and customers	30.8
Test marketing	24.4
Media selection plans	12.8
Consumer market simulation	12.8

SALES FUNCTION Activity	Percent of Firms Using EDP
Analysis of sales territories	83.3
Measurement of performance	80.8
Sales forecasting	75.6
Order-entry systems	74.4
Control of salesmen	64.1
Product pricing	43.6
Standard setting	43.6

MERCHANDISE-CLERICAL FUNCTION Activity	Percent of Firms Using EDP
Inventory control	91.0
Accumulation and storage of facts for future reports	88.5
Analysis of past and present sales in scheduling future production	85.9
Greater clerical efficiency and accuracy	79.5
Use of economic data as a corrective in scheduling production	39.7

Source: Random-sample study of 100 companies from *Fortune 500* based on answers supplied by 78 respondent companies. Study was conducted by Art Youmans, Jr.

creating a new product—from the idea stage to its introduction into the marketplace. Originally created for use in new product development, PERT has been used by management in many areas, resulting in time and cost reduction.

Briefly, these are the steps necessary in using PERT to find the most time- and cost-efficient way to manage a complicated project:

1. Identify all the jobs that make up the project.
2. Relate them to each other in a logical structure.
3. Estimate how much time and cost each step will take.
4. Feed this mass of data into a computer, which, if properly programmed, will produce as output a realistic budget and target date, with each step arranged in optimum order.
5. Periodically, utilize the computer to compare results, to date, with the original output and revise if necessary.

CPM (*Critical Path Method*)

CPM practitioners have developed supplementary computer-based techniques, such as RPSM (Resources Planning and Scheduling Method) and EAS (Expenditure Analysis System). As a result of this development work, CPM can generate more sophisticated cost and resource information than the PERT system. Both CPM and PERT are network techniques, and their diagrams look similar. However, CPM probes deeper and answers these three basic questions: (1) What jobs must be done? (2) By what date? and (3) By whom? Unlike PERT, CPM has proven particularly useful in plant construction.

Without the computer's ability to calculate and analyze data at superhuman speed, such time- and money-saving systems as CPM and PERT would be impractical on all but simple planning jobs.

Planning Short-Range (*Under Three Years*) and Long-Range Strategy (*Over Three Years*)

Failure to have a strategy consistent with the environment can result in costly failure for the company involved, as evidenced by Ford's $250 million loss with the Edsel.

General Electric utilizes computerized long-range forecasts to pinpoint its

expected sales to markets five and ten years ahead for its 100 product departments. These long-range forecasts allow GE to plan its resources on the basis
of future expectations and give GE top management a bench mark with
which to evaluate the annual short- and long-range plans, which are drawn
up separately by the 100 decentralized product departments.

Setting Market Growth Objectives

Companies may desire to grow by increasing sales of their products to present customers, by finding new customers for present products, by adapting
product lines to reach new markets, by developing new markets through
diversification, or in other ways. All of these strategies are distinct paths that
a company may take in achieving future market growth. However, a company may simultaneously pursue market penetration, market development,
and diversification.

By computer analysis, a company can set market growth objectives in the
following manner.

The company first determines which strategy or combination of market
penetration, market development, product development, or diversification
strategies would be the best method of meeting the company's needs and
long-run objectives. The computerized output from meaningful primary and
secondary data input can then provide much essential information upon
which market growth decisions may be based. For example, Exhibit 4–2 is
based on computerized output, which graphically reveals that corporate mar-

Exhibit 4–2
Market Penetration

SIC CODE	Number of Present Customers	Number of Potential Customers	Percent of Penetration
2514	22	517	4.3
2522	35	170	20.6
2531	42	421	10.0
TOTALS	99	1,108	8.9 Average

ket penetration to SIC 2514 customers is substantially lower than to SIC 2522 customers. The company can then combine this computerized output with other information in setting market growth objectives, which should not conflict with existing corporate strategies and objectives.

Setting Profitability Objectives

Computers are capable of assessing an almost endless number of variables (price, for example) associated with the selection of an optimum choice from among a number of alternatives. By matching corporate requirements against variables, an optimum combination can be achieved utilizing linear programming.

Other computerized mathematical models have been used to evaluate new products and analyze estimated probable sales and costs, life cycle considerations, cash flow discounting, sales effect of marketing mix variations, and in other ways. From these projections, profitability objectives can be set by management.

The computer can aid management in setting profitability objectives by evaluating the effect on profits and return on investment of such influencing factors as price levels, sales volume, product mix, changing wage and material rates, and cost reduction by means of such factors as methods improvement and pruning out unprofitable products.

The computer can also be used as a tool by marketing management in supplying information upon which decisions can be rationally made. With its great speed and accuracy, the computer has the potential to greatly improve information flow within a company.

USE COMPUTERS IN ANALYZING YOUR MARKETS!

The profitable life cycle for new products is shrinking at an accelerating rate due to technological advances, competitive activity, changing consumer preferences, and similar causes.

The U.S. market is becoming more complex and segmented. Competitors watch a rival's markets carefully, and often learn as much from the rival's test marketing as the rival himself.

Well-managed companies now realize that their survival and growth depend upon their speeding up their analysis of markets. The best way of doing this is by using the computer.

Test Marketing

Last year, more than $1 billion was invested in test marketing by American business. Although it is increasingly difficult to gauge potential success accurately from scattered markets that usually represent no more than 2 to 3 percent of the nation, test marketing still remains a key to a new product's future.

Some companies simply use the computer in test marketing as they would a clerk, in sorting, comparing, and analyzing sales in various test markets, test panel results, and consumer attitude and preference tests. Others (Du Pont, for example) employ the computer in a more sophisticated manner by constructing a mathematical model to simulate the marketplace, including the quantification of potential consumer reaction, competitive activity, various advertising expenditures, and other independent variables. By testing different alternatives on this model, Du Pont was able to predict how successful its new products might be under various competitive situations.

Market Segmentation

The purpose of market segmentation is to optimize profits returned on investment by isolating groups of people who will have similar responses to a company's promotional activities and for whom the purchase rate is high. After these target market segments are identified, promotional activities can be tailored to their needs.

Computerized warehouse withdrawal reports on local markets (that is, specific cities) are proving an enormous aid to companies desirous of segmenting their markets geographically. These monthly computerized reports enable sales managers to immediately pinpoint their strongest and weakest markets; product managers can gauge the relative impact of private labels on a market-to-market basis; and the relative impact of off-label deals as opposed to invoice deals can be measured for the first time. These computerized reports are available on magnetic tape or punched cards and can be used as input for a company's computerized market segmentation study.

Also especially valuable for segmentation studies are *Sales Management's*

"Survey of Buying Power" and Dun & Bradstreet's SIC (Standard Industrial Classification) data bank, which are also available on punched cards or tape.

Consumer Market Simulation and Mathematical Model Decision Making

Consumer market simulation is the artificial mathematical representation of a marketplace, with the elements of the marketplace quantified and reacting as they would in actual life.

The computer can be programmed to simulate purchasing behavior of households and individuals, to assign probabilities for product use in the next time period, and to come up with purchasing patterns of households and individuals in a particular sample. The results of this operations research technique can then be compared to actual store audits, region by region, to test their validity.

Mathematical model decision making is another operations research technique in which a model of a system is developed, incorporating measurements of risk to predict and compare the outcome of alternative decisions, strategies, and controls.

The operations of an entire business over a period of 400 weeks have been simulated on the computer, using only one minute of computer time. A quantified description of the company's operations, the economy, and the company's interaction with competitors within the economy is fed into the computerized model, which produces (as output) several alternatives for decisions about finances, manpower, product flow, and other items. From these alternatives, management has only to select the best ones. Some oil companies, for example, eliminate most of the guesswork in planning new service stations by simulating two or three years of operations at proposed sites. They then can select the site that promises the highest payoff.

This usage of the computer can be very important for managers since it allows them to test the consequences of various corporate decisions without actually committing resources.

Location of New Markets and Customers

The search for new markets and customers has been facilitated by the use of the computer by marketing managers and by the Commerce Department's

SIC System. The Commerce Department has assigned an SIC code (a government index) to businesses to indicate both the function and line of business in which the company is engaged. This SIC code can enable managers to locate new markets and customers in the following manner.

The first step is to analyze a company's sales records, locate the SIC codes for each customer, add percent of total sales for each SIC code, and break out each SIC classification geographically if desired. In this way, a company can classify its present market by industry and location.

The second step is to use government census reports and other secondary data ("Survey of Buying Power" or Dun & Bradstreet's SIC data bank, for example) to determine the potential market by industry and location. Comparing the results of step one and two provides a good idea of how the number of present customers compares with the number of potential customers in the marketplace.

With the advent of the computer, it has become a relatively simple task to locate new markets and customers by such techniques as SIC analysis, which can reveal untapped market potential.

Marketing Research

Marketing research is that research related to any phase of marketing, including test marketing, market segmentation, consumer market simulation, mathematical model decision making, location of new markets and customers, and media selection plans.

The speed of the computer in processing data is important. The sooner information is available about activities in the marketplace, the sooner corrective action can be initiated to remedy undesirable conditions.

Computers have been utilized by marketing managers in statistical analysis, especially in multivariate techniques (such as multiple regression and correlation) to study, simultaneously, the action of multiple variables—in processing of (questionnaire) survey results, in maintaining a data bank for future decision making, and in other ways.

Computerized data, used by market researchers, can be derived from internal data or can be purchased from numerous outside suppliers, such as The A. C. Nielsen Co., Audits & Survey, Inc., and MRCA, among others.

USE COMPUTERS IN ANALYZING YOUR SALES FUNCTION!

The computer's prodigious ability to digest millions of bits of information and to calculate at lightning speed the logic and interrelationships of seemingly unrelated data has been a useful management tool in analyzing the sales function.

Whether a task is the simple projection of historical trends, a sophisticated correlation of company sales with business indicators, the removing of seasonal factors from sales curves, or similar computations, computers can do it faster, more accurately, and in greater detail than any other method.

Sales Forecasting and Measuring Performance

Sales forecasting has been aided by the tremendous outpouring of statistical data in recent years. The Department of Commerce, trade associations, research organizations, and industry publications are but a few of the sources which send out a steady stream of socioeconomic data that are meaningful to business. The computer gives forecasters a ready tool with which to handle, select, digest, and manipulate these data.

The computer can aid a company in predicting future sales on the basis of past performance, the influence of outside factors, such as competitors, government restrictions, and other quantifiable variables. Obviously, the computer cannot make decisions, but can only speed the movement of data to the marketing managers, who then make the decisions, applying their own judgment to the computer printout.

If a company has accurate input and programs the computer to print out a logical sales forecast which is analyzed by managers with sound judgment, this company has a definite competitive advantage in the marketplace.

Sales forecasts can be used in scheduling production, in setting quotas, in hiring a sales force, in inventory control, and as planning tools by progressive management in creating future corporate strategy. Also, once the sales forecast is completed, it can become a useful check on the company's progress during the forecast year.

Sales forecasters can construct mathematical models, which consist of a series of forecasting equations based on the past and current history of a product. Sales forecasting models have been successfully utilized for products with a sales history in excess of one year.

Pillsbury's computer provides executives, at eight o'clock every weekday morning, with a complete analysis of the company's sales and inventory position as of closing time on the previous working day.

A major insurance company analyzes sales performance from every sales office on a daily, weekly, monthly, and annual basis and measures performance against the previous year's and the present sales goals. Data are summarized at corporate headquarters every Friday and are then mailed to area managers across the United States. On the following Monday morning, the area manager knows how his office is doing as compared to this period's quota and to past performance.

SIC analysis of a company's market penetration is another excellent way of measuring performance.

Monthly summaries of sales performance by territory, district, and region are helpful in sales control. A summary report of sales volume as compared with quota and of sales costs compared with budget keeps management aware of strong and weak spots.

Computers have proved effective in determining the best sales routes for traveling salesmen, routes which optimize their selling efforts. Given the necessary input, the computer can determine the route that minimizes the total distance, time, or expense in traveling through each of a designated set of points.

Such factors as time invested per sales call, number of calls per sale, miles traveled per sale, miles traveled, dollar sales, and cost per sales call are but a few of the possible ones a computer can measure that can prove helpful in the control of salesmen. With the help of the computer, the salesman may find himself traveling fewer miles, making fewer callbacks, rendering better customer service in less time, and making more income.

Setting Standards

Dorsey Laboratories set hiring standards for its salesmen by examining in detail the results of interviews and intelligence and psychological tests given present and former salesmen. With the help of a computer, the hundreds of bits of information about these salesmen were collated, and gradually group differences and similarities emerged. Since Dorsey estimated that it cost $20,000 to put one salesman in the field, any standards which screened out potential dropouts could mean additional profits for the company. In two years of operation, the turnover rate was reduced from more than 50 percent to 24 percent.

Standards can also be set for the following cost items, which can be compared by the computer: (1) cost per dollar of net sales, (2) cost per dollar of gross profit, (3) cost per unit sold, (4) cost per sales transaction, and (5) cost per order received.

In setting standards, the computer can easily be programmed to utilize the principle of exception reporting whenever standards are not adhered to.

Computers are utilized by marketing management in setting such standards as quotas, defining sales territories, and setting other standards which contribute to achieving the corporate goals.

Order Entry Systems

An order entry system is any system in which data on an order cause the computer to produce some related action as output, such as a shipping label, paycheck, invoice, credit rejection notice, refund, or sales-compared-to-quota report.

A computerized order entry system could automatically cause a shipping label to be typed, subtract the transaction file (orders) from the master file (inventory), compute salesmen's commission, and even reorder whenever inventory fell below a certain level.

Analysis of Sales Territories

Sales territories can be analyzed by SIC code, zip code, comparison of internal sales data with external data—such as that purchased from an outside supplier—and in numerous other ways. Firms might analyze their sales territories for numerous reasons, including segmenting their market, locating new customers and markets, or realigning sales quotas.

Product Pricing

Mobil Oil utilizes the computer to analyze market prices and then instructs its refineries to turn out whatever combination of products will be the most profitable.

Du Pont used a mathematical model to set the price for its leatherlike new synthetic, Corfam. After examining the computer's projections of the probable sales, competitive activity, profits and other variables at different prices, management set its product price at $1.10 to $1.25 per square foot, which is about the cost of top-grade calfskin.

In an indirect manner, EDP can affect product pricing by optimizing inventory control, which in turn can smooth out production scheduling and allow a company to cut costs and, perhaps, price its goods more competitively. Thus, although a respondent does not directly use the computer in product pricing, his product pricing may very likely be indirectly influenced by the computer.

USE COMPUTERS IN YOUR MERCHANDISE–CLERICAL FUNCTION!

Every firm must have enough inventory to meet the needs of its customers, but inventory maintained beyond this amount costs money needlessly, and thus reduces corporate profits.

It costs money to own and maintain an inventory. Generally, this cost is at least 10 percent per year and may run as high as 30 percent. Thus every $1 million of inventory, at the minimum, costs $100,000 annually.

The computer has great potential in the corporate merchandise–clerical function for cost reduction as well as for time-saving or lead-time advantage. Companies that get a constant flow of computerized information about inventory and sales can operate with much smaller inventories than they did in the past. With computerized inventory control, it is unlikely that a company will suddenly find itself with such excessive inventory that it is forced to cut back on production (and employment) until the inventory is whittled down.

Large grocery distributors, cooperatives, and chains have utilized the computer for tighter inventory control and then sold these computerized records of merchandise movement to corporate users.

The computer (EDP) is very well utilized by management in inventory control.

Greater Clerical Efficiency and Accuracy

It has been estimated that at least one-sixth of our gross national product is devoted to data handling. Computers make a tremendous contribution by doing this work more quickly, efficiently, and accurately.

The computer's main purpose is to reduce the cost of data handling. The cost squeeze has induced industry to replace many manual procedures by the more economical computer procedures.

Northrup Corporation's Norvair Division in Hawthorne, California, saved $1.8 million per year when it automated its data handling and paperwork. Norvair estimates that it saves 425 man-hours daily in its use of EDP.

Accumulation of Facts for Future Reports and for Scheduling Production

Many companies are developing a companywide data base, in which all data used in the company's various automated systems are stored in one location. This centralization of data makes it possible to provide management with information that otherwise would not be practical to obtain.

With the development of third-generation computers, with their mass random-access memory for storing data in a central location, their time-sharing capabilities, and remote terminal devices which give marketing management push-button access to facts, companies have begun developing their own management information system (MIS). This MIS stores facts for future reports and gives management the ability to control operations and make effective decisions by having facts available as fast as they occur.

Marketing research firms, trade associations, U.S. government agencies, and such organizations as The Roper Public Opinion Research Center maintain computerized data banks. These banks can prove useful to industrial companies as repositories for facts that can be combined with the corporate data bank to produce various corporate reports.

RCA used the computer in 1967 to adjust production of color TV sets and components when its sales forecasts proved incorrect. After analyzing its past and present sales on a computer and comparing the result with inventory levels, RCA noted that its inventory–sales ratio increased from 1.4 in December 1966, to 1.9 in March 1967. Production was immediately cut back in March 1967, and 2,600 workers were laid off. RCA spokesmen have stated that they feel that their production scheduling is performed at least 100 percent better by a computer.

In addition to being vital in scheduling production, the sales forecast is necessary in realigning sales quotas and territories, maintaining inventory and backup stocks, and ordering supplies and materials. Corporate profits, cash flow, manpower and materials requirements, capital equipment, and plant expansion are all predicted in the forecast. Overcasting can result in costly buildup of inventories. Undercasting can result in idle labor and equipment, costly overtime operations, and late deliveries to customers.

Analysis of past and present sales is a vital element in scheduling future production.

Economic Data as Correctives
in Scheduling Production

Celanese Corporation constructs custom-tailored input-output tables using economic data (GNP and others) issued by such governmental agencies as the Office of Business Economics. These tables allow Celanese to create mathematical models of its company and industry and to make assumptions about the future interrelationships with the industries it buys from and sells to, including industry-by-industry demand for their products. Since Celanese sells products to more than 100 industries, such a forecast, using input-output analysis, was deemed essential in order to supply economic data which could be used as a corrective in scheduling production. By continuously developing annual input-output tables, changes in the coefficients should alert management to both market and technological trends that prove valuable as correctives.

These input-output tables allow corporate management to examine and forecast effects upon its own operations of possible changes in the industries that use its products either directly or indirectly. They are generally custom-tailored by companies which purchase detailed input-output tables of the national industrial economy from a supplier of economic data. The purchaser then custom-tailors the tables to meet his corporate requirements.

The computer's dexterity in tracing hard-to-see relationships among complex data makes it an ideal means of using economic data as a corrective in scheduling production.

Most large industrial corporations are affected by economic data. A rise in the standard of living and a decrease in the personal income tax rate, for example, may result in additional sales for many corporations. In order to have available for sale the additional items that the corporation anticipates selling, corporations must use this economic data as a corrective in scheduling production.

*   *   *

Respondents to this 1968 random-sample study indicated that their major reason for using the computer was that EDP produced improved marketing information, which allowed managers to make more accurate decisions and therefore do a better job for their company and so contribute to increased corporate profits.

As every competent executive knows, making a decision involves taking a risk. However, when the computer furnishes improved marketing information, this risk is lessened, and the potential danger to the company due to error is reduced.

5

What Marketing Managers Really Need to Know About Computers

Roman R. Andrus

TODAY'S BUSINESS EXECUTIVE cannot escape awareness of the rapid growth and potential of the computer. He hears myriad stories of new, important, and often exotic computer applications. But he also hears rumors and occasionally reports of computer "horror stories." Salesmen, technical reports, and promotional literature bombard him with information about equipment and software. He is intimidated by a new alphabetized EDP jargon. There is a proliferation of computer conferences sponsored by trade associations, professional groups, consulting firms, universities, computer firms, and private individuals. A growing number of publications focus on the computer.

Is it any wonder that executives have felt a good deal of frustration about their relationship with the computer? The frustration has spawned the stories, the conferences, the journals, and the articles (including this one). But, hopefully, some sense can be made of the alphabetic and numerically coded hardware, the jargonized software, and the problems of communicating with programmers "from another world." There should be a sensible approach to learning about the computer and its role in marketing management.

Few executives would dare disregard the computer, especially in light of the tremendous impact which the machine has already had on so many other activities, ranging from the space program to banking and already including many marketing functions.

The real problem is anticipating and facilitating future computer applications, while avoiding the competitive losses or personal obsolescence which might result from failure to use the machine.

The purpose here is to categorize the types of information which are valuable to the executive in understanding and creatively using the computer and to suggest a priority by which he should approach their mastery.

What Can You Learn About the Computer?

There are basically three forms of computer expertise which the manager may acquire.

1. He may master the ever expanding catalog of available computer hardware. He may do this not only by unraveling the alphabetic and numerical mysteries of brand comparabilities, but also by becoming familiar with the generalized capabilities of available equipment, not only in terms of milliseconds, bits, and bytes, but in terms of task capabilities: what they can do; what you have to do to get it done; how much space, time, and expertise are required; and how much the job will cost. It is impressive to be able to cite technical differences between the Univac 1108 and the IBM 360-50 (and perhaps necessary for a member of the corporate computer acquisition committee), but cataloging this type of information should more profitably be the function of the respective computer salesmen.

It would seem useful for the marketing manager to trust what seems apparent—that equipment capabilities will probably far outstrip his ability to use them—and to focus his energies on other preparations for computer applications. The manager's major effort should be directed toward delineating the role which the computer will be expected to play in the firm and the tasks which it will be expected to perform.

2. The manager may develop computer language competence. This competence may take at least two forms: (a) the ability to use computer languages and (b) the ability to communicate with "computer people."

The executive may develop programming skills through mastering one or several of the currently available computer languages. For most executives, however, it is probably most desirable to hire this type of expertise, especially in light of the rapid evolution which computer languages seem to undergo and the common prediction that, within a decade, it will be possible to communicate directly with the computer using ordinary English, even in handwritten form. If an executive feels that he should learn a language, perhaps the simple BASIC language developed at Dartmouth and already adapted to several brands of equipment would be most practical.

The availability of time-sharing remote terminals, which may be used directly on the job, in the office, is probably the best argument for mastery of a computer language such as BASIC. It is also indicative that the manager must learn not only how to communicate with the machine, but, more important, he must learn what to ask the computer.

The executive may concentrate on the language of computer people, rather than on the language of the computer. His familiarity with their jargon will facilitate solution of the difficult problems of bridging the communication gap between the executive and the corporate computer staff. A side effect of this approach will be to equip the executive with an arsenal of impressive buzzwords which will be useful in dealing with his peers. Oscar Wilde's observation that "Nowadays to be intelligible is to be found out" is two-edged. A command of computer jargon will be useful not only in understanding hardware, software, and their disciples but also in creating a certain personal aura of expertise.

3. The executive may become a software expert. He may accomplish this through studying the multitude of available software packages offered by computer equipment manufacturers, universities, and consultants, and by a rapidly growing number of private firms dealing in software services.

This is probably the area where the executive may more profitably devote his energies, not in cataloging a wide variety of programs and services, but in identifying data processing solutions to specific marketing problems. To use Peter Drucker's terms, the computer is indeed an efficient, fast, and accurate "moron." Through software instructions, man gives the machine its brain. Instructions do not exist without the goals, tasks, or programs which generate them. This is the basic problem underlying management's use of the computer and its difficulty in communicating with computer people. Marketing computer instructions are meaningless unless they follow the specification of marketing functions. Marketing goals and procedures must be made explicit before they may become computer functions.

The First Priority: Noncomputer Knowledge

There is a certain mystique about computers which leads people to expect them to produce wonderful and incomprehensible solutions to problems which are yet undefined. Perhaps this is due to the machine's reliance upon electronics and mathematics, which are themselves largely mysteries to most people.

In spite of this mystique, however, it is commonly known that computers can do only those things for which they are programmed. If the computer is to make marketing decisions, whether they involve inventories, prices, media, or product design, it must be programmed to do so. If the machine is to make these decisions based on the informational inputs, criteria, and assumptions upon which the executive wishes decisions to be based, he must see that they are included in the program. No intuitive or other decision elements, regardless of how basic they are to the executive's own decision processes, will be used by the computer unless they are programmed.

This fact has led executives to forsake the "stupid" machine for its inattention to "obvious facts," and it has led computer programmers to make basic market assumptions. In fact, one programmer recently suggested, in all seriousness, that he was sure it would be much easier to make marketing executives out of programmers than to teach marketing executives to use the machine. Some people feel that this is pretty much analagous to letting the secretary make business decisions rather than teaching the executive to use the typewriter. Perhaps it is possible for programmers to continue to do the programming and for executives to continue to administer and to have the services of the computer in doing it.

How to Use the Computer Without Becoming a Programmer

If you make the realistic assumption that sufficient hardware and software capabilities can be made available, then the problem of integrating the computer in marketing is one of understanding and specifying marketing management processes—thus making them programmable—rather than one of mastering computer languages and hardware.

The reason that accounting, engineering, production, and even finance departments usually have greater access to and utilization of the computer than the marketing staff is that they have been able to define their activities in more objective terms than the current state of marketing decision making permits. In short, those activities are more programmable because of their more exact nature and the "cleaner," more specific, and measurable delineation of tasks, inputs, and goals. If marketing is to get greater utilization of the computer, its processes must also become more objectively defined. Criteria, alternatives, goals, and procedures must be identified. Fortunately, a number of analytical tools and approaches have been and are now being developed which will facilitate this progress. The manager concerned with greater computer marketing application can most profitably become familiar with these developments. Once specifically identified, marketing activities will readily lend themselves to computer execution.

The types of information which must be developed in order to make marketing activities more compatible with computer applications are essentially the same types of information which identify or develop the superior manager. He must be able to accurately identify goals and objectives; available resources and alternatives; and decision processes, procedures, and criteria. He may use a variety of approaches in the identification and specification of these items. These approaches, however, are not substitutes for familiarity with the tasks and environment of the marketing manager. Rather, they are devices for organizing and fully utilizing job familiarity and experience.

Perhaps the most valuable currently available tool for understanding marketing tasks is carried in the broad term, "systems approach." In general terms the systems approach involves an understanding of the elements and relationships of an interacting group of elements or institutions and their accompanying flows of information, influence, authority, or power. In marketing, this approach implies the application of at least five specific types of tools. They are (1) models, (2) decision theory, (3) information systems, (4) economic, behavioral, and organization theories, and (5) quantitative techniques.

Models. Models may be either descriptive or normative; that is, they may be used either as devices for analyzing and understanding an environment or for the purpose of determining the desirable action in a given situation.

Every marketing executive has some sort of implicit or intuitive model or conception of the nature of his operating environment and the determinants of expected success or failure of available alternatives. For example, an executive may visualize his market as consisting of a situation where prices which differ from those of a designated industry leader will not optimize profits. His decision approach would then consist of simply watching the leader's price and emulating any change which he initiated. In the same situation another executive might see governmental pressures and dealer reactions as having a strong effect on pricing effectiveness. In this case the decision model would include some sort of sequential or simultaneous response not only to competitor behavior, but also to the behavior of dealers and regulating agencies. (See Exhibit 5–1.) Until marketing theorists design general, all-purpose marketing models, the executive should work on modeling—that is, specifying the individual factors and their relationships—for his own unique decision environment. Logical flow models provide a useful approach to specifying and hence programming these relationships. The executive should attempt to develop models which make explicit his perception of his environment and relevant opportunities and constraints. The types of decision information gathered and processed will be dictated by the conceptual model which the executive holds of his situation.

Decision theory. The ability to recognize the processes by which an executive makes decisions is essential to the development of the explicit models discussed here. In the past two decades, a good deal of work has been done in specifying the nature of decision processes and in developing approaches for identifying and analyzing alternatives. These techniques are invaluable for modern management.

Information systems. The design of an efficient system for the selection, storage, and retrieval of management information provides two immediate benefits: (1) It avoids intrafirm information processing duplications, and (2) it provides executive time economies resulting from the instant availability of needed information, free from an overburden of irrelevant and frequently uninterpretable data. The opportunities for information system design utilizing the huge storage and rapid retrieval capabilities of the computer are obvious. But equally obvious is the fact that the design of an effective information system must be based upon an evaluation of the value and use of available information. If specific information needs are not identified, the process of collection and retrieval will be meaningless, if not impossible.

Organization, behavior, and economic theories. Just as it is important to understand the decision process and to facilitate the desired information flows, it is equally important to understand behavior and relationships within the economic system and within and between firms and individuals and their customers. Three academic disciplines offer a wealth of information about the executive's environment. Organization theory examines the ways in which information and influence patterns within a formal organization, such as a firm, affect its ability to accomplish its goals and those of its members. Such basic concepts as control, motivation, authority, and so on are the heart of this discipline. Economic theory is concerned with the way in which a

Exhibit 5-1
Follower Pricing Models

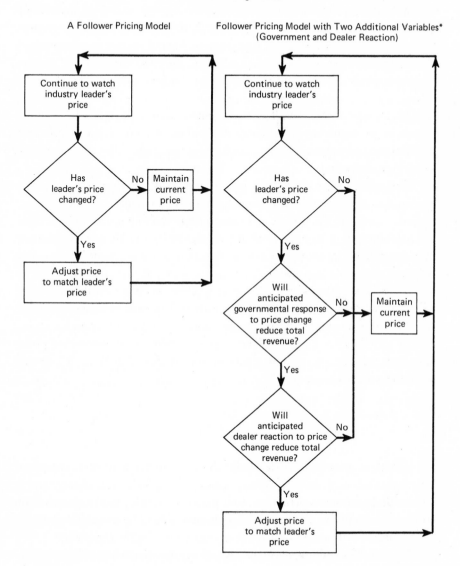

A Follower Pricing Model

Follower Pricing Model with Two Additional Variables*
(Government and Dealer Reaction)

*A large number of variables may affect the results of pricing decisions, including brand image consumer loyalty and response, supplier and dealer response, and governmental as well as competitive behavior. As the number of variables increases, and their interrelationships change and the sequence of their consideration is modified, the model itself will also be modified. However, the modeling approach will be the same.

society's resources are distributed. An understanding of it is essential in such areas as pricing, market forecasting, and competitive behavior. The behavioral sciences are concerned with explaining the actions of individuals and groups. They may be used, for example, to understand customer or supplier behavior, relationships of distribution channel members, promotional effectiveness, brand loyalty, and purchasing patterns. Organization theory, economic theory, and behavioral theories are essential to marketing management.

Quantitative techniques. The management science approach has yielded a number of significant techniques which allow for the quantification and manipulation of previously unspecified marketing (and other management) decision components.

The ability to specify criteria, inputs, and results was the basis for early applications of computer technology to accounting, engineering, the sciences, and other fields. It will also be so in marketing. Marketing, however, is characterized by a high degree of subjective, dynamic, and frequently intuitive decision making. Such techniques as Bayesian statistics, game theory, and heuristics allow for unproven, changing, nonoptimal inputs to be stated in specific (and hence programmable) terms. These techniques will be the basis for increased marketing computer application. It seems reasonable that the executive should understand the nature and capabilities of available quantitative techniques and models. The details of their use, however, are probably best delegated to staff nembers or consultants. Exhibit 5–2 presents several of these techniques.

What Should Be the Manager's Priority?

Given the possibility of learning about computer hardware, computer languages, software, systems theory, logical flow models, role theory, and a variety of quantitative techniques, and given the already heavy demands of current operations on an executive's time, how should he proceed to prepare for maximum utilization of the opportunities offered by the computer?

An attitude should be developed about the machine which is based upon understanding rather than upon fear and frustration. Its potential should be identified. The executive should attempt to learn about its capabilities just as he would about any other capital or personnel addition to his operation. The computer is a data manipulation device capable of storing and recalling information, sequencing activities, and "accumulating" (thus performing a

(*text continues on page 66*)

Exhibit 5-2
Quantitative Marketing Models and Techniques

Technique	Description	Application*
PERT–CPM	• Method for planning and control using a critical path technique.	• Schedule and cost control
Bayesian statistics	• Decision model utilizing personal probability in an explicit form. Allows for revision of old probabilities upon receipt of new information.	• Decisions involving expected risk.
Classical statistical analysis (probability)	• Probability sampling and multivariant analysis (correlation, multiple regression, factor analysis). Finds variable relationships.	• Marketing research and forecasting.
Time series analysis	• Arithmetic trend projections.	• Forecasting.
Econometric models	• Breakeven, cash flow, and demand analysis.	• Product and activity evaluation.
Allocation models	• Linear, nonlinear, integer, and dynamic programming; transportation and traveling salesman models.	• Allocation of scarce resources (time, manpower, money, etc.). Media, sales, scheduling, etc.
Brand-switching and waiting-line models	• Behavior predictive and scheduling models.	• Forecasting and scheduling.
Monte Carlo techniques and game theory	• Models for predicting competitive behavior under uncertainty.	• Competitive strategy evaluation.
Heuristic programming	• Use of decision rules or principles as constraints in problem solving. Computer "learns" for solving problem.	• Situations where useful nonoptimizing principles are applicable.
Simulation	• Computer representation of real situation. Dynamic, responsive model (may involve many other specific quantitative techniques).	• Media selection, inventory control, pricing, forecasting, management training

*Computer Approaches to Marketing Problems

Product Policy:
    New products:
        PERT–CPM
        Bayesian analysis
        Simulation (except DEMON and SPRINTER)
    Product mix:
        Linear and nonlinear programming

Advertising:
    Media selection:
        Linear and nonlinear programming
        Bayesian analysis
        Simulation (except high assay)
    Advertising appeals:
        Content analysis
        Semantic banks
        Pupilometric data analysis

Sales Management:
    Training:
        Simulation-business games
    Control:
        Data processing (feedback: reports, etc.)
    Forecasting:
        Time series analysis (including exponential smoothing)
        Correlation, regression, factor analysis, and discrimination analysis
        Simulation
        Markov analysis
Distribution Design:
    Inventory control and warehouse location:
        Linear programming
        Simulation
        Heuristic programming
    Scheduling: PERT–CPM
Marketing Research:
    Bayesian analysis
    Classical statistical analysis

Exhibit 5-3
Computer Preparation: The Executive Priority Table

Priority	Area	Type of Knowledge
1	The Firm's Environment Customers, competitors, products, markets, suppliers, etc.	• Parameters and opportunities for successful manipulation of the marketing mix.
2	Tools for Organizing and Specifying Experience • Models. • Organization, behavior, and economic theories. • Information systems. • Decision theory. • Quantitative techniques.	• Devices for specifying relationships. • Understanding of the internal and external environments of firm. • Provide inputs for marketing decision making. • Understanding of the processes and techniques of decisions. • Tools for specifying marketing decisions processes.
3	Computer Knowledge • Computer jargon. • Software. • Hardware. • Programming.	• The ability to speak the language of "computer people." • "Canned" programs available for a variety of general problems. • Technical and functional capabilities and brand comparability of available equipment. • Ranging from BASIC to elaborate special-purpose languages.

Logic of Priorities

1. A marketing manager must understand his decision opportunities and restrictions. At present there is no substitute for experience in manipulating the marketing mix in the marketplace. Knowledge of his marketing environment must be the manager's first priority.

2. Marketing theory provides a number of approaches which are useful in facilitating, specifying, and organizing one's understanding of the process of successful marketing decision making. These tasks are essential to computer programming of marketing activities. Models provide an analytical framework. Decision theory and organization economic and behavior theories provide reference concepts. Information systems provide data. Quantitative techniques assist in the translation of marketing activities into specific computer-manipulatable symbols.

3. Executive computer expertise, beyond that necessary to understand capabilities, communicate with programmers, acquire hardware, or impress one's peers, must rank far below an understanding of the environment and nature of marketing tasks. If the first two priorities listed above are accomplished, quantitative and computer skills should probably be left to staff personnel. It may safely be assumed that machine capabilities will not be a limiting factor in future computer applications—except on a cost basis.

Exhibit 5-4
The Marketing Manager's Model for Using the Computer

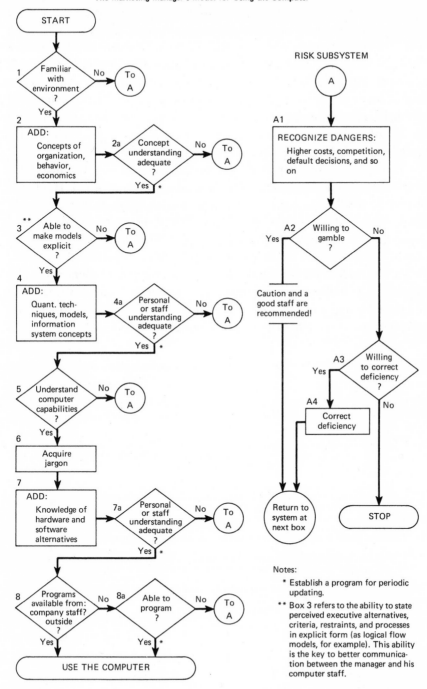

Notes:

* Establish a program for periodic updating.

** Box 3 refers to the ability to state perceived executive alternatives, criteria, restraints, and processes in explicit form (as logical flow models, for example). This ability is the key to better communication between the manager and his computer staff.

variety of mathematical and logical steps). It should be recognized that the presence of a computer does not provide a technique for problem solving. The computer is merely a tool for the execution of techniques which have been translated into software. And the executive should recognize that the computer will force him to be more precise in the delineation and performance of his own function and that of the marketing staff. The computer will not make an executive obsolete, unless his decision effectiveness, as a result of lack of understanding about his own function and environment or his ability to specify his perceptions, is already inadequate.

The answer to the preparation question appears obvious. The marketing manager should develop a keener understanding of his own job. He should attempt to develop the logical and detailed models of his own environment, alternatives, and parameters which will allow him to specifically state his goals, decision procedures, alternatives, and criteria. Having done this, he should find that he has not only increased his ability to perform his job, but he has also bridged the communication gap with computer programmers and increased his ability to use the machine. Exhibits 5–3 and 5–4 present a priority table and a flow-charted model for executives preparing to integrate computer operations into their decision processes.

PART TWO

Inventory Management
and Physical Distribution

6

First Conquest
of the Computer in Marketing

Evelyn Konrad

INVENTORY CONTROL AND MANAGEMENT, as a function, bears the closest similarity to problems of logistics in the armed services. And, of course, some of the most recent innovations in operations research came out of these activities two and three decades ago.

The chapters in this section will provide some insights into the veritable revolution that the computer has caused in inventory management. Its impact has ranged from simple take-over of clerical control functions to the development of an entirely new relationship between the source of production (or manufacturing) and the ultimate buyer of the product.

Many of the truly sophisticated computer applications to inventory management require and deserve separate treatment in books on the subject. And, indeed, such books do exist. However, for the marketing man seeking a clearer understanding of the many ways in which computer applications can improve the effectiveness and efficiency of the diverse operations within his domain, this section will serve to introduce some successful applications of computer models to the key questions in inventory management and control.

7

Trends in Inventory Management

Arthur B. Toan, Jr.

WHAT HAS BEEN HAPPENING to inventory management?

What part have computers and the techniques of operations research played?

Is the total impact measurable?

What industries (or types of inventories) have seen the greatest improvement?

Management has, in the past ten years, used a combination of old and new techniques to try to use its inventory dollar more effectively. In most instances, "more effectively" has been defined as substantially equivalent to "smaller in relation to sales." Not always, however, for the goals of improved inventory management can also result in increases in inventory—to provide better service to customers; to support a wider variety of products, often at least partially personalized through permitting selection from a range of options; to stabilize a workforce; to simplify production scheduling; to permit transportation economies; and so forth. Inventories constitute a buffer that provides a substitute for time and an opportunity for the economy of scale. Inventory reductions can be considered advantageous only in relation to the achievement of a balanced set of goals.

Factors Affecting Inventory Management

A number of factors—some old, some new—have affected inventory management. Among the old, for example, might be cited something as prosaic as the shortage of money, for as *The Wall Street Journal* headlined a couple of years ago, "Tight Money Prompts Firms to Hold Down Inventories." Working in the other direction can easily be such old-time problems as a fear of delays, strikes, price increases, and shortages—factors which would tend to override an otherwise strong desire to minimize inventory quantities.

Other factors, tending to reduce inventories overall, although not necessarily for a specific company, would be the following:

1. Faster transportation. This (a) reduces the time that goods are in transit and thus available to no one and (b) permits smaller stocks to be carried at the outer perimeters of the distribution system because of the speed with which they can be supplied from a central point. Air shipments are perhaps the most visible example of this approach.

2. Faster communications techniques. Alone or in conjunction with faster transportation, they permit the central producing or warehousing unit (a) to know more quickly and accurately what is happening in the market, (b) to react more quickly and accurately to such changes, and (c) to supply the market from new production or from smaller central inventories with what the market actually requires.

3. Better administrative systems (often computer based and utilizing better communications devices). These, among other things, record and transmit customer orders faster and more accurately, assist in shipping goods faster (with or without automated warehouses), schedule and control production facilities more tightly and more accurately, permit more rapid adjustments to meet new needs, and facilitate the purchasing process.

4. More flexible production facilities, at times using devices like numerically controlled tools. These facilities permit greater and more rapid adjustments of the production process and also facilitate matching sales requirements with production capabilities.

5. Increased recognition of the importance of good sales forecasts and improvements in the collection and analysis of more reliable market data.

6. The techniques of operations research (with or without computers). These techniques have helped to sharpen up sales forecasts, to make analyses of past usage more useful and more available, to make transportation and distribution systems more efficient, and to bring about a more rational and scientifically based understanding of the relative value and cost of the various forces which alternatively tug in the direction of larger or smaller inventories.

7. Changes in "business practices." Many retailers are trying to force wholesalers to carry more of their particular product, and wholesalers are pushing inventory down to the manufacturers, who in turn are pushing as much as they can of their inventory back on their suppliers. Coupled with this trend are changes in the number, size, and location of stores and in such intangibles as customer attitudes.

These are not all the forces at work; nevertheless, the list should serve to indicate (1) that many factors are operative and (2) that attempts to isolate the effect of any one or two sets of factors are bound to be rather hopeless on any across-the-economy basis.

Overall Indications of Inventory Management

One overall indication of the effectiveness of inventory management is the ratio of business inventories to monthly sales published by the U.S. Department of Commerce in its *Survey of Current Business.* Data about certain industries or classes of industries for certain selected years since 1960 are shown in Exhibits 7–1 and 7–2.

It is very difficult to generalize about progress by industries, particularly because of the wide variation in the efforts made by individual companies. By and large, one could state that those companies and industries which have been most aggressive and imaginative in their use of computers probably have also most improved their inventory management. In part, this reflects the importance of computers in inventory management; it also reflects the kind of atmosphere and drives within which efforts to improve inventory management are apt to flourish.

A further indication of the potential for improved inventory management may exist in the results attained through specific attempts to bring about inventory reductions in specific companies. They would seem to indicate that reductions of from 10 to 25 percent are somewhere between possible and

Exhibit 7-1
Ratio of Inventories to Monthly Sales

	All Manufacturing	Durable Goods	Nondurable Goods
1960	1.76	2.08	1.42
1962	1.70	1.97	1.42
1964	1.64	1.91	1.35
1966	1.62	1.85	1.34
1967	1.77	2.08	1.40
1968	1.70	2.01	1.33
7/31/1969	1.70	2.04	1.29
	Wholesale Trade	Durable Goods	Nondurable Goods
1960	1.23	1.69	.89
1962	1.16	1.57	.86
1964	1.13	1.49	.86
1966	1.14	1.49	.85
1967	1.22	1.61	.91
1968	1.20	1.54	.92
7/31/1969	1.20	1.54	.91
	Retail Trade	Durable Goods	Nondurable Goods
1960	1.43	1.95	1.20
1962	1.40	1.83	1.18
1964	1.40	1.86	1.18
1966	1.44	2.00	1.18
1967	1.47	2.03	1.21
1968	1.44	2.00	1.18
7/31/1969	1.50	2.11	1.23

Exhibit 7-2
Trends by Industries
(Dollars in Millions)

	1962		1964		1966		1968	
	Monthly Sales	Inventory	Monthly Sales	Inventory	Monthly Sales	Inventory	Monthly Sales	Inventory
Durable Goods Industries								
Stone, clay, and glass products	961	1,492	960	1,587	1,219	1,907	1,313	2,219
Primary metals	2,835	5,873	3,236	6,111	4,127	7,226	4,205	7,552
Fabricated metal products	1,859	3,861	1,962	4,251	2,576	5,415	2,848	6,287
Machinery, except electrical	2,366	6,486	2,808	7,558	3,890	10,248	4,837	11,310
Electrical machinery	2,301	4,900	2,517	5,388	3,400	7,930	3,529	8,560
Transportation machinery	4,453	6,799	4,969	7,908	6,273	10,762	7,014	13,939
Motor vehicles and parts	2,806	2,413	3,204	3,013	3,928	3,706	3,970	4,257
Instruments and related products	557	1,365	627	1,619	737	1,863	947	2,183
Nondurable Goods Industries								
Food and kindred products	5,577	6,028	6,324	6,030	6,644	6,922	7,513	7,370
Tobacco products	377	2,314	391	2,359	398	2,226	410	2,261
Textile mill products	1,263	2,886	1,484	2,837	1,634	3,072	1,788	3,539
Paper and allied products	1,314	1,800	1,426	1,885	1,701	2,185	2,017	2,384
Chemicals and allied products	2,449	3,818	2,798	4,003	3,400	5,230	3,872	5,937
Petroleum and coal products	1,433	1,736	1,516	1,745	1,700	1,861	1,856	2,118
Rubber and plastics	710	1,157	851	1,176	998	1,582	1,189	1,801

probable in a "company of average efficiency." Experience would also seem to indicate that these results, once attained, are not automatically held but require constant attention.

Effect on Capital

There is no question but that the demand for capital to finance inventories influences the capital and the debt structure and the return on investment of both a particular company and industry in general. It is also widely believed to affect the height and depth of cyclical swings. In a particular company, reductions in inventories can reduce the requirements for either short-term borrowing or more permanent types of capital.

They undoubtedly have done so in some cases. However, they are only one of many factors at work—not the least of which are inflation and the overall growth of the economy. Thus the effect of inventory changes is hard to single out. In most instances, factors other than improved inventory management would seem to be more important.

8

Inventory Management, Physical Distribution, and the Computer: An Overview

Evelyn Konrad

PHYSICAL DISTRIBUTION is the amorphous, hybrid marketing function that makes up for its lack of glamour by its vast impact not only on the profits or net earnings and the asset valuation of any manufacturing concern but on the total marketing function down to the firm's customer servicing capabilities.

What does physical distribution really mean? The National Council of Physical Distribution Management defines it as follows:

> The broad range of activities concerned with efficient movement of finished products from the end of the production line to the consumer. These activities include freight transportation, warehousing, material handling, protective packaging, order processing, market forecasting, inventory control, plant and warehouse site selection, customer service.

Let us look beyond the definition. Physical distribution is that part of the marketing function that presents the greatest challenge to company managements intent on finding meaningful computer solutions. The complexities involved in so doing are the result of diverse factors implicit in organization structure, the interrelationship of this so-called marketing function with the production and financial function in a company, and the gigantic economic implications of the problems involved in physical distribution.

Consider, for example, the fact that 25 to 50 cents of the consumer's average dollar is spent in moving goods. Equally significant and more obvious to the business community is the fact that physical distribution represents the third-largest cost component in meeting the demands for a company's products. This means that if physical distribution costs could be reduced, profits could be higher, price-earnings ratios could be improved (with all the implications of this formula on a company's cost of capital), and consumers be given bargains (with all the implications that this simple phrase carries for a company seeking to gain a competitive edge by improving its share of market).

Yet computer applications have brought into this area both the advantages and management head-scratching implicit in a wealth of cures that produce new illnesses. To illustrate this vicious cycle, let us consider briefly the implications of superbly computerized inventory control on production costs when the former problem is solved out of context from the total company picture.

Among the best-known computer applications, familiar to those responsible for inventory management, are economic order quantities (EOQ) and reorder points (ROP). These applications are based on simulation programs which program into the computer the company experience or track record of demand for inventoried products and then sample this total experience through a random generator within the simulation program and come up with a mathematically correct probability curve which tells inventory management when it requires a new supply of product. The effect of these systems has been to free corporate funds from unnecessary inventory, to reduce the cost of inventory storing and handling, and to show spectacular cost efficiencies in this phase of the operation.

But what has been the effect of these inventory savings on the entirety of the company operation and operating costs?

At times, it has been disastrous: The positive results produced in this critical area have often introduced new problems into other equally critical company functions. For example, the same economic order quantities that proved to be most efficient from an inventory control and cost viewpoint may have imposed an inefficient production cycle on the manufacturing process which all but wiped out the profits generated by the newly found inventory efficiencies.

Sometimes less measurable is the effect of EOQ on the company's customer servicing abilities. However, the link between inventory and the customer or consumer is self-evident to marketing management albeit sometimes less easy to document in terms of dollars and cents. Indeed, the fact that these detrimental results are somewhat more difficult to define and measure and more long-range makes them more important to consider when individual aspects of physical distribution functions are committed to computer solutions.

Do these cautions negate the use of computer technique?

Of course not. They do, however, impose on corporate management the responsibility to view problems and solutions not within their functional limitations alone but in terms of their overall meaning to company objectives. In brief, little purpose is served if the organ transplant is successful but the patient dies of seemingly unrelated complications.

Sophisticated management is certainly aware of this dichotomy, and management consultants have been known to deal with it implicitly many times when they have broadened a company question originally addressed to them to deal with the more comprehensive problems at stake. Nonetheless, the fundamental guideline may deserve restating. As F. R. Denham, principal of Stevenson & Kellog, Ltd., management consultants, explains: "The essential principle of physical distribution management is to expand management's horizon and to encourage it to think of traffic, warehousing, inventories, and production planning as elements in a system, which only operates effectively when all elements are in tune with each other."*

Given that these broader considerations have been taken into account and that the marketing concept has been applied to physical distribution—with all the customer and consumer orientation implicit in the marketing concept—then the computer does indeed make a genuine and measurable contribution to this function.

For example, one of the most computer-sophisticated consumer products manufacturers, General Foods, reevaluated its customer needs some years ago and found itself distinctly insensitive to supermarket buying policies and needs in terms of the ordering and shipping of its own products. At the

---

* *Handling and Shipping,* October 1967.

time, retailers had to order products from this giant food manufacturer not from one centralized distribution system but rather according to product lines, since warehousing and shipping were directly related to the firm's multiple manufacturing plants. Therefore, Post Cereals came from Battle Creek, Michigan, and Maxwell House Coffee from Hoboken, New Jersey, with all the order duplications and shipping delays implicit.

After applying computer techniques within a broader customer-need and company-system analysis, General Foods established 19 distribution centers —according to population concentrations and therefore major food retailer warehousing patterns. Each of these distribution centers carries the entire General Foods line. The solution sounds logical enough even on the surface, and the customer-service Brownie points earned by General Foods from this change in physical distribution are equally apparent. The genuine computer sophistication is not as easy to detect. However, it contributed enormously to all the stages of the study: the system analysis, the distribution center locations, the physical layout of these centers (based recognizably on linear programming technique), the inventory control and shipping system, as well as the order handling and processing stages now employed.

At times, computerization has made it possible to centralize warehousing entirely. For example, Westinghouse was able to replace numerous and scattered warehouses throughout the country with a single central computerized warehouse not only without sacrificing service to distributors but actually improving it. This central warehouse is linked to Westinghouse distributors by dataphone: This allows the distributor or buyer to put his reorder on an EDP card and insert the card into his local transmission machine with the knowledge that it is instantaneously processed at the Westinghouse central warehouse by the computer controlling the total inventory supply. Not only does this system make same-day processing the normal routine, but the same computer handles the distributor invoicing and instructions for order picking in the warehouse. For Westinghouse this has meant a reduction in its inventory, which is reflected in the company's balance sheet. Speeded delivery time is, in turn, reflected in the firm's customer servicing advantage, and accelerated cash flow is reflected in an increase of investment or expansion funds.

This Westinghouse system, which may well have other U.S. manufacturing company parallels, is also duplicated by a fascinating and unusually successful retail giant overseas.

At times, the ultimate by-product of highly computerized physical distribution systems has been to plunge the manufacturer knee-deep into the retailing operation. This fact is illustrated by the new major appliance marketing program of the General Electric Company: Under this program, the manufacturer, General Electric, has assumed the entire inventory burden from the retailer, supplying each retailer only with floor samples. The retailer, in turn, completes the sale, and then the manufacturer takes over with a series of completely vertically integrated services beginning with computer-dictated withdrawal of the sold appliance from the General Electric warehouse and ending with its delivery to the home of the buyer. This is followed by demonstration, installation, and, when necessary, servicing of the appliance.

This General Electric system is an extension of the real-time computer order processing system that became operational at General Electric's purpose control department in 1967, and its functions and ramifications are sufficiently broad to deserve additional explanation.

The real-time aspect of this operation is actually not yet totally pure in a computer-desk unit sense of the word but refers rather to the almost-instant processing capabilities of the total approach. Perhaps, as a matter of fact, it is consistent with the unfortunate promotional overtones of the computer world that this system was announced as a real-time approach to the computer, even though the technical ramifications implicit in this description are not fully exploited in practice. At this time, General Electric simply means that a staff of order-takers man the telephones at the General Electric purpose control desks from 7 A.M. to 7 P.M., to take into account West Coast time differences and that orders are handled immediately as they are received by mail, telephone, Telex, and RECOMM. While there is time efficiency in this approach, this does not actually qualify the system as a real-time system in which computer "talks" to computer and bumps lesser priority jobs according to instructions that have been programmed into the real-time system beforehand.

Nonetheless, the outcome of the General Electric approach is a current 48- to 72-hour shipping capability from the moment an order is received. This represents a 50 percent improvement in speed of servicing and approaches the department's objective of a 24-hour turnaround on all stock products.

Of course, the system also includes direct input from some 800 distributors nationally—many of these on a direct real-time approach. To do this job, General Electric employs $1.5 million of hardware including the GE-225 computer, Datanet-30 controller, three random-access memory files with a capacity of over 55 million characters, plus printers and teletypes. The order-processing operation employs 80 people including key punchers, edit clerks, and computer operators. Actually, this is a remarkably small number of people to handle the General Electric volume, which can be measured in several thousands of orders a week for some 7,500 different devices and renewal parts both at the Bloomington plant and in 12 warehouses throughout the country plus 6,000 catalog items, which are built on short notice upon ordering.

Here is an instance where the physical distribution system has a direct impact on a product and manufacturing cycle: For items that have to be manufactured, the computer determines manufacturing lead time, generates a workorder for the factory, and prints an order acknowledgement for the customer.

In addition to direct order processing, the computer system also maintains inventory records for Bloomington and the branch warehouses, issues manufacturing orders when stock minimum limits are reached, and daily comes up with the answers to some 500 to 600 customer inquiries on order status. Such inquiries used to take from one to three days to handle, but answers now are provided within 24 hours, according to L. F. Steinbach, the manager of finance.

The new system has speeded up shipments of products stocked in or to be made by Bloomington and also has eliminated considerable paperwork and most of the human error in order processing. And now process control can hold the line on order-processing manpower while handling a vastly increased amount of business.

The real-time system required 15 man-years of programming and systems work to bring it to its present advanced state. The new system was operated in parallel with the previous manual order-handling system for a year to insure smooth operation before the cutover to complete computer operation was made.

From such an extreme example, it becomes obvious that the computer has brought us to the brink of a new distribution and mass retailing revolution, which may in some product lines eventually entirely bypass the need for the independent retailer. This trend, however, may find its counterweight in other consumer industries, where the computerized giant retailer is already forcing a consolidation of the small, independent, and splintered manufacturers, such as certain fashion products and soft goods companies. In this area, a reverse trend has already become apparent.

Contrary to some appliance and hard goods industries where the manufacturer has been able to free a fractionated retailing community from the inventory burden, the computerized mass retailers, such as sophisticated chain stores and department house complexes, have forced the inventory burden in other product lines onto a fractionated manufacturing community that lacks the resources to carry the inventory risks.

Here's an example of the same fundamental order and customer servicing system as is implicit in the General Electric program, but this instance originates with the retail community to the detriment of the small manufacturer:

Today, the Neiman-Marcus or Macy buyer of women's at-home wear— through use of a centralized simulation program comparable to an EOQ system—does not need to order and stock an entire season's supply. It is physically possible for the buyer to key the order and shipping process to match current demand and sales patterns.

On the other end, however, are the dozen or more small manufacturers of these products who are no longer able to plan a whole season's product based on large one-time orders but are forced by competitive pressures to go along with the day-by-day whims of consumers in the aggregate, sacrificing as they do this the retail giant buyer's willingness to exercise judgment and risk just to keep this splintered Seventh Avenue community in business.

As a direct result of consumer-sensitive computer programs among the retail giants, these small manufacturers find themselves in an untenable squeeze between the giant retailers and the giant suppliers of fabrics—the former with their unwillingness to carry inventory and assume risks, the latter with both a price structure geared to large-quantity orders and the size and power to make this price structure stick.

Ultimately, this condition in a small industry, produced by computerization in the physical distribution function, may well speed the trend to bigness and to mergers within the mass apparel manufacturing business. However, those who see in this trend a threat to product diversification might take heart from the fact that computerization at other levels of the marketing spectrum is now making it possible to virtually individualize and actually customize mass-produced assembly-line products, such as cars. Thus, with the exception of those "Mamma and Papa" manufacturers who cannot find shelter within a larger company home, the final impact of this computer-produced trend on the consumer is not necessarily an inevitable reduction in choice or quality of merchandise. There may be room, though, for speculation about the consumer's welfare in the broader context, as computer applications in physical distribution begin to affect the ownership patterns in some industries. Certainly, many of these computer applications do tend to speed trends toward centralization and bigness, with all the implicit socioeconomic and political ramifications that may best be left to the soul-searching of dedicated future economists.

9

Physical Distribution and the Computer: How Can It and How Does It Work?

Evelyn Konrad

THE EXTENT TO WHICH computerization contributes to overall company profits is in geometric proportion to the management level at which the potential contribution of such computerization to decision making is fully understood.

This pseudo-mathematical proposition may sound like a mere truism couched in current buzzwords until it is measured against some current and documented evidence. In the business world, we find a dramatic example of this apparently self-evident contention in current applications to physical distribution problems.

This particular marketing function alone offers a large choice of mathematically sophisticated solutions to an incredible variety of logical business questions:

- ■ What is the best location of new warehouses in view of current and anticipated business and plant shifts and changes in transportation systems?
- ■ What is the best layout, in terms of both efficiency and cost saving, for a new warehouse?
- ■ How should merchandise be stacked and laid out within a warehouse for most efficient handling and least costly access to the merchandise in terms of manpower saving and customer servicing?
- ■ How precisely can inventory needs be anticipated in order to help level out production cycles and simultaneously back up the company sales effort?

These are typical and reasonable physical distribution questions that face management of manufacturing concerns daily and to which a remarkable number of managers have already found viable and meaningful computerized answers. Certainly, there is no shortage in the business community of brainpower to answer these questions; this talent also may be drawn from the vast government establishments and armed services' force of logistics experts, mathematicians, and operations research men among other professionals.

Indeed, inventory control models, which will receive detailed attention in later discussion, have already made an immeasurable contribution to more efficient marketing processes, more cost-conscious production planning, more precise valuation of company assets on the balance sheet among three key areas of improved business operation and decision making. However, while the impact of computerized mathematical models for inventory control would in themselves deserve a full-length book because of their enormous implications not only in marketing but toward freeing corporate funds for less speculative or more profitable investments than in the company's own product inventory, the full contribution of these models in a still broader context continues frequently to be impeded by management rigidities imposed through traditional institutionalized and functional decision making.

This may sound like a severe indictment on the surface. The accuracy of the indictment, on the other hand, emerges from a very singular and challenging case study.

Quelle

Quelle is one of the world's largest mail-order firms, with an annual volume of $350 million—a figure that assumes added significance when contrasted with the $575 million volume of Montgomery Ward and $2 billion annual volume of Sears, Roebuck.

Quelle was founded in 1927 and is headed by the same individual, Dr. Gustav Schickedanz, today. In 1941, at the start of the war, the firm was doing a $12 million annual volume. As a result of World War II, the firm virtually started from scratch once again. The significance of its recent origins speaks to the heart of the problem implicit in nearly all computer applications to the totality of business decision making: The management of Quelle was able to plan the new firm around the new technology, unhampered by organizational rigidities and institutionalizing of functions which inevitably creeps into the procedures and thinking of a more established firm.

It may not be surprising, therefore, that a top management executive for Montgomery Ward estimates that it would cost his firm $200 million to duplicate the Quelle system and success—a staggering investment regardless of the returns that it may generate. But more importantly, such an investment would require a vision and dynamism which even a J. C. Penney or Julius Rosenwald would not have the freedom to exercise within his current business context.

Before further evaluating the implications of the Quelle experience, let us trace it through all its diverse computerized and mechanized stages.

- Quelle handles the $350 million annual volume out of one centralized building housing all its computer facilities and mechanized equipment while Montgomery Ward requires nine separate warehouse locations.
- Quelle ships roughly five times the amount in daily volume to customers that Montgomery Ward does with less than one-tenth of the Montgomery Ward manpower.
- Quelle fills 99.8 percent of all orders on the day they are received while the U.S. mail order average is 92 to 94 percent of same-day fulfillment.
- Quelle generates more than a 20 percent after-tax profit since Quelle's entire payroll, including management, amounts to $8.2 million, or a little over 2 percent of annual volume as contrasted with 25 to 30 percent labor costs among the U.S. mail-order giants.

The profit and customer service implication of these facts are self-evident. The intimate relationship among warehouse location, inventory control, customer orders and shipments, and other pertinent marketing functions comes into sharp focus after an analysis of the total Quelle system.

The Quelle Delivery System

The cycle begins with the delivery of merchandise from the manufacturer to the mail-order warehouse. Like all mail-order giants, Quelle has a sufficiently large account with diverse manufacturers to be able to control varying terms of delivery, including the critical packaging of the merchandise. Quelle's use of this leverage is significant in that the firm demands and receives all goods in small standardized cartons precisely measured to fit into Quelle's complex and totally mechanized storage, inventory, and warehousing system.

All merchandise from manufacturers, except heavy appliances and other hard goods, is packaged in these standardized cartons, shipped on standardized skids, and moved on monorails to any available six-foot-square area in the compartmentalized warehouse.

A quality control system is exercised simultaneously through random inspection of 5 percent of each delivery. This is the job of 150 employees, better than one-third of them graduate chemists and engineers. This tight control system—one of the high-cost areas of labor—produces a proved saving: Quelle has a return rate from customers of less than 1 percent of all shipments contrasted with a 10 percent average for the return rate of leading U.S. mail-order houses. The disparity in returns on orders is too great to be attributed simply or cynically to the different national characteristics of the average consumer in Germany and in the U.S. And even if a greater selectivity or vacillation among American customers may somewhat boost the U.S. return rate, a substantial part of the disparity can inevitably be contributed to the effectiveness of Quelle's quality control system.

All Quelle shipments are placed into open squares without regard to the merchandise in the cartons. One six-foot square may well contain men's shirts; its neighboring square, a carton of toys; and a third adjacent square, a particular shipment of trousers. Immediately upon being placed in its particular location, each shipment is registered by computer control according to area and location of squares based on assigned space numbers which hang vertically over each square. These numbers are electronically tipped to horizontal position when the last item is removed from the basic carton.

In summer 1968, Emanuel K. Fruman, corporate packaging research engineer from Montgomery Ward & Company, visited and studied the Quelle operation. His comments on the importance of having manufacturers' merchandise arrive in standardized cartons may add insights to this stage of the Quelle operation:

> On the second and third floor of this mammoth building are located thousands and thousands of order-picking bins. In each bin there are two cartons, one of which is opened on its side as the means by which individual orders are filled, while the second is its immediate replacement. Since this box containing the ordered goods is put directly into the bin and used to fill orders, a tremendous internal handling of merchandise is completely eliminated.
>
> The reserve box in the bin is placed at a slightly higher angle to the first box; thus, when all merchandise has been drawn out of the first box and it is removed, the second box automatically slides into place. As this happens, a lever is automatically tripped, relaying this out-of-stock position to the computer, which in turn notifies the warehouse. Within less than five minutes after this information has been received, a reserve carton has been shipped from the warehouse via an overhead monorail conveyor and is directed into the proper bin area by a key punch operator who performs this function by coordinating the article number into the proper computerized bin position.

The workings of the entire mechanized and computerized system become clear through tracing the procedures from the time when a customer order comes in to Quelle. The individual items on each order are keypunched into the same computer which contains an up-to-the-second inventory record of some 40,000 SKU's (stockkeeping units) at all times. At this time, an information retrieval program goes to work within the computer. Thus, if a specific item ordered is currently out of stock, the computer selects four proposed substitutions which are printed out. This printout is automatically delivered to the desk of the buyer in the mail-order house so that he can choose the specific suggested item to be sent to the customer. In view of the substitution process, Quelle's less than 1 percent return rate is even more extraordinary.

To dramatize this example, let us picture a U.S. housewife ordering a particular model of toaster from the catalog of a U.S. mail-order house. In its place, the consumer receives another model, of assumed comparable quality and price range, with a notice that her original order could not be filled at the time and would require a specific delay in delivery. Although the toaster she does receive is one at an immediately higher price level in the catalog, she is charged only the amount that her original choice would cost. Contrast this approach with a simple notice that her order could not be filled—period or a notice that there will be a several-day or several-week delay. It may lead to interesting speculation in the U.S. marketing community as to whether Quelle's approach might generate more customer satisfaction among U.S. consumers.

As soon as the appropriate Quelle buyer has selected one of the four substitutions, the computer records this information on a separate sheet of paper including the page of the Quelle catalog where the item appears and the price of the substituted item. It isn't too surprising, therefore, that customers are equally pleased with the substitute merchandise, since they are receiving greater value than they expected. This technique may be a small factor not only in the low return rate but also in the firm's high level of performance—namely, Quelle's ability to ship 99.8 percent of orders within one day after their receipt.

How does the system overcome the fact that the average number of items ordered ranges between 10 and 15 totally unrelated selections? A hypothetical tour through the warehouse may help visualize the physical layout and warehousing technique. Contrary to the bin arrangement traditional in this country, frequency of turnover of items rather than their relationships as end products dictates general location in the varying six-foot squares. Therefore, adjacent bins may contain women's blouses, house slippers, drip-dry pillow cases, and men's slacks. Slower-moving items like sports jackets, raincoats, blankets, and toys may be neighbors in another section of the warehouse. Of course, it helps to picture a gigantic area accommodating literally thousands of bins with an open in-use carton below a semitilted reserve carton arranged in neat and seemingly endless rows. This arrangement clearly puts the fastest-moving items with the greatest turnover closest to the packing areas, while relegating the big-ticket or slower items to the farther regions of the mammoth halls. A thoroughly computerized technique for collecting the items during the subsequent stage makes it easy for one person to pick thousands of individual items during a normal workday without any waste motion.

The original customer order is processed by the computer, which in turn prepares individual picking tickets coded for the workers to take them from their bins. Every picking ticket contains the following numerical information: In the left-hand corner, it shows the bin number, and, in the right-hand corner, a consecutively numbered customer order. These customer order numbers play an important role in the operation of the equipment that was specially designed to carry all the diverse computerized multiple orders from every corner of the warehouse at a precise time to their eventual packing destination.

This equipment in itself deserves some explanation. Although it does not necessarily depend on the computer, it is an extension of the imaginative thinking of a technologically oriented management. Only complicated equipment, controlled electronically by the computer, can handle more than two million individual and uncorrelated items in any eight-hour shift. In operation, this equipment is reminiscent of a latter-day Rube Goldberg functioning in a 1970s version of Charlie Chaplin's *Modern Times.* In construction, it is simplicity in itself. In application, it captures the essence of the computer's potential contribution; namely, its astounding man-defying precision.

The Precision Equipment

After this teaser, what is this equipment? The actual equipment consists of thousands of constantly moving bins numbered in consecutive order, machine-controlled on a vertical track. Alongside the moving bins is another numbered master moving belt. When the belt number and bin number correspond to the last three digits of the customer order number, the employee who collected the diverse items from the order ticket places them into that bin. This process is repeated and duplicated in several critical areas throughout the warehouse building. Each individual customer bin moves along its cycle until it reaches the first floor. Here a conveyor containing a packing bin with the same three critical digits as the customer order moves along beneath the vertical bins and conveyor belt. Thanks to computer timing, the individual machine bin drops the chosen items into the moving packing unit at a rate of one item a second until all the merchandise collected by the other vertical bins throughout the warehouse has been placed into the packing container. At the end of its journey, this container carries the customer's entire order, including substitutions. At the appropriate point, it is joined by a computer-selected, cubic-sized corrugated carton, the right size for the total customer order. The container plus the packing crate arrives on a conveyor belt in front of the packers.

Those who see a hopeful sign in man's battle against machines in the use of human packers at this stage are destined for early disillusionment: Quelle's management has underwritten a variety of studies, which were to be completed in 1969, designed to eliminate man at the final packing operation.

It is at this point that the U.S. business community may well throw up its hands in despair and put this book into the circular file. It is inconceivable that such an operation—though obviously as technologically feasible in this country as it is in Germany—would be permitted by one of the many organized institutions that hinder management from fully capitalizing on the potential contributions of the computer—that is, the labor unions.

At this particular stage of mechanization, packers still remove the merchandise from the tote box, pack the order, and send it on its way on the conveyor unsealed. A senior inspector spot-checks one order in every 1,000, removing all the merchandise from the box and examining it against the original order attached to it. The open cartons continue on their way to another point of the assembly line where operators seal the carton with three strips of tape, attach a mailing label, and put on the required postage.

The entire operation for the large annual volume requires fewer than 1,000 people and only some 50 of these, highly educated specialists, check the quality of the manufactured products shipped to Quelle. The remainder of the personnel are able to handle the volume extremely effectively in an environment where the possibility of human error has been, if not totally eliminated, so reduced by computerization and mechanization as to be virtually negligible.

If there is a moral in this particular case study beyond the unquestionable sex appeal of a high-profit, labor-problem-free business climate, it may well appear in the next section of this chapter.

Management Prerequisites for Success

When a management has the vision and freedom of operation to view its business as a totality, an entire approach, staffing, and methodology can be developed based on the genuine capabilities of the computer. Frankly, when this rare condition does exist, the emphasis is not upon highly sophisticated and inventive mathematical formulas nor on supremely complex facilities. Rather it becomes possible to reduce the interlinking problems in any overall business operation to its genuine basic components and apply to their solution some seemingly innocent and simplistic answers whose sophistication becomes evident only when the results are produced.

If the American mail-order community has not adopted this particular dramatic computer application, it is not by any means because of superior German innovation or the technological gap between the United States and Germany, but rather because United States mail-order firms had both the advantages and disadvantages of being ongoing businesses at the time when their German peer faced a problem of rebuilding from scratch—albeit with the required capitalization.

The upshot is that many computer applications to distribution problems among diverse U.S. corporate giants are characterized by intricate and extraordinary mathematical sophistication used in infinitesimal problem areas relevant to the overall business operation. Equally supersophisticated mathematical models address themselves to equally splintered business problems in other functions, and their cumulative benefit to the corporation is, by definition, smaller than might be that of a simpler model addressing itself to a major and overall business problem.

Another by-product, of course, is the fact that this condition in U.S. business continuously reinforces the knowledge and communications gap between the top management community and those specialists with potential computer-based solutions to major problems. Few company presidents get intimately involved or terribly hot under the collar about the physical layout of a specific warehouse. It becomes harder to relate the genuine accomplishment in the narrow area to the broader need it might serve on the larger management scale.

To illustrate this communications gap, let us quote, somewhat unkindly, from a contemporary and extremely learned analysis of a warehousing location analysis. The section titled "Problem Solution" begins with these thought-paralyzing sentences.

Dynamic programming is particularly appropriate for investigating this type of multi-period problem. The best location plan is found by recasting the problem into the form of a sequence of single-decision events. Then, according to Bellman's "Principle of Optimality": In a sequence of decisions, whatever the initial decision, the remaining decisions must constitute an optimum policy with regard to the state resulting from the initial decision. That is, once the first decision is made, the decision for the second event is based on this first decision; then the third decision is based on the second, and so it goes until all events have been evaluated.

What this paper states is actually eminently logical. Its writer discusses an approach toward evaluation of all the costs implicit in deciding whether to relocate a warehousing operation and if so, where to. But it is difficult to imagine that even the most profit-conscious and conscientious company president will (1) plow through the jargon and (2) assimilate it sufficiently to figure out how this particular analysis might help him in solving other risk-laden decisions (whether in the marketing function or elsewhere) within his overall business responsibilities. Rather than dwelling with futile tenacity on the jargon barrier and frustrated development of overall computer applications to newly viewed and comprehensive business problems, let us use the Quelle experiment as an example for discussing current U.S. applications of computer solutions to the distribution function within the marketing process.

It is quite apparent, for example, that the Quelle warehouse layout and distribution of merchandise reached its peak of efficiency not through human accident but through careful computer planning. Such models dedicated to improving the physical layout of merchandise and cost efficiency in warehouses not only exist on the U.S. scene but are being applied remarkably effectively in the warehousing operations of many multiproduct manufacturers. The particular computer program that had been found useful in this area—linear programming—is one with near-universal application to any problem of efficient allocation of limited resources for specific objectives.

Translating our own jargon, this simply means that linear programming offers useful results any time management faces a question that can paraphrase any part of the following question: Into what areas in my warehouse should I place all my different products, which vary not only in size but in turnover, in order to keep costs of handling and time as low as humanly possible?

In order to induce those readers with limited interest in linear programming as such to continue reading, it may be worthwhile to point out that such programs have effectively managed to reduce annual handling costs by a range of 10 to 25 percent. Indeed, some large warehouses—including one with 300,000 square feet of floor space—were able to show yearly savings of $30,000 to $70,000. And the beauty of this particular program is that the input—that is, the information required to make the program meaningful—is neither mysterious nor difficult to compile. Basically, it consists of a diversity of cost factors and measurements which are readily available to those in marketing management who have the physical distribution responsibilities. These would include a list of all the products destined to be stored in the particular warehouse and a description according to some of the following variables:

- The mode of delivery, be it by truck or rail.
- The turnover ratio of the product—that is, the daily, weekly, or annual frequency with which a workforce requires access to these products.
- The size of the product, perhaps related into its warehouse space requirements by item and by numbers of these products generally stored.
- The number of operations, manual or semiautomated, required in the handling of each item or a specified quantity of these items within that category plus the relevant cost factors.
- More specific inventory carrying charges that could be reduced by more efficient warehouse layout.

The strength of linear programming in addressing itself to such a seemingly simple question is that this program can mathematically evaluate all these relevant factors in combination and come up with what the operations research community joyfully calls an "optimum solution."

This optimum solution, in effect, takes into account all the practical considerations, translates them into mathematical measurements or terms that were fed into the original mathematical statement of the problem and that defy being perceived or even evaluated either intuitively or through experience.

The result of such a problem may well be the seemingly contradictory adjacency of men's trousers to toy trains in the warehouse of a mail-order firm. It may be the proximity of precision equipment and nuts and bolts in a warehouse supplying a manufacturing plant. The end result, however, will be cost reduction through better use of space, through more efficient use of the manpower required to handle the products, and even through such less measurable factors as better fulfillment of requests for the warehoused products.

10

The Computer in Physical Distribution

Herbert W. Davis

THE RECOGNITION of physical distribution as a major management function occurred almost simultaneously with the rapid introduction of computers to the business world. It was natural, therefore, that computers be applied most widely in these new areas of interest, which were largely in the mechanical, recordkeeping functions. For example:

- Sales forecasting and the analysis of selling trends as orders are received.
- The preparation and updating of inventory records and the production of statistical and management reports necessary to replenish inventory, either at the central point or in a field warehousing system.
- Production planning and control.
- Receiving, editing, booking, and shipping of customer orders.
- Invoicing of shipments and the maintenance and control of accounts receivable.

- Preparation of sales, salesmen, and customer statistics and reports.
- Control systems for raw material, work in process, and finished goods.

More recently, however, the computer has had an even greater impact on distribution as it has become involved in the more complex matters involved in decision making as changes in physical distribution are planned and in operating warehouses and systems as they are implemented. The new applications are a direct result of recent technical developments in hardware, input/output devices, and mathematical programming.

The recent technical improvements have answered long-standing needs in the distribution field. Management has needed to improve control to get better inventory turnover and to provide more rapid reaction to changing sales demands. There has been a real need to improve the accuracy of sales and inventory records to support more advanced systems controls. It is in this area that the new input devices have been making major strides. A few examples may serve to illustrate how these new devices and techniques have changed the computer's role in physical distribution from simple record-keeping to its present central position in planning and control.

Determining the Proper Number and Location of Warehouses

With the rapid growth of national markets for their products, many manufacturers have been faced with the problem of determining how best to serve these markets. In developing a distribution system, the manufacturer has to balance many conflicting objectives. These objectives can be summarized into two basic categories:

Customer service. Customers usually demand prompt delivery. Frequently this requires that warehouses be located close to the market. How close, however, is a difficult question that cannot always be answered satisfactorily. A system with many warehouses, for example, tends to spread inventory thinly, and orders may not be filled completely. The irritation of receiving partial shipments frequently can offset the advantages of nearness to market.

Costs. Distribution warehouses are costly. To be located in every major market can increase inventories beyond bounds, as well as administrative, storage, handling, and transportation costs, and result in volume too low to be handled economically.

Further, transportation costs frequently are the largest single element in a distribution system. The number and location of warehouses sharply influence costs for shipments from plants to warehouses and from warehouses to customers. At best, the determination of the proper number and location of warehouses to balance all of these conflicts is an art. Optimum answers have seldom been achieved. Nevertheless, workable answers must be found.

The science of warehouse location has changed dramatically in the past ten years. Three methods have been used:

Manual. In this method, a plot is made of sales and production. This is usually done on a map to illustrate the relative location and magnitude of each. The planner then spots warehouses in the major market areas and calculates costs for several alternative systems. Separate analyses can be made of service. Management can then make a decision as to the proper number and location of warehouses to service the market. Mathematical methods such as the "moment arm" or "center of gravity" calculations used to determine the weighted center of regional or national markets are variations of the manual technique.

Heuristic. Some years ago, computers were used in an attempt to get better answers in the analysis of distribution systems. The heuristic approach provides a rapid calculation of many feasible distribution systems. Information concerning the market, plant sources, and warehousing and shipping costs are entered into the computer program. Through the means of simplifying rules (heuristics), the computer is able to set up a series of reasonable distribution systems to supply the market. It then calculates the cost for each system to determine the lowest cost arrangement. The heuristic method has been supplanted by more modern approaches because of its limitations, such as the lack of detailed information available in the final output.

Linear programming. This mathematical technique to develop optimum solutions to complex problems has been known for some years. Only recently, however, have computers been of sufficient size and speed to permit linear programming to be used to solve distribution problems. Today, however, this method is widely used. The method proceeds in three steps. First, given a distribution market system of a specific number of existing warehouses, potential warehouses, customers, plants, sources, and so on, the program generates an input matrix. The matrix contains all the data on locations, capacity, volumes, costs, and transportation. Second, a standard linear programming algorithm or solution is used to optimize the assignment of customers to warehouses to minimize operating and transportation costs. Third, an output report generator prints the information necessary to analyze, approve, and implement the solution. The reports show the warehouse which will serve each customer, the costs at each warehouse in the optimum system, and the transportation costs associated with each leg of the system.

The linear programming method has undergone gradual improvement and more recent models have been developed which allow for the introduction of nonlinear costs, such as those associated with administrative and building requirements.

The following example shows how one large manufacturer used a linear programming model to improve his distribution system. The company is a major processor of agricultural products, manufacturing food and industrial products. The raw products used can be purchased throughout the country. The company manufactures at several locations and ships finished products to approximately 150 public and private distribution warehouses throughout the country.

Total distribution costs for this company were as follows:

Inbound freight cost	$ 2,100,000
Plant storage and handling	2,500,000
Outbound freight	5,600,000
Field warehousing	1,800,000
Inventory capital charges	700,000
	$12,700,000

The company's management made a decision to reduce these costs. As a first step, each warehouse was analyzed, both as to volume and cost. The company determined that those warehouses to which shipments were made in less than carload quantities were uneconomic. Elimination of these reduced the distribution system by approximately 20 warehouses.

The elimination of these minor warehouses, however, had little influence on costs. The company then undertook the development of a computer model of the entire system. The resulting model showed that the company should reduce the number of warehouses to approximately 35 and that, by so doing, it would save over $2 million annually.

The computer model had one interesting ramification. The manufacturer could procure the basic agricultural products from many different sources throughout the country. The products were priced differently in each market area. The manufacturer had to pay for transportation to his plant, but he received in-transit credits for application against outbound transportation costs. In other words, his manufacturing plants were merely stopping-off places on the journey of the agricultural products from farm to consumer.

Through the use of the computer model, the manufacturer is now able to determine where he should procure the raw product to minimize total costs in the system. The model takes into account the raw material cost, the region where it is procured, the transportation cost to the plant, and the transportation credits accruing thereto.

The type of linear programming model used in this example has wide application to companies serving regional or national markets. For a complex system, it is almost impossible to calculate properly the optimum number and location of facilities to balance the conflicting objectives of cost and customer service. The linear programming model, coupled with the computer's calculating power, offers a modern solution to this problem.

Planning Storage Layouts by Computer

Mathematical programming techniques are just now coming into use in the preparation of warehouse layouts. It is possible with these methods to reduce manpower and space requirements by optimizing the location of the various warehouse functions. Some companies have even used computers to determine the best storage slot for an item after considering a whole range of factors.

A major industrial equipment manufacturer, for example, was faced with the need to consolidate three smaller warehouses into a single larger facility. He needed a plan to tell the warehousemen where each item should be located and what storage method (bin, pallet rack, bulk, or other) would be most appropriate. The typical method used to answer such questions in a new warehouse is to mark up a copy of the layout on the basis of the existing volume and space required for each item. This method has several drawbacks:

1. It requires considerable effort by engineers or warehousemen and can be quite costly and interfere with other projects or delay the move.
2. Sizing is based on existing volume of the item rather than the future levels the warehouse has been designed to accommodate.
3. The usual method has to be redone completely for each warehouse in a system and cannot be easily modified or reprofiled as volumes and product mix change.

The manufacturer decided to use a computer programmed to draw up the best layout available. The essence of the computer approach was that stock location and storage method should be determined on the basis of forecast activity for the future design level rather than on existing volume. Since the building had been designed in terms of projected rather than existing activity, it was logical to develop the stock location system in the same way—if it could be done accurately and within a reasonable budget.

Perhaps the most convincing argument for the computer approach was that the method proposed could be reused for other field warehouses and future volumes by changing only one entry per item—the average monthly activity of that particular item.

The computer program developed for the facility emphasized the establishment of good policy rules which the computer would consistently follow in determining the proper placement of items. The resources of engineering and experience were applied to developing a sound series of engineering rules and stock location criteria for the program. About 20 different rules were programmed. To give a brief picture of the kind of rules considered, the following are samples:

- Bin items placed on bin shelves in numeric sequence, top to bottom and left to right.
- Drawer items to be no more than five bin sections (20 feet) removed from position where they would have appeared in the bin sequence if they had been in bin-size volume (to minimize picker walking).
- Bins to be no more than 80 percent full in total; no single bin section to be more than 90 percent full.
- Drawers to be no more than 90 percent full.
- Pallet rack to be no more than 80 percent full; picking positions in pallet rack to be restricted to floor spots, with reserve pallets in upper rack positions.
- Special items not fitting normal storage pattern to be listed separately.

Three particularly critical criteria in the program concerned themselves with future levels of activity:

- Items to be placed into drawer, bin, pallet rack, or bulk based on size of item and quantity required in inventory in the design year.

- Space for future items to be provided every 5, 10, or 20 items depending on product line.
- Computer to list for editing all items scheduled to be stored in a method different from that now in use.

Input requirements for the computer program were relatively simple, consisting of item information and forecast factors. Item information included the stock number, the class of product, the size expressed in terms of facings and depth of the package, the average monthly usage, and the present storage method. Forecast factors included the months of stock of the item stored by product class and the activity growth of the item by product class. The use of product classes rather than individual items for forecasting was dictated by the number of items in the line.

Program output was designed to be understood easily by warehouse personnel. The first output report listed items in numerical sequence, described their inventory and storage characteristics, and indicated the type of storage to be used—that is, drawer, bin, shelf, rack, or bulk. The second output report shows specific locations in the warehouse with the stock arrangement and the storage configuration at each location. There is a one-page printout of each of the bin, pallet rack, and bulk storage locations. For example, for each bin section, the page shows the serial number of the bin with the number of shelves and drawers to be erected in that section. The printout then shows each shelf and drawer and lists the item stock number, quantity, and percentage of the shelf to be allocated to the item.

To a considerable degree the actual format of these printouts simulates the physical layout of each location and provides a schematic which warehousemen have no difficulty following, either in placing stock or locating it at a later date. This printout shows also the locations reserved for future storage of new items.

Finally, for management review, the program provides a summary printout showing the percentage of space actually filled, by type of storage and the percentages available for future expansion.

Computer programs similar to the one in this illustration have been prepared to determine such things as which items in a large warehouse should be closest to the shipping dock, how items should be placed on an automated order-picking line to balance the load on the system, and how departments and functions should be located within a building to minimize travel.

Improving Sales Trend Information

A manufacturer and distributor of high-volume consumer household products had a major problem of planning and controlling distribution on a nationwide scale. The correlation of sales trends to control manufacturing schedules was a basic part of this problem.

The manufacturer sells over 1,000 products. Volume of each product is high but tends to fluctuate sharply, influenced by price promotions and special deals. Shipment of products to customers is made from seven distribution centers. In the past, each center kept track of its own sales, calculated selling trends, and ordered additional merchandise to replenish inventory as necessary. If an item "took off," however, manufacturing plants could not keep up with demand from several distribution centers, and shorts would result. Even if the plants could meet the demand, suppliers frequently would fail to deliver vital supplies.

It was clear that coordinated efforts would be required to keep track of sales and production nationwide, to balance stocks, and to reallocate production of raw material supplies to cope with developing sales demand.

To do so, the company installed a data transmission system to interconnect by telephone lines the existing EDP system of 12 computers. Seven of these are located in distribution centers and are programmed for invoicing, sales statistics preparation, and other distribution tasks. Several times a day, these seven machines interrupt the billing function to accumulate daily sales. They calculate sales trends, compare these trends to previous forecasts and predetermined permissible deviations from forecasts, and transmit significant variations to computers located in the manufacturing plants and in the company headquarters.

The manufacturing computers accept the information transmitted from the various shipping centers, correlate it for regional trends, determine the effect on production schedules, and signal the need for revisions. Raw material needs to support production are updated, and the necessary information is transmitted to the central computer.

The headquarters computer calculates national trends, keeps merchandising informed on the progress of the sales campaign, and determines the need for revised forecasts for coming sales campaigns. It also directs the procurement of additional materials to support the plant production schedules, indicates the need for transfers of finished goods or supplies between locations, and maintains an overall control and audit on the entire network.

The company now has outstanding control of its entire inventory-distribution sales system. The major improvement came, not with computers doing routine invoicing and control operations, but with the data transmission system coupled with a sound plan for correlating events throughout the distribution system.

Direct Entry of Data to Computer Files

The great bulk of data entered into computer systems results from the keypunching of paper documents. There are three problems with this approach: First, it is costly because it requires duplicate work and double handling; second, it is slow because duplicate operations require time; third, keypunching frequently results in the introduction of errors to the system.

A number of new devices are available now to make original entries directly into computer records. Some companies, for example, use cathode ray screen units on which the operator can see the data being entered. CRTs are coming into use for order entry. The screen may contain an order blank. The operator merely fills in the appropriate blanks, verifies, and enters all the data simultaneously.

Many other devices are available. Some of these are teletype terminals or similar keyboard entry units, punch card, badge, or ticket readers, push-button telephones, optical scanners, and so forth. The number of devices is increasing rapidly as new techniques and equipment are developed to satisfy the widespread need.

The following is a description of a data entry system used by a major supplier of men's wear to a leading retail chain in the United States. It illustrates the power of these new devices in speeding up the flow of information and in reducing the incidence of error.

The manufacturer has installed a new computer-controlled management information system covering the entire range of physical distribution operations from the receipt of orders to the shipment of goods. As a part of this system, he has installed IBM 1050 terminals in the warehouse and in the customer service office. These are connected by direct telephone line to the IBM 360/30 in the main office.

The terminal in the warehouse is of primary interest. Finished goods are received from long-haul trucks and from adjacent plants over a conveyor system. Items are normally received in large cartons which contain several dozen assorted sizes of a single style garment. A handwritten label on the carton details the contents.

The IBM 1050 terminal is located adjacent to the conveyor. As cartons move past the operator, she enters the lot number and a complete description of the item, the production order number, and the quantity of each size contained. This information is transmitted directly to the computer by the IBM 1050 terminal.

The computer maintains a disk file record of all open production orders and the quantity in stock of each item. As the information is received from the IBM 1050 terminal, the computer performs an audit of the information. The entry is examined for logic, a cross-check is made of the production order number and the lot number, the sizes are checked, and if all is in order, the entry is made to the records. If an error is found, the operator's terminal is queried, and the data are resubmitted or the carton is opened and inspected. Only when the entry can be verified are the data entered into the disk file.

Under the former system, the handwritten label on the carton was removed, edited in the warehouse office, sent to the computer room, and keypunched, and the data were entered and tabulated. The entire paperwork process took between two and three days. With the new remote terminal, inventory is available for allocation to orders and for shipment to customers two to three days earlier than under the manual keypunch system. In addition, a great amount of cross-checking and counting of inventory, necessitated by the former inaccurate system, has been eliminated.

The inquiry station located in the customer service office allows access to any customer order in the computer file within a few seconds. Telephoned inquiries on order status can be handled promptly. The old system, with its voluminous files, required callbacks or letters to answer inquiries. Production can be planned with greater accuracy, using up-to-date inventory and order status information. Inventory levels can be kept at a minimum because of the rapid handling of the receipts and the allocation of goods by the use of the on-line terminals.

Data Transmission Systems for Order Processing

Almost every large-volume order processing system today has, at its core, a computer. No company can continue to avoid computers in this area. To be sure, impersonalized systems have created ill will with consumers. Nevertheless, electronic means offer the only sure method of handling ever larger and larger volumes of transactions.

Some companies, notably those in the mass retailing field, have combined massive computer power with data transmission systems to speed up the entire operation.

One chain, for example, relies upon store computers to determine stock replenishment needs. Through data transmission the store computers signal the central unit, which in turn prepares consolidated reports to aid buyers. The buyer makes decisions on new merchandise orders; the computer switching system then transmits the order to the vendor. Major outside vendors have their own computer equipment to receive and process the order information.

Two years ago, one large apparel vendor received 90 percent of his orders by mail. Today over 90 percent are received over wire directly at the computer. The paperwork reduction is impressive. The speed of handling is even more evident.

Another giant retailer has used computer magnetic tapes to transfer orders to vendors for several years. The receiving computer must have compatible tape drives and programming. Given this, however, the savings are most important.

Recently several trial installations have been made using push-button-type telephones to enter orders. The advantage of the telephone over other hardware is the low cost and ready availability of equipment. This method of order entry will have a wide application to field sales forces in the near future.

It is clear that those manufacturers prepared to join these purchase order transmission systems will have a decided competitive edge. The systems, in addition to improving internal operations, make it easier for customers to buy. Errors are reduced and shipment can be made more rapidly.

Planning and Scheduling

The changeover from one physical distribution system to another, the design and construction of a new distribution center or plant, and the introduction of a new computer system all present major strains and dislocations in an organization. Critical activities may be forgotten or delayed enough to jeopardize the entire schedule. PERT and CPM techniques have gained wide acceptance in minimizing such problems. The following describes how one manufacturer of goods which vary according to changing styles uses CPM techniques to sharpen the operations necessary to bring a new product line to market.

The company is a large manufacturer and distributor of cosmetics and household products. Each fall about 200 new or repackaged products are introduced. Initial sales are always heavy and success in filling the demand completely and on time is crucial to profits for the entire year.

Each of the 200 finished products requires the design, procurement, and manufacture of a multitude of raw materials, tools, molds, and packaging materials. Each item must be designed and approved and adopted for the line. Contracts must be let; vendors must be controlled; and the items must finally be delivered to a plant for final manufacture and assembly into finished products.

Between preparation of the initial designs in April and the delivery of products to a distribution warehouse in September, at least 20 individual actions or operations must be completed on every one of the thousands of items involved in the line. In total, approximately 20,000 operations must be performed during 100 working days—an average of 200 per day.

The basic problem of planning for the fall line is that there is too much to do in too little time. Actions can be missed, and the entire organization then must scramble to make up the lost time. According to the company executives interviewed, the problem was getting worse each year. Crises and a lack of time are inherent in this phase of business because the company wants to introduce new products as rapidly as possible. The impact on the organization of fall line planning was sharply reduced, however, by application of CPM techniques to every stage of the planning cycle.

The special problem presented to this company by the introduction of the fall line is not unique. A similar situation occurs in government procurement, in major building construction, and in the development of many consumer products. Control techniques were developed over ten years ago for computer applications in connection with several early ballistic missile programs. The general name given to these techniques for keeping track of developmental operations is either PERT or CPM.

The CPM system, together with a central computer system, enables the manufacturer to review progress rapidly and automatically on every one of the 20,000 operations being performed and to find those where failures threaten to delay introduction of the line. The system operates as follows.

Purchasing agents, vendors, and planning personnel lay out a plan and a schedule for developing and producing each item as it is adopted. The planning task is simplified by the preparation of standard operation sheets for each general class of product or item. For example, even though the specific design of a carton may not be known in April, it is clear that the carton must be designed, approved, plates made, flats printed, slit, and so on. The operations can be generally described and lead times established based on past experience with similar actions. This experience is summarized on the standard operation sheet. Normal lead times are shown. The concerned planners either confirm the standard operations and lead times or make modifications as they deem necessary.

The standard operation sheets for each specific product and raw material item are keypunched as the sheet is issued. The cards are then edited and read into the computer files. The machine then calculates and publishes two schedule dates for every operation—one when it ought to be done based on normal leads and one indicating the latest that it may be done. The latest date for an item action is the date beyond which the introduction of the entire line or the finished product will be affected.

The computer stores all the dates for all the actions for every product, package, raw material, tool, or whatever required for the entire line. The computer prints a list each week for each purchasing agent, vendor, and responsible company department or individual containing all the operations which should or must be completed that week. The list is accompanied by "turn-around" punched cards on which the operation is briefly described. Each responsible individual enters appropriate information on the card indicating completion of the operation, reschedule dates, or problems. The cards are then returned to the computer.

The computer analyzes the card entries showing completed operations and prints a critical list each week. The list tells executives where problems are developing by showing items not completed on time and the responsible department or individual. Corrective action to meet overall schedules can then be taken promptly. Nothing can be forgotten.

Later, after every product is complete and the line introduced, the computer reviews all the events which affected it and prints a list of those operations which actually determined the final completion date. It highlights schedule dates which were not met and those which delayed the product. This postmortem has proven invaluable in sharpening planning and control of the following season's lines.

Fall-line introductions are still difficult and still require the full efforts of many people. Performance, however, is much better and the impact of the work on each individual has been reduced. The entire organization is better controlled and works more effectively.

There are many other examples of how modern developments in computer technology are making computers more important in setting up and controlling physical distribution systems.

Simulation techniques, for example, are in their earliest stages of development in distribution. A large distributor of dry grocery products set out to design a modern distribution center. Following the preliminary engineering design, simulation was used to determine the best configuration of conveyor equipment and to determine the proper speeds and capacities of each segment to minimize jam-ups. The same simulation program is now used to train supervisors and control personnel in the proper operation of the system and to assign orders to a time slot in the picking-shipping schedule.

Computer programs have been developed to apply queuing theory to the design of truck terminals and docks. The number of docks, the speed with which each truck is serviced, and the rate of truck arrivals are the variables. Computers can weight these 15 factors and determine the right number of docks to hold the line to any given time or number of trucks.

Data transmission equipment is used extensively to trace rail car movements and to report the progress of a shipment toward the market. Manufacturers can now tie directly into the railroad computer systems for up-to-date information. A large fertilizer manufacturer ships cars on open bills-of-lading with later redirection as orders flow in the computer. This substantially reduces lead time.

Mathematical techniques and computers are being used to route trucks for local and long-haul operations. These methods offer real promise of reducing trucking costs while simplifying route accounting, finding more efficient routes, and improving service.

Applications are no longer limited by computer speed or memory capacity. New devices are insuring better quality and more timely input data. Mathematical methods, formerly theoretical, are now in everyday use in physical distribution.

11

The Role of Computer Forecasting in Inventory Management Systems

Allan Vesley

THERE IS LITTLE DOUBT that the major impact of computers in marketing has been in the area of inventory management and control. Whether the goal has been improved customer service or cost reduction, the results have been measurable and usually good. It is the purpose of this chapter to explore one aspect of such systems—the forecasting of future demand or requirements. It is here that the computational and "number-crunching" capabilities of the computer have been used to do a job in a fashion that would not have been possible in a precomputer era.

Inventory Concepts

A recent IBM *General Information Manual* defines inventory as "an aggregate or total mass of goods. . . . Inventory serves the function of making a company's internal operation relatively stable while providing service to customers."

While this is a traditional and partially correct definition, it is not as all-inclusive as it might be. An alternative definition describes inventory as "an idle resource of any kind provided that such resource has economic value." The advantage of this definition is that it is broad enough to include such things as plant capacity to meet future demands, toll stations to meet varying traffic demand patterns, airline seats, and any other item or capability that must be provided to meet future requirements.

An expanded view of the nature of inventory is useful in three ways:

1. It enables us to apply the valuable theoretical concepts that have been developed for the control of inventories of goods to a much wider range of problems.
2. It broadens our horizons by inviting us to apply techniques from other types of decision problems to the management of commodity-type inventories.
3. Miller and Starr, in their valuable book on inventory theory, *Inventory Control: Theory and Practice,* structure the analysis of inventory problems in terms of opposing costs.[1] Inventory policy is optimized by balancing the cost of carrying inventory against the cost of ordering it into stock. An optimum policy can be found when future demand is known and when a policy regarding a desired level of service is given. This desired level of service is determined by balancing the costs of being out of stock with the cost of carrying additional inventory to reduce the out-of-stock probability.

The application of inventory theory is one of the oldest examples of the use of management science or operations research techniques. However, traditional discussions on the subject of inventory control have dwelt on the determination of an optimum order strategy on the assumption that future demand is either known or can be estimated with some determinable degree of accuracy.

There has, therefore, been recognition of the great importance of forecasting future demand in applying inventory theory. However, the problem of how to forecast future requirements has been set aside as an entirely separate subject. In past years, this has lead to the development of a large number of reasonably scientific inventory control applications utilizing demand forecasts that represent "seat-of-the-pants" guesswork or informal or intuitive

---

[1] (Englewood Cliffs, N.J.: Prentice-Hall, Inc., 1962).

projections from history. In the meantime, considerable progress in the application of quantitative forecasting techniques was being made in noninventory problem areas. Combining of these improved forecasting techniques with traditional inventory control procedures is now producing major breakthroughs in inventory management.

The task of foretelling the uncertain future is a common denominator in a vast array of decision-making problems. Robert G. Brown, in *Statistical Forecasting for Inventory Control,* sheds considerable light on the nature of this activity by distinguishing between "forecasts" and "predictions." He states:

> I shall use the term forecast to mean the projection of the past into the future. Literally the word means "to throw ahead, to continue what has been happening." Prediction or saying beforehand will be reserved for management's anticipation of changes and of new factors affecting demand.[2]

Prediction does not readily lend itself to statistical or mathematical techniques. Unlike forecasting, it is not an extrapolation of the past into the future. This does not mean that prediction can only be done with a crystal ball or by unfounded guesswork. It does, however, mean that human judgment must be applied to find the assumed similarities and correlations between the entity being predicted and other entities recalled from past experience of the person doing the predicting.

Methods of Forecasting

Forecasting is often thought of as a more exact means of foretelling the future. We must remember, however, that it is based on the vast assumption that the future is in some way related to what has gone before. Forecasting can be done in one of two basic ways:

1. Assuming a relationship between an external event and the thing being forecast is known as *extrinsic* forecasting and is usually done by correlating a figure such as birthrates, freight car loadings, or housing starts to the entity being forecast on the theory that its behavior will lag behind that of the statistic being used but will be directly related to it.

[2] (New York: McGraw-Hill Book Company, 1959).

2. Forecasting the demand for individual inventory items is more likely to be done by extrapolating the past demand for that particular item into the future. This is called *intrinsic* forecasting in that the correlation assumed is the correlation of the future behavior of an item with its own past behavior.

Numerous methods exist for forecasting from historical data. The simplest approach involves averaging the past data and using that value as an estimate of the future (see Exhibit 11–1). A refinement on this approach is to develop a moving average in recognition (see Exhibit 11–2) of the fact that it is the most recent period of history that is most meaningful. A further extension of this idea as shown in Exhibit 11–3 involves the use of a weighted moving average in order to emphasize the most recent history even further.

Exhibit 11-1
Projection of Simple Average

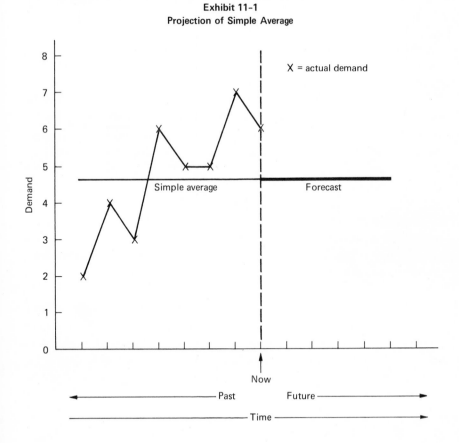

All of these approaches give a forecast that is somewhere within the bounds set by past values. Even if we assigned a weight of 100 percent to the highest observation from our past history, our forecast for the future, as shown in Exhibit 11–4, will be equal to the value of that observation but no higher. In order to recognize a trend in historical data and account for this trend in the forecast for the future, it is necessary to develop a line of best fit for the past history so that the slope of the line as well as its level may be extended into the future (see Exhibit 11–5). The development of any sort of simple or weighted average can only give us a horizontal or trendless forecast of future demand.

When the past data reveal that cycles or patterns rather than a linear

Exhibit 11-2
Projection of Four-Point Moving Average

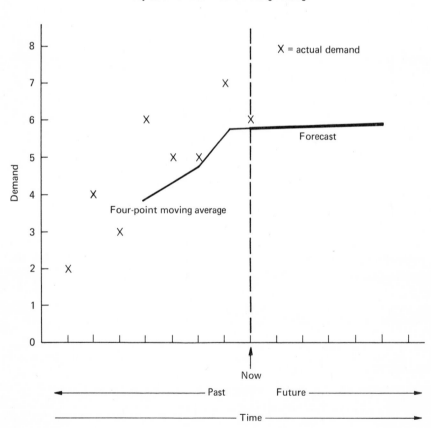

Exhibit 11-3
Projection of Weighted Moving Average

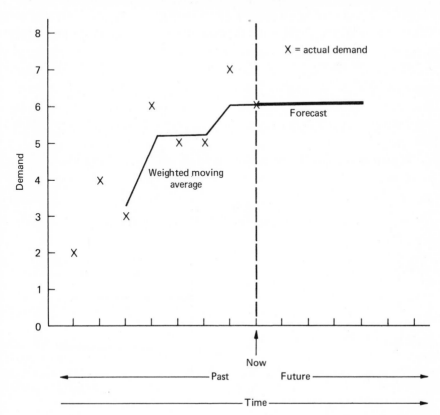

function best describe the history, it is necessary to employ higher-order curve-fitting techniques and then to extrapolate the best-fitting curve into the future in order to make a forecast.

Exponential Smoothing

In his book on inventory control, Robert Brown describes a method of forecasting that is especially suited to inventory problems. This method, exponential smoothing, has the advantage of reducing the amount of historical data that must be carried and makes it possible to control the weight given to current data. Exponential smoothing is a form of weighted moving average. A publication of the IBM Corporation describes this method as follows:

> Consider an item for which the pattern of demand can be classed as constant and for which data has been accumulated in monthly increments. One month ago, the average of demand was computed to be 19 units per month. This month the demand was, in fact, 21. We want to take advantage of this new information to revise the estimate of the average. Assume that the old records which yielded the average of 19 have been inadvertently destroyed, so that the new estimate must be worked out using just the two numbers, 19 and 21. Two things seem immediately apparent: (1) Because 21 is greater than 19, the new estimate of average should also be larger than 19 and (2) the amount

Exhibit 11-4

Projection by Assigning 100 Percent Weight to Highest Point

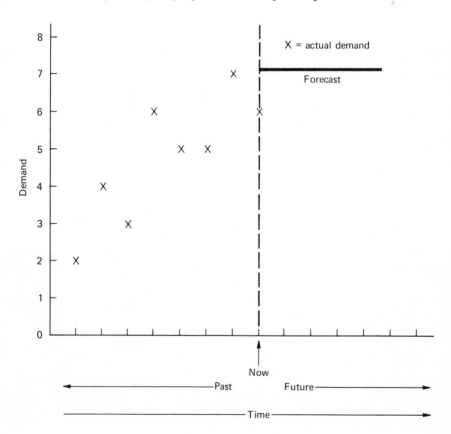

Exhibit 11-5
Projection by Fitting a Trend Line and Extrapolating It into the Future

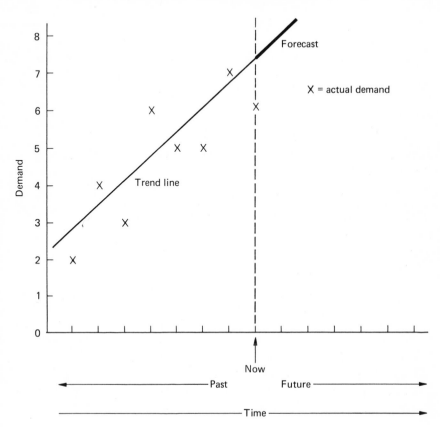

of change from 19 should be proportional to the difference $(21 - 19)$.

While these two statements explain exponential smoothing verbally, the following formula says the same thing:

New average = old average + a (new demand — old average)

(The Greek letter alpha, a, is commonly used to designate a smoothing constant between 0 and 1 which determines the influence of the new demand on the new average.) By controlling the weight of the most recent data, alpha simultaneously determines the average age of the data included in the estimate of average. The value chosen for the smoothing constant can be such that the estimate is very stable (low value) or reacts very quickly (high value).

If you use $a = .1$, and work through the formula, you should get a new average of 19.2:

$$\text{New average} = 19 + .1\ (21 - 19)$$
$$= 19 + .1\ (2) = 19.2$$

With a higher $a = .5$, there is a greater response to the new information:

$$\text{New average} = 19 + .5\ (21 - 19)$$
$$= 19 + .5\ (2) = 20.0$$

If the figures had been reversed so that the old average was 21 and the new demand 19, we would intuitively think that the new average should be less than 21 (the corollary of statement 1).

Solving the formula with $a = .1$

$$\text{New average} = 21 + .1\ (19 - 21)$$
$$= 21 + .1\ (-2) = 20.8$$

When $a = .5$

$$\text{New average} = 21 + .5\ (19 - 21)$$
$$= 21 + .5\ (-2) = 20.0$$

Obviously, a lower value of the smoothing constant introduces less effect from the new data. Correspondingly, the effect of older data persists for a longer period of time, though to an ever decreasing extent. With a value of $a = 0.1$, the newest data available make up 10 percent of the new average. One period later, the contribution is reduced to 9 percent, two periods later to 8.1 percent, and so on until 20 periods later when the contribution of the data is reduced to about 1 percent. With a high a such as .5, however, the contribution of a given piece of data is reduced much more quickly. Regardless of the value of a, the weighting of data follows what is called an exponential curve—hence the name, exponential smoothing.

Exponential smoothing can be used to do more than calculate the weighted average of past history alone. For example, it is possible to develop an exponentially smoothed average of the difference between each old average and its succeeding value. If there is a true trend in the data, that trend will be revealed in this fashion. It is also possible to develop an exponentially smoothed average of the differences between forecasts made and the actual demand experienced during the period forecast. Such a measure can be used as a tracking signal to determine whether or not the system is indeed forecasting future demand with acceptable accuracy.

Judgment and Prediction

There are many inventory control situations where forecasting from history alone does not produce adequate results. This is true in cases where:

- Seasonal variations are an important determinant of future demand history.
- The item being forecast does not have any previous demand history.
- The numbers comprising the demand history for an item are too small to permit meaningful extrapolation.
- External factors (for example, a promotional campaign) will have a greater effect on future demand than would the past history of the item.

It can be seen that the above characteristics are common to a great many inventory situations. In these cases, it is possible to combine the advantages of forecasting from history with the advantages of making predictions based upon other factors. This can be done by translating the prediction for the item into a pattern or profile. Brown, where discussing this approach to seasonal forecasting, refers to a seasonal item profile as a "base series." A profile or base series is used to represent the expected or predicted pattern of future demand. It does not attempt to indicate the quantity of demand at any point in the future, only the expected shape of the demand curve over a period of time. For example, where expected demand is known to be seasonal, its profile might be expressed by a series of numbers representing the percentage of total annual demand expected in each week in a year. In this case, the sum of the numbers in the profile would be equal to one. In the case of a brand new product, we might expect that demand will increase steadily and sharply for some period of time and then level off. In this case, we could develop a profile representing this function even though we are unable to estimate what the level of demand will be.

In effect, what we are doing is predicting the shape or direction of the demand curve rather than trying to give a quantitative estimate of what that demand will be during any given period of time in the future. The actual level of future demand remains to be determined by combining forecasting from history with the prediction represented by a profile. This is done by determining the ratio between actual demand and its appropriate profile point.

The calculation of the average of these demand ratios can be handled by using a weighted moving average or, more likely, an exponentially smoothed figure. This is done in exactly the same fashion that would be employed in using exponential smoothing to track actual history rather than the history of demand ratios. By the same token, we would apply a trend to our history of demand ratios and also measure our average error in order to determine whether the system is in control. The exponentially smoothed estimate of the demand ratio is then applied to future profile points covering the period for which a forecast is being made. The forecast of future demand is therefore the joint result of a *prediction* about the expected future requirements and a *forecast* based upon the historical data available.

A system such as this is applicable to inventory forecasting problems of any type. Obviously, if there is no past demand history whatsoever for an item, it becomes necessary to prime the pump by setting an initial order amount in order to experience demand and begin forecasting from it. The use of profiles in conjunction with forecasting from past demand data can be useful in cases other than those involving new items or seasonal items. For example, an established product without any seasonal fluctuation might best be described by a profile that is a straight horizontal line. However, if a major promotion were to be run for that item, it might be desirable to change the profile temporarily into an upward slope.

The System in Use

Examples of the application of these concepts to actual situations are plentiful. The management of inventories for the S&H Green Stamp Division of the Sperry and Hutchinson Company has involved the successful use of these techniques.

In his study of the value of a book of trading stamps, Professor Harold W. Fox of the University of Northern Illinois found, among other things "that the average premium's value is about $3.25 per book of S&H Green Stamps. This exceeds the stamps' average cost to users (merchants) by 21 percent." Several factors contribute to this high efficiency in moving goods through a distribution network. Computers contribute an important amount at the Sperry and Hutchinson Company.

In applying computers to operational problems, the trading stamp industry, as exemplified by S&H, has two important advantages. First, after a rather prolonged period of development (which still continues) S&H has become rather sophisticated in computer usage. Secondly, a trading stamp company operates with a limited assortment of items. This assortment changes little from year to year, and when it does change, the change is orderly and predictable. For instance, S&H has offered a certain blanket as a redemption item, practically unchanged, since the company was founded in 1896, 75 years ago.

Given its good start in the field, S&H has maintained the major share of the trading stamp business. Last year the S&H share was close to 40 percent. That is a volume of business in excess of $360 million. These characteristics provide a history upon which to base forecasts of future demand for particular merchandise.

One reason the company has maintained its position is its ability to provide good merchandise values to stamp savers at the times and places they want them. This is the key to success in the trading stamp field and worth a substantial investment of resources to attain. Efficiency in moving merchandise has a double value. It keeps costs down and saver enthusiasm up. Contrary to popular belief, one of the most costly problems to trading stamp companies is stock-outs. Stamp savers are not "captive" customers in any sense. Redemption centers are often some distance away, and savers who have spent months or years accumulating stamps are not happy when they cannot redeem them for an item they have long desired. Stock-outs mean more than just the loss of a sale for a trading stamp company. They may result in the loss of a customer for the family of stores that give the stamps or, at the worst, an out-and-out opponent for trading stamps. The attack on stock-outs begins with a commitment to automation.

A Description of the System

The objective of S&H's system is not to produce voluminous quantities of inventory control reports. Instead, it is designed to regulate the flow of merchandise through the company, that is, it is an inventory management system. The inventory system can be said to start at the 65,000 retail establishments that use S&H Green Stamps. These retail outlets represent every type of business from food stores and service stations to florists and lumber yards. S&H maintains more than 800 redemption centers at which the housewife can redeem her stamps for merchandise. The redemption centers are stocked from the eight warehouse locations.

When an item of merchandise is redeemed for stamps, a clerk in the redemption center enters the item number and book value on an adding machine with an optically readable register tape. These tapes are mailed to the computer center each night and provide the input needed to update inventory records and forecast future demand. If this results in a need for replenishment, the computer automatically writes a shipping order on the appropriate warehouse. Exponential smoothing techniques combined with the predicted redemption pattern for each item are used in forecasting future redemptions.

The forecasting activity begins with a man-made prediction of the seasonal variations in demand for each item. This prediction is expressed in a series of numbers representing the percentage of the total annual demand expected weekly throughout the year—a profile. Meanwhile, the computer system keeps track of all past demand. Actual estimates of future demands are determined by a combination of past history and the predicted profile submitted by the merchandiser. Once an initial profile is assigned to an item, forecasting becomes relatively automatic.

After using redemption transactions to update the file for each item, the system compares the remaining inventory with the forecast and determines whether or not an order should be placed. If the answer is yes, the computer order is transmitted over regular phone lines, producing a punched paper tape at the warehouse. The tape is then run through a teletypewriter, which creates warehouse picking orders and shipping documents.

Every redemption center and warehouse has its inventory records updated daily. The redemption store goes through its ordering cycle once a week. Warehouse inventory files are also updated by the computer system. The computer automatically subtracts items from the warehouse's inventory when it writes an order on the warehouse. Additionally, the warehouses report merchandise receipts, special orders, cancellations, and other transactions that affect inventory status by punching paper tape and transmitting it over telephone lines to the computer center. The tape then serves as input for updating the warehouse master files. Additional input is provided by the headquarters merchandise control group, which prepares changes to static information (initial profile assignments, package quantity, and so on) contained in master merchandise inventory files. Warehouses are replenished by ordering from suppliers and vendors. The forecasting system used here is similar to that used for forecasting store demand. However, actual order determination in this case must also take into account economic order quantities, delivery time, and such factors as transportation economics. Regional merchandise control groups are responsible for monitoring the performance of the system and for submitting changes to the rules which govern computer calculation of the store order.

In addition to writing orders, the computer system also produces periodic stock status reports for each warehouse and redemption store. The warehouse report shows the history of withdrawals and redemptions for each item and current data such as warehouse inventory, receipts, and open orders. The store report contains, by item, redemption history, and current-on-hand as well as ideal inventory position at a particular time, redemptions, orders not yet received by the store, and forecasting data. The stock status reports are used only for postmortem review of the performance of the system.

One warehouse in Chicago is totally automated. The computer produces order-picking sheets in the sequence of the slots in which the merchandise is kept for order picking. The computer must balance the orders over the various conveyer lines and schedule them to the truck docks. The cubic size and weight of each order is determined by the computer for the proper scheduling and use of trucks. Operations similar to those at Chicago are scheduled for other regional warehouses also. The S&H system, aimed at prompt redemption and good value to savers, represents a combination of many improved procedures.

*   *   *

Good inventory control theory and practice has been known for a long time. Electronic data processing increased the feasibility of applying inventory theory in a more complete fashion to the day-in, day-out control of individual items. In the same fashion, computer technology will continue to foster the use of mathematical and statistical techniques for forecasting inventory demand.

Uncertainty characterizes most business decision problems, including those related to inventory management. Inventory theory does not eliminate that uncertainty, but does enable us to take it into account while working toward the achievement of optimum solutions. Better forecasting strikes directly at the problem of uncertainty itself and thereby makes its contribution to the economic management of inventories.

12

•

The Marketing Manufacturing Gap

John W. Garofalo

How often in industry have statements been made such as these: "Our inventory is too high and must be reduced"; "Our customer service level is below par"; "Marketing is unable to develop a realistic forecast"; or "Whether a forecast is good or bad, the manufacturing plant is unable to supply the necessary products to satisfy our customers."

Today, this problem exists in many companies, both large and small. Management is plagued with high inventories, sub-par customer service, and inefficient plant operations. Many companies have resorted to elaborate data processing centers or management information system departments to assist them in resolving this problem. Improvements utilizing computer systems have helped companies' positions to a degree, but not to the expected or anticipated desired level.

The main cause for the limited results are that many companies cannot prepare a realistic, responsive, and accurate forecast for the production department. In most companies, usually the marketing or sales department prepares the forecast (a product or group-line one). In addition, it is usually highly inflated because marketing or sales people prefer to have an overabundance of stock available upon request. On the other hand, production people, responsible for operating the plant, like to schedule long production runs in order to reduce setup time.

The second cause of high inventories is that management is often afraid of changing existing procedures. Although management science techniques are available to industry, it is unfortunate that many people in responsible positions possess a limited knowledge of very basic algebra or statistics.

Because of these limitations, implementing a forecasting system becomes a tedious task. Responsible people who request a reduction in inventory do not want to devote the necessary time to understanding how a statistical forecasting system can benefit the company. To this type of management, whenever the phrase "statistical forecasting" is mentioned, the first words are: "It cannot be done"; "How can one forecast sales of new products?"; or "If forecasting is reliable, why are so many companies in the same position?" With this type of management, it is recommended that their present method of forecasting, if any, be continued. On the other hand, for the progressive management willing to improve its operation, statistical forecasting is the answer.

Prediction and Statistical Forecasting

Since statistical forecasting is a prerequisite for reducing inventory, it is mandatory that the difference between prediction and statistical forecasting be understood.

Demands for products are generated by a complex interaction of many factors. If the effects and combinations of each of these factors were known, a mathematical model could be built which would yield a very accurate estimate of future demands. Unfortunately, this is not the case. The effects of such areas as competition, advertising, and gross national product are not fully understood.

Prediction is judgment-guessing the future when there are no directly related events in the past on which to base such a guess. It is strictly intuitive. Decisions on whether to manufacture or not were made in the cases of such items as compact cars and cartridge-load cameras. Prediction requires a great deal of knowledge and understanding about what the item is, how it is used, future marketing plans, the probable effects of competition, the economic condition, and so on. There are some people who possess the ability to predict the future sales of an item, commodity, or stock very accurately if given enough time to study all the pertinent factors related to the item. Unfortunately, many companies produce hundreds of finished marketable items, and when one considers the package size, color, and locations involved, there may easily be half a million units to be controlled. Since there are not sufficient skilled people who have time to predict demands for each item, forecasters must resort to various types of statistical forecasting.

Statistical forecasting is the extrapolation of the past into the future. It is a sequence of numbers whereby one guesses what the next number in series will be. Later, as the next number becomes known, efforts are made to predict the succeeding one, profiting by the mistakes in the previous guess.

Arriving at an Average

In forecasting products for hundreds of items of the company, it is necessary to play the game of averages. There are various ways of arriving at an average. A type of average frequently used in industry is the moving average, whereby the most recent period of information replaces the oldest period of data. It is simply the average usage over a fixed number of time intervals. In the following example, the average usage rate based on the average of the past five weeks was 100.

$$\frac{100 + 90 + 110 + 80 + 120}{5} = \frac{500}{5} = 100$$

If the foregoing sequence of numbers occurred in a different sequence, such as 80, 90, 100, 110, 120, although the numbers are the same as before, the problem is different: Each week the demand has been greater than that of the previous week, so it is logical to assume that the demand in the sixth week is going to be at least 120 and probably higher. Thus the simple average of 100 would be a poor estimate of the next value in the sequence.

Another more difficult method frequently used for estimating an average is the weighted moving average, which assigns weights to each interval of data. A five-week weighted moving average, for example, might be made up of 30 percent of the demands in the most recent period, 25 percent of the demands in the next recent period, and so on to 10 percent of the period five weeks ago. The percentage or weight assigned to each interval of data must total 100 percent. With the first series of numbers, the result would be 100.5.

$$
\begin{array}{l}
30 \text{ percent of } 120 = 36.0 \\
25 \text{ percent of } 80 = 20.0 \\
20 \text{ percent of } 100 = 20.0 \\
15 \text{ percent of } 90 = 13.5 \\
10 \text{ percent of } 110 = 11.0 \\
\hline
\phantom{10 \text{ percent of } 110 = } 100.5
\end{array}
$$

With the second series, the result is 105.0.

$$
\begin{array}{l}
30 \text{ percent of } 120 = 36.0 \\
25 \text{ percent of } 110 = 27.5 \\
20 \text{ percent of } 100 = 20.0 \\
15 \text{ percent of } 90 = 13.5 \\
10 \text{ percent of } 80 = 8.0 \\
\hline
\phantom{10 \text{ percent of } 110 = } 105.0
\end{array}
$$

The two techniques for computing averages are commonly used in industry, but they have some major drawbacks. A good forecast should have stability in the face of random fluctuations or noise. At the same time, it should be responsive to real changes in demands. In order to have stability, long history files in both of these techniques are required. The second drawback is that the weighted moving average requires lengthy calculations. The third major drawback is that in both methods, the trend cannot be calculated. Therefore, if an item being forecast was moving upward or downward, with either of these methods, the change in direction would not be detected. An alternate method that overcomes the disadvantages of the other two techniques is exponential smoothing. This technique uses the least-squares method, initially, to select the forecast model. Simply, exponential smoothing is a technique comparable to weighted moving average. It has these features:

- The new value of the average is updated periodically as a weighted sum of demands in the period since the last review and the old average. Thus it is not necessary to keep and record all past demands, and the computer processing becomes more economical.
- The average is a weighted sum of all the past demands, with the heaviest weight placed on the most recent data.
- The method can be easily extended, with little additional computer processing effort, to detect trends and to compensate for them.
- It can be made to respond smoothly, automatically, and accurately to any anticipated changes in the pattern of demand.

- Using exponential smoothing, the basic equation to calculate the necessary and sufficient allowance for uncertainty in management estimates of the future is rather simple.
- The method is very easily adaptable to handle seasonal products.

The exponential smoothing equation that computes the average is

$$\text{New average} = a \, (\text{current demands}) + (1-a) \, (\text{old average})$$

As was outlined in Chapter 11, the Greek letter alpha, a, is commonly used to designate the smoothing constant that determines the influence of the new demand on the average. By controlling the weight of the most recent data, alpha simultaneously determines the average age of the data included in the estimate of average. The value chosen for the smoothing constant, a, determines how much of the past demand figures have any significant effect on the estimate of average. The smoothing constant value must be within the range 0 to 1. As in the case of the moving average, the more past data included in the average, the smaller will be the error in the estimate—provided, of course, that the basic pattern of demand has not changed during the forecast interval.

If a small value of alpha, say .01, is selected for the smoothing constant, the response will be slow and gradual, since it is based on the average of approximately 199 past months used to compare the expected demand figure. By contrast, a high value of alpha, such as 0.5, which corresponds to an average of three months' demand, will cause the estimate to respond quickly, not only to real changes but also to the random fluctuations.

In practice, it has been found that an alpha of 0.1 is a satisfactory compromise between a very stable system that fails to detect real changes and a nervous system that fluctuates with the demand. This value corresponds to a moving average of 19 months of demand.

Basic Demand Patterns

Basically, most history-of-demand data fall into one of three basic patterns—horizontal or constant trend, data that are increasing or decreasing in a particular direction, and cyclic, which repeat peaks and valleys in demand at nearly the same time every year. Determination as to which model best fits the history is made by using a technique of fitting a curve to the data. This is known as *regression analysis.* The exponential smoothing expression, thus far, has been used for estimating the average for a horizontal or constant forecasting model. Therefore, in an item that follows a steady rise or fall trend, the average would lag behind the demand. If the estimated magnitude of the trend were able to be computed, it would be necessary to make the corrections to eliminate this lag.

A method for approximating the trend is the difference between the new average and the old average. Random fluctuations in demand are, to be sure, bothersome but a simple method is readily available for estimating the average of a fluctuating quantity. The formula for the new trend looks very much like the exponential smoothing equation:

New trend $= a$ (new average – old average) $+ (1 - a)$ (old trend)

This method of computing the trend is in fact the least-squares estimate of it if the weights given to the demand in each previous month are the same as those used in the computing of the average. The correction for the lag due to trend can be expressed as:

$$\text{Expected demand} = \text{new average} + \frac{(1 - a)}{a} \,(\text{new trend})$$

Utilizing these formulas, it is necessary only to store the previous calculated values for the average and for the trend; therefore, the computer processing is minimal and rather straightforward.

As a rule, demand changes very slowly, so that a small smoothing constant is appropriate. But occasionally management may believe an important change is coming because of the introduction of a new product, a promotional campaign, the discovery of a new use for an item, a strike, or a recession. If management is able to predict a development of this nature, it can increase the value of the smoothing constant to an alpha of 0.3 or alpha of 0.5 for a temporary period of five to six months.

During that period, the statistical forecasting calculation will respond quickly to whatever changes do materialize. Later, when the new pattern of demand is established, the smoothing constant may be dropped back to its original value to provide greater stability and accuracy.

Note that it is not necessary for management to predict the magnitude or even the direction of the change. Management need predict only that a change will occur shortly. The forecasting calculation can detect and correct for the actual change that materialized in the demand for each item. In fact, a computer system can probably make the corrections more accurately than can the people making the prediction.

Up to this point, procedures to forecast horizontal and trend items have been discussed. In many companies, some products (though fewer than commonly supposed) have a true seasonal pattern of demand.

Seasonal Forecasting

In deciding to use a seasonal method for forecasting, two factors are important:

1. There must be a known and reliable reason for the heavy selling season to occur at about the same time every year.
2. The seasonal variation in demand should be larger than the random variation or noise. Most common methods of forecasting, when there is a seasonal pattern, depend on comparing the observed demand this year with the historical or predicted figures; this is known as a base series.

The best possible base series is one that has exactly the same pattern as the demand for the item being forecast will have. This condition very seldom exists. Therefore, a series that is higher when demand is high, lower when demand is low, and has about the same relative range of values is the ideal type. A commonly used method is the same-month-last-year method. The most familiar and the most obvious base series is the actual demand for the product during the corresponding month last year. The pattern of demand should show some rational change from year to year. If the changes are not too violent, the pattern observed last year can be used to advantage in forecasting the remainder of this year.

A successful method for applying the base series to obtain an item is to smooth the ratio of demand in the current period to the corresponding value of the base series.

Each month, compute the demand ratio. The ratio equals the demand in the current month divided by the value of the base series for the current month.

Compute the average, trend, and expected value of the demand ratio as described earlier for the nonseasonal demand. The expected demand for any future month is the expected ratio multiplied by the value of the base series for that month.

Error Measurement

In addition to knowing how to compute new averages and trends and project these trends into the future, it is necessary to have some indication as to the reliability of the forecast. Large cash expenditures are made on the basis of such forecasts. Disregarding errors of judgment, errors in a forecast are due to factors such as economic or marketing strategy. Knowing that a forecast is going to contain an error, a method must be developed to measure this error in order to establish the maximum reasonable demand which is equal to the expected demand plus an allowance for the forecast error.

To measure the forecast error, two values are needed. They are the average (also known as the mean) and the standard deviation. The average or the mean is the same value discussed previously. The standard deviation is a measurement of how much the errors cluster around the average or mean value. In forecasting demands, if a product had a small standard deviation, this would indicate that the product is very stable and predictable. On the other hand, a large standard deviation results in a volatile product. If both values are available—the average and the standard deviation for a product —conclusions can be made for the forecast of the product. That is:

- 68 percent of the time, the demands for this product would be less than the average plus one standard deviation.
- 95 percent of the time, the demands for this product would be less than the average plus two standard deviations.
- 99.8 percent of the time, the demands of this product would be less than the average plus three standard deviations.

The expression for evaluating the standard deviation is rather cumbersome because it involves the calculations of square roots. Therefore a more simple form that will approximate the standard deviation can be used—the mean absolute deviation—as follows: Obtain the difference between the current month's sales and the expected value that was computed last month. This difference is known as the current deviation. Then substitute the absolute value of the current deviation (the value taken as a positive value regardless of the sign) and evaluate the expression:

$$\text{New mean absolute deviation} = \text{current deviation} + (1-a) \text{ (old mean absolute deviation)}$$

The standard deviation is equal to 1.25 times the mean absolute deviation. This method can be used to estimate the standard deviation for each item that will give a practical current measurement of the variation of the product.

Two Control Tests

Thus far, the method for forecasting finished goods has been described, together with a method for evaluating horizontal, trend, and seasonal products and a means to measure the variation of a product. In addition to the above, two control tests are needed in a forecasting system.

1. The demand filter test detects demand values which differ from the forecast by some predetermined value.
2. The tracking signal test detects a forecast that is consistently too high or too low.

The demand filter test consists of testing whether the actual demand for the forecast period differs from the forecast for the same period by more than a specified number of MADs (Mean Absolute Deviation). The number specified reflects the desired degree of confidence that the difference between actual and forecast demand is a significant difference, rather than a difference due to normal random fluctuations. Limits that are frequently used are based on four MADs corresponding to over 99.8 percent confidence.

A demand filter trip occurs whenever a demand falls outside these limits. When the trip occurs, it is customary to bypass updating the forecast until someone has investigated the cause. Or the system can adjust the demands to fall within the specified limits. In any case, when the filter trip occurs, it should be brought to the attention of a knowledgeable person to investigate the cause.

If a system is forecasting properly, the demands should fall above the expected demand about half the time and below the expected demand half the time. If the sale falling below the expected demand were considered minus, and the sale above the expected demand were considered plus, they would tend to cancel each other. A running total of these errors should be very close to zero most of the time. A persistence on either the plus or minus side would indicate that the forecast is consistently too high or too low. In such a case, the forecast may not be tracking demands in the desired way, and there is a need to evaluate what has happened.

The mean absolute deviation provides the measurement of whether or not the forecast is tracking in a satisfactory manner. The equation for the tracking signal is:

$$\text{Tracking signal} = \frac{\text{sum of the deviation}}{\text{MAD}}$$

If the value of the tracking signal falls outside the limits of $+4$ or -4, which is equivalent to three standard deviations, the forecast is not tracking in the proper fashion.

Whenever the tracking signal trip occurs, the most common causes are:

1. Random occurrence, which requires no correction.
2. Significant change in the sales behavior. The corrective action required is to change the average to a new demand level. The sum of the deviations should be reset to zero.
3. The use of an inappropriate forecast model. The corrective action is to examine the forecast model.

In any event, when the trip occurs, notification of the trip should be made to a responsible person to initiate an investigation of the cause.

*   *   *

It is known that forecasting can definitely be improved by using exponential smoothing techniques. The method is especially adaptable to high-speed computers. It can routinely measure the expected demands. Measurements of error in the forecast by item can also be computed. Since a practical technique is available, companies should establish formal forecasting responsibilities. Marketing and sales departments should provide meaningful forecasts for special items, promotional items, and new products when past history cannot be a reliable guide for future activity. The production department should make routine forecasts, using the technique outlined for the run-of-the-mill items that contribute to the bulk of inventory investment. The production department should inform the marketing or sales departments of the groups of products that are important in planning the level of operation. With established responsibility and a forecasting system implemented, the most important contribution to improving the forecast is close cooperation between the marketing or sales and production departments. Therefore, the goal of progressive companies is to improve their forecasting and simultaneously develop sound flexible production control systems based on forecasting principles and characteristics.

13

The Computer and Physical Distribution in Service Industries

Evelyn Konrad

IT MAY SOUND LIKE A MISNOMER to discuss inventory control and physical distribution for service industries where the product is, by definition, a customer or consumer service rather than a warehoused product. However, not only do the concepts of physical distribution apply, but service industry faces, in addition, the added problem that it is frequently handling a service with built-in and instantaneous obsolescence. Cutting through the jargon, this simply means that the unsold places on an airplane scheduled to proceed on its regular route, like the unsold commercial time on a TV or radio station on its regular schedule, are obviously eternal losses to the airline management and radio and television station managements respectively.

It is not surprising, therefore, that the airlines—classical examples of service industry with a totally perishable product—with their vast capital resources were computer pioneers in this function, which can be described as a distribution and consumer service function. Certainly, the airlines have had an obvious stake. Without attempting to place a value judgment on the systems approaches of one company versus another, let us outline in some detail the remarkably sophisticated new computer "reservation" system initiated in 1968 by Eastern Air Lines: It may well live up to the enthusiasm of this firm's public relations men, who tout it as "the world's largest reservations system." Certainly it is fraught with valuable insights and lessons not only for marketing management of other airlines and other companies with comparable problems in service industry, but as a genuine real-time system, it also shows the way to the future to marketing management tackling physical distribution problems in major manufacturing companies.

Perhaps the magnitude of the airline customer servicing and "inventory"-plus-distribution problem may best be brought into focus by the following projections made in 1968 by W. E. Jenkins, division vice-president, reservations and telephone sales:

> In 1968, we will handle close to 35 million calls from the public; initiate over 5 million outgoing calls; place over 2 million internal calls; originate over 14 million teletype messages; receive over 21 million teletype messages, and produce over 21 million passenger records. The manual handling of this workload requires an average monthly headcount of over 3,500 employees.

> The size of our operation has doubled over the past four years—our passenger traffic and telephone calls will double within the next five and triple by 1975.

These facts and projections indicate why the airlines plunged into the computer world early and heavily. Where Eastern Air Lines' present program is concerned, the timetable began in fall 1964 when the firm created a joint research and computer sciences group to study the industry's and company's future reservations requirements, check the anticipated technology available for their fulfillment, and make recommendations. These conceptual recommendations were approved by Eastern Air Lines management in spring 1965, and bids and proposals from hardware houses were entertained at that time. These resulted in a firm proposal to top corporate management in 1965. By that winter, the company made its commitment to an IBM 360 Model 65 computer system. During the subsequent year and a half, Eastern and IBM worked together on the development of the program that is now operational.

Today, as this new airlines reservations system is being phased into operation, Eastern Air Lines reservations offices in Atlanta, Charlotte, Chicago,

Houston, Miami, Montreal, Woodbridge (New Jersey) Tampa, San Juan, and Seattle, it is not promotional hyperbole to say that "the slowest part of the new reservations system will be voice communications between the passenger and the reservations agent. The agent will have nearly instantaneous communication with the computer to retrieve information or make a reservation."

To those lingering humanists and antimachine idealists within the marketing community, it may restore some hope to find out that one byproduct of this system—albeit not the most important—is to translate passenger identification back from numbers into the individual given names. This refinement of computer sciences, although not physically earth shattering, may eventually inspire those ruling over "university customers"—that is, their students—to program into their computer system that small but dignity-restoring tape required to restore to rebelling university students their names instead of using social security numbers and other ciphers. Suffice it to say, it can be done. Indeed, Eastern Air Lines is in the process of doing so for nearly 20 million passengers a year.

Possibly out of public relations-inspired sensitivity, Eastern management is so proud of this small but tender human wrinkle in its multimillion-dollar computer system that it has called this system the passenger-name record system. This name, however—in deference probably to the machine's continuing conversational limitations—is reduced to the PNR system for those who prefer present-day jargon.

A rose by any other name, however—or ARBAON, as we say in the computer world—the system does "free our agents to answer customers' inquiries more promptly, completely and accurately," according to Robert B. Parsons, vice-president–computer sciences. He adds,

> For the first time since the computer revolution began, we are able to restore the individual's identity. Instead of a number, he is once again a name with his own individual needs. To utilize this new system for maximum benefit and to provide the best possible customer service, this investment will have to be met by the recruitment and training of additional men and women to handle the public's increasing travel demands.

These comments offer an insight into the sociological and institutional hangups within the business and broader U.S. communities in that they shrewdly second-guess continuing and often-times articulated fears of more and more massive computerization—namely, the fears of the man in the street that he is indeed becoming a cipher and the fears of the labor establishment that union power is indeed being eroded through management's ability to replace manpower with machine power.

Whether these fears are founded or just philosophically interesting may not be totally relevant to the dimensions, workings, and pragmatic effect of Eastern's PNR system. Today, this new research computer system is being phased-in in Miami while the present Eastern computer operation in Charlotte, North Carolina, is completing its transformation into a new Eastern Air Lines Operational Data Center. These facts may not be terribly reassuring to the unions directly concerned with the union's airline personnel, but the construction community can take heart from the fact that this project calls for a $22 million building program at Miami International Airport, which includes a separate Computer Sciences Building specially designed to house the batteries of computers and support equipment required by the system.

This system stores information on 1,300 daily flight segments, including time of departure and arrival, meals, class of service, fares, and other details. The system monitors the preparation of each passenger's itinerary to insure that all details are in order, automatically reserving the desired number of seats on Eastern and connecting airlines. Later innovation may include the printing of tickets for transmission to customers either by mail or by teletype.

Key components of Eastern Air Lines' passenger reservations system are three of IBM's most powerful computers, one of the world's largest IBM electronic file systems, and 2,250 television-like display terminals.

"The new passenger name record system is so responsive that the reservation agent can handle a telephone inquiry with virtually no pause or interruption in the conversation," said Bob Parsons, Eastern's computer vice-president. "She simply keys in the inquiry as the passenger asks the question, and the information flashes on the screen in less than a second."

Cutting through the technical complexities, the key application involved in this program is actually a real-time information retrieval system. Such a system is based fundamentally on the machine's ability to match data and review and search out data on so-called DO-loops when these are programmed in.

This is the same fundamental capability which is destined to revolutionize not only the publishing business but the entire communications industry and to spawn a new generation of businesses and consumer services as soon as entrepreneurial skills catch up with the technical expertise to develop fresh marketable concepts. Peculiarly, it is largely the hardware manufacturers' suicidal penchant for their own jawbreaking jargon that is delaying this application of managerial and entrepreneurial know-how to geometrically increase the need for the manufacturers' high-priced product by applying it to the development of fresh concepts and services.

A small case study based on decade-old, more or less futile attempts to introduce information retrieval concepts into a supposedly sophisticated segment of service industry—that is, advertising and communications—once again serves to underscore the fears, conservatism, and institutionalized hangups that militate against computer-based improvements.

It is self-evident that the television or radio station, whether in an urban center or in the hinterland, which is forced to air any major program segment with unsold commercial time has lost forever the opportunity to generate gross income from the sale of this commercial time to any advertiser. Technically, a central clearing house for all TV and radio station time availabilities has been feasible for ten years or more.

In practice, a number of small, albeit skilled, software houses have lost their shirts and their investors' enthusiasm in futile attempts to buck the institutionalized structure of those currently controlling the buying and selling of commercial time—the advertising agencies and the station representatives. Pressured by major advertisers and by a number of economic factors beyond the limitations of computerization, agencies have continuously looked into computer applications of diverse sorts. A diversity of media selection models are currently operational in agencies.

However, the computerized handling of radio commercial time inventories—by a centralized availabilities bank—is still far from a reality. The reasons are obvious: It wasn't the carriage manufacturers of the 1900s who encouraged and backed the development of the automobile. Nor is it likely that station representatives would join in an effort undermining their critical function: selling time. There may also be a latent suspicion among media directors that the existence of a centralized availabilities bank would make it feasible for advertisers to plug in directly and bypass the agency. Whether this would be the logical outcome is really immaterial. The most recent development in the advertising industry—the advent of media buying services and the abdication of agencies of this function—may be the first economic step toward computerized and centralized time availabilities.

According to the station representatives, such an information-retrieval-based computer and inventory and distribution system would obviously put them out of business. In brief, they aren't dumb about computerization; they are simply steeped in more or less enlightened self-interest and activated by a tenacious sense of self-preservation.

The handwriting is certainly on the wall. Indeed, some of the new young software houses offering media and advertising applications, such as Marketronics and Telmar, are on the brink of offering such a service. When it begins to make economic good sense to a major segment of this industry—be that segment the sellers or the buyers of time—then it will be a matter of very little time indeed before centralized availabilities are a fact.

PART THREE

Marketing Research
and New Product Development

14

Marketing Research

Evelyn Konrad

IT IS NOT UNUSUAL for a new industry to go through a stage where vertical integration is the keynote of individual firms' growth. This type of expansion has certainly been characteristic of the computer industry from its inception.

Computer Software and Marketing Research

The mutual attraction of computer software giants and marketing research firms has been simply an extension of the natural affinity between suppliers and leading customers. In this instance, of course, the marketing research firms were viewed, fairly accurately, by major software houses as not only large but potentially growing customers. That is not to say that these marriages between marketing research giants and major computer software suppliers have lived through unmitigated marital bliss. Indeed some corporate divorces have already occurred despite the obstacles that such divorces face. One of the earlier cases in point may well have been the marriage between C-E-I-R and the American Research Bureau—the latter a highly specialized marketing research firm that provides syndicated TV and radio rating information. This marriage, despite the overt logic, was headed for troubled times from the moment that former British "whiz-kid" of the Churchill era and founder–owner of C-E-I-R, Dr. Herbert W. Robinson, swapped stock with James W. Seiler, founder–owner of ARB, back in 1961. Within four years, a disillusioned Jim Seiler pulled out of ARB with his top brass in tow, reflecting not only disillusionment with a stock deal that had resulted in a lower market value than anticipated but also the more deep-rooted problems afflicting two segments of the computer industry that are particularly characterized by volatile and prima-donna managements. The fact that an overextended C-E-I-R subsequently was merged into the aggressive and expanding Control Data Corporation is part of history.

Although the ARB and C-E-I-R merger may have been one of the earliest, it was rapidly followed in the second half of the 1960s by the submergence of virtually every other major marketing research firm into often younger, but more rapidly growing, computer software houses. Cases in point include the Politz-Computer Sciences marriage and the stock trade-based merger between Brand Rating Index and Arcata National Corporation.

One of these mergers has already become unglued as Computer Sciences Corporation sold Politz, in 1969, to Ad/Mar Research Company at a fraction of the original price for which they bought it three or four years earlier. Others are destined to suffer some disillusionment if software parent companies discover that their market research investments have been principally in one-shot prima donnas who are rarely capable of developing another product such as the original one that zoomed them into a temporary popularity. Fashions in the marketing world being as short-lived as they are, it is rather likely that the software firms invested in marketing research companies at a time when each of these was either at its height or just beginning its decline.

Currently, the only two leading holdouts seem to be the A. C. Nielsen Company and Audits & Surveys.

Indeed the vertical merger fever has also extended into such peripheral marketing research areas as statistical tabulating services. Among these, Informa-Tab, Inc. became a subsidiary of Advanced Computer Techniques Corporation, a software house with a number of management applications bordering on marketing research.

What impact have these corporate mergers within this segment of the computer industry had on the art and science of marketing research? To what extent have they affected the state of the art? And is today's marketer of products and services any better off in this universe of combined facilities than he had been in the days of more numerous independent research services?

These questions lend themselves to critical analyses and appraisal couched in a great number of qualifying statements. But, on the whole, it may not be an exaggeration to say that the principal beneficiaries of these mergers may well have been the short-term stockholders rather than the marketplace.

The reasons for this sweeping indictment are complex albeit apparent: Ever since the rise of the A. C. Nielsen Company in the 1930s, marketing research firms have grown from single methodological insights on the part of the owner–founders into an increasing share of the market based on superficial permutations of the original theme. Few, if any, have had the vision to obsolesce their own basic service; indeed, like most maturing industries, they have spent their resources on more and more elaborate marketing of the basically identical product.

If computer software houses began wooing the marketing research industry because of their hunger for new computer application, then they were doomed to meet with disappointment. Virtually every major marketing research firm continues to be dominated by the same men and same thinking which launched the business in the first place.

If the computer software houses, on the other hand, thought they were buying a captive and major customer, then the moves may have made excellent business sense at the outset. By the same token, they added to the software houses' responsibilities for programming sophistication and investments for conversion as new generations of computers forced the introduction of process changes.

Unfortunately, in marketing research, as in any other business activity that is predicated on creativity and new insights, the mere addition of facilities and routine programming resources neither guarantees nor generates new approaches to old and new problems.

The Effect on Consumer Industries?

The upshot for the multitude of consumer industries who rely particularly heavily on marketing research? More of the same with few, if any, improvements that can be or have been passed on to the customers.

Obviously, these are observations that refer principally to those segments of marketing research that consist of churning out, on a syndicated basis, historic information concerning the flow of goods and the penetration of media. While these segments of the marketing research business account for its largest dollar volume, they never have provided the most stimulating or freshest answers. Rather, these are the segments of marketing research that provide the sine qua non statistical backup that is required for decision making. This is not the kind of marketing research data that lends itself to a new look at the changing dynamics of the marketplace or changing conditions within media.

Several Marketing Failures

Those computer-based innovations introduced into this area of marketing research to date have so far been economic failures. Two cases in point are the costly introductions of two computer-based flow-of-goods measurements: (1) SAMI, owned by Time, Inc., and (2) SPEEData, owned by Computer Applications, Inc. Each of these had intended, in effect, to take on Nielsen's Food and Drug Index in a major frontal attack, since Nielsen's $50 million-plus volume in this service (even taking into account Audits and Surveys' success story in this field) was substantially unchallenged.

Both SAMI and SPEEData were attempting to provide marketers with flow-of-goods measurements based on supermarket warehouse information retrieval. The problems, however, were twofold: Both services began on a local basis, but marketing men do not usually buy a new syndicated research service based on spotty or sporadic city coverage only. When evaluating the brand's competitive position, marketing men seek an essential national overview. Today SAMI continues to be a basically local service. SPEEData, on the other hand, after some four years of being in operation, announced in October 1969 that its coverage of warehouses is sufficient for it to be a national reporting service. The service was now based on withdrawal information from 300 warehouses in 30 contiguous marketing areas covering the United States. It is important to realize that this form of national coverage, based on adding markets, is not to be equated with a sample design that has been developed for national coverage in the first place.

A second flaw or weakness that may have slowed the progress of these two flow-of-goods measurements is the fact that the data based on warehouse shipping information lacked the demographics concerning the purchasers which are essential to intelligent analysis.

In April 1970 the board of directors of Computer Applications announced that the operations of SPEEData, Inc. were being discontinued immediately, although investments amounted to approximately $11 million. Additional losses to the software house will result from the fact that SPEEData had been a substantial customer of E.B.S. Data Processing, Inc., another subsidiary (more than 80 percent) of Computer Applications, Inc.

The Input-Output Matrix

The genuine innovations have come painfully and frequently at great cost from several other sources, all almost inevitably interlinked with the academic world. For example, Dr. Wassily Leontief's input-output matrix, originally the result of "pure" research into the nation's economy, has begun to have interesting and dramatic applications to marketing and marketing research. Heavily depending on the computer's ability to manipulate matrixes and perform linear algebraic operations, input-output theory does provide hopes for the possibility of predicting the required magnitude of independent variables in order to accomplish a given overall goal. Translated into English, this simply means that the Celanese Corporation marketing management, for example, has learned to use this application in order to determine how much effort this manufacturer should put into diverse categories of products that are actually used as components or ingredients by other industries. By being able to anticipate ultimate demand more accurately, management has gained an invaluable planning tool.

One of the best-known input-output models, the Maryland Model, run by Clopper Almon, Jr., econometrician and former associate of Dr. Wassily Leontief, studies the commodity flows between 93 industries. The resultant 93 × 93 grid produces annual forecasts and nearly 10,000 separate commodity flows between industries. The figures are possibly more impressive than the actual data. As Dr. Leontief himself admits, the finer the breakdown the more unreliable the data: ". . . sometimes it's better to have not very reliable information on something which you want to know than very reliable information on what you do not need to know. It's really a problem of choice."

A far more serious deficiency implicit within input-output forecasts—and perhaps intrinsic in virtually every attempt to predict the economy to date —is the unpredictability of technological improvement or change. However, a good chunk of creative effort on the part of economists is addressing itself to this very question. Thus Arthur D. Little's economist, A. George Gols, has been systematizing the judgment of some 200 or more of his company's engineers and technological experts concerning future technological developments and feeding these judgments into the input-output model in the hopes of adding precision to the essential technological change coefficient of industrial and economic growth.

Whatever their individual merits and capabilities, input-output models today swamp the business scene much the way simulation models seemed to proliferate during the early part of the 1960s. While the Maryland Model forecasts long-term average growth rate, the Wharton School econometricians forecast short-term swings in the economy.

But at the risk of glib iconoclasm, it may be worthwhile to point out that the science—or more precisely the mathematics—has outstripped the art of economic and market research to the point of near-absurdity. And the danger to corporate management and marketing management, in particular, is in the temptation to become so overly involved with the possibility of constantly counting the number of angels who dance on the end of a pin that we forget to ask whether any such angels are indeed there, and if they are, whether it matters very much.

The simple fact is that the unquestionable accuracy, speed, and computational sophistication of the computer and the intellectual beauty of elegant and pure mathematical formulas can combine to lead marketing management down a garden path.

15

Beyond the Pitfall

Emanuel H. Demby
and Louis Cohen

A MARKETING RESEARCH firm's client, a prominent maker of packaged goods, informed the research firm, "I know you're going to build a model to solve this next problem. But don't tell us about it. There is a fair amount of prejudice against models in this organization."

Another such client, a well-known marketing consultant, invariably goes in the other direction. No matter how one might approach the solution of a problem, he invariably asks for a model—and no amount of persuasion will convince him that anything less than a model can solve his problem.

Before approaching the practical application of marketing models, it is necessary to start, first, with the practical problem of semantics and people.

A Problem of Semantics

The term "model" can be glamorous or deadly depending upon the biases and backgrounds of the people with whom you are talking. And when you try to define the term—as a mathematical representation of a real-life situation—you only reinforce either the receptivity or the negative feelings about the model.

Marketing research experience has indicated the problem is that the model presents a conceptualization challenge that is difficult to meet not only for marketing men but for researchers as well.

Really, virtually all analysis in marketing research is based on a model —even the cross-tabulation of data to some extent, if we care to work out the mathematics of relationships between the variables under study. A discriminant function analysis, a Q-Analysis, a cluster analysis, and related multivariate analyses are involved in model building. The model is a reordering of data in order to visualize the dynamics in a given situation—to see the impact of A upon B, B upon C, and so on. Or one can say that the model is a constant reordering of data to enable researchers to play what-if games, simulate, and begin to understand better the potentials of cause and effect relationships—not that it can ever really be said that the cause is found.

The problem is in the word "model." It attracts and repels, depending on the listener's orientation.

Recently, MPI pioneered in the development of psychographics—it has been said that its national probability sample of the United States, in which the marketplace for the spending of discretionary income was segmented into creative and passive consumers, was really the first large-scale psychographic study ever conducted. Now MPI could have said that it built a model —a model of discretionary income use in the U.S. But since the trend, the fad if you will, in marketing and marketing research has been toward segmentation studies, MPI said that it had accomplished the psychological segmentation of the U.S. consumer. Indeed, that is what it was. Calling such a work a model might have produced a very sharp division between those who respond favorably and those who respond unfavorably to the word "model." Fortunately, aware of the temper of the times, MPI said that it had done segmentation research, and the acceptance of the psychographic approach is growing.

In general, the model builders have been the beneficiaries and victims of semantics, depending upon who the communications target was.

The purpose of this chapter, then, is twofold:

1. To discuss practical applications of mathematical models to marketing.
2. To discuss a practical way of getting marketing management to work with mathematical models.

There are a number of complaints about the model:

- "The findings are unrealistic."
- "How do you know this is so?"
- "Models have formulas all right, but just try to apply them in real life."
- "The model builders are not practical people."

Well, let's admit it; a lot of complaints are valid.

Problems with Models

When a model is in the hands of a mathematician who is not marketing-oriented (by our standards, not his), you are likely to get some unusual output.

Like the mathematician who recommended that a cosmetics manufacturer optimize his advertising by concentrating on 28-year-old women. (It had to be patiently explained to him that while 28-year-old women might, indeed, represent the optimal age group in the marketplace, there were not enough 28-year-olds to support a national advertiser.)

Another problem of the mathematician in operations research for marketing is that he speaks a language of his own. It is therefore difficult for the plain-talking marketing executive to learn whether the model makers are for real or whether they just engage in complex computer exercises.

Finally, we have the pure-research model problem experienced by a major record company. Its mathematician built a model which found that the name of the artist on the label had nothing to do with how well the record sold. The computations may have been technically correct, but, as any marketing man or researcher who knows his salt will tell you, most records depend on the glamour and name of the star on the label.

So much for the flip side.

Building a model is not, of course, an automatic process. It is not, really, very much different from doing good research—except that your tools are so powerful, you need to know what you are doing before you do it.

Some of the most successful marketing models do not come up with revolutionary findings, but all should make marketing sense and common sense. If the findings do not make marketing sense, researchers should go back to the drawing board to find out why they do not. A recent project will illustrate this point.

MPI built a model of usage of a particular toiletries product not long ago. Several mathematicians wise in the ways of operations research theory worked on it, and the construction was sound. When researchers looked at the printout, however, they saw at once that something was probably wrong.

Early in MPI's work on the product, it had carried out classic motivation and marketing research and already knew quite a bit about the product. The model findings did not coincide with this knowledge.

When researchers went back to the early steps in the model, they recognized the problem: Men and women were lumped together as a single group —and a single model was built—when, in reality, they represent two very different markets with different buying motivations.

Once the sample was separated into these two natural market segments —a separation apparent to a marketing man, but not so obvious to a mathematician—it was possible to build a model for each. The models, with this assistance, unearthed a previously untapped market. The client is preparing a new campaign to reach this market right now.

As just stated, some of the most productive models do not produce totally new findings. This was the case in the model just discussed. The project was conducted in a European country. As researchers were developing the recommendations based on the model output, they realized the marketing approach recommended was exactly the same as that used five years ago by a brand in the United States to move from a small share of the market to the number one position. Of course, the approach would be new in the country in which the study was made. The fact that MPI's recommendation was not completely new, that there was a substantial success story in the United States thanks to a similar marketing concept, was a key point in management's decision to go ahead with the approach suggested by the marketing model.

One point being made here is that, in many cases, a single marketing model is not enough to explain all consumer behavior.

An implication of this point is that the mathematician or statistician who builds the model needs the marketing-oriented researcher as much as the researcher needs the model builder. A great deal of marketing judgment and knowledge of the marketing problem is necessary before a successful marketing model can be built. The mathematician and the researcher need each other.

Another important implication is that preliminary research is necessary —that is, marketing and motivation research—before a successful model can be built. Only by total immersion in the subject area are researchers likely to build a marketing model which offers practical solutions to pressing marketing problems.

The Need for Marketing Research

Basically, the preliminary depth and marketing research is needed for the following three reasons.

First, such research can determine the important marketing segments (for example, sex) for a product about which to develop models. In one project for a mail-order gift company, researchers found that what they thought was a single business was really two businesses—one that sold gifts through catalogs and one that sold gifts through advertising in publications —even though both involved mail-order gifts. By combining the catalog business and the publications business in a single model, results were obtained that related to neither. Only by constructing separate models for each business were the marketing problems of each solved.

Second, preliminary research is necessary to discover *all* the factors with possible relevancy to sales, so that they are included within the model framework. In a model of operating room supervisors (nurses), one of the critical variables explaining sales of surgical supplies was "attractive salesmen." Without preliminary research, no one would have included this factor in the model—and if you do not include a factor in the model, you cannot test its importance.

Third, preliminary research makes sure one can understand the model output. A model of canned processed meat was built. One factor which the model showed critical to sales was that it should be seen as "not salty." If no preliminary depth research had been done, this finding would have been taken too literally. In reality, the factor explained why women used the canned product mainly for guests, despite its having a poorer image than the fresh smoked meat. Preliminary research showed that the regular smoked meat is sometimes too salty and the result is a cooking debacle, which not even the best cook can save. To paraphrase a famous slogan, women feel they can be sure if they use the canned product. There are many marketing implications to this "not salty" factor which are not apparent unless the product area has been thoroughly researched.

Another means of insuring that a marketing model project will result in practical findings is to make the project a team effort, with management very much on the team. Here is an example of how this team approach worked in helping to insure success for the model during a study for a company selling industrial products.

Preliminary research indicated that the company's business potential centered around six important market segments. However, the management members of the team maintained that their sales force was limited and could not be increased at the present time. Without this advice from management, the project might have produced some interesting, but perhaps not too useful, findings. The management members also developed some excellent practical applications of the findings, and the entire marketing efforts for the following year were a direct offshoot of the marketing model developed for the company.

Another company wanted to find out whether it should enter the home-heating market in one of the European countries. It would have been, at first glance, relatively easy to survey the market and find out how many people would switch from coal to oil and how many would choose central heating rather than room heating. In fact, researchers did this—and, at the same time, gathered data on the image of central versus room heating and coal versus oil heating. The question that might be asked is, Why wasn't this enough? Why bother building a model when we could express to the client in a very simple table that X percent said they might switch from coal to oil, that Y percent would rather have room than central heating, and the reasons behind each of the researchers' opinions were the frequency of reasons given for each possible decision?

The answer is that it is a bad policy to trust consumer intention statements. They are interesting and even useful, but they cannot be trusted. According to a psychographic study of American consumers, the passive consumers—who are the larger part of the population—will tell you they intend to buy something and then do not, while the creative consumers who may not yet have made up their minds about what they might purchase buy as soon as the impulse hits them. Thus, for purposes of forecasting, it is necessary to develop the model in order to understand what predicts purchasing, even among those who have not yet made a commitment.

In the case of the heating model, attitude variables were more powerful than demographic and socioeconomic factors in predicting. By using the discriminant function analyses technique, it was found that when projective test results were used, researchers were correct 91 percent of the time in saying that the respondent was a user of coal as compared to just 77 percent when demographics were the basis of the model.

In the case of predicting an oil user, the projective test result model was correct 76 percent of the time, as compared to only 45 percent when demographics were the data base for the model.

From the point of view of the client, this was a very central finding—which might not have been as discernible without the aid of a model.

If attitudes were more important than demographics in predicting the use of coal or oil, then it was possible to conceive of the potential market for oil heating as much larger than that which existed in that country at that particular period of time. While demographics cannot be changed, attitudes can be.

The power of the model to predict was even greater when the choice between room heating and central heating was presented.

Again, two models were built—one employing attitude variables and the other employing demographic variables.

In predicting whether an individual had central heating, the attitude model was 99 percent correct when the person had coal at home and it was 100 percent correct when the person had oil.

On the other hand, the demographic model was correct 75 percent of the time in predicting that a coal user also had central heating and only 45 percent correct in predicting that an oil user had central heating.

On this basis, the marketing program to convert coal users to oil and also to central heating was developed.

The models played another important function. Since attitudes were more critical than demographics in predicting fuel and heating system, the variables making the greatest contribution to the heating decision were able to be isolated. And from these, a marketing program was built.

Basically, the researchers were dealing with four concept categories:

1. Self-identification factors—in essence, the user image.
2. Product attribute factors—or product benefits.
3. Communications factors—advertising and distribution.
4. Functional recognition factors—the extent to which a respondent felt one fuel or another, one heating system or another, could be rated as needed.

Both sides of the equation were examined—what it was that kept a person with coal and what it was that might turn a person toward oil. This was done because bridge concepts were necessary. And if the models built were to come anywhere near real life, they had to portray the dynamics, the problems, that would confront the client.

The analysis of the interrelationship between these factors would be impossible, in terms of costs and man-hours required, without the computer. The program itself is a remarkably simple and easily available package program that measures the relative impact of diverse related variables upon each other.

In explaining use of coal, self-identification variables accounted for 36 percent of the total variation. If a respondent said that coal was for "people of my age," chances are that, despite any expressed liking for oil, he has remained with coal. Now, this is important, as the model suggested and later marketing efforts proved to be true. Just selling a person on oil was not enough; it was necessary to deal with such factors as self-identification.

Thus, if a respondent said that oil was for "people of my age" and maintained that oil is for young people and coal is for old people, chances are that he had made the switch from coal to oil.

Product attributes explained 46 percent of the total variation in the coal model. If a respondent saw oil as reliable, chances are that he has switched to oil. On the other hand, if coal is seen as convenient and economical and having no unpleasant smell—one of oil's negative product attributes—then the chances are that the respondent has resisted the chance to switch to oil and has remained with coal.

Communications awareness explained 13 percent of the variation for people remaining with coal and not switching to oil. This factor was expressed by a statement that coal has many nearby dealers (without, at the same time, saying the same thing for oil). This correlated with seeing coal in frequent advertisements and with the belief that the coal dealer knows repairmen for the stove.

Thus there was a reason why people would not switch from coal to oil—and there were two ways of analyzing the many-nearby-dealers response.

1. Those with coal do indeed have more nearby coal dealers than oil dealers.
2. Those who have not switched to oil feel comfortable about remaining with the status quo. They know about coal dealers but not oil dealers.

The objective analysis—that the nearby coal dealer response meant there were really more coal dealers nearby than oil dealers—is untenable. Most coal dealers in this particular country also sold oil. Indeed, there was a .79 correlation between coal being seen as having many nearby dealers and oil being seen as having many nearby dealers. Thus analysis of the model indicated some anxiety on the part of coal users about moving away from the status quo—coal—even if they realized that oil is superior as a heating fuel.

Functional recognition was the final conceptual factor that explained 5 percent of the variation in the coal model. If a respondent said that coal was needed rather than oil, chances are that he has remained with coal.

Once more, there is a status quo and inertia problem. Certainly, the respondents knew that oil can do a better heating job. In fact, many of the coal users say that oil is superior to coal—indeed, in this model, those who still use coal say they really want oil.

Because the client's objective was to convert those in the available market, only responses from individuals who said that they really wanted oil were included.

But change is difficult—and the answer to the problem came from the other side of the discriminant function analysis model—switching from coal to oil.

The problem was not one of selling the virtues of oil to people who already knew its merits and were ready to move. Rather, the problem was that of building a self-identification bridge, of making it possible for fearful people who wanted to become customers to buy.

The model's basic contributions are these:

1. It cut through 57 different possibilities for action and narrowed the marketing problem to a single one among a highly desirable target group.
2. It taught the client the value of isolating market target groups and running campaigns on a hierarchical order—with first attention to high prospects and last attention, if any at all, to the low prospects.
3. It increased the ability to communicate the findings to people in the field—general management, advertising and marketing directors, sales personnel—all of them isolated from headquarters in the United States and devoted to the myth of superior American research.

All in all, the model reduced the anxiety in the decision-making process.

Were the researchers right?

Oil sales went up on a consistent curve, and the client made a lot of money with a relatively small advertising investment but with excellent copy and excellent selling platforms for the salesmen.

MPI experience with the marketing model has been mainly in the development of marketing platforms. But MPI has moved into some other areas too.

For a major pharmaceutical company, MPI built a discriminant function analysis model to predict what kinds of men would make good salesmen. Turnover dropped from 40 percent to 8 percent, and the promotional pool for managers increased from 5 percent to 10 percent, to say nothing about the money that the company saved by cutting out all those psychological tests that didn't work.

More recently, MPI built a model to predict the chances that a man would make a good store manager and then another one to predict that a man will remain with the company if he becomes a good store manager. The client in this case was one of America's large appliance and tire chains, and the program is too new to report results. But the model provided not only a formula for prediction but also a key insight.

If a man was a college graduate, the chances were high that he would become a successful store manager sooner than a man who was not a college graduate. On the other hand, the college graduate was more likely to quit after becoming successful, whereas the man who was not a college graduate was more likely to stay with the company.

The model even considered a man's appearance. Short, fat men were more likely to stay. This makes sense. The handsome guys probably have more confidence about switching jobs.

The reader is probably familiar with MPI's original work in psychographics, which involved the building of a model of how Americans spend discretionary income. Here we may be getting closer to that very dangerous area of media selection. What the psychographic model does show is that there are two vastly different segments of the population and that they differentiate around social orientation. Whether a man is outwardly or inwardly oriented socially will predict a great deal about how often he will buy a car, how many extras he will put in a car, how many new electrical appliances he owns, how active he is politically and religiously, where and how often he will travel, how many different alcoholic beverages he will have in his house, and how often he will serve them.

The implications here appear to be great for marketing, for creative advertising work, for product development, and possibly for media selection.

The model is not suggested as a panacea. Only one or two out of every 100 studies deserves a model. The model should be used mainly where the data are good and provided in depth and where the problem requires sharp delineation between decision alternatives.

The marketing model is a powerful technique which can be used to understand some of the forces acting in the marketplace. However, it is too easy to make the mistake of viewing the model not as a technique but as the marketplace itself. One model theoretician said he saw life as a series of multiple correlations, while another saw it as "dimensional space." It is too easy to make the mistake of moving from the simile to the metaphor.

Seeing the marketing model as the marketplace rather than as just a technique leads to error, because it may place the researcher in an unquestioning or unskeptical mood.

In summary, the mathematical model can be an extremely powerful tool whose use in the marketing department has been stalled because of *a gap in communicating its story to marketers* (researchers do not state their story clearly enough, and they do not state it in the language of the marketer) and because of *a credibility gap* (too many of the findings and recommendations that result from marketing models do not make marketing sense, and some do not even make common sense).

16

Computers and Models in the Marketing Decision Process

Peter J. Gray

IN ORDER TO AID MANAGEMENT DECISION MAKING, all marketing tools and methodologies have to be developed so that they can be explained and understood by the decision maker. Such a constraint is extremely challenging to most operations research analysts. Nevertheless, most models have to meet certain criteria and answer such questions as the following:

- Is the model logical, rational, and consistent?
- Is it well organized and procedural so that all steps can be traced?
- Is it quantitative, explicit, and unambiguous?
- Can it be reproduced by others so that the solutions will be standard?
- Is it dynamic over time and can it be simulated by changing the values of the variables?
- Can it be tested for accuracy and reliability?

The marketing models developed to date range from simple computer methods of identifying prospects by geographic location, size of firm, and industry to more complex salesmen allocation models.

The computer has been and is used extensively within Xerox Corporation for a variety of marketing purposes. Early uses of computers were for billing and shipping, sales forecasting, and inventory control. Recently there has been a proliferation of marketing applications for computers within the company. Such applications include prospect identification, pricing, market potentials for new products, competitive analysis, and sales allocations. Continuing efforts are being made to improve the models for many of these applications and to develop new models in such areas as new product simulations, input-output analyses, and decision theory. This chapter contains brief descriptions of some of the models that have been successfully developed and used to provide marketing management with better inputs for decision making, relative to both current and future products.

Xerox is an extensive user of a variety of commercial data bases such as the Dun's Market Identification File, Newsfront, and other census data bases on magnetic tape. These commercially available data bases, plus customer surveys and field interviews, provide the basic raw materials to develop a series of models for estimating market potentials for new products. Many of these models involve correlation analysis using a step-wise regression program in an attempt to match the characteristics of current customers with those of the purchased data bases. The results are used by market research, product planning, product marketing, and other groups to refine market estimates and to develop market plans and programs.

New Product Evaluation Models

The evaluation of new market opportunities is a vital prerequisite to new product planning. Many ideas are submitted for consideration as viable products, and some logical, consistent method must be employed to evaluate and sort out the good and profitable opportunities from the less practical ones. A series of models were developed to evaluate such new market opportunities by considering all the significant factors that might have a bearing on the marketability of the product, application, or service.

A multivariate model was developed to quantify all defined exogenous and endogenous variables affecting the market for new products. Quantitative values are assigned to each variable, and the model is simulated by modifying the values of the variables. Results of iterative simulations are then tested for reliability using probability values to provide a degree of confidence in the value of any solution and to determine the level of accuracy of the results. This model analyzes market potentials using utility theory to assess alternatives and preferences by considering in quantitative terms the impact of competition and alternative methods.

It is assumed that a prospect or group of prospects will select the alternative that maximizes the expected benefits at the least cost. Therefore, the greater the value of the product to the market, the larger the expected proportion of potential users. Essentially, this model is a logical procedure consisting of an organized arrangement of steps. It contains both known and unknown elements; however, all the components of the model are quantifiable and therefore can be stated in mathematical form, simulated on a computer, and reproduced because the assumptions are explicitly stated, unambiguous, and consistent. Thus the results can be tested and checked for reliability. The model is dynamic over time rather than static and relies on the application of rational inputs based on the best available statistics and other information.

An attempt is made to identify all pertinent variables acting as either constraints or enhancing factors on the various forecast levels. Among such factors affecting demand are the following: size of the sales force, complexity of the market, advertising and marketing strategies, product capabilities, and limitations versus alternatives in regard to pricing, technological and economic changes, competition, and so on.

Prospect Identification Model

Another model was developed to help define and choose major prospects within selected industries. Market research and product marketing specified the criteria for selection of major prospects from available data bases. This model is sufficiently flexible to allow the specification of a significant number of criteria, such as progressiveness of the firm in terms of growth rates in, for example, sales, assets, earnings, and number of employees; rates of return on investment over a period of time; number and types of computers installed and level of sophistication by types of applications used; and expenditures in such areas as research, experimentation, development, and plant and equipment.

This factor of progressiveness helps to distinguish leaders and innovators within an industry and size group. Another criterion used to help define key prospects is that of size of the firm in terms of multiple locations, subsidiaries, and divisions. An additional important factor is the relationship between prospect firms and Xerox customers measured by the number and type of copiers and duplicators installed, revenues generated, and growth rates over time. Different weights are assigned to each of the criteria with generally more weight being given to progressiveness than to the size of the firm.

Forecasting Model

In 1967, the Xerox forecasting program was developed. This program extrapolates a time series using five different forecasting techniques and evaluates their relative performance. The input to the program is the time series, parameter values, and control information. The program is extremely easy to use, requires no knowledge of the computer or any of the programming languages, and accepts free format input punched on 80-column cards. Other attractive features are variable output precision, automatic selection of optimum smoothing constant values, and a fully edited output report. Internal arithmetic is performed using significant digits only, an approach that contributes substantially to the success of the program.

The five different forecasting methods in the program are

1. Moving averages.
2. Least squares.
3. Simple exponential smoothing.
4. Exponential smoothing with seasonal corrections.
5. Exponential smoothing with seasonal and linear trend corrections.

The performance of each of these methods is measured in terms of the sum of the squared deviations of the forecast from the actuals. The program accumulates the squared deviations from the same periods in each case to insure a valid comparison among the forecasting methods.

Competition Model

Another vital concern of marketing management is the problem of competition. Good market intelligence is required to determine possible market strategies of competitors and to develop adequate counterstrategies. A model was developed to enable Xerox to simulate competitive capabilities over time. Data collection included a complete company profile of expected competitors, including each company's sales, profits, employees, growth rates, production facilities, marketing capabilities, product lines, technological skills, and other measurable data. A series of assumptions was developed relating to sales strategies that could have an adverse impact on Xerox markets. For example, it was assumed that a competitor would attempt to penetrate existing Xerox markets by offering customers cost reductions based on lower prices. It was further assumed that the competitors would establish branch offices in major metropolitan areas, and they would expand to new cities if such key branches were successful. Xerox also estimated that its competitors also knew the scope of the market and therefore would staff sales offices according to market potentials as well as existing Xerox business in those areas. Sales coverage was calculated using different mileage rings around major metropolitan areas. Various levels of pricing were calculated and a cost comparison was made between products. With this input information, the model was simulated to determine various degrees of competitive impact on the machine population and on the potential markets within the defined geographic areas. Furthermore, by changing pricing and marketing strategies, Xerox could determine the proportion of the competitive impact that could be negated.

This model was instrumental in bringing about significant changes in Xerox marketing strategies. For example, additional stress was given to promoting total customer service, national sales coverage capability, flexible pricing plans, improved delivery dates, revised sales commission systems, improved sales training, and so on. These strategies served to lessen the impact of present and potential competitors.

The Salesmen Allocation Model

A traditional problem of any marketing organization is the profitable and optimum allocation of salesmen and technical personnel. This problem is closely related to the question of how many sales and service people are required. However, in many instances, marketing management attempts to solve both these problems by applying rough rules of thumb. As a result, business is lost, opportunities are missed, and selling costs are unnecessarily excessive.

Early in 1967, at the request of marketing management, Xerox started work on a computer model to allocate salesmen or technical service personnel to optimally cover a specified geographic area. Input for the model was available from the customer data base of customer types, revenues per customer, and products purchased by customer. This information was matched with secondary source data available on magnetic tape.

The model was developed as a result of the joint efforts of market researchers, programmers, salesmen, and operations research analysts. The scope of the task includes the ability to handle geographic areas of arbitrary sizes and shapes, customers differing in revenue size and organizational structure, salesmen and technical service people with different capabilities, and varying costs of marketing and service. The model was designed to either minimize the number of salesmen or technical service representatives required, maximize the potential revenue, maximize the territory covered, or maximize the percentage of customers and prospects contacted.

In the initial planning stage, the entire sales area is laid out with definite boundaries to insure that the salesmen cover only the areas desired. The second step is to determine what data are available so the proper optimization criteria can be chosen. That is, a company may not be able to maximize revenue in its coverage if the only data it has available are the number of customers. Also, data on the effectiveness of the sales force are needed (for example, the number of calls per day expected). The final planning step is to decide in what time period the company wants the entire sales area covered —six months, one year, or whatever.

Once the data and market areas have been assembled, this information needs to be prepared for computer processing. A grid of intersecting horizontal and vertical lines is laid over the sales area to divide it into smaller units or cells. The size of each cell depends on the degree to which the input information can be broken down geographically and the desired accuracy to which each salesman's area is defined. The grid lines can follow any shape as long as the intersecting lines completely envelop each cell. This means that the individual cells do not have to be regular, but can be counties, postal zones, states, or whatever.

Once the grid is laid out, it can be used as a guide for laying out the assembled data. Within each cell the expected number of customers, the expected revenue from these customers, and the expected number of calls per day per salesman must be known.

There can be several "levels" of this information for each cell to distinguish between such items as national accounts, present customers, or potential customers. In the areas where salesmen won't be used, a zero entry will effectively keep the area from being included in the analysis.

The first step in the computer computation is to take the input data and determine an equivalent revenue per call for each cell and each level within a cell. This means that if it takes an average of six calls to sell one unit of product X at an average monthly revenue of $180, then the average monthly revenue per call is $180 for six calls or $30 per call.

The expected revenue per call from a customer, the expected number of calls per day by a salesman, the maximum time allowed a salesman to cover his territory, and the number of customers at the various levels or calls are all data derived from the input information for the analysis.

The basic philosophy is to go after the highest revenue per call first. Once the potential of that cell has been realized, the salesman moves to an adjacent cell with the next highest revenue per call. The process of adding cells incrementally to the salesman's area by maximizing his revenue is continued until his maximum time limit is reached. The set of cells covered constitute his sales area. After the sales area has been determined, the realized revenue is subtracted from the potential revenue of the overall grid. This will reduce some cells to zero. A new sales area is then found with the grid's next highest revenue per call. When all the cells have been reduced to zero, the entire area of the grid has been covered and the analysis completed.

The computer printout covers such information as the individual sales area, its salesmen, its expected revenue, and its number of customers.

In most cases, there will be "extra" cells left over, which will not be considered worth grouping into complete sales areas. This information would be available along with the percent of region covered, percent of potential revenue covered, and percent of customers reached.

A point to remember is that this approach is only a tool to help the manager work more effectively, not a total solution to the problem. Its output is only as accurate and reasonable as the manager's input.

Pricing Models

Pricing changes may make it advantageous for existing customers as well as prospects to purchase equipment rather than lease it. Traditional breakeven analysis can easily be applied to determine whether a single piece of equipment can be economically justified under conditions of lease or purchase. However, when multiple units are involved, each generating different levels of volume, the problem becomes more complex. Furthermore, many companies have rules which govern the purchase versus lease of equipment, and these rules differ among companies. For example, methods of depreciation, cash flow calculations, returns on investment, tax write-offs, and so forth are treated differently from one company to another because no single accounting method or set of standards has been established throughout industry. Some companies such as banks, life insurance companies, and some government agencies are favorable to outright purchase rather than leasing, while others would rather lease equipment even when the installation life of the proposed equipment exceeds the calculated break-even point. The Xerox pricing model was designed to be flexible, so that calculations of lease versus purchase could be accomplished for specific large customers and prospects. Such factors as the estimated life of the installation after date of purchase, the purchase price of the machine, and the volume of the installation serve as the inputs to the model for any individual company. Therefore, purchase or lease costs can be calculated along with the monthly usage required to break even.

For example, the customer data base shows that company X has eight units of product A, five units of product B, and three units of product C, and each unit has different usage patterns, monthly rentals, and installation dates. The monthly cost of purchasing these units is calculated by dividing the sum of the total purchase and service costs (minus credits) by the estimated number of months the equipment is expected to be used after purchase. Total savings are derived by subtracting total monthly purchase costs from total monthly rental costs and multiplying the result by the expected usage period in months. Therefore, it is possible to calculate lease versus purchase costs for each machine, model, location, customer, and industry group, or for all customers.

A related problem was to estimate and forecast the total number of customers and units of equipment that would be purchased rather than leased for any price change. Using the same input factors, we could predict, with variable degrees of accuracy, the proportion of existing customers that would fall into each category. Such analyses enable marketing managers to develop better forecasts of revenues and profits and help to improve the planning process.

Customer demand for a particular model and type of business machine is a function of its price, the prices of substitutes, what customers are used to paying, and other variables. With certain products, there is a positive cross-elasticity of demand so that if the price of a newer model increases, the quantity demanded of the earlier model increases because of substitutability. However, price increases sometimes cause customers to evaluate alternative suppliers, and competition can reduce the quantity of machines demanded from a specific supplier. Therefore, competition and pricing models were developed to help define the impact of the changing business environment.

If each existing competitor had the same strength as Xerox and its products were similar in every respect, then Xerox's share of the market could be expressed simply by:

$$P \cdot \frac{1}{1+x}$$

where P is the market potential and x is the number of competitive machines already present in the market. However, there is a competitive threat from firms whose entry into the field is either imminent or probable, and the probability of their entry can be stated as $p_1, p_2, \ldots p_y$. Then the equation can be modified as:

$$P \cdot \frac{1}{1 + x + \sum\limits_{i=1}^{y} p_i}$$

where y is the number of probable competitive entries into the market.

We have to account for the fact that each competitor does not have the same strengths and that most products are dissimilar in some respects. Although prices and costs of alternative products are probably the most significant factors in the assessment of competitive impact, many other important parameters had to be considered. These parameters include, among others, machine features and capabilities, vendor capabilities and relationships with customers, equipment design characteristics, timing of introduction of products, and technological strengths. A matrix of competitive equipment and significant parameters is constructed, and a factor is assigned to each competitive machine ranging from zero to a maximum of

$$(1 + x + \sum\limits_{i=1}^{y} p_i).$$

If for any particular parameter a competitive machine is approximately equal to Xerox's, then the factor would be assigned a value of one. Therefore, the factor of a parameter such as equipment cost is calculated using the equation:

$$A = \frac{a_1 + a_2 \ldots + a_x + p_1 a_{x+1} + p_2 a_{x+2} + \ldots p_y a_{x+y}}{X + \sum\limits_{i=1}^{y} p_i}$$

where $a_1, a_2, \ldots a_x$ represent subfactors for existing competitive machines, and $a_{x+1}, a_{x+2}, \ldots a_{x+y}$ represent probable competitive entries. Similarly, factors for the other parameters may be calculated. Each parameter is given a weight depending on relative importance, and the factor for all parameters is:

$$F_1 = \frac{A \cdot W_a + B \cdot W_b + \dots}{W_a + W_b + \dots}$$

and the competition factor:

$$F = \frac{1}{1 + x + \sum\limits_{i=1}^{y} p_i} \cdot \frac{A \cdot W_a + B \cdot W_b + \dots}{W_a + W_b + \dots}$$

where W_a is the weight for A, W_b is the weight for B, and so forth. Then expected share of the market (S) is the market potential times the competition factor or:

$$S = P \cdot \frac{1}{1 + x + \sum\limits_{i=1}^{y} p_i} \cdot \frac{A \cdot W_a + B \cdot W_b + \dots}{W_a + W_b + \dots}$$

This model becomes extremely complex as the number of competitors, types and models of equipment, and parameters are increased. Therefore, the computer was used to provide rapid solutions to each problem, and it was possible to simulate the results by changing the weights and values in the matrix.

*   *   *

A variety of marketing models have been described, but these models represent only a small portion of the total efforts being expended toward the improvement and development of new methods and techniques for improving and aiding management decision making. A major challenge is the integration of a series of these models into a marketing information system. However, the general approach to date has been to develop specific models to solve particular problems and aspects of marketing. Attempts are being made to create models which become modular components of a general marketing information system.

Xerox management is receptive to the development and application of practical marketing models. Most of these models were developed to fill a need for more logical, quantitative methods of evaluating and analyzing marketing problems pertaining to new products, pricing, competition, and sales analyses. Marketing judgments are still applied to provide the inputs and assumptions used in these models; therefore, the marketing manager is actively involved in the decision-making process.

17

The Use of the Computer in New Product Planning

Robert D. Dahle

In a large corporation, new product programs may grow out of developments in several areas. Within the structure of Xerox Corporation, new product programs have resulted from developments in one or more of these four major areas: (1) advances or discoveries of new technologies within the Research and Advanced Engineering Division; (2) special applications developed by the advanced development departments within an operating division of the corporation; (3) identification and product specification by a divisional or corporate staff business development and market research group; and (4) direct adaptation of ideas brought to the corporation by outside firms or individuals.

The new product program which is described in this chapter represents one of the most sophisticated developments of the integrative modeling concept within the corporation to date but is not by any means an isolated case. Engineering design simulations for mechanical and electrical systems are in daily use as an integral part of product design; the corporation utilizes both generalized and detailed simulation models for long-range financial planning at the corporate, divisional, and regional levels; and the models are in use for the detailed management of the huge copy machine rental population. Financial and engineering modeling has been a natural way of business within the corporation. However, until the inception of the new product program described here, computerized models were not being used extensively in a systematic way to aid in the development, analysis, and implementation of a product concept from market research through engineering design and field installation.

Recent articles have reported that the computer has not had much impact on top-level decision making in the United States. Even though the use of the computer has increased the executive time available for decisions and the evaluation of alternatives, it has not substantially affected the way decisions are made or increased the validity of the information used in making decisions. Some of the predictions made about future computer use were:

- Greater computer influence at divisional versus corporate level.
- Greater computer impact on larger companies as opposed to smaller.
- Greater impact on content of specially prepared information to support specific top management decisions.
- Significant increase in the use of simulation models in exploring alternate courses of action, particularly in evaluating alternative long-range plans, product lines, and pricing decisions.

A specific example of how these predictions are becoming a reality at Xerox Corporation is contained in this chapter.

Basic to the development of this product concept was the old salesmanship maxim of "find a need and fill it." The original task was to identify a market which could provide the economic basis for a substantial new product venture and then to refine information about this market to discover a product need which matched technologic capabilities and could meet corporate profit objectives. Thus, the computer models are the results of an active new product program within the corporation. The purpose of the program is to enable Xerox to become a worldwide leader in creating products and services for obtaining and communicating information in a new market area. The planned introduction date is still several years away, so the models have yet to withstand the validation test of time.

Reasons for Developing the Modeling System

The reasons why this system of computer models was developed are threefold. The first and most practical reason is the desire for maximum utilization of the scarce manpower available for new product program planning. In its embryonic stage, a new product program can command little manpower until its potential worth can be argued convincingly. Conversely, it is often difficult to do all the work necessary to gather sufficient data, develop equipment performance objectives, and analyze market potential in order to develop convincing product concept arguments until enough manpower can be brought to bear on the program. The process is therefore what has been called a "bootstrapping" technique of painfully moving ahead—perhaps not being able to do the most thorough job along the way—until management has been convinced that the assignment of sufficient people to get the job done is justified. Many tedious and repetitive calculations were envisioned as this program developed. As changes were made in product specifications because of technological and market definition refinements, the effect of these changes on other program aspects had to be calculated. Computer models seemed to be the answer to the repetitive calculations, and the models could also provide a means of drawing together all aspects of the program so that the effect of a change in one parameter could be seen in the resulting changes upon the other. It also appeared possible to utilize manpower from other departments in the design, programming, and implementation of the models.

The second reason is that the use of simulation models is a competent way of identifying and solving business planning problems as well as communicating program progress. The methods described are not standard procedures in most businesses, yet much is being written about them in business journals. By making an honest effort to apply "advanced methods," management may have more confidence that the recommendations for program developments were developed on a sound basis through evaluation of alternatives by the program planning staff.

Third and finally, because simulation methods for new product programs were not generally in use at Xerox, it was felt that there could be much beneficial use in other company operating divisions. Thus, at the start, the project was seen as an opportunity to prove the feasibility of the models in a staff program (where there might be less penalty for failure than in an operating division concerned with short-range profitability) and then to utilize the work in developing a product division. Participants from other divisions had the chance to observe the modeling objectives and to keep any programs developed as part of the project general enough for widespread use in other areas.

A not-unimportant aspect of this project was the cooperation of the separate departments and the manpower within them. The project was an opportunity to show that departments could cooperate and work together on an informal basis for the purpose of overall company achievement. This modeling development has been from its inception a "bottom-up" project rather than a "top-down" project. A major selling job was needed many times to get top management to continue their support of this interdepartmental effort, rather than the usual situation of top management forcing cooperation between the analytic units.

Modeling a New Business Program

Most industrial product modeling efforts are directed toward the evaluation of technical specifications and trade-offs associated with the product rather than the effect of the product upon its environment. However, engineering characteristics are, from all points of view, extremely important in relationship to their effect upon the system within which they are to be used. Unless product development is carried on in conjunction with an investigation of the synergistic effects of product and environment, program feasibility may substantially change during the design phase.

The analysis techniques which formed the basis for modeling the new business program consist of four basic steps. First, a detailed description of the environment of the product is developed and validated. Second, various product concepts are introduced into this environment, and their effectiveness in mitigating physical problems as well as their economic feasibility at this level are evaluated with respect to the total market opportunity and the ability to meet corporate profit goals. Specifically, an attempt is made to determine what set of conditions must exist if the corporation is to gain a specific share of market in face of competition and yet meet the profit goals of the corporation. This basic process is illustrated in Exhibit 17–1.

To carry out this basic system, the following models were developed:

1. Product operating environment simulator.
2. Equipment reliability model.
3. Machine operating cycle simulator.
4. Product pricing model.
5. Demand forecasting model.
6. Bayesian marketing research planning model.
7. Market model.

The output of the market model and some of the information on product characteristics are used by a corporate financial model to generate cash flow analysis and compute return on investment. The interconnectedness of this system of models is illustrated in the flow diagram of Exhibit 17–2.

The succeeding sections of this chapter describe the specific models on an individual basis including the uses of each model, and then some of the experiences encountered during the design of the models are related. Finally, the

Exhibit 17–1
New Product Analysis

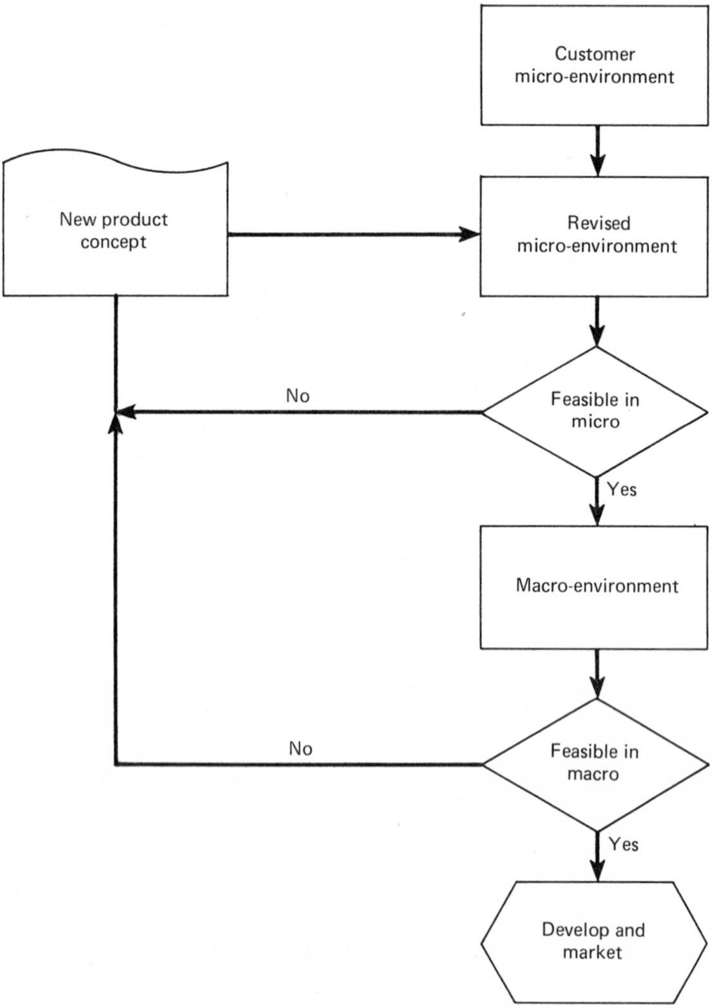

Exhibit 17-2
Integrative Modeling System

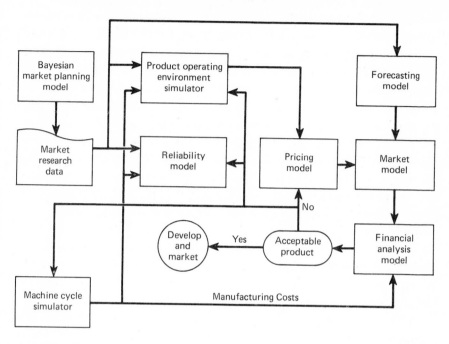

reactions of management and expectations for the future use of the models are discussed.

Because of the proprietary nature of this new business program, the exact nature of the project must remain confidential. A soil-testing laboratory provides a suitable surrogate for illustrating the nature of the analytical system.

Product Operating Environment Simulator

The general objective of this model is to simulate the effect of the planned new product upon its environment. Analyses of competitive products can also be run using the same logic. A principal input to the construction of the simulator is market research data which define the nature of the environment. Another input is the assumed performance characteristics of the product, tempered when information becomes available by the results of the machine cycle and reliability simulators.

A soil-testing laboratory operates as a job shop in which all work entering must be uniquely tagged for later identification at a reassembly point. The soil samples are then broken into tagged subsamples to be analyzed at the various chemical analysis work stations. Tagged results are collated, and a report concerning the soil sample is prepared and sent to the requester of the analysis. To illustrate the type of results which are obtained from this model when tested for validity, see Exhibits 17–3 and 17–4.

Points of interest in Exhibit 17–3 are the point of peak labor utilization, expressed in minutes, located between 1 and 2 P.M., and the "percent done" column on the far right side of the exhibit. The difference between the tests done versus the samples done is also of interest, since all tests must be completed before a sample can be released and reviewed by supervisory personnel. Because there are different rates for each test, the number of tests completed is initially faster than the number of samples completed. Based upon this workload, a minimum of 13 persons working a fully productive hour plus supervisory personnel is required to operate this lab during the day. If casual time were allowed during the day, several additional employees would be required. Casual time is the time used by employees for personal requirements, casual conversations, and other nonproductive actions.

The results from a single chemical analysis station give some idea of the type of information obtained at this level of operation. Data for a 24-hour period are shown in Exhibit 17–4. Essentially the same information is presented here as in the summary table, but additional information such as the queue size at the end of each hour, cumulative analysis time for the various labor categories, and actual test completion rates is also included. This station illustrated in Exhibit 17–4 operates only sporadically during the second two shifts of the day. Labor utilization characteristics such as this can be interpreted as requiring either part-time employment or the shifting of an employee to another station which opens at a later hour and does a small number of tests for an hour or two to finish off the employee's day. Data for a work station which is opened later in the day and is run for only a short period are shown in Exhibit 17–5.

When a new product that combines the testing done at three stations into one station is introduced into the environment, substantial changes occur in the results. Data for a new lab operating setup as compared to the manual setup are shown in Exhibit 17–6. By comparing the two sets of data, one can appraise the physical effects of the two different operating systems. A large reduction in labor occurs as a mechanization of some stations is substituted for manual operation. For the 24-hour period, the reduction is a factor of 20.

(text continues on page 178)

Exhibit 17-3

Soil Samples Tests—Summary Table

Summary of Entire Lab—To Completion Time

Lab Opens 8 A.M.

Time	Analysis Actual	Calc + Record Actual	Setup + Cleanup Actual	Totals	Samples			Tests		Percent Done	
					In	Rel	Out	In	Out	Samples	Tests
8– 9 A.M.	51.8	13.4	57.7	122.9	229	79	1	245	13	0	5
9–10 A.M.	293.9	102.7	90.1	486.7	236	115	10	380	142	4	37
10–11 A.M.	432.0	183.5	34.0	649.5	242	148	41	511	286	16	55
11–12 A.M.	445.6	201.1	39.3	686.0	248	186	72	639	432	29	67
12– 1 P.M.	438.3	239.1	0.0	677.4	256	221	116	768	577	45	75
1– 2 P.M.	457.6	276.2	28.5	762.3	262	255	150	896	716	57	79
2– 3 P.M.	490.3	242.1	0.0	732.4	267	266	193	941	836	72	88
3– 4 P.M.	325.4	155.6	0.0	481.0	274	274	219	977	911	79	93
4– 5 P.M.	107.9	45.0	305.0	457.9	278	277	237	993	942	85	94
5– 6 P.M.	116.5	37.3	156.8	310.6	279	278	244	996	961	87	96
6– 7 P.M.	190.1	30.5	5.0	225.6	280	280	251	1008	978	89	97
7– 8 P.M.	68.0	37.0	0.0	105.0	283	283	257	1022	996	90	97
8– 9 P.M.	60.4	11.6	0.0	72.0	284	284	262	1023	1001	92	97
9–10 P.M.	67.7	30.4	0.0	98.1	287	287	270	1033	1015	94	98
10–11 P.M.	49.6	24.9	0.0	74.5	289	289	279	1035	1025	96	99
11–12 P.M.	120.9	37.1	0.0	158.0	292	291	285	1052	1042	97	99
12– 1 A.M.	129.3	33.3	335.5	498.1	294	294	291	1066	1054	98	98
1– 2 A.M.	233.0	51.5	189.0	473.5	296	296	292	1080	1073	98	99
2– 3 A.M.	103.9	37.5	0.0	141.4	298	298	295	1089	1084	98	99
3– 4 A.M.	56.0	27.1	13.1	96.2	300	300	298	1097	1091	99	99
4– 5 A.M.	30.8	17.9	0.0	48.7	302	301	299	1101	1096	99	99
5– 6 A.M.	51.0	13.8	0.0	64.8	304	304	300	1104	1099	98	99
6– 7 A.M.	49.9	22.3	5.0	77.2	306	306	302	1116	1105	98	99
7– 8 A.M.	131.9	39.1	269.5	440.5	308	308	304	1124	1116	98	99
24 Hr. Total Labor Cost	4501.8 157.56	1910.0 66.85	1528.5 53.50	7940.3 277.91							

Table 17-4
Soil Samples Tests—From a Single Station

Test No. – Potassium
Station Opens – 8:30 A.M.

Time	Analysis		Calc + Record		Setup + Cleanup		Totals		No. Rec'd Cum.	Left In Queue	No. Done	Percent Done
	Actual	Cum.	Actual	Cum.	Actual	Cum.	Actual	Cum.				
8– 9 A.M.	11.8	11.8	1.5	1.5	16.2	16.2	29.5	29.5	28	18	3	10
9–10 A.M.	45.8	57.6	14.5	16.0	0.0	16.2	60.3	89.8	44	10	32	72
10–11 A.M.	32.8	90.4	27.0	43.0	0.0	16.2	59.8	149.6	61	1	54	88
11–12 A.M.	35.8	126.2	17.1	60.1	0.0	16.2	52.9	202.5	75	1	73	97
12– 1 P.M.	41.6	167.8	16.8	76.9	0.0	16.2	58.4	260.9	93	0	91	97
1– 2 P.M.	34.9	202.7	15.8	92.7	0.0	16.2	50.7	311.6	109	0	107	98
2– 3 P.M.	11.8	214.5	7.6	100.3	0.0	16.2	19.4	331.0	115	0	115	100
3– 4 P.M.	14.6	229.1	4.0	104.3	0.0	16.2	18.6	349.6	119	0	119	100
4– 5 P.M.	0.0	229.1	0.0	104.3	45.0	61.2	45.0	394.6	120	0	119	99
Shift Total		229.1		104.3		61.2		394.6	120	0	119	99
5– 6 P.M.	1.6	1.6	1.0	1.0	20.1	20.1	22.7	22.7	120	0	120	100
6– 7 P.M.	9.8	11.4	1.0	2.0	0.0	20.1	10.3	33.5	121	0	121	100
7– 8 P.M.	3.2	14.6	2.0	4.0	0.0	20.1	5.2	38.7	123	0	123	100
8– 9 P.M.	0.0	14.6	0.0	4.0	0.0	20.1	0.0	38.7	123	0	123	100
9–10 P.M.	1.6	16.2	1.0	5.0	0.0	20.1	2.6	41.3	124	0	124	100
10–11 P.M.	0.0	16.2	0.0	5.0	0.0	20.1	0.0	41.3	124	0	124	100
11–12 P.M.	3.2	19.4	2.0	7.0	0.0	20.1	5.2	46.5	126	0	126	100
12– 1 A.M.	0.0	19.4	0.0	7.0	45.0	65.1	45.0	91.5	127	0	126	99
Shift Total		19.4		7.0		65.1		91.5	127	0	126	99
1– 2 A.M.	14.9	14.9	2.0	2.0	20.1	20.1	37.0	37.0	128	0	128	100
2– 3 A.M.	1.6	16.5	1.0	3.0	0.0	20.1	2.6	39.6	129	0	129	100
3– 4 A.M.	1.6	18.1	1.0	4.0	0.0	20.1	2.6	42.2	130	0	130	100
4– 5 A.M.	0.0	18.1	0.0	4.0	0.0	20.1	0.0	42.2	130	0	130	100
5– 6 A.M.	0.0	18.1	0.0	4.0	0.0	20.1	0.0	42.2	130	0	130	100
6– 7 A.M.	1.6	19.7	0.6	4.6	0.0	20.1	2.2	44.4	132	0	131	99
7– 8 A.M.	1.6	21.3	1.0	5.6	45.0	65.1	47.6	92.0	133	0	132	99
Shift Total		21.3		5.6		65.1		92.0	133	0	132	99
24 Hr. Total		269.8		116.9		191.4		578.1	133	0	132	99
Labor Cost		9.44		4.09		6.70		20.23				

Exhibit 17-5

Soil Samples Tests—From Another Station

Test No. — Phosphorus
Station Opens — 1:30 P.M.

Time	Analysis Actual	Analysis Cum.	Calc + Record Actual	Calc + Record Cum.	Setup + Cleanup Actual	Setup + Cleanup Cum.	Totals Actual	Totals Cum.	No. Rec'd Cum.	Left In Queue	No. Done	Percent Done
8- 9 A.M.	0.0	0.0	0.0	0.0	0.0	0.0	0.0	0.0	4	4	0	0
9-10 A.M.	0.0	0.0	0.0	0.0	0.0	0.0	0.0	0.0	9	9	0	0
10-11 A.M.	0.0	0.0	0.0	0.0	0.0	0.0	0.0	0.0	10	10	0	0
11-12 A.M.	0.0	0.0	0.0	0.0	0.0	0.0	0.0	0.0	12	12	0	0
12- 1 P.M.	0.0	0.0	0.0	0.0	0.0	0.0	0.0	0.0	16	16	0	0
1- 2 P.M.	21.7	21.7	0.0	0.0	5.5	5.5	27.2	27.2	19	8	0	0
2- 3 P.M.	58.4	80.1	1.1	1.1	0.0	5.5	59.5	86.7	19	0	1	5
3- 4 P.M.	38.2	118.3	21.6	22.7	0.0	5.5	59.8	146.5	22	0	20	90
4- 5 P.M.	0.0	118.3	3.2	25.9	0.0	5.5	3.2	149.7	22	0	22	100
Shift Total		118.3		25.9		5.5		149.7	22	0	22	100
5- 6 P.M.	0.0	0.0	0.0	0.0	0.0	0.0	0.0	0.0	22	0	22	100
6- 7 P.M.	25.9	25.9	0.0	0.0	0.0	0.0	25.9	25.9	23	0	22	95
7- 8 P.M.	0.0	25.9	1.8	1.8	0.0	0.0	1.8	27.7	23	0	23	100
8- 9 P.M.	0.0	25.9	0.0	1.8	0.0	0.0	0.0	27.7	23	0	23	100
9-10 P.M.	0.0	25.9	0.0	1.8	0.0	0.0	0.0	27.7	23	0	23	100
10-11 P.M.	0.0	25.9	0.0	1.8	0.0	0.0	0.0	27.7	23	0	23	100
11-12 P.M.	0.0	25.9	0.0	1.8	0.0	0.0	0.0	27.7	23	0	23	100
12- 1 A.M.	0.0	25.9	0.0	1.8	10.0	10.0	10.0	37.7	23	0	23	100
Shift Total		25.9		1.8		10.0		37.7	23	0	23	100
1- 2 A.M.	10.6	10.6	0.0	0.0	5.5	5.5	16.1	16.1	24	0	23	95
2- 3 A.M.	0.0	10.6	1.8	1.8	0.0	5.5	1.8	17.9	24	0	24	100
3- 4 A.M.	0.0	10.6	0.0	1.8	0.0	5.5	0.0	17.9	24	0	24	100
4- 5 A.M.	0.0	10.6	0.0	1.8	0.0	5.5	0.0	17.9	24	0	24	100
5- 6 A.M.	0.0	10.6	0.0	1.8	0.0	5.5	0.0	17.9	24	0	24	100
6- 7 A.M.	0.0	10.6	0.0	1.8	0.0	5.5	0.0	17.9	24	0	24	100
7- 8 A.M.	0.0	10.6	0.0	1.8	10.0	15.5	10.0	27.9	24	0	24	100
Shift Total		10.6		1.8		15.5		27.9	24	0	24	100
24 Hr. Total		154.8		29.5		31.0		215.3	24	0	24	100
Labor Cost		5.42		1.03		1.08		7.54				

The information provided by this analysis gives some idea of the amount of labor substitution which can then be utilized in developing a pricing strategy for the product. The obvious increase in speed, coupled with improved accuracy and greatly reduced labor requirements, creates an improvement in the physical environment that can also be capitalized upon in the pricing strategy.

The improvements in speed of sample completion also permit a more rapid turnaround time for each sample. While substantial early-morning

Exhibit 17-6
A New Operating System

| | Total Time | | Percent Done | | | |
| | Manual | Combined | Manual | | Combined | |
			Samples	Tests	Samples	Tests
8- 9 A.M.	122.9	27.4	0	5	0	4
9-10 A.M.	486.7	21.1	4	37	6	30
10-11 A.M.	649.5	62.9	16	55	10	64
11-12 A.M.	689.0	26.2	29	67	28	90
12- 1 P.M.	677.4	21.6	45	75	50	95
1- 2 P.M.	762.3	33.3	57	79	76	98
2- 3 P.M.	732.4	77.4	72	88	95	98
3- 4 P.M.	481.0	23.3	79	93	96	99
4- 5 P.M.	457.9	17.6	85	94	96	99
5- 6 P.M.	310.6	2.3	87	96	97	99
6- 7 P.M.	225.6	8.1	89	97	97	99
7- 8 P.M.	105.0	8.1	90	97	97	99
8- 9 P.M.	72.0	2.8	92	97	97	99
9-10 P.M.	98.1	2.3	94	98	98	99
10-11 P.M.	74.5	2.4	96	99	98	99
11-12 P.M.	158.0	2.3	97	99	98	99
12- 1 A.M.	498.1	16.4	98	98	98	99
1- 2 A.M.	473.5	4.0	98	99	98	99
2- 3 A.M.	141.4	2.6	98	99	99	99
3- 4 A.M.	96.2	36.6	99	99	98	99
4- 5 A.M.	48.7	3.4	99	99	98	99
5- 6 A.M.	64.8	9.2	98	99	98	99
6- 7 A.M.	77.2	8.1	98	99	99	99
7- 8 A.M.	440.5	19.4	98	99	99	99
24 Hr. Total	7,940.3	438.9				
Labor Cost	277.9	15.4				

gains are not made by mechanization (there is even some loss before noon), the effects of mechanization on throughput are dramatic in the early afternoon. Thus we begin to gain some appreciation of the way in which the introduction of a mechanical device might expand the use far beyond our initial expectations or may actually change the environment. It is entirely possible that the decreased labor requirement might change the whole way of conceptualizing the function. For instance, a different quality of labor may be used in a mechanized environment than is required in the manual laboratory.

In addition to its use in business planning, the environmental simulator can be utilized in marketing the product. A simulator provides a good way of communicating the expected effect of the product upon the customer's present methods, work schedule, and manpower requirements and permits the salesman to control a powerful sales tool.

Equipment Reliability Model

The objective of the equipment reliability model was to investigate the interaction of product operating time, failure rates, repair requirements, and serviceman utilization. Given assumptions concerning machine part failure rates, repair time, installations per sales territory, and servicemen per sales territory, the model simulated:

1. Number of machines awaiting service at any time.
2. Down time for these machines.
3. Time required to repair these machines.
4. Average utilization of servicemen.

These calculations were useful as input for an engineering trade-off analysis on design cost for a certain level of product reliability versus corresponding service costs and customer satisfaction. Also, this model helped to determine the number of machines needed per customer if at least one operating machine was desired at all times.

A very gross simulation model was developed to compute this information. The model was gross for two reasons: (1) The data available on failure rates were approximate, and (2) detailed models to generate this same information when more refined information became available were under development in another division of the corporation.

Estimates of down time were used to condition the throughput of the equipment studied with the operating environment simulator. Consequently, this model became an integral part of the operating environment simulator.

Machine Operating Cycle Simulator

The objective of this model was to aid in the detailed design of the product concept. The model provided information to the engineering-design personnel in the same manner as the environmental model provided information to the market analyst. In this case, the environment was the internal operation of the soil testing machine, rather than the soil testing laboratory.

In many corporations, construction of this type of simulator is the only simulation work undertaken during the development of a new product program. Traditional engineering use of this simulator was contemplated for the model, but it was later seen as part of a much larger planning system.

Product Pricing Model

Pricing strategies considered for the new product ranged from a monthly rental charge based upon the time the product was in use to a combination of minimum monthly rental charge plus a processing charge related to a number of soil samples processed daily and a charge for each individual determination made on the sample. Comparisons among these various pricing strategies and variations within each strategy would have involved laborious manual calculations. To further complicate the problem, it was suggested that no price charged for a soil test be either greater than that charged for the alternative method or less than the cost of performing the test.

Formulation of the model was made considerably easier when several arbitrary rules were developed and accepted. Multiple-product pricing, under conditions of market uncertainty with respect to individual determinations, was reduced to a rather straightforward iterative procedure. The solution of the pricing problem as additional soil analysis determinations become available is more and more difficult. Certainly, treating the marginal values of each determination as a function of their average cost will not suffice for very long, especially if there is a real difference between the value of the determination to the users. Results from this model are used directly in the market model and in product financial evaluation.

Bayesian Market Planning and Research Model

The objective of this model was to use Bayesian methods to determine the level of expenditures justified for up to three years of new product and market research planning work. The method used is illustrated by Wroe Alderson and Paul Green in *Planning and Problem Solving in Marketing.** Inputs to the model include the expected reliability of information, research and development expenditures, a priori probabilities of a favorable market, the expected cost of business planning work, the opportunity cost of capital, and anticipated payoff of the product (profit over the product's life). To determine whether planning expenditures are justified, present values of the program with no planning expenditures were compared with the present values if assumed planning expenditures are made.

The model was used to run various analyses of sensitivity to determine the effect of variations in some parameters when others were held constant. For example, a hypothetical case, as shown in Exhibit 17–7, illustrates what was done. The model was set up to vary the expected payoffs for each case. For expected profits of $2 million, the assumed expenditures for business planning would have been justified, since program present value with the information obtained exceeds present value with no further information. The optional action is just to do the first year of business planning. However, if the payoff from this program really exceeds $2 million, then the value of additional information does not justify any further business planning. Thus the model has been used to show the implications of the assumptions underlying it.

As the program progressed, more completely defined probabilities were used which extended the model's capabilities beyond the simplified level presented here. The model also can be used to determine the effect of the planning-group budget when changes occur in R&D or any of the associated variables affecting the budget.

Demand Forecasting Model

During the period prior to market introduction, market research interviews, consisting of three to ten years of past annual soil testing volumes obtained through sequential sampling of potential customers, will be collected so that each new set of data can be used to expand the base and update a

---

* (Homewood, Illinois: Richard D. Irwin, Inc., 1964), pp. 210–235.

Input Assumptions				
Time	Expenditure			
0	200,000.			
1	300,000.			
2	500,000.			
3	0.			

	Conditional Revenue Table			
	Demand (1)	Demand (2)		
Go	-0.	-0.		
No-Go	-0.	-0.		
A Priori Probability	0.60	0.40		

Opportunity Cost of Capital = 0.10

Survey No.	Cost	Cost Period	Results Period	Reliability
1	40,000.	0	0	0.70
2	60,000.	1	1	0.80
3	80,000.	2	2	0.90

PRESENT VALUE				
Revenue	0	1	2	3
1	0.	0.	0.	0.
2	15,627.	131,091.	108,705.	98,753.
3	466,416.	446,643.	483,258.	460,840
4	917,205.	877,205	906,999.	878,271.
5	1,367,994.	1,327,994.	1,330,741.	1,306,055.
6	1,818,783.	1,778,783	1,754,482	1,747,829.
7	2,269,572.	2,229,572.	2,178,224.	2,189,602.
8	2,720,361.	2,680,361.	2,625,815.	2,636,422.
9	3,171,150.	3,131,149.	3,076,604.	3,084,506.
10	3,621,938.	3,581,938.	3,527,393.	3,532,590.

five- to seven- year market-projection equation. The number of field interviews planned in any single year will be influenced by the market-planning analysis information from the Bayesian model.

A regression model was designed to project testing volume for each individual determination, with the independent parameters being various customer characteristics and a time parameter. While the initial emphasis will be on projecting national and regional testing volumes by size of customer, as more data become available, projections will be refined upon a geographical basis. Validation of this regression model has been particularly difficult since the total time span of the base data used in development was relatively small and the predictability validations were hard to make.

As has been explained elsewhere, the pricing of individual determinations on a soil sample was made using a rather arbitrary set of rules. The demand prediction defined in this model does not presently attempt to predict a price response but attempts to project present usage into the future under fixed price or proportional price changes. Since the pricing model assures, perhaps incorrectly, that the cost of performing a given set of soil tests will never be greater than competitive costs, the lack of an adequate treatment of the effects of price on quantity demanded can lead to underestimation of the market. Planning for market introduction will have to take this underestimation into account through specific studies of demand elasticity.

Market Model

The objective of the market model was to provide a means for calculating the annual revenues from the new product, given an assumption about market share. Other inputs to the model included labor and time required to process the soil tests for both the new Xerox product and competitive products obtained from the environment simulator, a Xerox pricing plan from the pricing model, and a projection of future demand for processing tests for each size of customer. The output is designed to be used as input to the financial analysis model. It is desirable to be able to obtain a new estimate of annual revenue quickly if the program inputs change. In addition, the first portion of the output model is intended to be presented to the potential customer as a sales tool which compares the operating costs of the Xerox product versus a competitive product which the customer may have in the lab or under evaluation for purchase. For future use in marketing, the model was designed to be expandable to a regional, state, or city basis. It could then be used for setting up sales territories, estimating required sales and service men, and setting sales quotas.

The market model (see Exhibit 17–8) was designed to compare costs for each test done by manual methods as compared to an automated ("machine system") method. Labor and supplies costs are first allocated depending upon the quantity of testing done by the particular lab, size (small, medium, or large), the time allocated to the test, and the estimated supplies expended by each individual method. The actual cost to do the quantity of tests demanded by the lab workload and overhead costs of the lab are allocated to each test. Supplies, labor, and total costs are summed and compared within the model. The least expensive method, based upon the data entered, is designated, and total costs are multiplied by the number of customer laboratories in the market data base.

If the overall costs of the machine method are too high, the output may be examined on a test basis to determine whether cost of the new product exceeds the cost of the machine. The unit cost of each method and the cost differences point up the comparative advantages quickly. Changes can be made in pricing plans for an individual test or group of tests until overall test processing cost equals or is less than that of competition.

Reactions to the Modeling System

Because implementation is always one of the major stumbling blocks to use of an integrative modeling approach, actual experience in developing this modeling system and an idea of the actual time, effort, and practical problems involved have been presented. There are usually several product development programs going on at any one time. Funds and manpower for these programs are always scarce and must be allocated on a priority basis. Also, the mortality rate of new product programs is very high, and investment in these programs is high risk. Thus any assignment of resources is under continuous review during the product's development.

All the models described resulted from the informal cooperation of two or more individuals from different divisions. The business analyst and the modeling analyst worked together over a period of time to design and evaluate a useful environmental simulation model. The business analyst defined the purposes of the model, specified the available information (input) and the desired output format, and was generally responsible for the usefulness of the model for business planning purposes. The modeling analyst pro-

Exhibit 17-8
Market Model

Test	Manual System			Machine Manual System Allocated*			
	Non Labor Cost	Labor Cost	Total Cost	Machine Tests	Non- Labor Cost	Labor Machine Cost	Total Cost
1	0.72	1.50	2.22	M	3.00	0.49	3.49
2	2.40	4.88	7.28	C	3.75	5.20	0.95
3	1.30	2.93	4.23	M	2.70	2.46	5.16
4	0.27	1.33	1.60	M	1.63	0.43	2.00
5	2.00	2.65	4.65	M	2.20	3.08	5.28
6	1.65	5.75	7.40	M	1.80	3.69	5.49
7	0.11	1.00	1.11	M	0.40	0.25	0.65
8	1.05	3.43	4.48	C	1.65	5.20	6.82
Total	9.50	23.45	32.95		17.13	20.80	37.95
Overhead Costs			100.00				75.00
Grand Total			133.				113.

*Allocation based upon total time for test per unit of time; M—Xerox machine, C—Competitive machine

	Composition of Unit Costs						
1	0.36	0.75	1.11	M	1.50	0.25	1.75
2	0.16	0.33	0.49	C	0.25	0.35	0.60
3	0.26	0.59	0.85	M	0.54	0.49	1.03
4	0.27	1.33	1.60	M	1.63	0.43	2.00
5	0.20	0.27	0.47	M	0.22	0.31	0.53
6	0.11	0.38	0.49	M	0.12	0.25	0.37
7	0.11	1.00	1.11	M	0.40	0.25	0.65
8	0.07	0.23	0.30	C	0.11	0.35	0.46
Total	1.54	4.86	6.40		4.77	2.66	7.43
Avg. Unit Cost Without Overhead		0.51492				0.59250	
Avg. Total Unit		2.07742				1.76448	

Test Number	Unit Cost of Manual Method	Unit Cost of Machine Method	Difference (Manual-Machine)
1	1.11	1.75	-0.64
2	0.49	0.60	-0.11
3	0.85	1.03	-0.19
4	1.60	2.06	-0.47
5	0.47	0.53	-0.06
6	0.49	0.37	0.12
7	1.11	0.65	0.46
8	0.30	0.46	-0.16

Year 1, Level 1

Total Size of the Market	100.0
Xerox Share	20
Net Supply Revenues	342
Gross Machine Revenues	208
Gross Supply Revenues	342
Total Net Revenues	550
Annual Net Revenues	143,000
Annual Gross Revenues	143,000

vided logic design and ·programming support after being satisfied that the purpose of the model made sense to him.

There have been several formal presentations concerning these models. The first few were made to sell various groups on the value of using simulation models in a new product program. The first presentation was made to the technical team shortly after the feasibility of the environmental simulator was proved with a first-cut, relatively inefficient simulator. The engineers were in the early stages of product conceptualization and felt the need for a good description of the product's environment. A principal technical consultant was present who had several years of full-time responsibility for the performance of jobs in such an environment using manual procedures. The objective of the presentation was to show that the environment could be described by a computer model and that such a model was a practical tool for business analysis–engineering development. The consultant agreed that his "job shop" had been faithfully represented by the model. All present agreed that modeling held promise for future helpfulness and that further work in that direction was to be encouraged.

The next presentation, shortly thereafter, was made to the middle management groups to stimulate their enthusiasm and support for the effort ahead—bringing several models to operational status. This was also a successful presentation, resulting in increased cooperation and a spreading reputation of a well-planned project.

About nine months of work on the modeling system passed. The environmental simulator, pricing program, and reliability model became operational. In particular, several good runs on the environmental model were available, and another presentation was made to the technical team. A thorough discussion of the model's capabilities resulted, and several suggestions for further analyses were made. In particular, the ability of the model to compare systems operation of competing products in the environment, as opposed to just comparing product specification, was recognized.

In addition to fulfilling their original purpose, the models have proved to be a good tool for communicating the objectives, methods, and progress of the business development program. In particular, these approaches to business planning have engaged the interest of financial control and planning people whose opinions of any new business venture are valuable in gaining top management support.

The business development team found that developing models forced them to know the product and marketing environment well. The models enable the thinking-through of detailed plans in an organized and complete manner. Invariably, in designing and running the models, areas were identified where new or more complete information was needed.

In general, the business planning and corporate modeling people associated with this program felt that they were helping to increase the corporation's experience in simulation modeling. Those working on this new product development felt that the effectiveness of models as decision-making aids will increase gradually through better communication of the quality of input data and working of the computer models. All believe that these techniques will have widespread application within the company in the near future, and familiarity should encourage the acceptance of models as components of the decision-making process.

Future Marketing Payoffs

As was implied earlier, several of the models designed for planning new products will be useful to or easily converted for the use of a marketing organization. When selling begins, the environment simulator will be used to show the customer how his present and future workload can be handled by Xerox product-versus-manual or other automated methods. The first section of the market model will also be used to estimate market potential on a sales territory basis for the setting of sales quotas and evaluation of salesman performance. At this level a program can also be designed to estimate needed salesmen, service loads, and potential revenue per placement. The pricing model will help Xerox approach the market with the correct mix of prices related to use and will help in quick evaluations of proposed pricing changes. The Bayesian model may prove useful in future marketing planning and research budgets for the marketing organization.

18

The Computer's Role in the Discovery and Development of Product Opportunities

E. J. Sandon Cox

IN THE FOLLOWING TWO CASE HISTORIES, a computer was used in both the batch mode and the time-sharing mode to discover new product opportunities and to develop some of these opportunities to the point of launch.

CASE HISTORY NO. 1

Company: Taylor Soaps-Perfumes Limited, Toronto, Canada.

Subject: A project undertaken to diversify Canada's oldest producer of soap products into new product areas.

Taylor Soaps-Perfumes Limited started operation in Canada in 1865. In recent decades, this small Canadian company, doing less than $5 million annual business, has concentrated its efforts in the production of private brands of soap. At the same time, it has maintained a small share of market for its own brands of toilet soap. Mr. Taylor, the third-generation owner–manager of this business, perceived that it was necessary to diversify the company operations to obtain the growth rate he desired.

For this reason, Applied Management Sciences, Limited (AMS) was engaged to search out new opportunities. Initially, no constraints were placed upon this product development company in its attempts to seek new ventures. Such diverse areas as aircraft, plastics, and cosmetics were considered. Some of the original areas of investigation still remain possibilities for future diversification.

These early investigations, which were largely conceptual exercises, indicated that initial expansion should come about through an extension of the existing expertise and the distribution system into product lines not then manufactured by Taylor Soaps.

The most obvious opportunity area was the liquid detergent market. Historically, the liquid detergent market has opposed the conceptual trends in the powdered detergent market. While primary emphasis with powders has been on increasing strength, the opposite situation obtained with liquids. This is not to say that the major manufacturers of liquid detergent were stressing the relative weakness of their liquid detergent, but rather that their very definite emphasis on the cosmetic benefits of their liquids implied a negation of their cleaning power.

This rather curt summary of the conceptual exercises that led to opportunity recognition belies the fact that significant inputs were obtained from a marketing psychologist.

It then became necessary to build operational models of the Canadian detergent market. Without these models, the developer has no way of assessing the financial possibilities inherent in a new product entry.

In order to establish the model of the market, data were obtained from two sources: A. C. Nielsen and The Dominion Bureau of Statistics.

Trend Analysis

The vitally important trend information regarding the overall movement of the market and brand share interchange within the market was obtained by using less than $20 of computer time on a General Electric 430 time-shared computer utility. The marketing use of computers is perhaps one of the most economical uses made of the computer today.

General Electric has published excellent support documentation for its regression analyses and curve-fitting programs that were used for this trend analysis. By using the computer in time-sharing mode, the marketing manager, like the scientist, maintains control through involvement in the experiment that he is running. The development policy requires one person to maintain a complete awareness of all aspects of a project. This would not be possible without the use of the time-shared computer.

Administrative Control by Computer

The many complexities of product development require a sound program of administration to insure that all components of the development dovetail into place at the proper time. Many articles have been written concerning the use of critical path methods (CPM) or their probability equivalent, PERT, as control mechanisms. A critical path model for the Taylor diversification program was developed at the beginning of the study.

The critical path is a logical extension of a bar chart. By linking together development activities that are dependent on one another, rather than leaving these activities unconnected, as they are on the bar chart, the manager can see at a glance the progress to date of his project. The graphic representation of this chart is often referred to as a network diagram.

We find, however, that the final network, or CPM, often is very different from the original network. In spite of this, the discipline of a network plan is an invaluable part of early planning and development. Fortunately, the time-sharing computer has come to our rescue again by providing a very efficient method for weekly updating and alteration of the network model. Some say that it is not worthwhile computerizing the CPM routine for less than 100 activities. But there seems no justification for the selection of this particular number of activities, nor are such statements made with a knowledge of the ease of use and low cost associated with running CPM on the time-shared utility. The particular system AMS uses has the added benefit that the weekly update need not be printed out on the terminal connection. The data are stored on disc and subsequently dumped on the line printer. This particular option allows the user to avoid lengthy connect time with the computer merely to obtain printing output. The actual graph—that is, the network diagram—is easily prepared by a clerk.

The use of critical path methods not only provides the manager with a disciplining mechanism and a control function, it also provides him with a guide for decision making. One output from the critical path program is a time listing of cash flows. These cash flows provide the input for a cash flow model which becomes the primary model for the development program. Another benefit of this method is that key decision points are highlighted on the CPM. The primary purpose for highlighting these decision points is to insure that the manager recognizes that a decision made at a given point in time commits him to a known expenditure of personnel and financial resources.

Interactive Discounted Cash Flow (DCF) Analysis

Once the administrative program, based on the CPM, is created, a cash flow model of the project can be built. In this case, the model is known as the profitability index calculation and is used to determine return on investment. A computer program has been written for the GE 430. The input parameters are:

1. The type of cash flow.
   (a) Rising.
   (b) Declining.
   (c) Even.
   (d) Instantaneous.
2. The time period over which the cash flow occurs.
3. The relevant factor.
   (a) Depreciation.
   (b) Capital cost allowance.
   (c) Tax rate.
4. The cash flow.

The output of this program can take several forms, at the option of the person interacting with the program. Since interaction involves no programming, anyone can obtain the desired output or change the input conditions. The following outputs are obtained by simply typing in the appropriate number from 1 to 7.

1. The user inputs two profitability indexes (PIs), which are correctly referred to as discount rates, and the computer then calculates and prints the two present dollar values of the project for the given discount rates.

2. The second option operates like No. 1 with the addition that all input cash flows are printed out showing the present value of each cash flow.

3. This option computes the unique profitability index solution for the series of cash flows. The DCF rate of return (PI) is a bench mark for comparing one project with another.

4. Option 4 allows the user to change one or many of the original cash flows entered into the computer. This allows one to change all input parameters for a given cash flow, say in consumer research (a 20 percent increase, perhaps, with a change in timing), and instantly see the effect of this change on return on investment. This measuring of effects caused by different dollar values and different timing is referred to as sensitivity analysis. Options 6 and 7 permit sensitivity analysis to take place under different input conditions.

5. After measuring PI for the different conditions created by options 4, 6, and 7, the manager may want to restore the plan to its original form. By typing in the number 5, the computer rereads the original input file and deletes changes made by 4, 6, and 7.

6. When dealing with a marketing plan, one is frequently faced with the problem of product life cycle. Option 6 permits one to temporarily delete selected cash flows at either end of the time period. This allows the user to assess the sensitivity of a project to changes in anticipated life or in R&D expenditure and capital expenditure.

7. In some instances, only the amount of a cash flow will need to be changed, leaving all other input data as originally entered. If the user is only changing a cash flow value, he would use option 7 rather than option 4 to do his sensitivity analysis. This option is useful to the marketing manager who wishes to evaluate different levels of promotional expenditures and sales returns.

Similar programs are available on most time-sharing systems.

As mentioned, the profitability index calculation uses the discounted cash flow technique. The primary objective, once it was determined that a market gap did exist, was to evaluate the most profitable way to enter the market given the strategy considerations that obtained at that time. The initial financial analysis indicated that the profitability targets could not be achieved without establishing a dedicated production line. This was somewhat surprising in view of the great excess of liquid detergent production capacity in Canada.

As the development of the product progressed, a significant change occurred. At the six-month point in the development program, it became obvious that the necessary production equipment would not be available in time
for the scheduled launch date. The financial program was then run again,
using new inputs which covered the possibility of temporarily having the
product produced by an outside supplier. This particular program allows one
to evaluate such alternatives in a few seconds of computer time. To any manager who has been involved in the calculation of the discounted cash flow
rate of return on a marketing plan without the aid of a computer, this will
hardly seem believable. Nevertheless, it is true that the time-sharing computer permits us to evaluate many alternatives at once. A good clerk can
work through a typical DCF marketing plan in about one day without a computer. The initial data entry takes approximately ten minutes of terminal
connect time and usually about three to six seconds of actual computer time.

This computer program also permits probabilistic treatment of the market forecast that is fed in. However, for most purposes, this much-touted
approach is not, in fact, practical. The additional cost of computer time to
perform the probabilistic operations on the market forecast is negligible. The
real problem at present is the lack of appreciation by the decision making
manager for the value of the probabilistic approach.

In the Taylor Soaps case, AMS was presented with the problem of assessing the cost and effects of alternate sources of supply. The consultant's job
was made very much easier because the available alternatives were evaluated
with less than ten minutes of terminal connect time. An outside supplier was
chosen, and the scheduled launch date was maintained.

Special Programs

During the course of this particular project, two specialized computer rou-
tines were written. The first routine written was a sample allocation program
which allowed AMS to structure a data base for in-home product testing.
Rather than attempt to design a large probability sample, it was decided to
experiment with a new approach. As the product was placed in homes, the
data obtained during the qualifying interview were fed into the computer and
analyzed on a day-by-day basis to ascertain how the structure of the sample
population was building. When undesirable skewness was noted, the person
placing the samples was redirected to another district in the metropolitan
area where there was a higher probability that the respondents required to

balance the data base structure would be found. This technique is known as dynamic sample allocation.

A second special program was written to allow AMS to ascertain the net profit possibilities for various combinations of trade pricing, dealer allowances, case costs, and shipping costs. The output allowed AMS to select an optimum case price based on the anticipated early shipping pattern. This particular program was written in the Dartmouth language, BASIC. It took an hour to construct the program, and the necessary output was obtained with approximately five minutes of terminal time. Many such routine calculations are very easily handled with the BASIC programming language. More advanced programs are written in FORTRAN IV and are stored in their object code form. Storing the program in object code results in considerable economy when the program is used frequently, as one avoids the cost of recompiling for each run.

Summary

This first case has been selected to show how pragmatic the use of the computer can be. No attempt has been made to discuss the underlying theory behind any of these techniques.

The computational cost associated with this project during the nine months from the initial analysis of the market to putting the product on supermarket shelves was less than $50. No doubt, some wag will say that no analysis worth its salt can cost so little. Unfortunately, such thinking is very closely related to the Parkinsonian humor so prevalent in business today.

The Taylor brand of liquid detergent is today achieving the objectives established following the original analysis. The minimum DCF objective set for the product was 30 percent after tax. Early results suggest that this target will be exceeded during the projected five-year life span of the product.

CASE HISTORY NO. 2

Company: Imperial Tobacco Sales Limited.

Subject: Project Horizon.

The second case study indicates the role the computer can play in a very large multidepartmental marketing organization. In the Taylor case, we saw how a small private company with an aggressive owner–manager used the computer to develop a more sophisticated marketing program than would otherwise have been possible. In this case, a very large and complex organization operates the computer to make better use of its underutilized assets, such as extensive sales and consumer research data.

The project began in 1968. Some of the outputs of the study have developed into ongoing projects in their own right to this time, especially in the area of the marketing use of the computer (that is, building stochastic predictor models) where AMS has continued to study opportunities.

To put the problem into the proper perspective, note the relative size and activity of Imperial Tobacco Limited. *The Financial Post* reported that Imperial Tobacco Limited in 1967 had net sales of $393 million and net profit of $13 million on an asset base of $189 million. While the major activity of Imperial Tobacco Limited has been in tobacco products, they have diverse interests in such areas as food distribution, education, and beverages.

However, like most large organizations, Imperial Tobacco Limited at times finds itself drowning under the mass of data that accounting and consumer research systems can produce. Top management recognizes the problem, but the solution is not always clear. This situation, which exists in many large companies, is, at one and the same time, the consultant's dream and nightmare. The dream is that masses of data, which are really the record of past experience, will, on scientific analysis, yield new insights into the reality of the marketing world around us. Fortunately, the dream comes before the nightmare, which arises when one attempts to process data to get information.

Before moving into a discussion of actual techniques used in Project Horizon, let us outline how the stage was set for this study.

Setting the Stage

Imperial Tobacco has participated for several years in a semiannual consumer research study known as *8M's*. This is a low-overhead survey, a statistical sample of the Canadian population, done every spring and fall by Canadian Facts, Limited. The low overhead of this survey is achieved through multiindustry participation. Sample size is large, approximately 8,000 respondents, and well documented. Real characteristics, along with extensive demographic data, have always been collected in the *8M's* survey. More recently, perceived product characteristics have also been measured, either in binary form or as data values on a monadic scale. Anyone familiar with the treatment of segmentation analysis will recognize how valuable an asset a series of surveys like the *8M's* can be.

Prior to Project Horizon, each *8M's* survey was regarded as a snapshot in time. Although the most recent survey was always compared with the prior survey for selected measures (like the male–female ratio of brand adherents) no attempt had been made to treat the total series of surveys as a time series, that is, as a movie instead of a snapshot. It was hoped to reprocess these surveys in the computer to obtain a moving picture of market activity and segmentation analyses.

The consumer research group at Imperial Tobacco also attempted to develop within the executive body of the company an appreciation of the sociological undercurrents extant in Canadian society. To achieve this end, the company arranged a symposium, away from its headquarters, which was attended by many of the senior executive group. Speakers were invited to come to the session and present a point of view, vis-à-vis the role of tobacco in the 1970s. Papers were given by a sociologist, an anthropologist, a marketing psychologist, a statistician, a packaging design team, and others. These different points of view provided a very useful concentration of stimuli.

Having thus set the stage for Project Horizon, both as a problem for the computer and as a problem for people concerned with the cigarette market, the actual activity of Project Horizon began. The following techniques represent the computer aspects of Project Horizon.

Trend Analyses

Trend analyses were performed on different types of data. An obvious starting point was the historical sales trends based on shipment data that the company had on hand. In this case, the computer was used in time-sharing mode to perform the analysis. Experience with the data suggested that the most meaningful output was obtained by a curve-fitting program. For the historical sales data, an exponential curve fitting routine provided projections and growth rate per period. The growth rate, which can be equated to the value of the exponent in the curve equation, subsequently proved very useful. Other types of data were also analyzed for their trend information. For example, AMS looked for such short-term trends as filter cigarettes versus plain and Virginia tobacco versus menthol. These latter data were acquired from the *8M's* data base.

Perhaps the most significant single program in this project was one written to perform a univariate analysis on the consumer demographic age. For this particular problem, approximately 100,000 data cards, representing 80,000 respondents, were loaded onto tape. This tape was then processed in batch mode using a COBOL program. A typical graphic representation, a histogram, is shown in Exhibit 18–1.

Exhibit 18–1
Percent Product Users Found in Each Age Range

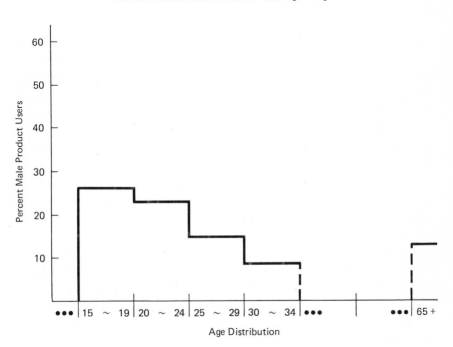

A univariate analysis can be represented by a histogram. As shown in Exhibit 18–1, for each brand covered by the survey, and for males and females, AMS ascertained the percentage of adherents found in each five-year age range. For a number of reasons, no measurements are made below 15 years of age.

Prior to this study, the age data, which were very detailed on the original survey, were grouped together so that a detailed picture of the age distribution within each brand was not available. By reprocessing the data to obtain uniform age intervals, one is presented with the opportunity to relate other factors to a given response within an age range. It must be remembered that these are the responses of some 80,000 individuals. Even when we divide these 80,000 individuals into various brand users, we still end up with significant numbers of male or female users for each brand in the market. Responses to over 25 different brands, segmented by the cigarette characteristics—plain, filter, short, king size, super king—are recorded in this survey. Exhibit 18–1 represents one brand for one of the two sexes for one of the ten surveys put together for this study. One would certainly hesitate to attack such a large data base without the use of a computer.

Operations Research—The Computer and Marketing

It was mentioned earlier that the output of the trend analysis provided, among other things, a mathematical description of the growth rate for each brand for each time period under study. Operations research, which originated during World War II, is a term used to describe the bringing together of several scientific disciplines to bear on an organizational problem. The various inputs to Project Horizon would certainly qualify this study to be called an operations research analysis, except that the term "operations research" nowadays has come to mean a much more narrowly defined activity. Today, operations research most often refers to a specific mathematical relationship—that is, a mathematical model—developed to represent some type of organizational activity, whether it is the overhauling of jet engines or the movements of products from manufacturer to consumer. It is unfortunate that the meaning of the term has been changed. Very valid work remains to be done in the field of marketing based on the earlier definition of operations research. At the same time, the more esoteric models developed for the microbusiness situation have added new possibilities for a total understanding of the marketing environment.

In this particular study both the earlier concept of operations research and the more narrowly defined present-day idea were operative. In the introduction to this case study, the various disciplines called to bear on Project Horizon were noted. Now, let us demonstrate how a very simple mathematical relationship can have great significance to the marketing man.

The growth rate per period, originally found in the trend analyses, was felt to have some relationship to the numbers of smokers found in different age ranges. This hunch was followed up by using the computer to compare the growth rate per period for selected brands with the percentage of adherents found in different age ranges. A significant relationship was discovered, when the growth rate was converted to the growth rate index, which is described on this page.

The actual brand names shown in the graphic relationship of Exhibit 18–2 are concealed. Two effects are noteworthy: the first, a threshold effect; the second, the nature of the relationship between the growth rate index and the percentage of adherents for a brand found in the rather narrowly defined age group of 15 to 19.

The threshold effect is indicated by the fact that a brand with less than about 5 percent adherence in the 15 to 19 age group is actually a dying brand. Since these brands have a negative growth rate index, the operation of a peer group acceptance is suggested.

The growth rate index, which is a measure of the numbers joining or leaving that particular brand in the time period being studied, is often referred to as a momentum trend. It is quite simply the growth rate per period multiplied by the current brand share, the result being changed to a useful number system. As one moves up the curve to the right—that is, in the direction of increasing growth rate—there is a decrease in the use of broadcast media by the more successful brands. The marketing implications are indeed profound.

Exhibit 18-2
Product Growth–Decay Versus Percent of Users in 15 to 19 Age Range

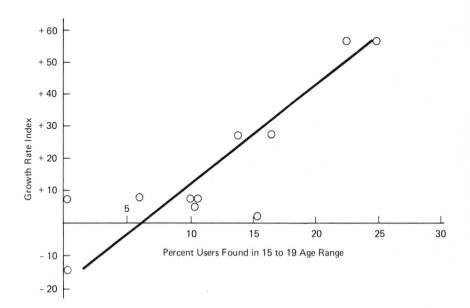

Summary

Unlike a true scientific analysis, certain brands were excluded from the above relationship. Marketing is not yet a science, and the judgment of knowledgeable people in the field should be brought to bear on any given problem. In the given instance, there were brands which, on the subjective judgment of the analyst, were excluded from the relationship. These brands, when included, created a confusing picture near the crossover on the horizontal axis. It is suggested that a large-scale marketing study of this type make use of the judgment and professional abilities of the managers on the scene.

An obvious implication of the Project Horizon type of study is that there are ways to attack the problem of effective communication for a given brand. The computer can play a very significant role in detecting underlying relationships. One must also seek new opportunities from such a study. For the purpose of this chapter, which was to demonstrate how the computer can be used in both batch and time-sharing modes by a large corporation, we let the case rest. Opportunities were discovered, and it is to be hoped that relationships useful to product managers working with a given brand were found.

THE FUTURE OF THE COMPUTER IN MARKETING

Almost certainly within the next decade, we shall see a much greater use of the computer as a tool for searching out new relationships among the many variables of the marketing process. The most significant work in the near future probably will come through the application of the techniques of numerical taxonomy to large data bases. Numerical taxonomy is often referred to as cluster analysis in current marketing research papers. However, cluster analysis has its origin in the field of biology where the term "numerical taxonomy" has been used for many years. Essentially, the taxonomists are divided into two camps in biology, and one sees the same process occurring today in market research. There are those taxonomists who believe that they perceive relationships between selected variables in the population base. They then use the computer to seek out these perceived relationships; that is, to supply numerical measures of a subjective prejudgment. There are also taxonomists who suggest the computer should be allowed to search out all interesting groupings based on two or more variables. AMS subscribes to the second point of view, and its programming efforts are presently directed along those lines.

Decision trees have been used in situations where risk and outcome can be very complicated. AMS took the basic concept of a decision tree and modified it to use subjective probabilities supplied by managers with knowledge of the market. The technique draws together the many parameters of product design and requires the manager to focus his attention on the probable acceptance of any given characteristic by a specific segment of the population. The data so collected from different managers are processed by a computer routine to supply those branches of the tree which, in total, have the highest chance of succeeding with the target group. The technique was not at first computerized. But even in the early stages of development, this technique shows promise in the development of new brands.

In the next decade there should also be greater development of game theory in application to marketing problems. Even the simple models now available give rise to an understanding of market activity. Perhaps their most immediate use is in their ability to make the manager realize the great complexity of his market and its problems. By defining the limits of his knowledge, game theory focuses the manager's search for new information into channels that are most likely to provide improved understanding.

Another important future role of the computer is information retrieval. Information retrieval techniques already exist which allow the user, either in the batch mode or the time-sharing mode, to selectively recover data from large data bases. Dr. Stanley Shapiro has coined a very apt phrase for this use of the computer; he refers to it as "mining the data base." The change in emphasis from the processing of data to the data itself is a significant one. The relative inability of early computers to handle extensive programming resulted in a de-emphasis on the data content and an excessive interest in the systems design that processed data to give the manager information. Unfortunately, managers very often are not sure exactly what information they do want. With the relatively rigid systems design of the past, they did not have the opportunity to browse through the corporate data base and to explore their hunches. This unhappy situation is rapidly reversing as the power of computers increases and the cost of accessing a data base decreases. Even the medium-size time-sharing utility has provision for loading 2,000 files, each file having up to 50 fields and each field having up to 26 values, or alternatives. Using this particular program, we have been able to browse through the data base to find significant new associations of data elements where the data can be quantitative or qualitative. Programming techniques are advancing rapidly in this area. Ultimately, well-developed techniques of information retrieval will be necessary to support advanced numerical taxonomy procedures. However, even at the existing state of art, companies with large data bases ought to be designing their computer systems to support the marketing effort of the company.

Computers in the 1970s will no longer be merely an accounting tool but rather a diagnostic and predictive operator for the marketing arm of a corporation.

PART FOUR

Pricing

19

Competitive Pricing

Evelyn Konrad

THERE ARE TWO MARKETING FUNCTIONS to which computer models are ideally suited. One of these is the inventory control function discussed previously. The other is the continual problem of competitive pricing.

However, while excellent examples of inventory control applications abound, it is remarkably difficult to find an application to competitive pricing that a sophisticated management group is willing to share with other management readers. In few areas of computer application is there as strong a sentiment concerning confidentiality, and in no area is there a greater reluctance to share a proprietary package.

The reasons are obvious: Certainly, as soon as a competitor knows what a firm's decision parameters are for changing product prices and under what given circumstances they will initiate or react to a price change, the model becomes, in effect, useless.

An even greater reason for the aura of mystery and exclusivity surrounding corporate pricing models is the "Nervous Nellie" attitude of corporate legal departments. Not that this attitude lacks a rational base. After all, pricing has long since been used as a thermometer of economic ill by all those in government concerned with the continuation of our free enterprise system. The watchful eyes of the Federal Trade Commission and Justice Department lawyers are forever upon the marketing community, and pricing is a tangible variable that is easier to isolate and investigate than some other aspects of competitive marketing strategy.

There are, of course, a diversity of areas in which the computer is used for pricing. Not all of these are as sensitive as competitive pricing. Here then is a bird's-eye view of the actual or future role of the computer in pricing in relation to the following areas:

1. Projecting, estimating, and forecasting price elasticity of demand: What will be the volume of sales at various prices?
2. Simulating competitive economic behavior at various future prices, and estimating the profit consequences to the firm and industry: If we cut prices by $X or $Y or $Z, to what extent would each of these reductions discourage further expansion of industry capacity and what would be the effect on our return on investment in the next five years?
3. Modeling the future pattern of industry prices based upon the life cycle patterns of related products: Since our new synthetic fiber is similar in newness and functions to "Fibron," what are the chances that its price history will parallel that of Fibron and what will be the sales and profit consequences if it does?
4. Analyzing the historic bidding patterns of competitors in order to predict the future range of their bids for various major contracts: If the cyclical pattern of bidding of each of our competitors for these large construction projects is repeated on the present project, what does this suggest about our bidding strategy today to get that job?
5. Modeling the entire competitive cost, price, and resource structure to determine the extent and durability of each competitor's vulnerability to various possible price reductions: Given the cost structure and balance sheets of each of our competitors, how long would they resist following us down in a price reduction, and how long would they stay in business if we cut prices by various amounts?

How do each of these methods work and what is required to put them to work?

In discussing price elasticity of demand, Professor Theodore Levitt of Harvard University Graduate School of Business Administration comments:

It didn't require the invention of the computer for people to use the concept of price elasticity of demand in their business strategies. It's an old and sometimes even useful concept from old and sometimes useful economics textbooks.

What has kept it from being terribly useful until now is that the simplifying assumption that it has entailed so thoroughly deprived it of realism that no self-respecting business manager would have much to do with its use. The concept in its pure form requires the assumption that all competitive products are identical and perfect substitutes for yours, and that customers both know this and are completely flexible and mobile in their capacity at any moment to switch from one seller's product to another's.

The austere scholars who invented the concept of price elasticity of demand were not so uninformed or insular to think that the conditions that were required for the concept had very commonly existed. Their pure theory of demand has been accepted by economists for years as a sort of underlying truth not because it is indeed truth, but because we suspect that it was too hard to find out what operable truth really is.

The computer now helps us overcome this problem. Its capacity for simultaneous storage and manipulation of numerous variables enables us to do what was impossible before. Instead of repeating the unrealistic but necessary old question "All other things held fixed, what would happen to sales if prices fell X percent?"—it is now possible to ask "With everything we know about competitors, consumers, and market conditions, what would happen to sales if prices fell X percent?"

In short, the computer enables us to be more realistic than we've ever been. The only trouble is that in order to answer the question as we now in this new age phrase it, we must first gather and store into the computer "everything we know about competitors, consumers, and market conditions." Unfortunately, this includes more than simple descriptive materials—such as the size of markets, income of consumers, market shares and price lists of competitors. It includes behavioral information as well —such as the historical pattern of competitive responses to various types and sizes of price changes, measures of relative loyalty of various consumer goods to particular brands, responsiveness of consumers to various special appeals under given conditions of price change. Moreover, not only does the more realistic modern computer-based question require these inputs, but for each it requires a predictive coefficient—a statement regarding the chances that in the future various consumers and competitors will behave in the ways that studies of past behavior or inclinations suggest are likely.

The following chapter on a competitive pricing model by Dr. Franz Edelman provides excellent insights for marketing management into the analytic process preceding model building and the actual uses of such a model. Although the case study used is hypothetical, it is so thoroughly steeped in the real considerations facing marketing management that no loss in knowledge or understanding occurs because the facts and figures have been disguised to preserve the essential confidentiality of the material.

20

Competitive Pricing—
A Systematic Approach

A Case Study in the Application of Practical
Mathematical Models to Pricing Problems

Franz Edelman

THE GENERAL PRICING MODEL provides a means for systematic analysis of the relationships among many factors relevant in realistic pricing decisions.

The information required for use by the model covers a wide spectrum of marketing issues and is not basically different from that considered in traditional approaches to pricing. The model has the added capability of serving as a high-speed, economical means for pretesting as many pricing alternatives as required to determine the likely effect of each on the company's competitive position. The systematic aspect of such analysis leads to mutual consistency among the various alternatives, breadth of scope, and a maximum degree of objectivity.

While this model is still exploratory, it can furnish valuable additions to the store of information available to management for application to competitive pricing situations.

The material in this report is presented on the basis of a hypothetical case study to best illustrate the salient features of the approach, what is involved on the part of the user in the application of this model, and the sort of assistance which this model can give.

Since its inception some years ago, this model has gradually evolved from its initially very simple structure to one which is progressively more extensive. This evolution has always been prompted by requirements of the users, who are, primarily, operating marketing professionals, and it is to be expected and hoped that this trend will continue. Only in this way will this tool continue to develop and give a valuable service to marketing personnel.

The primary requirement of continued evolution of a practically useful management technology is a high degree of management involvement in and commitment to sensible and practical developments of this type. This implies that responsible marketing executives should make it their business to get to know and understand management models of this type, to participate personally in their testing and refining. This will insure that the emerging management technology is indeed responsive to their genuine requirements and will become a meaningful and important part of the marketing decision processes.

The Problem—A Qualitative Statement

The APEX Corporation has pioneered the development, manufacture, and sale of a commercial product. Until recently, APEX had virtually sole ownership of the market. During the past year or two, competition has entered the field seriously, and the APEX market share is currently at 80 percent. Competition is continuing to build up its capacity, and APEX management has sound reason to believe that competition may announce a price reduction sometime during the coming year. APEX management agrees that whatever favorable brand preference and company image APEX may enjoy, these factors alone will not suffice to protect APEX's market and profit position. Nor will stronger advertising and promotion campaigns, by themselves, provide adequate countermeasures. It is therefore decided that price may have to be used as a tactical weapon and that a thorough study of this issue be undertaken.

APEX management has essentially two broad courses of action. It can adopt a "wait and see" approach with the intent of counteracting a competitive price move when and if it occurs. Or, it can take the initiative by making an offensive price move, taking into account, of course, a now almost certain competitive reaction.

A comprehensive analysis is therefore requested by APEX management, for which it enlists the aid of a technical and business-oriented task group. The objective of the study is essentially to answer the following two basic questions: (1) Which of the two broad courses of action is more appropriate? and (2) If an offensive move is indicated for APEX, what should it be?

Some discussion leads to the general agreement that the measure of "appropriateness" shall be APEX's profit and market share position with the prevailing industry price structure. That is to say, if the APEX profit position cannot be materially improved by an APEX price change in either direction, in the absence of competitive pricing action, then the "wait and see" approach would be considered appropriate. In that case, the analysis must supply the information required to allow APEX to take an immediate counteraction, once competition has made its move, geared to produce the best possible position for APEX under the new circumstances.

While it is agreed that an offensive APEX price move, in the face of uncertainty concerning competitive reaction, has the primary objective of leading to the best possible profit position, APEX management also wants to know the projected effects of the combined pricing actions on two variables of major importance: market share and factory load. The magnitude of the likely competitive reaction is also to be assessed, inasmuch as it is bound to affect APEX's offensive move in the first place.

A Matter of Balance

It must be understood at the very outset that the true purpose of a good and practically useful management model is not to dictate or even strongly suggest a specific course of action. In particular, the pricing model described in this report does not determine a specific pricing decision which is, in some sense, the "best" decision. The true function of the model is and should always be to assist the responsible executive in formulating and evaluating the tradeoffs which are the focal issues of every decision process.

These tradeoffs are almost always very complicated. They involve many variables, tangible and intangible. They involve uncertainty as well as risk. They apply to a wide spectrum of different operating conditions. A well-conceived modeling approach to the analysis of complex tradeoff situations focuses on the primary elements of the tradeoff.

In the case of competitive pricing, the basic elements are profit and market share, with price being the control lever of the marketing executive for achieving the desired balance. Clearly, this conception is an oversimplification of the issue for two main reasons. First, price is not the only lever with which profit and market share can be affected. Factors such as distribution, product quality, company image, advertising and sales promotion activities, and many others play a vital role in this process. These factors are, of course, recognized and do enter the model presently under discussion in an implicit manner. Their effect is to modulate the influence of price on the profit/market share tradeoff. Second, profit and market share are certainly not the only two relevant performance measures. Here again, the present model will evaluate other measures of effectiveness for examination by the decision maker. The model focuses on profit and market share because they appear to be the highest-ranking performance measurements relating to pricing decisions.

The assessment of uncertainties is one of the very important contributions which a modeling approach can make to more effective decision making. It is not enough to assess and evaluate this tradeoff under a specific set of assumptions and circumstances. This is so because it is impossible for even the most experienced and knowledgeable operating manager to pinpoint with certainty some of the information required for the operation of the model. This refers primarily to the judgmental type of information which relates to customer attitudes regarding brand loyalty and the like, as well as to competitive posture regarding the imminence and size of potential price moves. As a result, some of the input information required for this model should be supplied not as single values but rather as a possible range of values which might conceivably be experienced. It is then the function of the model to ascertain the sensitivity of the outcome—the profit/market share tradeoff—to changes in these uncertain input quantities. Clearly, a variable which affects the result only slightly needs to be specified only approximately. This is valuable information because such a variable does not justify much in the line of market research expenditures. On the other hand, a variable which is very critical to the outcome—that is, one to which the tradeoff is extremely sensitive—does warrant considerable expenditures leading to the refinement of this information for more reliable results.

In any event, the model, through such sensitivity analysis, informs the marketing executive of the possible spread of outcomes, which is caused in part by the uncertainty contained in the input information. It thus helps the executive gain additional insight into the basic relationships that underlie the decision process. In addition, it helps him assess directly the incremental value of market research information intended to sharpen the judgments required for model operation.

Overall Model Structure

The overall model structure is roughly as described here. Price, as the explicit factor in the product–market environment, affects market share according to the rules and assumptions enumerated later on in the report. Price and market share together interact with total industry demand according to the concept of elasticity assumed in the model. Market share and industry volume combine to determine each competitor's unit volume, which in turn leads to income, cost, and profit for the participants in the industry.

This model description is of course an oversimplification. The model also monitors capacity limitations and contains decision rules for the allocation of overflow volume, that is, unsatisfied demand.

Model Sectors

The model divides into five basic elements. The first sector analyzes the price–volume response of the market as a whole to price changes by either or both participants.

The second sector of the model deals with the market share balance among the competitors as this is affected by relative price movement among them.

The third sector analyzes the effects of volume on the internal characteristic of each firm, specifically on income, cost, and profit measures.

The fourth sector is concerned with an explicit assessment of the posture of competition in regard to likely price movement, whether offensive or in response to a previous price move.

Finally, the fifth sector relates the results obtained so far to one another and presents them for inspection by the management user.

Each sector is based on one or more assumptions, which are subject, to varying degrees, to verification through actual results from the field. Here again, the sensitivity analysis plays a very important role. Through model experimentation, it is possible to ascertain the effect of changes in these assumptions on the outcome of the analysis. The relative sensitivity of each assumption will give an important clue to the most productive allocation of research funds for the purpose of refining and improving the structure of this management model.

It is therefore clear that experimentation through use of the model must be supplemented by experimentation in the field. The former serves to point to market research of maximum relevance and productivity, while the latter serves to validate and make practical the management laboratory concept underlying models of this nature. This cycle of hypothesis, experimentation, validation, and, thereby, improved hypothesis is surely the essence of the so-called scientific method upon which all of our discussion is based.

The remainder of this report will discuss these five model sectors, one at a time, using the case study as a vehicle of this discussion.

Some Quantitative Background Information

Before going to the first sector of the model, it is necessary to give some general quantitative background of the case study. (See Exhibit 20–1.) The

Exhibit 20-1
Current Industry Status

CURRENT OPERATIONS	COMPANY	COMPETITOR
UNIT PRICE ($/UNIT)	100.00	95.00
UNIT B-E COST ($/UNIT)	70.00	70.00
VARIABLE COST PORTION (%)	75.0	70.0
PRODUCTION CAPACITY (UNITS)	1,000.000	600,000
FREE MARKET SHARE (%)	80.0	20.0

current status of this industry is that the APEX product presently sells for $100 per unit, while the competitive product sells for $95 per unit. Both APEX and competitive products are estimated to have a unit breakeven cost of $70. It is estimated that 75 percent of this cost is volume variable in the case of APEX Corporation, while only 70 percent is estimated to be variable in the case of the competitive product.

APEX has an annual production capacity of one million units, and competition, which is just now beginning to build up its capacity, is presently operating under a production capacity of 600,000 units per year.

The term "production allocation" refers to the manner in which either competitor would respond to a limited-capacity situation, should this arise. That is, production allocation refers to a policy option which can be exercised by either participant when or if he becomes unable, for capacity reasons, to supply the demand.

Finally, as was indicated earlier, APEX still maintains an 80 percent market share under the prevailing conditions described here.

The remainder of the quantitative information required for the operation of the model will be introduced with each of the model sectors.

Sector 1—The Market Structure

The present version of the model assumes a very simple structure of the market. One portion of the total market, the free market, is available to all competitors who compete for market share. Relative price changes in this segment of the market can result in changes in the market share balance, as well as changes in total demand.

The company captive market segment is that segment in which potential customers have access only to the APEX product. While market share is therefore not relevant in this segment, APEX price changes can alter the demand for the product in the captive market, in accordance with elasticity data supplied by the user and described later on in this report.

The competitor's captive market is that segment of the market in which potential customers have access only to the competitive product. The total demand in the competitor's captive market depends upon the prevailing competitive price, and the elasticity in this market segment need not be the same as that in either of the other two market segments.

The size of each market segment is determined by customer demand and measured in product units. Geographical boundaries are not taken into account in this version of the model.

In addition to the preceding descriptive statements, two basic assumptions are made which underlie the structure of this portion of the model.

It is assumed that the demand in the free market is dependent upon both APEX and competitor prices. It is furthermore assumed that APEX and competitor prices combine to form an average industry price. This average price concept is arrived at by weighting each price by the respective market share of the participant. This assumption hypothesizes that the competitor with the larger market share has a greater leverage on the total industry than does the competitor with the smaller market share.

It is assumed that the price–volume response of the captive markets depends only on the prices of the respective participants in these markets and are otherwise uncoupled.

It is quite clear that these assumptions are not yet substantiated in any rigorous sense. They do, however, appear reasonable and seem also to be those assumptions which underlie many actual pricing decisions made in the traditional and more or less intuitive manner.

As was said earlier, each of the assumptions, and particularly the first, should be examined more carefully and subjected to some tests wherever and whenever feasible.

Under the prevailing conditions, as shown in Exhibit 20–2, the potential

Exhibit 20-2
Free Market Conditions

INDUSTRY CHARACTERISTICS	FREE MARKET	COMPANY'S CAPTIVE MKT.	COMPETITOR'S CAPTIVE MKT.
DEMAND (UNITS)	800.000	200.000	100,000
AV'G PRICE INCREASE(%)	10.0	10.0	10.0
DEMAND REDUCTION (%)	20.0	5.0	
AV'G PRICE REDUCTION(%)	20.0	20.0	20.0
DEMAND INCREASE (%)	10.0	5.0	

demand in the free market amounts to 800,000 units per year. This market is still considered to be in a phase of gradual growth, the rate of which is likely to be accelerated by an industry price reduction. It is expected that an average industry price cut of 20 percent would result in a rather modest 10 percent market expansion. On the other hand, it is pointed out that the market is relatively more sensitive to potential price increases. It is also judged that a 10 percent average industry price increase would affect the market growth rate adversely by as much as a 20 percent reduction in market size.

The APEX captive market segment consists of a potential demand of 200,000 units per year. This market segment is described as being considerably less responsive to price changes. A 10 percent price increase would result in a 5 percent reduction of demand, while a 20 percent price reduction could use only a 5 percent increase in the demand for the APEX product in its captive market. As is to be expected, the captive market is less elastic than the free one.

The competitor's captive market, amounting to 100,000 units per year, is seen as totally inelastic over the range of price changes being contemplated. This means that the size of this market is expected to remain unchanged over the entire range from a 10 percent price increase to a 20 percent price reduction.

Fifteen quantitative inputs are used by this portion of the model to structure price–volume relationships for each of the free market segments as a function of both APEX and competitive prices.

All the model outputs are displayed and evaluated most conveniently in the form of the rectangular array shown in Exhibit 20–3. Before getting into specifics, general understanding of the results will be greatly facilitated by a preliminary examination of this exhibit.

Every row in this array represents a specific APEX price level, relative to the currently existing price ($100 per unit in this case). The first element in each row indicates the percent change from this current price. The fourth row from the top has a zero entry there and therefore corresponds to the status quo, that is, $100 per unit. Negative percentages, of course, denote price reductions.

Exhibit 20-3
Output Evaluation

RUN DESCRIPTION: APEX CORP., WIDGET TYPE 012

FREE MARKET DEMAND(UNITS)

C O M P E T I T O R   P R I C E   C H A N G E S (%)

		30.0-	20.0-	10.0-	ZERO	10.0	20.0
C	(%)						
	30.0-	931,649	923,145	927,659	927,659	927,659	927,659
O							
M	20.0-	898,168	880,000	872,805	876,230	876,230	876,230
P							
A	10.0-	885,811	852,406	836,824	830,604	833,239	833,239
N							
V	ZERO	948,207	842,367	813,608	800,000	770,474	781,396
P	10.0	948,207	895,639	805,312	697,047	640,000	618,043
R							
I	20.0	948,207	895,639	851,696	663,693	565,246	522,045
C							
E		PRICE	VOLUME		PRICE	VOLUME	
		DOWN 20%	UP 10%		UP 10%	DOWN 20%	

Every column represents a competitive price state. The top element in each column indicates the percentage change from the prevailing competitive price ($95 per unit in this case). The fourth column from the left is headed by a zero element, and, therefore, this column corresponds to the prevailing competitive price. Again, negative percentages indicate price reductions.

Each element in the array now corresponds to the free market demand which is expected to be experienced under pricing conditions indicated by the particular row and column in which this element appears. For example, the element in the zero row and zero column is 800,000, which is the free market demand under the prevailing prices as specified previously. Note that the element in the row and column headed by −20 is 880,000 units, according to the input specification of a 10 percent demand growth under an average industry price reduction of 20 percent. Conversely, the element in the row and column headed by 10 is 640,000, in accordance with the specification of a 20 percent demand reduction under a 10 percent average price increase.

According to the first assumption of this model sector, the free market demand depends not only on price levels but also on the market share breakdown which these price levels produce. This is the reason why the elements on the right-hand end of the first row, for example, are equal to one another (927,659 units). In this region, we have APEX price reductions combined with competitive price increases, and therefore the competitive market share has decreased to such a small value that the competitor's leverage on the market has virtually disappeared. In other words, the market demand has become independent of the competitor's price and is determined almost entirely by the APEX price level. Conversely, the lower elements in the first column are all equal to one another (948,207 units) because at this point we have APEX price increases combined with competitive price reductions, and now the APEX market share has been reduced to virtually zero. This now means that the free market demand has become insensitive to APEX prices and is determined only by competitive price levels.

The array in Exhibit 20–3 displays the free market demand as it was affected by the combination of APEX and competitive price actions. Sector 1 also produces the demands in both the company captive and competitor captive market segments shown in the array format of Exhibit 20–3. Finally, the three demands are added up to display the total industry demand as a function of price. These results are now held in the model and are made available for subsequent calculations.

The next sector is that of market share balance. It is pointed out again that the order in which the model segments are presented does not correspond to the order with which items are computed within the model. Clearly, preliminary market share results must be computed for use by Sector 1 of the model in calculating market demands. Therefore, the calculations in Sector 2 are actually carried out before those of Sector 1.

Sector 2—The Market Share Balance

The present version of the model makes use of the simplifying assumption that all of competition can be aggregated into a single entity called "the competitor." This is one of two or three basic areas in which additional model complexity should gradually evolve through professional marketing participation in the model formulation efforts. On the other hand, this assumption has so far not limited real use of the model and has, in fact, had some actual advantages over having to specify information on a competitor-by-competitor basis.

The second basic hypothesis relates to the market share mechanism as it is affected by relative price changes among competitors. It assumes that if both competitors change their prices by equal percentages, all other market factors remaining the same, then the market share balance between them will be unchanged. This is an assumption which should also be examined closely and ultimately tested in a real world environment. The formal description of this mechanism requires some more definition.

The Relative Price Differential

Relative price differential (RPD) is measured by the difference between APEX and competitor percentage price changes. The zero point on the axis (RPD = 0) represents the current price situation. The region to the right of this point shows APEX as relatively higher priced than competition compared to the present situation, and, in the region to the left, APEX is priced relatively lower than competition compared to the present.

Extreme RPD occurs when either competitor is priced out of the market. This variable serves as a reference value in that it defines the extreme ranges within which any pricing action is likely to take place.

In this case, it was judged that the APEX product has some competitive advantages, due to superior product quality, company image, and other factors. It is judged that a 30 percent RPD would result in pricing the APEX product virtually out of the market, while a –20 percent RPD would have the same effect on the competitor product. (See Exhibit 20–4.) The difference between these two percentages represents the pricing advantage enjoyed by the APEX product.

This range then represents the total field in which, going from left to right, the APEX market share in the free market segment would decline from 100 percent to zero. It now remains to ascertain in what manner this market share decline is expected to take place. To accomplish this, two more definitions are required.

The major RPD is here defined to be approximately one-half of the extreme RPD. (See Exhibit 20–4.) This is the second of three points at which the brand loyalty characteristics of the typical customer are to be estimated.

Specifically, this judgmental information refers to the market share retained by either participant (as a percentage of his current market share) if he were to implement a major (in the present usage) price increase relative to his competitor. The second assumption of this model sector stipulates under what conditions of price movement the market share balance remains unchanged. For that reason, a major relative price increase by APEX is equivalent to an equal relative price reduction on the part of competition in the market share sense. The total industry demand does, of course, differ in

Exhibit 20-4
The Relative Price Differentials

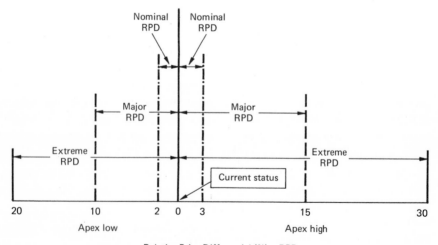

Relative Price Differential (%) – RPD

these two situations, because they clearly lead to different average industry prices.

The 2:1 relationship between extreme and major RPD is not mandatory, and the user may choose the ratio which he finds most convenient from the viewpoint of making sound brand loyalty judgments. It is recommended that it be in the general vicinity of the midpoint to insure proper shaping of the market share relationship.

The final definition relates to expected customer behavior under small price changes. It is recommended that the nominal RPD be defined to be approximately 10 percent of the extreme value. (See Exhibit 20–4.) This three-part formulation of the market share relationship was originally suggested by one of the operating marketing managers as an improvement of the existing version that would make it more suitable for his particular needs. This change has been meaningful in all situations encountered since then, and it constitutes a general improvement of the model.

Specification of behavior under both nominal and major price differentials is necessary for fairly obvious reasons. There are products and markets whose market share balance is not very sensitive to nominal price movements, while it is, at the same time, very sensitive to major ones. Conversely, there are products and markets that are extremely sensitive to nominal price movements, so that the differential impact of a major price move is a comparatively secondary contribution.

The information required for this formulation is described as follows:

It has been judged that customer brand preference, based on relative product quality, company image, and other factors, favors the APEX product. This is now quantified as a function of price as follows.

The maximum relative price increases (extreme price differentials) for APEX and the competitor are 30 percent and 20 percent respectively, as shown in Exhibit 20–5. The nominal relative price differential is left to the user, although, as has been stated previously, 10 percent of the extreme price differential is recommended. These are the values selected in this study. The market share retention, as percentage of current market share, is judged to be 95 percent for both APEX and the competitor in response to a nominal price differential. Major RPD is 50 percent as recommended. It is judged that under a major price movement APEX would retain 75 percent of its current market share, while under the same conditions the competitor would retain two-thirds of his current market share. Again, this difference is evidence of the favorable position enjoyed by the APEX product.

These ten quantities are now used by this sector of the model to structure the relationship explained in the sections that follow.

The Market Share Relationship

The curve (shown in Exhibit 20–6) generated by the model now represents the best estimate of the effect of relative pricing on market share. It obviously satisfies the requirements implied by the quantitative assessments of the previous exhibit. The curve indicates, going from left to right, total possession of the market for APEX when APEX is priced 20 percent below competition.

Exhibit 20-5
Market Share Response

MARKET SHARE RESPONSE	COMPANY	COMPETITOR
MAX. RELATIVE PRICE INCR.(%)	30.0	20.0
NOMINAL PRICE INCR. (% OF MAX.)	10.0	10.0
MARKET SHARE RETAINED (% OF CURRENT)	95.0	95.0
MAJOR PRICE INCR. (% OF MAX.)	50.0	50.0
MARKET SHARE RETAINED (% OF CURRENT)	75.0	67.0

Exhibit 20-6
Relative Pricing's Effect on Free Market Share

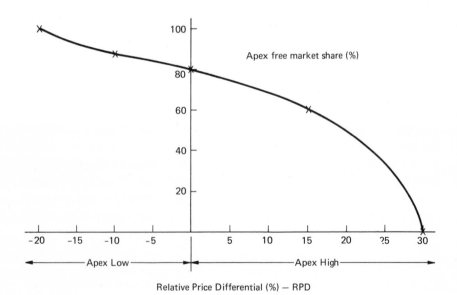

Relative Price Differential (%) — RPD

Exhibit 20-7
Output Evaluation

RUN DESCRIPTION: APEX CORP., WIDGET TYPE D12

COMPANY SHARE OF FREE MARKET(%)

```
        C O M P E T I T O R     P R I C E    C H A N G E S (%)

            30.0-    20.0-    10.0-           10.0      20.0

      (%)
C    30.0-    80.0     86.3   (100.0)   100.0    100.0    100.0
O
M    20.0-    66.7     80.0    86.6     100.0    100.0    100.0
P
A    10.0-    48.9     66.7    80.0    ( 86.6 )  100.0    100.0
N
Y                      48.9    66.7     80.0      86.6    100.0

P    10.0                      48.9     66.7      80.0     86.6
R
I    20.0                               48.9      66.7     80.0
C                                      ( 60 )
E            EXTREME  RANGE            MAJOR  RANGE
```

When APEX is 10 percent below competition (major RPD), the competitive market share has declined from the original 20 percent to two-thirds of that value or 13.3 percent. This leaves APEX with an approximately 87 percent market share, as shown.

The status quo is indicated by the 80 percent APEX market share on the vertical axis.

When APEX is priced 15 percent above competition (again major RPD, this time favoring competition), the APEX market share is reduced from 80 percent to three-quarters of this value, 60 percent as shown on the exhibit.

When APEX is priced 30 percent above competition, its market share is reduced to zero, as specified.

Sector 2 of the model is concerned with generating this curve which, in addition to possessing the properties just outlined, must also obey some other straightforward rules, such as requiring that any participant's market share cannot increase with increasing price. Exhibit 20–7 translates this into the required form for representing separately APEX and competitive price actions.

Exhibit 20–7 uses the same representation as was used previously for free market demand. This time, the elements in the array indicate the APEX share of the free market. Note again the element in the row and column headed "Zero" is 80 percent for the APEX market share under prevailing conditions. The circled elements in the array indicate the values which correspond to the bounds specified in the input. The elements along any diagonal from upper left to lower right are identical because of the assumption that identical relative price changes on the part of both APEX and the competitor will leave the market share balance unchanged. The figure of 86.3 percent (instead of 86.6 percent as in the remainder of the diagonal) results from a small excess demand at that price combination of 12,000 units which APEX is unable to supply.

The model is now ready to determine the unit volumes available to each participant, provided he has the required production capacity, and to examine the effects of volume changes on the internal operations of both APEX and its competitor.

Sector 3—The Internal Volume Effects

This sector of the model is concerned primarily with carrying out three analyses. First, having now both market share and industry volume under any set of hypothetical price conditions, the model computes unit volumes for both participants and checks to see whether these are feasible from a capacity viewpoint. If either participant turns out to be capacity limited, the model will recompute market share balance, total demand, and a new unit volume. The model will apply the decision rule concerning how the product shortage is to be treated.

When the actually achievable unit volume has been determined for both APEX and the competitor, then the total fixed cost burden is spread over this volume on a per unit basis, and the new unit cost is determined for each.

Finally, total cost, income, and profit figures are developed for both APEX and the competitor for every possible pricing combination within the specified ranges.

Basic Assumptions

The first assumption relates to a policy option which can be exercised by either participant when he becomes capacity limited. This is a four-way option, designated by four different values of the appropriate decision variable.

Suppose that APEX encounters a product shortage of 100,000 units and that APEX's unit volume in the free market accounts for about 75 percent of the total, the remaining 25 percent being used in APEX's captive market. The possibilities under the option are as follows.

An assignment of top priority to the free market segment. This means that the captive market segment will not be supplied until all demand in the free market segment has been satisfied to the maximum possible degree. In this example the entire shortage of 100,000 units would be assigned to captive market.

An assignment of top priority to the captive market segment. This means that the free market segment will not be supplied until all demand in the captive market segment has been satisfied to the maximum possible degree. The entire shortage is assigned to the free market.

An assignment of equal priority to both the captive and free market segments. This means that excess demand will be prorated for the captive and free market segments in direct proportion to the potential sales in each segment. In this example a shortage of 75,000 units is assigned to the free market and 25,000 to the captive market.

A priority assignment favoring that segment of the market, captive or free, which has the larger potential sales. Excess demand will therefore be prorated to the captive and free market segments in inverse proportion to the potential sales in each segment. In this example, a shortage of 25,000 units will be assigned to the free market and a 75,000 shortage to the captive market.

The second basic assumption in this model sector relates to the inter-competition disposition of the unsatisfied demand. It states that a participant may pick up additional volume caused by the inability of his competitor to meet the demand. The amount of this volume will depend upon the relative price position of the competitors in accordance with the market share relationship already described.

It is also assumed in this sector of the model that the total fixed costs are allocated evenly over the total volume, regardless of its size. Obviously, this assumption breaks down for very large deviations from current operations, but it turns out that, in all practical applications of the model, the extremes do not really come into play. This is also an assumption which is very easily modified by allowing for a number of fixed cost plateaus, one for each different range of volume.

This model sector produces seven outputs, all of which are produced in the array or matrix form previously illustrated.

APEX Pretax Profit

The final portion of this sector combines income, cost, and volume information to produce the impact of APEX and competitive pricing on the
APEX profit position. Again the matrix display is used to show (see Exhibit
20–8) the compound effect of prices on the variable displayed, in this case,
company (that is, APEX) pretax profit.

Exhibit 20-8
Company Pretax Profit

```
RUN DESCRIPTION:      APEX CORP., WIDGET TYPE D12


                                              COMPANY PRE-TAX PROFIT(K$)


                  C O M P E T I T O R    P R I C E    C H A N G E S (%)

                   30.0-     20.0-    10.0-        10.0      20,0

              (%)
    C     30.0-   2,127.0  2,800.0  2;800.0  2,800.0  2,800.0  2,800,0
    O
    M     20.0-   7,541.4 10,435.0 11;860.9 12,800.0 12,800.0 12,800,0
    P
    A     10.0-  (9,214.7 14,284.9)18;079.5 19,948.6 22,800.0 22,800.0
    N
    Y            5,200.0-14,361.6 20;564.3 25,200.0 26,493.5 31,916.3

    P     10.0   3,775.0- 3,775.0=18;863.2 22,945.1 25,665.0 27,000.4
    R
    I     20.0   2,461.7- 2,461.7= 2;461.7=19,440.1 22,974.4 25,728.7
    C
    E
```

Since each column represents a competitive act, over which APEX can
exert no control, the largest profit value occurring in each column has been
specially indicated, as shown in Exhibit 20–8 as the best possible outcome of
an act of nature, so to speak. These maximum values indicate desirable responses on the part of APEX to possible competitive price moves, where the
desirability of each response is based on best possible profit performance.
This array indicates that, in this particular case, it would not be to APEX's
advantage at all to respond to any competitive price move in the upward
direction. It also indicates that APEX would not be motivated to move downward until the level of competitive price reduction reaches about 20 percent.
And in that case, the best APEX response is a price reduction of only about
5 percent. Note again that these relationships are based on the criterion of

maintaining the best possible *profit position* and do not yet take into account directly the *market share position* of APEX under these conditions.

Sector 4—The Nature and Posture of Competition

This sector deals with APEX's assessment of the nature and posture of its competition. The assumed opponent is primarily one that is concerned with minimizing risk under uncertainty and represents essentially a conservative position. As will be seen later on, this assumption is not essential to the use of the model, nor is it in any way a built-in constraint. It is simply good practice to consider, as one of the possible cases, the condition under which the opponent acts on the same degree of intelligence as does his antagonist.

It is recognized that business decisions are not always logical and rational. Nevertheless, it is desirable, if not essential from the risk point of view, to have the *means* for applying rationality.

It is therefore equally essential to have the means for assuming that APEX's competitor is not only capable of rational behavior but also makes, in turn, the same assumption about APEX. This assumption, too, is not a constraint built into the model but simply a means for exercising a specific judgment.

Five outputs describe the competitive status. The first four are listed here and are not shown in detail. Again, each output is presented by the model in matrix form, so that the compound effects of pricing can be readily ascertained. The final output of this sector is shown in Exhibit 20–9.

Competitor Pretax Profit

This array of competitor pretax profit, as a function of both APEX and competitor prices, represents the picture that APEX's competitor would see if he were, in fact, using a similar technique of modeling his pricing situation. The only difference is that, to the competitor, it is the APEX pricing decisions, represented by the rows, which are the events which he, the competitor, does not control. The competitor would therefore be interested in the maximum values of his profits along each row of the array. These are circled in Exhibit 20–9.

It is interesting to note that, while APEX has no motivation at all from the profit improvement point of view to initiate price changes, the competitor has a great deal of motivation to initiate a price change, as is indicated by his profit potential of $8,864.70 arising from a 20 percent price reduction. This substantial increase is, however, realizable only as long as APEX does not respond to this price reduction. It is now interesting to see what sort of move–countermove situation develops by comparing the two pretax profit arrays developed by the model. (See Exhibit 20–10.)

Move–Countermove

Exhibit 20–10 is a composite of the relevant portions of the two pretax profit arrays shown previously. The left-hand portion shows APEX's profit and the right-hand portion, that of the competitor. To recap, in the left-hand portion, the maximum values of the columns are relevant, while in the right-hand portion, it is the maximum values in the rows which are of importance.

The left-hand portion clearly indicates that APEX's profit position of $25.2 million cannot be improved by an offensive price reduction. This is, of course, due to APEX's preeminent position in this market. On the other

Exhibit 20-9
Competitor Pretax Profit

```
RUN DESCRIPTION:      APEX CORP., WIDGET TYPE D12


                                    COMPETITOR PRE-TAX PROFIT(K$)


               C O M P E T I T O R     P R I C E     C H A N G E S (%)

               30.0-    20.0-    10.0-              10.0      20.0

        (%)
   C   30.0-    449.2-  ( 624.5 ) 1,810.0-    860.0•    90.0  1,040.0
   O
   M   20.0-  1,529.3  1,992.0  ( 2,458.9 )  860.0-    90.0  1,040.0
   P
   A   10.0-  4,213.1 ( 4,911.7 ) 4,298.8  4,259.8    90.0  1,040.0
   N
   Y          5,040.0 ( 8,864.7 ) 8,088.9  6,500.0  5,820.0  1,040.0

   P   10.0   5,040.0 10,740.0 (13,213.5 ) 9,828.0  7,194.0  6,423.2
   R
   I   20.0   5,040.0 10,740.0 (16,440.0 )14,744.2 10,547.1  7,826.6
   C
   E
```

Exhibit 20-10
Move-Countermove Situation

APEX PRETAX PROFIT COMPETITOR PRICE				APEX PRICE CHANGE (%)	COMPETITOR PRETAX PROFIT COMPETITOR PRICE			
-30	-20	-10			-30	-20	-10	
2,127.0	2,800.0	2,800.0	2,800.0	-30	-449.2	(624.5)	-1,810.0	-860.0
7,541.4	10,435.0	11,860.9	12,800.0	-20	1,529.3	1,992.0	(2,458.9)	-860.0
(9,214.7)	14,284.9	18,078.5	19,948.6	-10	4,213.1	(4,911.7)	4,298.8	4,259.8
-5,200.0	(14,361.6	20,564.3	25,200.0)	ZERO	5,040.0	(8,864.7)	8,088.9	6,500.0
-3,775.0	-3,775.0	18,863.2	22,945.1	10	5,040.0	10,740.0	(13,213.5)	9,828.0
-2,461.7	-2,461.7	-2,461.7	19,440.1	20	5,040.0	10,740.0	(16,440.0)	14,744.2

hand, a competitive price reduction of 20 percent would enhance the opponent's profit position from $6.5 million to approximately $8.9 million. This indicates a high likelihood that the competitor, in his present position, is surely entertaining notions about possible price reductions in order to capture a larger segment of the free market. A question for APEX management to assess is just how large a reduction in price to anticipate. There are now two possibilities. The first is that the competitor will make a price move which, in the short term, will give him his best profit position and that he will make this price move without considering the possible reaction on the part of APEX and the effect of this reaction in turn of his own profit position. If he takes this extremely short-range point of view, he could be expected to reduce his prices 15 to 20 percent and go for broke, so to speak. Clearly one might also infer from this that, in doing so, he is underestimating APEX. If he does this, then APEX's profit position will deteriorate as indicated; and furthermore, there is absolutely nothing APEX can do to counteract this. APEX's best response, in the sense of profit maintenance, is a counterreduction of 5 percent or so. The outcome of the entire procedure is the often-encountered situation of price and profit erosion of a gradually maturing product.

The other possibility is that the competitor can anticipate, by doing his own analyses, what the APEX counteraction might be to any of his moves and so reflect this counteraction back on his own profit position. If he acts in this manner, he can clearly see that it is within APEX's power to respond to a 20 percent price reduction with a 10 percent price reduction, leading to an APEX profit position of $14.3 million. This is only slightly below the best possible in profit but has the advantage of recapturing all or most of the market share which would otherwise be lost to the competitor because of his price leadership. If APEX were to respond in this manner, then the competitor's profit position would, in fact, be considerably worse than it was prior to the move–countermove situation. Instead of improving his profit position from $6.5 million to $8.9 million, he has now gone from $6.5 million to $4.9 million in profit. Knowing this in advance, the competitor would obviously reason that a 20 percent price reduction is too ambitious because a reasonable response on the part of APEX would wipe out all of the gains expected and turn out to be a very expensive pricing maneuver. It would therefore be far more rational for the competitor to consider a price reduction in the 10 percent range. This would, in the absence of an APEX countermove, increase the competitor's profit from $6.5 million to $8.1 million. Furthermore, this price reduction should not cause APEX to respond, as is indicated by the third column in the left-hand portion of the exhibit, as long as profit is the primary motive in the APEX decision.

The competitor, in the full knowledge of all the facts, would therefore consider a reasonable compromise in which he would trade off 10 percent of his profit potential ($8.1 million vs. $8.9 million) for a higher degree of price stability and a lower risk of damaging competitive reaction.

The problem facing APEX management now is to assess the posture of the competitor, and this is the subject of Exhibit 20–11.

Likelihood Assessments of Competitive Actions

Exhibit 20–11 contains the judgmental information, provided by APEX marketing executives, pertaining to the likely competitive actions. These judgments are made by APEX management, using the information which has been supplied by the pricing model up to this point.

Thus it is judged by APEX management that there is a 60 percent chance that the competitor will indeed behave in accordance with the results of the previous analysis—that is, make a price reduction in the 5 to 15 percent range. On the other hand, it is considered possible, to the extent of a 20 percent likelihood, that the competitor might go further and lower prices by 15 to 25 percent. There might even be a remote chance (5 percent) of his going beyond that. Finally, APEX judges, there to be a 15 percent likelihood that the competitor will stand pat for the time being, and there is no chance of his actually increasing prices.

The elements in this array are all input quantities specified as judgmental information by the marketing managers who have the widest experience with and best intuitive feeling for this particular pricing situation. These judgments are used later on by the model to effectively discount the model results corresponding to the particular competitive price level to which they apply.

It is clear that the likelihood assessments of competitive action are themselves affected by the element of uncertainty. It is precisely the function of the model to assist the manager in assessing this uncertainty as well. All that would be required to do this is to specify a variety of such judgments and to ascertain the model's response to all of them. This will indicate the model's sensitivity to changes in this variable in this particular situation, and it will indicate to what degree a refinement of these judgments is indicated as essential.

The model has now completed all its basic functions and is ready to relate the outputs of the first four sectors to produce the final results.

Sector 5—Interactions and Results

The model produces 17 different output matrices. The first four give the unit demand by market segment and in total for the industry.

The next five matrices relate to APEX's market performance in this par-

Exhibit 20-11
Likelihood Assessments

Price Change (%)

Greater than −25	−15 to −25	−5 to −15	+5 to −5	+5 to +15	Greater than +15
5	20	60	15	0	0

Likelihood (%)

Exhibit 20-12
Market Share, Income, and Profit Relationships

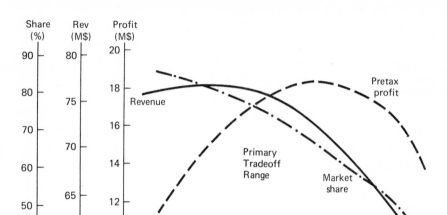

ticular pricing situation. APEX's share of the free market, APEX unit sales in the free and captive markets, and APEX's capacity limitation, if any, as it affects the free and captive markets.

The next four matrices deal with the competitor's market performance and give his unit sales in the free and captive markets as well as his excess demand in both.

The last four arrays relate to profit performance. They include APEX's sales income, unit cost, and pretax profit, as well as the competitor's pretax profit—all as functions of prices.

As was pointed out earlier, every one of these 17 output arrays is discounted by the model, according to the likelihood assessments made by APEX management, to produce the "expected" outcome in each case. This is illustrated using three major model outputs: market share, sales revenue, and profit.

APEX price is plotted against APEX pretax profit in K$ (thousands of dollars). This curve peaks just slightly above the $95 level and declines fairly rapidly on either side. (Exhibit 20–12.)

This relationship contains all the effects considered by the model, including the uncertainty assessment of competitive posture. In this context, the variable plotted here is the APEX profit expectation, in the light of the competitive uncertainty discussed earlier.

We now add the revenue curve and the corresponding scale in K$. This curve peaks near an APEX price of $86.

The range between the two peaks is quite narrow because of APEX's predominant market share position in this industry.

Now superimpose the market share relationship over those of profit and sales revenue. Note again that all three relationships are based on the management expectations of a certain stated competitive behavior relating to pricing.

The tradeoff among these three variables represents the essence of any pricing decision.

The Primary Tradeoff Range

The APEX price position is currently represented by the $100 point on the horizontal axis. The range which APEX has available to itself for price movement is divided into three parts. The first and most important area is the primary tradeoff range, indicated as the shaded area on Exhibit 20–13.

Exhibit 20-13
Primary Tradeoff Range

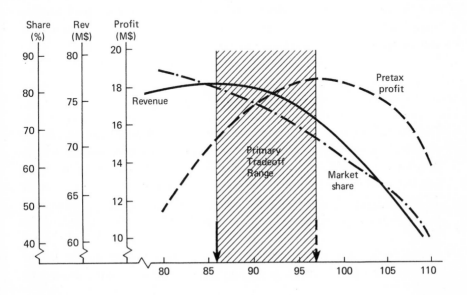

It is the range between the two points at which first revenue and then profit reach maximum values. It is, in other words, the range within which profit, revenue, and market share can be traded off against one another, depending upon the management requirements and business objectives of the moment.

All the space to the left of the primary tradeoff range can be called the secondary tradeoff range. It is secondary, in the sense of being less desirable, because in this range additional market share points must be traded off against both profit and revenue dollars. Note that in the primary tradeoff range profit dollars could be traded against both revenue dollars and market share points, while in the secondary tradeoff range both profit and revenue dollars must be traded for additional market share points. The secondary trade-off range becomes even less desirable as the market share curve continues to flatten out, thus making an ever declining marginal contribution.

The entire space to the right of the primary tradeoff range is clearly of no interest at any time, since in it all three variables, profit, revenue, and market share, decline simultaneously.

It is interesting to note that it can be shown quite rigorously that the price at which maximum revenue occurs is always below that which produces the largest possible profit. This means, as can be expected, that market-share-oriented objectives generally lead to lower prices than profit-oriented objectives whenever the two are substantially different. The width of the primary tradeoff range is clearly representative of the difference between these objectives. It is to be expected that this width and, therefore, these differences are considerably larger in business areas in which APEX has a much smaller share of the market. It is in these businesses that the differences between market share and profit objectives are most relevant.

The Tradeoff

To summarize this picture in a simple table describing this tradeoff, Exhibit 20–14 is what the pricing problem looks like to a first approximation. Obviously, this does not contain a good many of the intangibles, but it describes the essence of the issue. It says that APEX has room to maneuver between $86 and $97 per unit, that at the low end, it maintains current market share with a pretax profit of $15 million, and that at the high end it gives up 12 market share points but gains approximately $4 million in pretax profit. Within that range each market share point costs roughly $333,000 of pretax profits. This is simply the approximate price tag for maintaining market

Exhibit 20-14
The Tradeoff Table

	At $86.00	At $97.00
Pretax profit (M$)	15	19 (max)
Sales income (M$)	77 (max)	73
Market share (%)	80	68

share in the face of broadening competition and a tightening economic environment. It is now the executive's task to select that point within this range at which the profit–market share balance is considered the most appropriate.

In response to the basic questions asked by APEX management and mentioned at the beginning of this report, the analysis indicates that (1) the prevailing APEX price is such that no appreciable profit or market improvement can result from changing it, as long as competition remains pat (this would indicate that a "wait and see" attitude is appropriate) and (2) the most likely competitive price move, when it occurs, will be in the neighborhood of 10 percent. This can be expected to reduce APEX's market share and profit positions.

APEX's most appropriate countermove designed to protect its profit position would still be to remain pat even in the light of this 10 percent price reduction. If, on the other hand, market share protection is the primary objective, then an APEX countermove of approximately 10 percent would be indicated, subject to the understanding that this would be attained at a cost of approximately 10 percent of APEX's profit potential at this new position.

In summary, a defensive strategy appears to be clearly indicated for APEX. The nature of the response depends, as it always must, on the specific management objectives which are relevant at the moment. It is not the role of the model to formulate these objectives, but rather to highlight and display the nature of the tradeoffs involved. The manner in which the options are then exercised is clearly the prerogative of management.

*   *   *

The pricing model described in this report represents an initial attempt to provide a means for systematic analysis of a number of important marketing problems.

The work is still exploratory, and the model will continue to develop along productive channels, provided that managers of marketing operations and staffs continue to participate in this development through personal involvement—by becoming acquainted with this approach, by trying it out on an actual problem of current interest, and, most important of all, by suggesting improvements and giving general guidance based on actual application.

One final point should be stressed again. It is not the purpose of this model to determine an optimum pricing decision in any sense of the word. The real world is far too complex and the model far too gross an approximation for this to be a realistic objective. In any event, it is clear that the decision-making responsibilities will always rest with the executives. Instead, the true purpose of the model—and indeed of any sensible and practical operations research methodology—is to assist the executive in sharpening his judgments and improving his insights, thus to enable him to make better and more informed decisions.

PART FIVE

Advertising and Promotion

21

The Gordian Knot of Advertising

Evelyn Konrad

P ERHAPS THE LARGEST NUMBER and broadest diversity of computer applications to marketing problems exist in advertising and promotion. However, possibly because of their great diversity, these applications do not lend themselves easily to generalized analysis, criticism, and commentary.

Unlike inventory management areas, where a set number of techniques address themselves easily to grouped chores, computer applications in advertising and promotion areas are more different from each other in approach, value, and merit than computer applications or EDP techniques answering nonadvertising questions in totally divergent industries.

Because of this wealth of diversity, this section does not pretend to even touch on the many areas within advertising and promotion in which computers are making contributions. Indeed, even the discussion of the role of the computer in media selection may be considered only indicative and incomplete.

Another indication of the challenge this diversified area poses to anyone attempting to cover all the computer applications in it may be indicated by the fact that five new software firms offering diverse advertising applications and packages have sprung up in New York alone between the time when the manuscript for this book was begun and the time when it was completed. In brief, the problem of surveying this area exhaustively is complicated not merely because there are so many opportunities for diverse computer applications within the advertising function, but also because so many aggressive, young entrepreneurs with programming skills still consider entry into this part of the industry challenging and reasonable in terms of the start-up cash required.

The purpose of this section, therefore, must be stated more modestly than claiming to be an overview of this entire field. While it is not exhaustive, it does, however, touch upon those computer applications which, in the view of the editor, have had the most far-reaching impact to date and one or two examples that may stimulate fresh areas for advertising management exploration.

22

Advertising Media Models: Their Uses and Limitations

Lawrence F. Young

DURING THE PAST TEN YEARS, management scientists have applied their two most potent weapons, mathematics and the computer, to the problem of selecting advertising media. In this chapter, we will examine the media problem and the results of this effort.

To better gauge this effort, the power of the computer and mathematics should first be seen in perspective. In an age of technological accomplishments, the computer stands out as possibly the most significant one. Mass media have made its wonders known to nearly everyone: Computers can diagnose diseases, control missile systems and space shots, keep inventory and accounting records, write poems and songs, "scientifically" determine which boys should meet which girls, and do a seemingly endless list of other things. In all of these things, the computer has too often been viewed as if it were a monkey riding a bicycle—whether it does the trick well is not noticed as much as the fact that it can do it at all. The Sunday supplement kind of popularizing has established the new conventional wisdom that machines can already "solve" many complex problems and ultimately can be expected to do almost anything. The view of the computer as a superbrain may give rise to as much human jealousy as it does admiration. (Do you feel some perverse satisfaction when a computer system mixes up your charge account?) Is the computer as omnipotent as some claim or as awesome as many fear?

The fuller explanation behind the computer's more impressive accomplishments, as well as some of its spectacular pratfalls, lies not in the machine itself but in its human manipulator. For all its complex circuitry and speed at number juggling, the computer is only a tool. It requires a human master to plan and control its use. Organizing the machine so that its speed and ability to manipulate data can be made to do a useful job or "solve" a problem requires a high level of human ingenuity and knowledge of the details of the application. Therein lies both salvation and the rub. We need have no jealousy of the machine, only a higher sense of challenge that our own skills will enable us to use its power well.

Our other awesome weapon, mathematics, is also a passive tool. It is a concise and powerful medium for expressing and manipulating ideas about real or imagined things. It is a language, and as such, requires someone literate and knowledgeable to use it to convey anything sensible.

If the media selection problem has not been completely reduced to a mechanical solution technique, we should seek the reasons for the limitations in other than the tools of mathematics and the computer. The major limitations of media models are traceable to the unavailability of the required laws of consumer behavior. The sparseness of basic theory prevents us from finding "scientific" answers to other marketing problems as well. Without the foundation of well-developed theory based on experimentation and observation, mathematics and the computer can provide no new truths either in marketing or in other major problem areas. Marketing theory must ultimately focus on human behavior, and, whether individually or in the aggregate, human behavior is still incomparably less predictable than physical phenomena.

While the computer is far from being a magic box, and makers of mathematical models have no special direct line to the knowledge of the gods, let us clarify the benefits of the proper uses of models and the computer to the media planner and the marketing executive. The business executive is, after all, not a scientist and cannot afford the rigors of scientific proof before each decision he must make. Neither can he delay his decisions until the appropriate theory has been developed. The executive is a risk taker by virtue of his need to continually choose alternative actions without benefit of complete information. If mathematics and the computer can aid the executive in better understanding his own assumptions and in being consistent in his analysis of risk situations, they will have done the only job one can expect of them in the current state of the art of marketing.

With this criterion for success, we find, paradoxically, that media models that are simpler and limited in scope have been successful more often than global and more complex models. This is not accidental; it is the natural result of the media decision maker's need to impose considerable judgment on a model's solution. In order to be able to separate factors that the model has and has not considered and to make judgments about the mutual effects of both kinds of factors, the media planner requires a relatively simple model. Otherwise, he must abdicate a portion of his responsibility either by accepting a model's incomplete solution on misplaced faith or by imposing modifications on top of the model's results without fully grasping their significance.

Media Selection: The Problem and the Process

Like many of the most complex analytical problems, the essential bare bones of the media problem can be very simply stated: The media planner must select a number of vehicles—specific newspapers, magazines, TV shows, and so forth—to carry his ads over a predetermined period of time, and he must specify how many and which ads will be placed in each vehicle at each point in time the vehicle is available. He must do this within a prescribed total advertising budget and in a way that will "effectively" expose some appropriate target audience (or audiences) to his advertising messages.

To expand on this general problem definition, let us examine two sample statements, statements A and B. These are the kinds of statements that are commonly set down as initial guides to media planners in an advertising agency. A critical analysis of these statements may clarify some of the major problems in media selection.

Statement A. Our target audience is the young housewife with preschool or elementary school-age children. We will require the impact and demonstration power of TV to introduce this new cleaning product. A basic layer of national coverage will be attained by participating spots in daytime network TV supplemented by selected nighttime network prime time participations. To the basic layer of national coverage attained by network TV participations, we will build the frequency necessary to achieve brand awareness over the two-month introductory period by a heavy spot TV schedule in major markets. For the subsequent ten months, spot TV will be used at a reduced level sufficient to remind consumers and maintain brand awareness levels.

Statement B. Our special appeal is to a target audience of upper-income, better-educated, over-35, male "opinion leaders." Our purchase proposition requires extensive copy and will be carried in two-page spreads in national and regional print media. In addition to attaining high concentration and reach in the target group and maintaining adequate frequency levels, we must utilize vehicles that will provide suitable editorial environments and prestige in order to enhance the believability of our message. Insertions should be scheduled over the campaign year to provide continuity and aware-ness rather than a sudden surge and fall-off of impact.

The above statements of guidelines to a media planner can be examined in two different ways. One way to look at them is to consider that they really convey a set of code words and phrases. If looked at in this way, the coded instructions are not meant to convey literal, complete, and consistent infor-mation for selecting media according to rigorous, measurable goals and constraints. Instead, they merely serve as indicators of preestablished types of media plans that will be acceptable for the situation. In other words, the state-ments need not provide specifications for an analytical problem solution. In-stead, they need to be translated by an experienced media man into one of many possible variations of a prototype plan that other experienced media planners will find appropriate. The planner's experience and knowledge are exercised by understanding what prototype plans are feasible and which vari-ations are appropriate.

This is not to denigrate the media planner if this is how he actually ap-proaches the problem. It is not necessarily an easy way to proceed. Also, if an alternative, more formally analytical, approach is not *possible,* the media planner cannot be faulted for falling back on variations of past actions of ex-perienced practitioners in his field. The media planner is, however, to his credit, not content with this approach. He is lately more vocal about his de-sire to apply his experience at a more analytical level and his need for the relevant data and theory that will enable him to do so.

To see something of the sources of his discontent, examine statements A and B as if they were literal specifications instead of coded instructions to repeat previously established patterns. The management scientist, with his focus on rational decision making, would try to extract and clarify the defi-nitional and logical relationships in the statements of media planning goals. If one looks at the statements in the manner of the management scientist, there are some obvious questions.

1. What are the primary and secondary goals?
2. What are the constraining factors?
3. Can we derive the relationships needed to measure how well particular plans will attain the goals without violating the constraints?
4. Can we specify a method, mathematical or otherwise, to derive the plan that will *best* meet goals without violating constraints?

If we are to define a rational, analytical approach to a solution, we must have workable answers to, at least, the first three questions. When we have a satisfactory answer to the fourth as well, we are extremely fortunate. To explore the feasibility of such an approach, we have extracted and categorized some of the basic elements in the media selection problem from the two prior statements and expressed them in a table.

The extracted problem elements listed in the table make it apparent that these problem definitions are lacking in several respects. If the media problem is to be approached analytically, the inconsistencies in the stated goals must be rectified. There must be one measurable quantity to be optimized as a goal. This goal measure can be made up of more than one problem element (variable), so long as each element's respective relative contribution toward the overall goal is specified. If two or more goals are opposed to one another, their relative tradeoff values must be specified.

The first three questions of the management scientist cannot be satisfactorily answered. Goals have neither been related to one another nor have they been distinguished from constraints. In addition to the elements listed in Table 22–1, other concepts embedded in the problem statements have no clear definition or standard of measure. These include

- Impact.
- Editorial environment.
- Prestige.
- Believability.
- Continuity.

How, then, if the management scientist finds the media problem poorly defined, has the media man been living with it? The answer lies mainly in the fact that, in the simpler precomputer days, these problem definitions were never held up for comparison to such rigorous standards. As coded indicators of plan types they were adequate. In addition, the media man has had to focus a large part of his efforts on merely implementing his general plans by buying media at advantageous discounts and package rates. Indeed,

TABLE 22–1
MEDIA PROBLEM ELEMENTS

Element	Relevance	Consistency
Attain basic national coverage.	Stated as a goal, but level of coverage undefined.	Network TV does not distribute coverage equally in all markets.
Build frequency necessary to achieve awareness.	Stated as a goal, but frequency relationship to awareness is not rigorously defined.	This may be at odds with attaining coverage.
Reduce level sufficient to remind and maintain awareness.	Adequate levels undefined.	Reduced frequency may also reduce reach and concentration below acceptable levels; tradeoffs are undefined.
Attain high concentration in the target group.	Stated as a goal.	This may be at odds with attaining reach.
Attain high reach in the target group.	Stated as a goal.	This may be at odds with both concentration and attaining adequate frequency.
Maintain adequate frequency levels.	Stated as a constraint but adequacy measure undefined.	This can be at odds with spreading insertions out over the year.

the flexibility and complexity of media rates themselves have been largely undefinable or insufficiently stable for inclusion in a model. Even if all other concepts and problem elements could be better defined, the institutionalized rate complexity and bargaining aspect of media buying is likely to remain a largely extraanalytical aspect of the media problem.

Thus far, there has been no mention of an inseparable but often separately considered aspect of media planning—the message to be carried. McLuhan notwithstanding, the medium isn't the only message—or at least it doesn't automatically sell the advertiser's product. It has been argued occasionally that media can be evaluated in consideration of the "average" message to be carried, or some particular message "type." In this way, the media planner has, in a sense, factored out the effect of the message and can consider only relative audience delivery values for a given media schedule. The assumption of an average factorable message effect is at best, however, only an approximation of the real effect on the consumer, and may be a bad approximation. Media and message are likely to interact—in other words, the joint effect can be quite different from the sum (or even the product) of the separate effects of medium and message. No adequate data or theory for such interaction is available. If it were available, it still might not be feasible to include this type of interaction in a media selection model because of the large number of possible message–medium combinations.

The media planner is limited by necessity to rely heavily on intuition in gauging many of the effects of alternative media plans. Many loose concepts of "goodness" in media planning, such as impact, environmental effects, and continuity, can be addressed only in a general directional sense. In the absence of precise measures for many aspects of media planning, the media analyst has focused his quantitative analyses on the two things he can at least partially obtain objective estimates of—how many people are exposed and how often they are exposed to a medium, the old standby media bench marks of reach and frequency. Around this nucleus of reach and frequency estimation, the media planner must build his plan with little more than intuition and an occasional special finding in the sparse body of published results of media research experimentation.

Media Models: The Major Types Extant

The major types of media models fall into the following categories:

1. Media plan *analysis* models.

    a. Simulation models.
    b. Statistical estimation models.
  2. Media plan *selection* models.
    a. Basic linear programming (LP) models.
    b. Extended or special LP or other optimization models.
    c. Heuristic models.

Estimating by Simulation

The analysis models are aimed at estimating the results of alternative given media plans. The estimated results are generally measured in terms of the net number of different people (or households) in some defined target group that are included in the audience of the media plan (net reach) and the number reached or exposed at each level of exposure (exposure frequency distribution). These models do not automatically generate or indicate new plans, they merely provide estimates of the reach and frequency outcomes of given plans. They are, however, useful in producing improved new plans by enabling the media man to examine more alternatives at a more detailed level than he could without a computerized model. The more extensive of the analytical models, both in scope of output data and in the size and scope of the media plans that can be analyzed, are the simulation models.

Some controversy has been generated over media simulation models because of the methods employed to generate their basic building blocks, which are the exposure probabilities of individual persons to individual media vehicles. Although some statistical estimating models, primarily the Beta model, have a firmer theoretical foundation, they are not practicably applicable to large media schedules, that is, the most important schedules of large advertisers. This generally leaves the planner with the media simulation model as the only operationally feasible computerized tool to extensively measure the basic audience dimensions of his major advertising plans.

Despite initial controversy on simulation development methods, there is now general agreement that simulation is a useful and flexible tool when reasonable and carefully implemented development steps are taken to develop the basic probability estimates at the core of the simulation model. Several simulation models have been developed. This chapter will refer to the media simulation developed by Lawrence F. Young called SCANS (SChedule ANalysis by Simulation); however, its general features are representative of other media simulation models as well.

What Is Simulation?

Simulation is a special kind of experimentation. Instead of experimenting on the "real thing," whatever the real object of interest happens to be, an artificially designed substitute or stand-in is used. The stand-in may or may not resemble the real thing. More often than not, it doesn't look anything like it. That is unimportant, but what is important is that the substitute reacts in some manner analogous to the real thing. This analogous reaction or group of reactions is built into the stand-in in a simplified and elemental form. A combination of elemental, predesigned reactions can result in a total outcome that is not predesigned or even predicted. The artificial stand-in can be experimented with by feeding it different situations and noting how it reacts. By summarizing and analyzing these observed reactions, one can often learn something new about how the real system may react.

There are many examples of simulation. In one standard example, the substitute (an airplane model and a wind tunnel) does look very much like the real thing. In another familiar case, the substitute (the ground flight trainer that imitates real flying conditions but can be "crashed," for example, without physically harming the trainee pilot) looks a little less like the real thing.

But when the general purpose digital computer is used as a means for simulation, the substitute no longer looks at all like the real thing. Inability to watch what goes on inside a computer and see an obvious similarity to the real process being simulated lends an extra aura of mystery to a computer simulation.

But if we can put aside lack of familiarity with the mechanical workings of the computer and examine only the logic of a computer simulation, we find that computer simulation models are usually quite simple in their basic logical structure. This is no consolation to the computer programmer or the person who pays for developing the simulation program. The process of creating a computer program to perform the simulation logic and present the results is still time-consuming and costly and calls for painstakingly detailed work. This is often also true for formulating and testing the simulation logic. But when the computer simulation is finally complete and operational, its logical structure can usually be straightforwardly expressed and understood.

This relative simplicity is not accidental; it is a result of the nature of computer simulation. The kind of situation in which computer simulation is appropriate is illustrated by the following example. Suppose we are studying a worldwide cargo transportation system, and we want to answer the following questions—

- Under what conditions do unusually long delays occur? Where do they occur? How long do they last?
- How will different rules for establishing priority affect the overall performance of the system?
- How will changes in shipping schedules affect the overall performance?
- If we increase the capacity of cargo planes but decrease the number of planes, what will be the result?

The list of questions can go on and on.

To study this system, we could try to write down mathematical formulas that relate all the important variables, substitute different quantities, and solve the equation. This would certainly be a desirable thing to do, but with such a complex system, it is almost never a practical approach. There are just too many elements to tie together in the form of mathematical summary statements.

But we need not form any very complex mathematical equations if all we do is to follow every item of cargo on its journey through the system. All we want to do is to keep track of where it goes and how long it stays in each place—in short, to keep a detailed history for each item. If we can do this for all items and accumulate the result, we will be able to measure how the system behaves.

Since it is physically impossible to try out different approaches and record the results on the real system, we build a substitute. The substitute is coded for a computer and therefore not recognizable to the naked eye. But the codes just represent all the elements in the real system, such as units of cargo, planes, and trucks. Also we must represent the basic operations that take place. In order to simulate this system, all that need be well formulated are the individual elements of the system, the sequence of events. Usually these individual operations can be well approximated by mathematical relationships or a set of decision rules.

This kind of situation is typical of those that can profitably be studied by the method of computer simulation. That is, the elemental operations can be formulated pretty well, but the overall relationships are either too cumbersome or insufficiently understood to be dealt with directly. But even dealing with many simple individual occurrences and having to sum things up would itself be too cumbersome a task without the speed of the computer.

The computer, then, is a tool we use because of its speed, accuracy, and versatility in carrying out instructions. The logic of the simulation consists of little more than defining rules for behavior of each elemental operation and for performance of each operation in some sequence. The rest is a matter of recordkeeping and summarizing results.

SCANS

The events being simulated in the SCANS model are the exposure (or nonexposure) of each individual in the population to each use of each media vehicle in a schedule. As it occurs, each individual's exposure or nonexposure is recorded, and finally, summaries of reach and frequency of exposure can be produced for any prescribed group of individuals.

The simulation approach simplifies the problem of estimating for a group by keeping track of individual people's exposure and then summarizing the results in various ways. Here again, the essential feature of simulation that makes it a versatile and powerful tool is that when it is too complex or impossible to treat some process as a whole, we can break it up into its elemental components, simulate the behavior of these components, record, summarize, and analyze the results.

With SCANS and other simulation models for media, the difficulties of developing a flexible and accurate method to analyze mass exposure directly are circumvented by simulating exposure of individuals and then aggregating the recorded results.

SCANS provides basic measurements of reach and frequency of exposure of prescribed magazine and TV schedules for specified groups of individuals. These measurements are primarily used to compare several different schedules in order to—

1. Conclude which alternative schedules come closest to the desired objectives of the media planner.
2. Gain insights and indications of how various differences in schedules affect the basic reach and frequency patterns that are of interest to the planner.
3. Use the results to indicate what further alternatives should be examined.

The emphasis on the use of the simulated results is on comparisons among alternatives rather than on the absolute numbers associated with a single plan. In simulating the process of individual people being exposed to specific media vehicles in a schedule, every factor that might affect the outcome in a real-life situation has not been included. We have attempted to create a simulation process that would be affected in close proportion to the real-life effects of changes in media schedule. The reasons for this approach are several. First, in attempting to introduce every factor that can exist in real life, the many assumptions called for multiply the unreliability of the simulated outcomes. It is better to consider fewer factors (the factors that are most likely to be of greatest significance in affecting outcomes) and get reasonably good results, than to try to consider everything and make the process hard to manipulate because of unnecessary complexity.

Even when greater detail can reliably be introduced, there is still the economic question of the value of doing so. Increased complexity is not only more costly to the developer of an operational system, it is more costly to the user of the system. If a refinement in informational output is not worth this additional cost, we are better off without the added detail.

Beyond these technical and economic considerations, there is a key need of the planner—to make a decision among alternatives. A rational choice among alternatives can be made if the planner can either *rank* the value of each alternative or measure the *relative* value of the alternatives, even if absolute values remain unknown.

SCANS results are primarily used to examine relative differences, but SCANS also produces good to excellent estimates of reach and frequency for individual plans where comparable survey data are available as a validity check.

SCANS utilizes a machine language file of specially designed data representing descriptive facts for a sample of individuals. This artificially constructed sample is designed to be representative of the adult populations of the United States and can be viewed as a proportionately scaled-down version of the total adult population.

The simulated sample contains 3,892 adult individuals. (A separate sample of 1,500 teenagers has also been created.) Each individual is represented by a tape record containing certain basic demographic data and open space provided for the addition of any data that are thought to be especially relevant.

The basic data include all of the following factors (as is shown in Exhibit 22–1)—

Exhibit 22-1
The Simulated Population: Coded "People"

Identification Code No.	Sex Code No.	Family Income Code No.	Age Code No.	Education Code No.	Urban-Rural Code No.	Region Code No.	Employment Code No.	Magazine Reading Habits
								Look Magazine
0015	1	4	2	5	1	1	1	.9
	=	=	=	=	=	=	=	=
	Male	$10,000 or more	35 to 49 years old	College Graduate	Urban Area Resident	New England Resident	Employed	Subscriber, Reads 9 out of 10 issues on average

etc. →

- Sex.
- Age group.
- Census region of residence.
- Education.
- Income category of individual's family unit.
- Family size.
- Employment status.
- Urban-rural-farm classification.
- TV set and home ownership.

Space is also provided for adding data of special relevance and can be utilized and varied according to individual client needs. Special-purpose computer programs have been developed for the statistically controlled assignment of such new data. For example, an automobile advertiser may have demographic descriptions of new car buyers and their choice of car body types (that is, station wagons, sedans, convertibles, or whatever). These car body choices can then be coded and statistically assigned to the simulated sample of individuals.

The addition of this kind of special information depends on whether it can be made available to us and whether such information can be directly related to any of the characteristics already assigned to the sample population.

In addition to the assignment of demographic and marketing characteristics, methods have been developed to estimate and assign data related to the reading, TV viewing, listening, and similar habits of each individual. These media exposure data are in the form of average probabilities. For example, a specific housewife may receive a weekly subscription copy of a particular magazine. If it is estimated that, on the average, she reads nine out of ten issues of the magazine, her exposure probability for that magazine would then be recorded as .90. Similarly, exposure probabilities can be estimated for all other magazines and assigned to that housewife.

Her probabilities of watching television for every quarter hour of the day can also be estimated. In addition, we can estimate the same housewife's probability of watching each particular show if she is watching TV at a given time.

These basic elements of information enable us to follow each individual through a period of time (such as a month or a year) and record each instance of exposure.

The basic information the SCANS user must specify covers the alternative media plans to be simulated. Each plan to be simulated is presented by listing the media vehicles and specifying which weeks each vehicle is to be included in a schedule covering a period up to 52 weeks long.

Up to 20 plans may be simulated at the same time by SCANS. If more than 20 schedules are to be simulated, a second run, and possibly a third, can be made in sequence.

For each schedule to be simulated, the user can specify a number of demographic groups that are important as marketing targets. There may be several different demographic groupings and combinations of these groupings which are all significant to the advertiser. Any of these groupings that can be directly defined in terms of the basic characteristics assigned to the simulated population need only be specified in order to have output results produced for each of these groups. Up to 12 groups can be requested in a single run.

An example of such a list of demographic breaks required by a particular user would be as follows—

1. All adult females.
2. All urban adult females.
3. Urban adult females 18 through 34 years of age.
4. Urban adult females 35 through 49 years of age.
5. Urban adult females over 50 years of age.
6. All college graduates 18 through 34 years of age.

If requirements include additional demographic breaks that are not included in the basic characteristics already assigned to our sample population, then special assignments can be made. This can be done as long as relevant data are available and time and cost permit making the special assignments called for.

The key elements of the media simulation are the exposure probabilities which are estimated and assigned to each simulated individual.

These probabilities are computed for each individual's exposure to—

- Each national magazine.
- Each Sunday supplement.
- Each half-hour of the TV day.
- Each TV network show appearing in each half-hour.
- Each area of local media.

The procedure for deriving these probabilities is itself a mathematical model that provides a "best fit" of the results with available survey data.

The data ingredients of the probability estimating process include—

1. Syndicated media research data sources on—
   ■ Vehicle's average audience sizes.
   ■ Limited data on vehicle's cumulative audience.
   ■ Vehicle's audience demographic descriptions.
   ■ Extent of TV viewing by time of day.
   ■ Attitudes toward vehicles.
   ■ Other standard syndicated media research data.
2. Special published studies covering many of the subjects listed in the preceding point.
3. The judgment of seasoned professionals in media research.

The results of the probability estimating procedure are verified by using them in SCANS runs and comparing the results to the available bench marks derived from direct research and past experience.

Random Outcomes (Monte Carlo Technique)

For some, the use of these probabilities may be unfamiliar, but the meaning of the probability itself is, however, not a new concept. When we state, for example, that a person has a probability of reading *Life* equal to .75, we simply mean that we would expect that person to read 75 out of 100 issues, on the average.

It is possible to simulate that person's exposure to *Life* by spinning a wheel (as shown in Exhibit 22–2). If three-quarters of the wheel is labeled "reads" and one-quarter is labeled "doesn't read," we can obtain a random outcome. We could repeat the spinning six times, record the result each time, and in this way we will have simulated the individual's exposure to six issues of *Life*.

An equivalent way of simulating this would be with the use of random numbers. Because of the gambling wheel analogy, this method has been called the Monte Carlo Technique.

Random numbers could be used in the following way. Suppose we have a list of random, two-digit numbers as follows:

Random Numbers

67	17	—	—
39	81	—	—
01	92	—	—
42	36	—	—
63	61	—	—

This table can be visualized to go on to contain millions of these random digits. Because these numbers are random, we expect any two digits to occur in the list as often as any other two digits. There are 100 different possible two-digit combinations, that is, all the numbers from 00 up to 99.

Therefore, we can simulate our *Life* reader's exposure as follows. Since he has a probability of .75 of reading, we can set aside 75 out of the 100 possible two-digit combinations to signify "reads," and the remaining 25 numbers would mean "doesn't read." For convenience we can assign these two-digit numbers in this way—

Exhibit 22-2
Random Probability Outcome

Individual # 0015 has a
.75 probability of reading *Life*

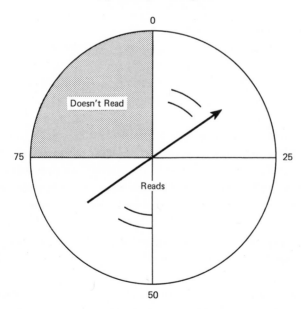

00 to 74:   Reads
75 to 99:   Doesn't read

We then proceed by selecting some arbitrary starting place in the random number table, say the third number in column one. This is 01, meaning "reads." If we were to start with this and simulate exposure to six issues we would obtain these results:

	Random Number	Meaning
1.	01	Reads
2.	42	Reads
3.	63	Reads
4.	17	Reads
5.	81	Doesn't Read
6.	92	Doesn't Read

In the actual computer procedure used, almost exactly this kind of procedure is followed to obtain random outcomes governed by the assigned probabilities. One procedural difference is that, for the sake of efficiency, a special computer subprogram is used to generate one random number after another instead of reading these numbers from a table. As each random response is simulated the results are recorded and later summarized. (See Exhibit 22–3.)

The heart of the simulation process is obtaining the random outcomes in the logically simple way illustrated.

Selection Techniques—The FAST Model

Simulation of a number of alternative plans can be a valuable tool for the media planner in selecting his final recommended media schedule. However, simulation alone will not uncover the most efficient plan for meeting the planner's goals if he doesn't happen to choose that particular alternative plan to simulate. In many cases, the best plans may represent considerable departures from past practice and intuition and therefore are unlikely to be simulated unless they were previously generated by a selection model.

For these reasons, the planner would benefit from a selection model that would serve to efficiently generate a media plan, given the planner's goals and the situation's constraints. One such model developed by Lawrence F. Young and in use in conjunction with the SCANS simulation model is called FAST (Frequency Aimed Selection Technique). FAST comes under the category of a special nonlinear mathematical model that can be transformed into a form solvable by linear programming. Although LP is used within the FAST system, the FAST model is unlike the more standard LP media models described later.

FAST is designed to perform the following tasks:

■ To select a feasible media schedule which will deliver a minimum number of underexposed and overexposed individuals and as many individuals as possible in the most desirable range of number of exposures. (Note: A feasible schedule is one that does not violate a budgetary limit, limited issuance of media vehicles, or other important constraints.)

Exhibit 22-3
Steps in Running The Simulation

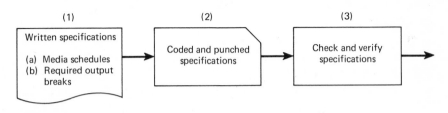

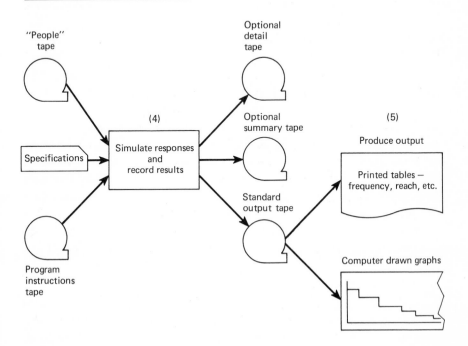

- To attempt this focusing on number of exposures while still producing an acceptable result in terms of overall net reach.
- To define a prime (first priority) target group, and, if necessary, a second priority target group and a third priority target group and to define the most desirable range of exposures for each of these groups.

The FAST Model and Method

Data required. The method requires the existence of a representative sample of individuals, each with an accompanying set of vehicle exposure probabilities for all media vehicles to be considered. These are the same basic data required by the SCANS media simulation system. These data are basic input and are used in conjunction with a problem definition that includes the following:

1. A list of eligible media vehicles and the maximum number of times each vehicle can be used in the schedule.
2. Unit costs for each vehicle and the maximum total expenditure (budget) amount.
3. Demographic definitions of the target priority groups and the most desirable exposure level for each group.
4. A definition of the relative importance of the three priority groups.

The method. Phase 1 is the generation of the model and parameters. This is a computer program which uses the input data and problem definition described above to generate a linear set of equations, inequalities, and an objective function. This equation system includes a subset of equations which are similar to the so-called normal equations of linear multiple regressions analysis. These modified normal equations control the "frequency aiming" aspect of the selection by computing the statistically expected number of exposures for each individual in the simulated sample.

Phase 2 is the optimization of the phase 1 Model.

Phase 1 produces its output in the exact format required by the LP 90 or MPS 360 system. LP is used in phase 2 to generate a mathematically optimal solution to the phase 1 model.

Phase 3 is simulation.

The media schedule indicated by phase 2, after rounding the indicated number of insertions to whole numbers and spreading out the buys over a calendar year, is run through the SCANS simulation model. Alternative schedules generated by direct human judgment or other methods can also be simulated so that comparable measures of each alternative can be examined. In this way, we can get an immediate evaluation of the FAST-generated schedule.

In practice, we have usually recommended the use of SCANS first to simulate last year's plan or other alternatives before the media planner attempts to set down his goals and specifications for FAST to select new "optimal" plans. This provides the planner with a departure point and a contextual framework to define feasible frequency goals within his budget. The FAST-generated plans are then submitted to SCANS for simulation. The usual sequence is to run SCANS, then FAST, then SCANS again.

Both systems have been updated and expanded several times to meet client needs. At the present time, the entire process of SCANS-FAST-SCANS can be completed within five days, enabling the user to do an initial review of prior or theoretical future plans, select optimum schedules, and conduct the final analysis of modified plans for recommendation to the client.

The systems have been used on several hundreds of schedules and have been found to have special benefit to the advertiser who is investing more than $1 million in mass media. By selecting an optimum range of exposure frequency and discounting extremely light contacts and inordinately heavy exposure, the advertiser can often realize a 5 to 15 percent reduction in the advertising budget necessary to meet his objectives.

A Summarized SCANS-FAST Case History

An automobile advertiser wanted to efficiently reach and impress key new car-buying prospects during an eight-week introductory campaign.

The series of steps shown in Table 22–2 involving the planner, models, and the computer were carried out.

The "traditional" plan started with was labeled plan A and consisted of a list of 21 magazines including mass, business, and selected technical interest books, with two to five insertions in each publication. The total cost of this schedule was $1,805,000.

As an evaluation yardstick, the ranges of exposure frequency over the eight weeks were designated as follows:

- Excessive—16 or more exposures.
- Ideal—8 to 15 exposures (1 or 2 per week).
- Adequate—5 to 7 exposures.

- Inadequate—1 to 4 exposures.
- Never reached—0 exposures.

Three plan Cs, each representing minor modifications to plans produced by the FAST model at alternate budget levels, were simulated and compared to plan A. The computer simulation provides estimates of the number of

TABLE 22–2

A SCANS-FAST CASE HISTORY

Steps	Man	Implemented by Model and Machine
1. Preliminary media plans, including "traditional" plan, were specified.	x	
2. Preliminary plans (plan A) were simulated to estimate how often key groups of consumers were exposed to advertising.		x (SCANS)
3. Specifications of frequency goals for three target groups were made. First priority target group was men 35 to 49, earning over $8,000; second priority was men 18 through 34 earning over $8,000; and the third priority was men 50 and over earning over $8,000.	x	
4. Optimal plans (plan B) were generated to reach the above target groups at frequency goals of between 8 and 15 exposures.		x (FAST)
5. The FAST-generated plans were modified, and a modified set of plans (plan C) was simulated to estimate exposure delivery to the target groups.		x (SCANS)
6. The simulated C plans were examined and compared to select a final recommended plan.	x	

people exposed at each level of exposure; these data were summarized for the following comparison:

	A ("*traditional*")	C^1	C^2	C^3
Plans:				
	Percentage of primary target group exposed in each exposure range			
Never	5.8	5.8	6.5	5.8
Inadequate	13.0	8.0	18.8	9.4
Adequate	22.5	26.1	34.1	32.6
Ideal	39.8	42.7	29.0	38.4
Excessive	18.9	17.4	11.6	13.8
	100.0	100.0	100.0	100.0
Plan Cost	$1,805,000	$1,707,000	$1,002,000	$1,412,000

The C plans, produced by the FAST model, differed from plan A in both the magazines included and the number of insertions used in each magazine. Some business and technical books were removed from the schedule; some mass books had reduced numbers of insertions; and some outdoor publications were added to the schedule.

All three C plans represented improvements to traditional plans at comparable budget levels. C^1 can be seen to deliver more in the adequate and ideal levels and correspondingly less in the lightest and heaviest exposure levels for about $100,000 less than plan A. C^2, given only about $1 million as a budget, did not deliver quite enough exposure. C^3 was chosen as providing acceptable exposure delivery at a saving of $393,000 compared to the traditional plan. Plan C^3 delivered 61.6 percent of all three target groups combined in the adequate or ideal range of exposure, vs. 53.5 percent delivered by plan A.

The conclusion on this case was the recommendation and use of plan C^3 because it efficiently reaches more new car-buying prospects. (The $393,000 saving was reallocated to special market promotions for an added side benefit of this analysis.)

This case illustrates the cooperative interaction between man, model, and machine leading to useful results. The results were made possible by allowing the planner to fully exercise his judgment, aided by the new foundation and insight provided by models that were not too global in scope to be digested and modified by the user.

LP Media Models

Because of their historical importance and because variations of the basic LP media model are still in use by some agencies and advertisers, the general character of LP and a basic LP media model need to be described.

The basic problems which can be solved by LP consist of the following:

1. *A defined goal or objective.* The goal is simply to make a decision resulting in the best possible outcome for the decision maker. The outcome must be measurable in terms of some single variable. A variable frequently used to measure outcomes of business decisions is the cost resulting from those decisions. Everything affecting cost is measured in dollars, and the goal can then be defined as the selection of a decision which will result in costing the decision maker the least possible number of dollars. The least number of dollars is, in this case, the best possible outcome. All variables affecting the value of this single cost variable must be expressed mathematically in a single equation called the objective function.

2. *A set of rules or restrictions.* The goal of the decision maker must be reached without violating some set of rules which restrict his actions. Such restrictions may arise from several causes. Such causes may, for example, be company policy, limited availability of resources, customer requirements, or government regulations.

The rules may take the form of specifying exact quantities which must be conformed to, or they may specify maximum or minimum quantities which govern some aspect of the decision maker's course of action. For example, in a decision problem involving a choice of the best mix of products to manufacture in order to maximize profit, there may be some restrictions specifying exact quantities, such as exactly 500 units of product A and 750 units of products B and C.

Restrictions such as these are called equalities and can be represented mathematically as $A = 500$ and $B + C = 750$.

Other restrictions in the product mix problem may specify maximum or minimum quantities which must be conformed to, such as up to, but no more than, 900 units of product D and at least 300 units of products E and F combined.

Restrictions such as these are called inequalities and can be represented mathematically as $D \leqslant 900$ and $E + F \geqslant 300$. The symbol $\leqslant$ means less than or equal to and the symbol $\geqslant$ means greater than or equal to.

All such rules restricting the decision maker's actions must be stated explicitly. Such mathematical statements are referred to as restrictions or constraints.

3. *Existence of linear, or to-scale, relationships.* Each variable affecting the value of the objective function or any of the restriction equations must produce a linear, or to-scale, effect.

This can be illustrated by the following simple example. If it costs $2 for each unit of product A that is manufactured, 5 units of product A will cost $10, 6 units will cost $12, 10 units will cost $20, and so on. Expressing the number of units of product A that will be made as an unknown variable, X_a, the linear relationship of the cost of product A to the number of units of product A would be mathematically represented by

$$2X_a = C_a$$

where C_a is the total cost of making product A.

In any LP problem, all of the variables must produce this kind of linear effect on whatever is being evaluated, whether it is cost, profit, or something else. If, for example, the goal is to minimize total cost, and there are three possible products—A, B, and C, whose unit costs are $2, $1, and $5, respectively—an equation representing total cost would appear as follows:

$$2X_a + 1X_b + 5X_c = \text{total cost}$$

where the Xs represent the number of units of products A, B, and C, respectively, that will be made.

It is important to recognize that in real problems, the relationships are not always linear. *When a linear model of these relationships is not a close enough approximation to real behavior the problem may not be suitable for an LP solution.* Fortunately, many practical problems do have this characteristic of linearity or approximate linearity.

4. *Only nonnegative values are permitted in the solution.* It is a characteristic of most LP problems that only nonnegative solutions are sought. For example, we can only make a positive number of units of product A, or none at all; negative amounts having no real meaning in this case.

Mathematical proofs and the computational procedures relating to LP are available in many textbooks. It will suffice here to state that mathematical procedures exist which will determine the best (or optimal) solution to any properly formulated LP problem. Furthermore, the computational prcedures of LP have been programmed for electronic computers and are available to anyone who wishes to use them.

An Illustrative LP Media Model

The media planner must decide on a criterion that will measure how well any schedule utilizes the available funds. That is, in accordance with our previous definition of a goal, he must specify a single variable which he would like to optimize. Assume that the media planner decides that his goal should be to obtain as many effective exposure opportunities as he possibly can without exceeding the $1 million allotted for media purchases.

The word "effective" is used to indicate that the media planner is not just interested in total exposure opportunities. He would like the exposure opportunities to be directed against the advertised product's most likely purchasers and to be carried in appropriate vehicles in appropriate buying units. The appropriateness of vehicles and buying units is, in turn, measured by as many factors as the media planner considers significant. These factors might include such things as the editorial climate of a vehicle, requirements imposed by the length and style of the selling message, special marketing services offered by a vehicle, and other such factors which the media planner usually considers. All of these factors, some or all of which may be intangible and subjective, can be combined into a single numeric score for each eligible buying unit in each vehicle.

We will call this score S in general, and S_1, or S_2, or S_3, . . . to denote the specific score of each buying unit in each vehicle being considered. This numeric score can then be used to mathematically weight the total expected audience obtained from a specific buy just as the word "effective" grammatically modified our statement of the goal. However, this score accounts for only part of the required modification, the remaining part being a measure of the degree a given vehicle will direct messages against potential customers in the desired proportions. This must also be measured numerically. We will label this score F_1, F_2, F_3, . . . to denote the specific scores for each vehicle.

The respective S and F chosen to represent these two numeric ratings can be made, for convenience, to stand for the subjective media qualities (S) and the fit of vehicle's audience distribution to desired distribution among potential customer groups (F).

If we then weight the total expected audience by both F and S, we will have a measure of effective exposure opportunities. To extend our symbolic representation of the goal, we define the following:

- *E* is the expected audience or exposures obtained from a single media buy of a given unit in a given vehicle.
- *W* is the weighted effective exposure opportunities obtained from each single purchase of a given unit of a given vehicle.
- *X* is the number of units of a specified type to be bought in a given vehicle.

The weighted effective exposure opportunities obtained from a single purchase, *W*, can then be expressed as follows:

$$W = F \times S \times E$$

The purchase of several such insertions, where *X* is the number of insertions, will result in the weighted effective exposure opportunities *X* times. This total is *G*, and *G* can be mathematically expressed as

$$G = W \times X$$

We can refer to *G*, as defined, as the gross exposure opportunity score, and the sum of all such *G*s obtained from a given media schedule is the quantity we wish to maximize.

The Greek letter Σ (sigma) is used as mathematical shorthand to represent a sum. Our statement of the goal can then be expressed mathematically as

$$\Sigma G = \text{Maximum}$$

In the above equation, the verbal statement of the goal has been translated into a mathematical expression which is called the objective function in an LP model.

To complete the translation of the problem, we must specifically state the rules or restrictions which govern the choices open to the media planner. These statements, translated into mathematical expressions, will be the restriction equations of an LP model. To begin with, we have already stated the restriction of the available funds. If we now state the cost of each unit which can be bought for our schedule, the total cost of each buy (neglecting discounts for the present) will simply be the unit cost times the number of insertions (or broadcast announcements). Symbolically, if *C* is the total cost of a buy, *U* is the unit cost, and *X* is the number of units, the cost of a buy will be

$$C = U \times X$$

If the costs of all buys in a schedule are added up, we can then state the cost restriction as

$$\Sigma\,(U \times X) \leqslant 1{,}000{,}000$$

This states that the cost of the entire schedule must be less than or equal to $1 million.

Other obvious restrictions to the media planner's actions are that all of the Xs (the number of insertions for each buy comprising the schedule) must be nonnegative. That is, either he buys no units in a vehicle or he buys some positive number of units, negative buys having no significance. This is mathematically stated as

$$X_i \geqslant 0$$

(where the i in X_i signifies any specified X).

All other restrictions depend on the circumstances of the specific problem. Let us assume some circumstances to illustrate this, bearing in mind that no attempt will be made to set up an exhaustive list of the possible restrictions that may appear in a real-life problem. The important point here is that we can specify as many restrictions as we believe have any bearing on the problem. So long as all of these restrictions state linear or to-scale relationships, the LP model is not limited in the number of restrictions which can be handled.

One restriction may be, for example, that the client always buys at least six full-page, black-and-white insertions in magazine A and expects the agency to continue this practice. This means that regardless of any other evaluation of this buy, we must run at least these six insertions. Of course, this media alternative may have sufficient value on its merits to indicate that more than six insertions should be included in an optimal schedule. If the media alternative of a full-page black-and-white insertion in magazine A has been labeled as possible buy number 1, then this restriction is stated as

$$X_1 \geqslant 6$$

Another restriction might be that at least $500,000 must be spent in television. If media alternatives 2, 3, 4, 5, and 6 represent all the eligible TV buys (specified time units on specified TV stations), then this restriction can be stated as follows:

$$U_2 X_2 + U_3 X_3 + U_4 X_4 + U_5 X_5 + U_6 X_6 \geqslant 500{,}000$$

where the Us represent the unit costs and the Xs the number of units to be bought.

Other restrictions will arise from the total number of buys which are possible during the campaign period. For example, if the period is one year and alternative 7 represents a full page in a monthly magazine, we cannot buy more than 12 of these insertions. This is represented as

$$X_7 \leqslant 12$$

There are several major problems of omission and commission connected with the simple LP media model of the type just described. One serious problem is the lack of linearity of such relationships as reach and frequency to the media schedule. Methods have been suggested to overcome some of these difficulties. However, these and other special methods introduce both mathematical and logical complexity into the model, making it difficult for the media planner to impose his judgment on the results. Also, these special methods often require too much computer time to make their use cost feasible. The convenience of the generally available LP computer programs, however, still make LP a method to be considered for special media planning problems. Lawrence F. Young has used a special formulation of LP for allocating gross advertising weight among local TV and radio stations where geographic weight distribution according to prescribed goals was the factor of main importance to an advertiser.

Heuristic Methods

Other major media models in use for the most part come under the heading of heuristic models. A heuristic model is one that does not guarantee an optimal solution by means of a mathematical proof. It instead uses mathematical or logical rules to seek a *nearly* optimal solution, or one that is at least better than an intuitive or trial and error solution would be.

Such models include the high assay model (Young & Rubicam) and the incremental analysis model (developed by Jack Landis and Lawrence F. Young for J. Walter Thompson). Both models have similar approaches to selecting media in that media units are selected one at a time, in sequential steps until some stopping point (such as spending the entire budget or attaining some goal level such as 80 percent reach) is reached. At each step in the selection process, all remaining available media units are evaluated to determine which one will contribute the greatest total weighted value for the least expenditure. That "best" unit is then selected and the process is repeated to select the next unit. This process is logically simple but the evaluation computation can be made as complex and extensive in scope as the model designer cares to make it. In practice, however, it has been the author's experience that complexity of scope, when provided for the user's application at his option, is generally not used. That is, the user will leave most of the optional input factors in the model set at neutral or their default positions. This is, again, because of the planner's need to understand the solution so that he can apply his judgment in modifying it.

*   *   *

In summary, media models are now viewed by their users in much more realistic perspective than in the first heady days of the 1960s, when many saw the demise of the media planner as imminent at the hands of a computer directed by a mad model builder. It is more widely realized that many unanswered questions in advertising and marketing theory make human judgment indispensable in formulating media plans. Models are, however, still being used, less now for their promotional value and more for the platform of more extensive evaluation of alternatives provided for media planners. The SCANS and FAST models, as examples, have been run at Dataplan for several hundred media planning applications. This continuing usage speaks for itself in attesting to the usefulness of computerized models to marketing managers.

23

MSPS and Media Planners

Tom Teng-pin Yu and Leslie M. Harris

MEDIA SELECTION AND PROGRAM SCHEDULE (MSPS) is a nonlinear mathematical model that uses simulation techniques designed toward optimal solutions in media selection.

Although the first announcement of the use of mathematical models in media planning was made in 1961, computers have not revolutionized media departments, media selection cannot be "scientifically" controlled, and individual judgment still remains the key element.

That point settled, advertising agencies are still moving ahead in their attempts to make more effective use of computers. The major function of MSPS is to maximize the marketing effectiveness of an advertising program, that is, to obtain the maximum possible impact on the pertinent marketing target with a given set of restrictions and within a given advertising budget.

Once this optimal schedule is composed, other media or marketing problems can be formulated and tested accordingly, and more objective and intelligent decision making can be derived or confirmed. The computed media schedule can be systematically and inexpensively tested as the new research results become available. Related media problems or tests can be easily performed in order to analyze market competition, variations in product packaging, pricing, copy content, and so forth. The periodical processing and continued research may show a clear indication where, when, and how a new schedule should be formulated. As a long-term objective, this model can be used as a base to integrate other related research and analysis into a total information and decision system for all advertising and marketing efforts.

A Brief History of Media Model Building

To consider the media selection problem in its proper context, a brief background of the history of advertising models in media selection may prove helpful.

1. *Simulation.* The simulation technique was first offered as a computerized media service by Simulmatics Corporation of New York. It estimated reach and frequency of a media schedule through simulation carried out by a computer. The model consisted of a panel of 2,944 individuals representing the population of the United States. The reach, frequency, and demographic distribution are generated for a list of media. The objective of the model is to calculate the number of people each of these schedules would reach and with what frequency.

2. *High assay media model.* In 1961, Young & Rubicam started work on what they called the high assay model, which was designed to test effectiveness in terms of media data, product information, market environment, and the time element based upon consumer-product behavior, consumer-media behavior, and consumer-advertising behavior. The goal of the model is to reach an optimal media schedule within budget limitations by considering the dynamic and interactive effects of audience reached, purchasing cycles, switching rates, and other market phenomena.

3. *Linear mathematical programming models.* The linear programming technique represented the first attempt to improve media effectiveness. These models were of two general types: C-E-I-R's media-matrix and BBDO's original and revised models. BBDO's revised model was designed to derive a media plan that would come as close as possible to achieving an optimum schedule (instead of maximizing exposures to the most effective advertising vehicles, which the original model did). The built-in constraints as the major input data are estimated indexes (C-E-I-R) and the REU (rated exposure unit) (BBDO). The latter are estimated values assigned by the agency experts as the effective audience to be exposed to an individual advertisement.

4. *Other models.* In addition, a number of other models have been re-

ported. They include the London Press Exchange's media model called CAM (computer assessment of media), which utilizes computer simulation to assess alternative television and print or print or television schedules submitted by media planners and the COMPASS or COUSIN system. COMPASS stands for computer optimal media planning and scheduling system. The model was basically a simulation system aimed at reach, frequency, and product usage. The project was originally supported by ten advertising agencies as a cooperative venture and programmed by the Diebold Group.

Basic Approaches

This list is by no means exhaustive. In general, the basic approaches used in building media models may be classified into four major groups: mathematical programming, iteration, simulation, and statistical methods.

1. *Mathematical programming.* In mathematical programming, media models have been formulated as linear programming, nonlinear programming, integer programming, and dynamic programming. These consist basically of two parts: the objective function, which is defined as the goal set for the media problem, and the constraints, which reflect the physical limitations of the problem in question.

When a media problem is formulated in nonlinear programming, integer programming, or dynamic programming form, it is generally oversimplified, and hence the result of such mathematics has relatively minimal practical value, although it is theoretically valid. The LP model was among the first group of media models developed. In practice, the model's usefulness is restricted mainly because the model has been unable to accurately measure media or vehicle duplications and is often obligated to use inaccurate or artificial data.

2. *Iteration or marginal analysis model.* The basic idea behind the iteration approach is that the additional vehicle that demonstrates the highest incremental impact on a schedule is included. The model will repeat its analysis until the budget is fully utilized and a schedule is completed. This approach attempts to optimize a schedule, level by level, according to the criterion selected by the media user. The virtue of this system is its ability to cope with the problem of duplication between media and vehicle exposure levels.

3. *Simulation technique.* The simulation technique is based primarily on using a perfect or near-perfect sample of the defined domain of the subject.

The advantage of simulation is that it takes the full complexity of the media-audience behavior or media-product-audience behavior into consideration. A good simulation system is expected to deliver correct and stable results every time. In conceptual terms, the simulation approach to the problem of media selection is a relatively satisfactory one. However, while the simulation approach is very useful in testing the relative merits of existing schedules, it has proved to be very difficult and expensive in building a media selection model because of its technical complexity and the numerous trials required to access sample data.

4. *Statistical method.* In general, the statistical approach is primarily used to fit an empirical formula to survey data. Then the model is employed to extrapolate information and parameters beyond the surveyed level of exposure of multiple media combinations. The usefulness of this approach is limited by the difficulty of dealing with a large amount of information, the statistical problem in deriving average parameters from the large amount of data, and the reassemblying problem in calculating the results from each level of computation. Since the capacity of modern computers is limited, the required computation and memory storage are often prohibitive.

In general, model building is extremely difficult, especially in the use of high-powered nonlinear mathematics. One major problem is that there is almost no previous experience in this uncharted territory. The initial stage of model building has been used to confirm or to test some basic concepts or theoretical foundations. Gradually, we hope to learn more from the behavior of the model itself than we now know from actual experience.

The Conceptual Design of IRC's MSPS

The framework, structure, or theoretical foundation of IRC's MSPS has been carefully designed and tested and is based upon the practical knowledge of media buyers and media planners. The framework and structure of the MSPS model consist of a number of mechanisms, devices, options, subroutines, and alternatives. All components are designed and programmed in a modular sense, and all possible interfacing mechanisms are integrated.

The theoretical foundation of this model is a binomial distribution function. The whole set of nonlinear mathematical equations are formulated and solved for n level of duplications, for each vehicle, or for a combination of multiple media vehicles. A large number of probabilities and parameters associated with each vehicle and each sample representation are solved for each of the levels. Each sample representation has its demographic and attribute identity. All duplications are performed at these detailed sample levels. All these probabilities, parameters, and other information are the input data to this model and will correctly compute all assigned functions. During the evaluation or selection, all these probabilities and parameters must be maintained intact in order to produce stable and faithful duplications, and yet they must be dynamic enough to fit in ever changing environments and adjust automatically to changing interfacing effects.

The duplication mechanism must always satisfy a sufficient number of functional relationships or mathematical equations for any number of exposure levels or any number of multiple media combinations. These mathematical equations are:

1. For a single issue of a magazine or a single telecast of a TV show, the net reach of the exposure must be equal to the average reach.
2. For more than one exposure level, the net reach of the schedule must be equal to the summation of all audience reached under all different frequencies.
3. The gross impression of a schedule is the summation of total audience reached for each frequency multiplied by the cardinal number of the frequency. For example, if a magazine is used twice, the gross impression is equal to the audience reached one time multiplied by one plus those reached twice multiplied by two.
4. Average reach must be equal to gross impression divided by the level of exposure. For example, for four issues of a magazine, the average reach equals the gross impression divided by four.
5. Average frequency must be equal to gross impression divided by net reach.
6. Demographic distribution must be equal to the weighted means of all vehicles and their respective exposure levels.
7. The audience reached in the household, individual population, or demographic groups (for example, region or age) must not be more than the equivalent size of the United States population.

The mechanisms and controls of the MSPS provide a set of necessary conditions for the correct performance of the model. The above equations are additional checks for the accurate duplication mechanism of the model. These seven mathematical equations are the real checks against available data to insure correct performance as well as to offer assurance for those levels where there are no actual available data to be checked. These seven equations should serve as minimum requirements to be met by any media model.

The major input data used in this model are reported by the standard survey services. Of course, a user may substitute his own estimates in place of the syndicated data. Once these input data are used, all output produced by the model will faithfully conform to them and satisfy the seven functional conditions for any level or any schedule attempted.

The selection mechanism of the MSPS is basically a marginal analysis approach. Each exposure level to be added to the schedule is the result of a complete marginal analysis of all available vehicles. Only the optimal one will be selected each time according to the selection criterion preset by the user. The process will be continued until the advertising budget is fully utilized. The operation of the selection mechanism may be best described by Exhibit 23–1.

Once a schedule is composed, the output produced is organized into mean-

Exhibit 23-1

The Flow Diagram of the MSPS' Selection Function

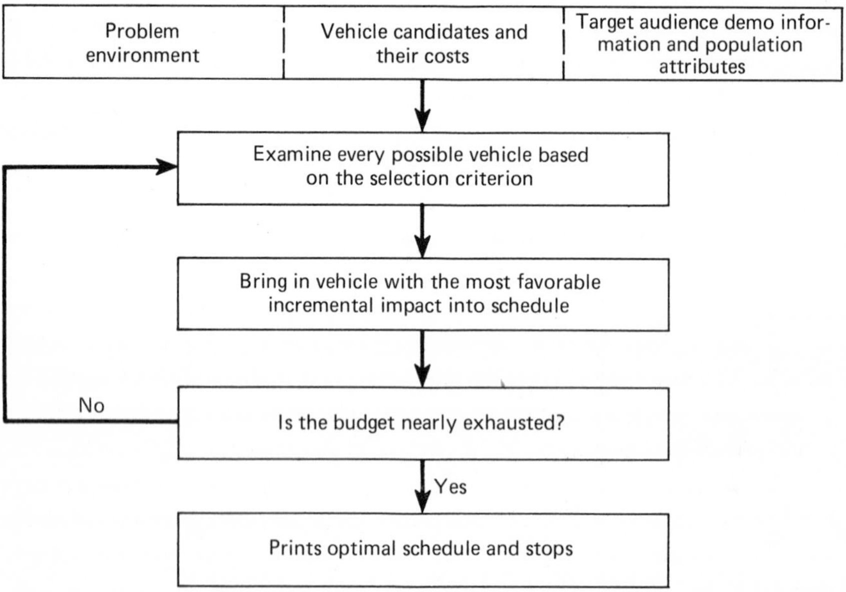

ingfully designed tables for all major demographic audience breakdowns. To show how MSPS works, we will examine a sample problem and its processed output later in this chapter.

What Kind of Problems May Be Solved by MSPS?

MSPS is a realistic model designed to process as many as 150 vehicles in one processing with multiple media and multiple exposure levels. It has been used in four phases of advertising activities: media planning, media selection, media evaluation, and media or marketing research. As mentioned before, the components of the basic model are integrated and programmed in modular fashion. This capacity permits interfacing with other existing computer systems for additional problem solving. The standard version of the model has demonstrated its capability to solve the following problems in media selection or schedule testing.

Media selection and program schedule. Given the target audience, selection criterion (net reach, average frequency, CPM (cost per thousand population), or a combination of the last two), campaign period, vehicle candidates suggested, demographic or subdemographic composition, cost structure for each vehicle suggested, and weighting value for the average reach of each vehicle candidate, the model selects the most favorable vehicle based on the selection criterion for each level of exposure added and composes an optimal schedule to meet the stated marketing objectives and budget limitation. The output indicates how the model selects each vehicle from the suggested candidates, adds each level of exposure to the schedule, and accumulates both total cost and total net reach. For each processing, a user may present the minimum or maximum level to be selected for each of the vehicle candidates suggested.

Testing existing program schedule. An old or existing media schedule, with its known vehicles and exposure levels, may be tested by this model for its reach and frequency as well as other information for each demographic or subdemographic group.

Testing new program or schedule. The testing of a new concept or a newly formulated schedule is handled the same way as processing an established schedule except that the list of vehicles and levels of exposure are preselected by personal judgment or other research findings.

Alternative media plans. For each media selection and program schedule, a number of alternative media plans may be requested and will be produced and reported. Each alternative media plan can exclude any vehicles, and a new media schedule is composed without using the excluded vehicles. The reason for requesting alternative media plans is that some TV shows or radio programs may be completely booked for ads and it is advisable to have some standby, substitute media plans.

Building reach and frequency time series for the product advertised. Each time period, say, every other month, an established schedule for an advertised product will be processed with the up-to-date tape if telecast media are used. The output obtained is deseasonalized and plotted and is accumulated as a time series.

This time series is very important for media research and marketing study because the continuous data can reveal significant trends and information for sales analysis. When a sufficient amount of data has been collected, a quarterly index may be computed to facilitate comparative marketing research.

Measurement of industry advertising. Based upon published data by major advertisers in a given industry for each advertised product, a periodical processing can be undertaken to report the magnitude and fluctuations of industry's advertising effort.

Industry advertising effort usually shows a considerable pulling power for the sales of a member advertiser. The changes of the combined schedule may reflect a pattern of a new trend or new philosophy, which serves as a leading factor in determining an advertiser's new budget as well as new strategy reflected by the criteria selected for a media schedule.

The same type of processing may be performed to measure competitive efforts. In this case, local spot media as well as print should be focused upon for careful examination. The obtained output, together with market potentials, market shares, consumer behavior, and other economic data in association with sales records, forms a meaningful basis for marketing analysis.

Effectiveness report. Based upon the information of returned coupons or warrants, surveys, and special studies, a user may have a knowledge of the correct percentage of the audience reached from each of the vehicles—who are the users or buyers of the product advertised. A computer analysis may be conducted by inserting such percentages as weighting values for each vehicle used, and the output so obtained is considered to be an effectiveness reach report.

Forgetting or remembering report. If the forgetting or remembering rate of each vehicle's reach is known, a report for this purpose may be obtained by using the rate as a weighting value for each vehicle used.

Noting score report. Based upon the published noting score and an estimated audience's recognition of the ad in each vehicle used, a report may be obtained by employing the noting score as weighting values in the computer processing. This list of applications is by no means exhaustive. It merely reflects the usefulness and flexibility of the MSPS model and helps the user to formulate his own problem and to process it in his own way. MSPS has also demonstrated its usefulness in other areas.

Substitution device. Users may substitute their own estimates for the reach, frequency, and demographic distribution of the audience reached by trade magazines, radio programs, local newspapers, and other media.

For example, if a user knows the data for a particular radio program that is not reported by the standard services, he may substitute the TV data for the radio program by adjusting the average reach proportionally if the TV show has the same percent distribution of frequency and demographic information. The substitution device enables users to include all possible media or vehicles in the analysis.

Weighting value device. The weighting value device in the model is a useful tool in problem formulation and problem solving.

For example, if a user puts a five-color, full-page ad on the front page of a leading magazine, and he has the knowledge that the current average reach of the magazine is 10 percent more than reported by a syndicated service; a five-color ad should attract 3 percent additional audience; and the front-page position would add 2 percent extra; thus the weighting value for this vehicle will be $1.100 \times 1.030 \times 1.020 = 1.156$. A weighting value may then be used in order to correctly reflect a group of actually existing phenomena.

Weighting value for demographic groups. By a weighting device built into the model, a user can create his own demographic or subdemographic configuration.

For example, if a firm is conducting a campaign in the North East region and its findings indicate that in low-income households, only 20 percent are effective buyers of the product advertised, and in the upper-income group, only 85 percent, the user may weight the lower-income group and the upper-income group by 0.200 and 0.850, respectively, and eliminate other groups.

For those who are working with local market problems, it is relatively easy to combine the built-in devices. For example, a firm is currently conducting a campaign for its product in the Tri-States market area located in the North Central region, and he has a good knowledge about the relative reaches for both the Tri-States market area and the North Central region in each of the national or local media used. By means of substitution, elimination, and weighting, the computer processing can provide the correct results.

Syndicated product or brand tapes. Although the model utilizes all standard demographic classifications, optional analysis can be added by syndicated product tapes. For example, a user may be interested in evaluating a more highly defined audience for his product, for example, women in the 35–49 age group, college-educated, working part-time, living in the suburban part of the North East region, their husband not present, having children in the 6–17 age group, and attending church regularly.

Extended target audience definition. A user may select any target audience information from the product tapes as additional restriction of his target audience.

Product usage. If a user's product or products are selected from syndicated tapes, a new set of output, based upon the users of the product or products advertised, will be provided.

Ten major regions. If Simmons' product tapes are used, the user may request and obtain a report of the audience reached in the ten major regions.

Major metropolitan areas. A user may select and obtain reports showing the audience reached in any or all of the major metropolitan areas available on the tapes.

Special reports. If a user has a product tape which contains a set of special data collected by the syndicate's service through a special arrangement, such as *Look* magazine's zip code, an output of this nature may be requested and obtained!

The preceding five sets of output as well as the output produced based upon the reach and frequency of the optimal schedule can be obtained in a single processing. In addition, MSPS may be used to compute other important information as well.

Find heavy users. By analyzing the information on a syndicate's product tapes, MSPS can statistically determine the characteristics of the heavy users of the product.

Find a group of the most favorable vehicles for the product. Based upon the syndicate's product tapes, MSPS can select the group of vehicles that reach the highest level of audience for the product.

The last two forms of computer analysis can be obtained from a market survey. It is often the case that the computer processing is more economical.

The Importance of Planning
Media Schedules More Scientifically

The contributions of advertising in a capitalist economy have long been under ardent debate, and it is likely that the social merits of advertising in this country will be eternally discussed by the economists. However, it is generally recognized in the business world that advertising has been one of the major factors in helping us to achieve higher economic levels. The objective of the advertising industry is improvement of the welfare of our economic world as well as the profit maximization of our business world.

In general, the advertising effort may be classified into planning, media selection, advertising measurement, and control. The aspects of these endeavors of most concern to us are media planning and media selection. The importance of planning and selection is increased by the following considerations.

The close relationship between advertising and industrial growth. Based upon statistical data, the marketing of major consumer products such as foods, drugs, automobiles, cosmetics, soft drinks, liquors, and tobacco products are highly dependent upon sales promotion and advertising. And these are the very industries which constitute the major portion of the private sector of our economy.

Advertising—the general feature of oligopolistic or monopolistic competition. The industries mentioned here are either oligopolistic or monopolistic in this country. In these industries, sales promotion and advertising are essential in creating brand differentiation.

Aggregate advertising expenditures. Aggregate advertising expenditures have grown from less than $6 billion in 1950 to more than $18 billion in 1968.*

Relationship between advertising and economic growth. The urgent problem is now how to improve the quality of services performed by advertising and how to reduce the operating costs of these efforts. Some advertising agencies are beginning to feel that media planning and media selection can be handled more scientifically, and the cost of performing these services can be considerably reduced.

Research—a bottleneck of modern advertising. Since the development of Agostini's Formula and Metheringham's Estimate, high hopes have existed among the advertising professionals that a realistic media model may soon be built, which is capable of more effectively handling media planning, media selection, advertising measurement and control, and media or marketing research problems.

In the past years, rewarding results have been obtained from operations research, management sciences, information technology, and modern com-

* Seymour Banks, Ronald Reisman, and Charles Yang, *Advertising Age,* March 3, 1969.

puter technology. Various systems or models have been built for production scheduling, inventory control, transportation or distribution, investment analysis, product or brand switching, sales forecasting, and so forth; but researchers have faced an impasse where media planning, media selection, or marketing is a subset of the domain to be investigated. An optimal schedule or even a semi-optimal schedule for an advertising effort, as generally conceived, can bring actual sales or effectiveness of the campaign and media performance much closer. More scientific media planning and media selection is becoming increasingly essential.

In summary, like any other system or model, MSPS does have its limitations. MSPS is intended to be a useful tool for a media expert, not a panacea in itself. Further improvement of this model depends upon better input data collection and better scientific techniques. The former will depend upon the efforts of media data surveys, and the latter may be centered upon the progress made in the rigorous application of more advanced mathematical concepts to the problems of advertising planning and advertising strategies.

THE SAMPLE PROBLEM

Exhibit 23–2 is the output of a test run from the MSPS model. In this run, CPM is used as the selection criterion, and the cost structure of the vehicles used is arbitrarily assigned. The purpose of this run is merely to demonstrate the functions or features of this model. It is not the intention to weigh the relative merits of the vehicles used.

The early copies of the 1968 Simmons publications on reach, frequency, and demographic distribution may be used to check the accuracy of the sample output. Other surveys or special studies may be used if they are comparable and consistent with the Simmons publications.

Exhibit 23–2 is self-explanatory. However, the following brief explanation may be helpful. The description follows the same sequence as the sample output.

A. Input data. The input data prepared by the user are printed out in this section. There are eight statements describing the scope and nature of the processing.

B. Computing flow—step by step. This section shows the actual performance of the selection conducted by the model, step by step. Each additional level or additional vehicle added is the result of the complete analysis of the available vehicle candidates based upon the selection criterion. The level

(*text continues on page 293*)

Exhibit 23-2

Sample of IRC Computerized Media Selection and Programming Schedule

IRC-MSPS
(2,000.)

IRC

1969

Sample Example of IRC Computerized Media Selection and Programming Schedule.
This Processing Is Prepared by
Innovation Research Corporation

U.S. Individual Population Section

Units: Cost = $00
CPM = Dollar
Audience = 000

A. INPUT DATA

1. Selecting Media for Optimal Schedule
2. Campaign Period: Starting Week 1, Ending Week 36
3. Number of Preassigned Vehicles = 2
4. Total Number of Vehicles = 9
5. Selecting Criterion: $ Cost per Thousand Net Reach
6. Total Ad Budget is $5,000
7. The Media Vehicle Information:

Vehicle Name	Starting Week	Max Level Per Week	Max Level Per Month	Regular Rate	1st Disc Rate	2nd Disc Rate	1st Disc Level	2nd Disc Level	Preassign Level	Weighting Value	Summer Rate	Xmas Rate
Preassigned Vehicles												
Family Circle	1	0	1	274	249	224	5	10	3	1.000	1.000	1.000
Look	1	0	2	380	350	315	5	10	2	1.000	1.000	1.000
Vehicle Candidates												
Family Circle	1	0	1	274	249	224	5	10	3	1.000	1.000	1.000
Good Housekpng	1	0	1	232	211	190	5	10	0	1.000	1.000	1.000
Life	1	1	0	387	352	319	5	10	0	1.000	1.000	1.000
Look	1	0	2	380	350	315	5	10	2	1.000	1.000	1.000
McCall's	1	0	1	359	326	293	5	10	0	1.000	1.000	1.000

A. INPUT DATA (cont)

Vehicle Name	Starting Week	Max Level Per Week	Max Level Per Month	Regular Rate	1st Disc Rate	2nd Disc Rate	1st Disc Level	2nd Disc Level	Preassign Level	Weighting Value	Summer Rate	X-Max Rate
Vehicle Candidates												
Newsweek	1	1	0	172	161	149	5	10	0	1.000	1.000	1.000
Reader's Digest	1	0	1	513	466	419	5	10	0	1.000	1.000	1.000
Time	1	1	0	211	192	173	5	10	0	1.000	1.000	1.000
Women's Day	1	0	1	260	231	203	5	10	0	1.000	1.000	1.000

8. Options Selected:

Alternative Media Plan	Deleted Vehicle
1	Life
2	Time

Seasonal Index for TV Show(s) is Not Used.

B. COMPUTING PROCEDURE – STEP BY STEP

Vehicle	Level Added	Unit Cost	Total Cost	Total Net Reach	Total Exposure Level
Family Circle	3	274.	822.	22,838.	3.
Look	2	380.	1,582.	59,414.	5.
Life	1	387.	1,969.	66,096.	6.
Life	1	387.	2,356.	70,294.	7.
Life	1	387.	2,743.	73,465.	8.
Life	1	387.	3,130.	76,152.	9.
Look	1	380.	3,510.	78,505.	10.
Life	1	352.	3,722.	80,748.	11.
Life	1	352.	4,074.	82,859.	12.
Life	1	352.	4,426.	84,859.	13.
Life	1	352.	4,778.	86,761.	14.
Life	1	352.	5,130.	88,574.	15.

(Optimal Schedule)

Vehicle Selected	Exposure Level
Family Circle	3
Life	9
Look	3

The Net Reach for Each Vehicle is the Marginal Net Reach.
The Total Net Reach is the Sum of the Net Reach of Each Vehicles.

Vehicle	Net Reach	Gross Reach	Avg Reach	Known Reach	KR/AR	Avg Frequency
Family Cicle	22,838.	39,905.	13,302.	13,299.	1.000	
Life	57,360.	296,583.	32,954.	32,920.	0.999	
Look	7,960.	95,586.	31,862.	31,834.	0.999	
Total	88,146.	432,040.				4.901

Total Cost for Optimal Media Plan = $5,130.

D. ALTERNATIVE MEDIA PLAN(S)

1. Deleted Vehicle   Life

Vehicles Selected	Exposure Level
Family Circle	3
Look	13

Net Reach = 89,601.
Gross Reach = 454,045.
Total Cost for This Plan = $4,917.

2. Deleted Vehicle   Time

The Vehicle is Not Selected in the Optimal Schedule, Hence No Alternative Media Plan is Needed.

F. OUTPUT BY DEMOGRAPHICS

Distribution of Frequency by Sex and Age

Freq/Age	Male Under 2	2-5	6-11	12-17	18-34	35-49	50+	Female Under 2	2-5	6-11	12-17	18-34	35-49	50+	Total
1	0.	0.	0.	0.	4,637.	3,887.	4,363.	0.	0.	0.	0.	3,532.	2,960.	3,323.	22,701.
2	0.	0.	0.	0.	1,582.	1,364.	1,900.	0.	0.	0.	0.	1,983.	1,709.	2,381.	10,920.
3	0.	0.	0.	0.	656.	598.	768.	0.	0.	0.	0.	1,737.	1,584.	2,034.	7,378.
4	0.	0.	0.	0.	388.	360.	303.	0.	0.	0.	0.	1,221.	1,133.	954.	4,358.
5	0.	0.	0.	0.	445.	406.	395.	0.	0.	0.	0.	724.	661.	642.	3,273.
6	0.	0.	0.	0.	828.	729.	765.	0.	0.	0.	0.	828.	730.	765.	4,645.
7	0.	0.	0.	0.	1,438.	1,242.	1,149.	0.	0.	0.	0.	1,313.	1,134.	1,409.	7,326.
8	0.	0.	0.	0.	1,894.	1,621.	1,309.	0.	0.	0.	0.	1,754.	1,502.	1,213.	9,293.
9	0.	0.	0.	0.	1,794.	1,534.	1,120.	0.	0.	0.	0.	1,761.	1,506.	1,100.	8,815.
10	0.	0.	0.	0.	1,164.	1,001.	682.	0.	0.	0.	0.	1,273.	1,094.	746.	5,961.
11	0.	0.	0.	0.	474.	413.	263.	0.	0.	0.	0.	628.	547.	349.	2,673.
12	0.	0.	0.	0.	100.	89.	51.	0.	0.	0.	0.	194.	173.	99.	707.
13	0.	0.	0.	0.	7.	6.	3.	0.	0.	0.	0.	33.	31.	14.	94.
14	0.	0.	0.	0.	1	1.	0.	0.	0.	0.	0.	3.	3.	1.	8.
15	0.	0.	0.	0.	0.	0.	0.	0.	0.	0.	0.	0.	0.	0.	0.
Total	0.	0.	0.	0.	15,407.	13,252.	13,072.	0.	0.	0.	0.	16,984.	14,767.	14,669.	88,154.
Net Reach															
Pop (000)	0.0	0.0	0.0	0.0	15,407.	13,252.	13,072.	0.0	0.0	0.0	0.0	16,984.	14,707.	14,669.	88,154.
Percent	0.0	0.0	0.0	0.0	100.00	100.00	100.00	0.0	0.0	0.0	0.0	100.00	100.00	100.00	100.00
CPM	0.0	0.0	0.0	0.0	33.30	38.71	39.24	0.0	0.0	0.0	0.0	30.21	34.74	34.97	5.82
Gross Impression															
Pop (000)	0.0	0.0	0.0	0.0	78,030.	67,441.	57,213.	0.0	0.0	0.0	0.0	87,695.	76,330.	65,429.	432,154.
Percent	0.0	0.0	0.0	0.0	506.44	508.92	437.69	0.0	0.0	0.0	0.0	516.35	516.90	446.03	490.23
CPM	0.0	0.0	0.0	0.0	6.57	7.61	8.97	0.0	0.0	0.0	0.0	5.85	6.72	7.84	1.19
Frequency															
Average	0.0	0.0	0.0	0.0	5.06	5.09	4.38	0.0	0.0	0.0	0.0	5.16	5.17	4.46	4.90
Std. Dev.	0.0	0.0	0.0	0.0	3.56	3.55	3.38	0.0	0.0	0.0	0.0	3.42	3.40	3.20	3.29
C.V.	0.0	0.0	0.0	0.0	70.30	69.68	77.27	0.0	0.0	0.0	0.0	66.20	65.72	71.68	67.02

F. OUTPUT BY DEMOGRAPHICS (cont)

Distribution of Frequency by Lady of House (Adult Women)

Freq/Age	Employed			Unemployed			Other			Total
	18-34	35-49	50 +	18-34	35-49	50 +	18-34	35-49	50 +	
1	2,387.	2,001.	2,246.	141.	118.	133.	1,003.	841.	944.	9,815.
2	1,224.	1,055.	1,469.	81.	70.	97.	678.	585.	814.	6,073.
3	937.	855.	1,097.	72.	66.	84.	728.	664.	852.	5,355.
4	644.	597.	503.	50.	46.	39.	527.	489.	412.	3,308.
5	433.	396.	384.	29.	27.	26.	261.	239.	232.	2,026.
6	542.	477.	501.	33.	29.	30.	254.	223.	234.	2,323.
7	867.	749.	693.	52.	45.	41.	394.	340.	315.	3,497.
8	1,149.	984.	795.	69.	59.	48.	536.	459.	370.	4,469.
9	1,138.	973.	711.	70.	59.	43.	553.	473.	346.	4,366.
10	805.	692.	472.	50.	43.	30.	417.	359.	244.	3,113.
11	383.	334.	213.	25.	22.	14.	220.	191.	122.	1,523.
12	110.	98.	56.	8.	7.	4.	76.	68.	39.	466.
13	16.	15.	7.	1.	1.	1.	16.	15.	7.	79.
14	1.	1.	1.	0.	0.	0.	1.	1.	1.	7.
15	0.	0.	0.	0.	0.	0.	0.	0.	0.	0.
Total	10,638.	9,228.	9,147.	681.	592.	590.	5,664.	4,946.	4,932.	46,419.
Net Reach										
Adult Women (000)	10,638.	9,228.	9,147.	681.	592.	590.	5,664.	4,946.	4,932.	46,419.
Percent	100.00	100.00	100.00	100.00	100.00	100.00	100.00	100.00	100.00	100.00
CPM	48.22	55.59	56.08	753.08	865.83	869.32	90.57	103.71	104.02	11.05
Gross Impression										
Adult Women (000)	54,971.	47,772.	40,850.	3,496.	3,044.	2,615.	29,228.	25,514.	21,963.	229,452.
Percent	516.73	517.68	446.58	513.21	513.74	443.10	515.99	515.82	445.36	494.30
CPM	9.33	10.74	12.56	146.74	168.54	196.19	17.55	20.11	23.36	2.24
Frequency										
Average	5.17	5.18	4.47	5.13	5.14	4.43	5.16	5.16	4.45	4.94
Std. Dev.	5.26	5.27	4.58	5.22	5.23	4.54	5.26	5.25	4.56	5.04
C.V.	101.85	101.84	102.47	101.78	101.76	102.39	101.85	101.85	102.48	102.02

F. OUTPUT BY DEMOGRAPHICS (cont)

Distribution of Frequency by Employment Status

Employment Freq.	Employed (129,115.)	Unemployed (4,050.)	Other (63,483.)	Total (196,648.)
1	15,346.	907.	6,449.	22,702.
2	6,739.	446.	3,735.	10,920.
3	3,981.	305.	3,092.	7,378.
4	2,298.	179.	1,882.	4,358.
5	1,959.	132.	1,182.	3,273.
6	3,038.	184.	1,423.	4,645.
7	4,838.	289.	2,198.	7,326.
8	6,089.	366.	2,838.	9,293.
9	5,697.	348.	2,770.	8,815.
10	3,772.	236.	1,953.	5,961.
11	1,632.	106.	935.	2,673.
12	402.	28.	277.	707.
13	46.	4.	45.	94.
14	4.	0.	4.	8.
15	0.	0.	0.	0.
Total	55,841.	3,532.	28,781.	88,154.

Net Reach

	Employed	Unemployed	Other	Total
Population (000)	55,841.	3,532.	28,781.	88,154.
Percent	100.00	100.00	100.00	100.00
CPM	9.19	145.26	17.82	5.82

Gross Impression

	Employed	Unemployed	Other	Total
Population (000)	272,981.	17,210.	141,960.	432,151.
Percent	488.85	487.31	493.23	490.22
CPM	1.88	29.81	3.61	1.19

Frequency

	Employed	Unemployed	Other	Total
Average	4.89	4.87	4.93	4.90
Std. Dev.	4.99	4.97	5.03	3.29
C.V.	102.07	102.06	102.03	67.02

F. OUTPUT BY DEMOGRAPHICS (cont)

Distribution of Frequency by Sex

Sex Freq.	Male (96,582.)	Female (100,066.)	Total (196,648.)
1	12,887.	9,814.	22,702.
2	4,847.	6,073.	10,920.
3	2,022.	5,355.	7,378.
4	1,050.	3,308.	4,358.
5	1,246.	2,026.	3,273.
6	2,321.	2,324.	4,645.
7	3,829.	3,497.	7,326.
8	4,824.	4,469.	9,293.
9	4,449.	4,366.	8,815.
10	2,848.	3,113.	5,961.
11	1,150.	1,523.	2,673.
12	241.	466.	707.
13	16.	79.	94.
14	1.	7.	8.
15	0.	0.	0.
Total	41,731.	46,420.	88,154.
Net Reach			
Population (000)	41,731.	46,420	88,154.
Percent	100.00	100.00	100.00
CPM	12.29	11.05	5.82
Gross Impression			
Population (000)	202,684.	229,454.	432,151.
Percent	485.69	494.30	490.22
CPM	2.53	2.24	1.19
Frequency			
Average	4.86	4.94	4.90
Std. Dev.	4.96	5.04	3.29
C.V.	102.10	102.02	67.02

F. OUTPUT BY DEMOGRAPHICS (cont)

Distribution of Frequency by Age

Age Freq.	Under 2 (8,846.)	2-5 (17,715.)	6-11 (24,321.)	12-17 (21,629.)	18-34 (38,370.)	35-49 (40,995.)	50 + (44,773.)	Total (196,648.)
1	0.	0.	0.	0.	8,169.	6,847.	7,686.	22,702.
2	0.	0.	0.	0.	3,565.	3,073.	4,282.	10,920.
3	0.	0.	0.	0.	2,393.	2,182.	2,802.	7,378.
4	0.	0.	0.	0.	1,609.	1,493.	1,256.	4,358.
5	0.	0.	0.	0.	1,169.	1,067.	1,037.	3,273.
6	0.	0.	0.	0.	1,656.	1,459.	1,530.	4,645.
7	0.	0.	0.	0.	2,751.	2,376.	2,198.	7,326.
8	0.	0.	0.	0.	3,648.	3,123.	2,522.	9,293.
9	0.	0.	0.	0.	3,555.	3,040.	2,220.	8,815.
10	0.	0.	0.	0.	2,437.	2,096.	1,428.	5,961.
11	0.	0.	0.	0.	1,102.	959.	612.	2,673.
12	0.	0.	0.	0.	295.	263.	150.	707.
13	0.	0.	0.	0.	40.	37.	17.	94.
14	0.	0.	0.	0.	3.	3.	1.	8.
15	0.	0.	0.	0.	0.	0.	0.	0.
Total	0.	0.	0.	0.	32,392.	28,020.	27,742.	88,154.
Net Reach								
Population (000)	0.	0.	0.	0.	32,392.	28,020.	27,742.	88,154.
Percent	0.0	0.0	0.0	0.0	100.00	100.00	100.00	100.00
CPM	0.0	0.0	0.0	0.0	15.84	18.31	18.49	5.82
Gross Impression								
Population (000)	0.	0.	0.	0.	165,731.	143,776.	122,647.	432,151.
Percent	0.0	0.0	0.0	0.0	511.63	513.12	442.10	490.22
CPM	0.0	0.0	0.0	0.0	3.10	3.57	4.18	1.19
Frequency								
Average	0.0	0.0	0.0	0.0	5.12	5.13	4.42	4.90
Std. Dev.	0.0	0.0	0.0	0.0	5.21	5.23	4.53	3.29
C.V.	0.0	0.0	0.0	0.0	101.89	101.88	102.52	67.02

F. OUTPUT BY DEMOGRAPHICS (cont)

Distribution of Frequency by Education

Education Freq.	GS or Less	1-3 Yr HS	4 Yr HS	College or Higher	Total
1	2,574.	4,053.	8,725.	7,350.	22,702.
2	1,238.	1,950.	4,197.	3,535.	10,920.
3	837.	1,317	2,835.	2,389.	7,378.
4	494.	778.	1,675.	1,411.	4,358.
5	371.	584.	1,258.	1,060.	3,273.
6	527.	829.	1,785.	1,504.	4,645.
7	831.	1,308.	2,815	2,372.	7,326.
8	1,054.	1,659.	3,571.	3,009.	9,293.
9	1,000.	1,574.	3,388.	2,854.	8,815.
10	676.	1,064.	2,291.	1,930.	5,961.
11	303.	477.	1,027.	866.	2,673.
12	80.	126.	272.	229.	707.
13	11.	17.	36.	31.	94.
14	1.	1.	3.	3.	8.
15	0.	0.	0.	0.	0.
Total	9,996.	15,739.	33,879.	28,541.	88,154.

Net Reach

	GS or Less	1-3 Yr HS	4 Yr HS	College or Higher	Total
Population (000)	9,996.	15,739.	33,879.	28,541.	88,154.
Percent	100.00	100.00	100.00	100.00	100.00
CPM	51.32	32.59	15.14	17.97	5.82

Gross Impression

	GS or Less	1-3 Yr HS	4 Yr HS	College or Higher	Total
Population (000)	49,004.	77,154.	166,080.	139,912.	432,151.
Percent	490.22	490.22	490.22	490.22	490.22
CPM	10.47	6.65	3.09	3.67	1.19

Frequency

	GS or Less	1-3 Yr HS	4 Yr HS	College or Higher	Total
Average	4.90	4.90	4.90	4.90	4.90
Std. Dev.	5.00	5.00	5.00	5.00	3.29
C.V.	102.05	102.05	102.06	102.06	67.02

F. OUTPUT BY DEMOGRAPHICS (cont)

Distribution of Frequency by Profession

Profession Freq.	White Collar	Skilled Laborer	Unskilled Laborer	Not Employed	Total
1	4,190.	666.	3,466.	14,380.	22,702.
2	2,016.	320.	1,667.	6,917.	10,920.
3	1,362.	216.	1,126.	4,673	7,378.
4	804.	128.	665.	2,760.	4,358.
5	604.	96.	500.	2,073.	3,273.
6	857.	136.	709.	2,942.	4,645.
7	1,352.	215.	1,118.	4,640.	7,326.
8	1,715.	273.	1,419.	5,886.	9,293.
9	1,627.	259.	1,346.	5,584.	8,815.
10	1,100.	175.	910.	3,776.	5,961.
11	493.	78.	408.	1,693.	2,673.
12	131.	21.	108.	448.	707.
13	17.	3.	14.	60.	94.
14	1.	0.	1.	5.	8.
15	0.	0.	0.	0.	0.
Total	16,272.	2,587.	13,458.	55,838.	88,154.

Net Reach

	White Collar	Skilled Laborer	Unskilled Laborer	Not Employed	Total
Population (000)	16,272	2,587.	13,458.	55,838.	88,154.
Percent	100.00	100.00	100.00	100.00	100.00
CPM	31.53	198.34	38.12	9.19	5.82

Gross Impression

	White Collar	Skilled Laborer	Unskilled Laborer	Not Employed	Total
Population (000)	79,767.	12,680.	65,976.	273,728.	432,151.
Percent	490.22	490.22	490.22	490.22	490.22
CPM	6.43	40.46	7.78	1.87	1.19

Frequency

	White Collar	Skilled Laborer	Unskilled Laborer	Not Employed	Total
Average	4.90	4.90	4.90	4.90	4.90
Std. Dev.	5.00	5.00	5.00	5.00	3.29
C.V.	102.05	102.03	102.05	102.06	67.02

of exposure, total cost, and total net reach will be gradually accumulated until the total advertising budget is utilized or less than $15,000. The level of $15,000 is an artificial cutting-off point which may be changed if necessary.

C. Output summary. The net reach used in this section is a marginal net reach, and the total net reach is the summation of the marginals. The average reach computed is obtained from the derived gross impression. The known reach is the average reach published by Simmons. The ratio of KR/AR is the ratio of the last two, which reflects the seven mathematical conditions discussed in the text and shows a discrepancy, if there is any, between them because of demographic group exclusion, weighting, or the application of weighting values to the average reaches of the vehicles used. If none of these adjustments or weighting applies, the number reported in that column may be 0.999 or 1.001 for each of the vehicles. This merely indicates the gaining or losing of one-tenth of 1 percent as a result of the rounding errors of the lengthy computation. In a normal case, each of the numbers should be 1.000.

The model is one of a few which may show the result of sequential effect for large schedules (slightly different results may be obtained if a different sequence is followed) and the rounding errors. In normal cases, the sequential effect is too small to be recognized even though it is there. For the final report, the vehicle sequence (rather than level by level) is employed because it is much closer to reality. (See Tables C and F in Exhibit 23–2.)

D. Alternative media plan. The first alternative media plan is computed by eliminating *Life*. The second one is intended to eliminate an additional vehicle, *Time*. Since *Time* is not selected in the optimal schedule, no alternative schedule is actually produced. The alternative media plan differs from the optimal schedule, because some vehicle was eliminated from the vehicle candidate pool. It is possible, under an unusual circumstance, for the alternative media plan to show a favorable result because the complex discount or cost structure of the final schedule could not be anticipated during the process of selection where optimization is performed level by level. Exhibit 23–2 illustrates this. At the cutting-off point of the optimal schedule, the cost for the nine issues of *Life* is its first discount rate and for the three issues of *Look,* its premium rate.

However, the 13 issues of *Look* in the alternative media plan is based on its second discount rate. In addition to that, the ratio of the second discount rate to the first discount rate is 90.0 percent for *Look* and 90.6 percent for *Life*. Otherwise, the optimal schedule is still optimal, based upon the vehicle candidate pool, the selection criterion, and the rules of the game.

F. Output of the optimal schedule. Between D and F, there is E, which is reserved to report the selected input information from a syndicate's tapes, which are not used here for this case.

Under F, there are seven output tables. The total reach, total gross impression, average reach, and average frequency may be checked against those reported by syndicates. The demographic distributions may also be checked by multiplying the syndicates' demographics and the marginal net reach of each vehicle selected.

Under each subdemographic group, CPM is computed based upon the total cost of the schedule. This is very useful when a particular subdemographic group is the coverage as the target audience. However, if the whole population is designated as the target audience, a proportional adjustment of CPM may be performed either by the ratios of the census reports or by the actual reaches among them, and the resultant findings should be comparable with the CPM reported under the total column of the output.

Computing or processing time. The described sample problem (see Exhibit 23–2) and its output attached are processed on an IBM 360–75 computer. The computing time (actual processing time) is two minutes.

24

The ARTS System

Joel N. Axelrod and A. R. Solomon

T<small>HERE IS</small> an innovative computer-based system at Xerox that uses the acronym, ARTS. This acronym stands for advertising reporting test system. The system is currently in the process of being phased into operation as a working tool for advertising management. Even on the basis of minimal experience, it can be said with confidence that a system of this type is of significant value to the industrial advertiser when determining the recipients of his direct mail advertising and monitoring the resultant sales effect of this advertising.

Before proceeding to the solution, let us examine the problem that ARTS was designed to solve. Sending out direct mail to a significant number of addresses is an expensive undertaking. Yet in most cases the industrial advertiser does not know the effect of his mailing. Did he send the mail to genuine prospects? Did he send duplicate mail to some prospects while totally missing others in his target market? How many of the prospects to whom the mail is addressed subsequently become customers? Does the revenue from these customers justify the expense of the mailing? Although conceptually the answer to each of these questions is very simple to determine, pragmatically, the large data bases and the lack of an adequate analytic framework make the task very difficult. As a result, the usual practice is to make decisions without a factual basis. The advertiser assumes that the direct mail pays for itself, pointing to individual instances in which he can positively state that advertising was the cause of the prospect's becoming a customer or at least a contributing factor. While reassuring to an anxious ad manager, individual case histories are hardly an adequate basis for decisions regarding significant expenditures of money on direct mail.

Clearly, a procedure was needed that would enable Xerox to select the target for direct mail and then to establish whether direct mail contributed positively to the marketing effort.

The Solution

The first step was the establishment of a numbering system that enables the company to interrelate the various files. For example, there are files organized by establishment and files organized by type of equipment. By the use of a cross-reference system, in which each establishment is assigned a unique number, the company can identify which customers have what types of equipment. This gives Xerox the capability to use direct mail selectively. Xerox might, for example, send out a description of a new use to all current customers for the 2400 copier/duplicator or announce the availability of an accessory for the 720 copier to all users of this equipment. This represents a significant step from the prior practice. Previously, for example, mailings were sent to all machine locations, with the result that at least one major customer received more than 200 copies of the same material.

The necessity for cross-referencing is, of course, a function of the complexity of the Xerox product line and the size of the customer list. With a single product and a limited list of customers, such a procedure would be superfluous. But with multiple products and a growing number of customers, it is wise to establish such a system early in the game. Xerox's experience gives credence to the belief that it is far cheaper to start off with a good numbering system than it is to institute the system once the files are massive. It already has spent over 250 man-months of clerical time plus substantial supervisory time adding a numbering system to the files—without fully bringing the files up to date. (Once the files are up to date, an ongoing effort will be required to keep them current. This is true no matter when the numbering system is introduced.) The significance of these numbers is that they are many times the incremental effort that would have been required to put in such a system when Xerox was a far smaller firm.

The numbering system used involves the identification of the industry and zip codes in which the company operates, the company size, and also the relationship of the particular establishment to any parent company. It is a logical progression to apply this same type of numbering system to purchased mailing lists, thereby greatly increasing the power of the ARTS system. That is, this step makes it possible to determine where the opportunity for advertising to noncustomers is greatest. Xerox has developed programs that enable programmers to simply run a customer list up against the mailing lists, producing a printout which might say that 5 percent of this mailing list are customers, 25 percent of that list are customers, and 45 percent of another list are customers. Furthermore, customers and prospects can be sorted by company size so that, by matching, the potential placements represented by the prospects on the list can be assessed. If the best current customers within a particular industry have specifiable characteristics, then it is a straightforward extrapolation to say that noncustomers with similar characteristics represent the best prospects for new business. On this basis, Xerox could then decide to go after those markets which it had served least, assuming the company did not feel there were intrinsic reasons why those markets were not good prospects. Additionally, the computer was programmed to print out lists of the best individual prospects based on extrapolating from current customers. These are used by Xerox salesmen and by field sales management. An example of these kinds of output is shown in Exhibits 24–1 and 24–2.

The next step is a mailing to prospects within a particular market. These mailings invite the prospect to send in a card if he is interested in discussing Xerox products further with a salesman. As the returns come in, the number assigned to the responder establishment is identified, creating a new tape. At a later point in time, this file is run against the customer file to determine how many responders became customers. Knowing the size of the original mailing, Xerox is able to calculate the proportion of new customers yielded by the particular mailing.

The effort described here clearly is an expensive undertaking, involving large amounts of manual sorting and coding. The process need not be so expensive, if one is willing to give up some features of the system. Assume for the moment that, rather than having a list consisting of prospects in a market based upon coding all customers and then subtracting them from the similarly coded mailing list, only mailing lists for several industries exist. Rather than numbering all customers, one possibility here is to number the mailing lists and then just new customers as the orders come in. Subsequently, by running the new customer list against the mailing lists, one could determine

Exhibit 24-1
Mailing List X

Region —
Branch —
SIC —

No. of Employees	No. of Customers	No. of Prospects	Total No. of Establishments
Unknown	13	96	109
Under 10	0	330	330
10 – 19	1	183	184
20 – 49	3	126	129
50 – 99	4	27	31
100 – 499	7	35	42
500 – 999	0	1	1
1,000 – 2,000	3	3	6
2,001 – 3,000	1	0	1
Over 3,000	0	0	0
Branch Totals	32	801	833

how many of these prospects had been converted to sales and what market, geographic area, and size were producing the highest yield. If one were doing the type of direct mail advertising that did not require or solicit a customer response but merely sought to create an awareness or a positive attitude toward a product, this would be necessary. The loss in this process as opposed to the Xerox procedure lies in not analyzing which markets to advertise to by direct mail in the first place.

Perhaps a more normal use of direct mail advertising is to develop leads by asking potential prospects to send in some sort of reply. If this is the case, it is possible to significantly reduce the cost of manual coding. Instead of numbering entire mailing lists, one simply gives numbers to those prospects who send in a reply card and to all new customers. Subsequently, by running the new customer list up against the list of people who responded, it is possible to determine how many of them were converted to customers and what proportion of each mailing list resulted in new customers.

What Price Glory?

A natural question at this point is, What will a system similar to ARTS cost to develop and operate? There is no categorical answer since each advertiser has unique problems, and, more importantly, the quality of his programming and systems support may vary radically. What one systems analyst can do in one month takes another four months, if his background is less appropriate or if he just lacks the necessary talent.

In this case, the design work was completed after three man-months of effort—part of which was contributed by graduate students in operations research who were working at Xerox to gain experience. (The use of graduate students and undergraduates in systems development work has been highly beneficial to both Xerox and the students. They gain real-world experience, and Xerox gains a fresh viewpoint that otherwise would have been lacking. In addition, the company is able to identify real "comers" to whom it can make offers once they have been granted their degrees.)

The programming for the ARTS system was done outside the firm on a contract basis. The elapsed time for completion and debugging of the programs was three months, at a cost of $12,000.

Within broad limits, the cost of systems and programming work for a system similar to ARTS should be comparable to what Xerox experienced. There is, however, one additional element, previously noted, which is likely to vary dramatically in scope from firm to firm: the physical work of coding customer or prospect lists.

Exhibit 24–2
Prospect Card

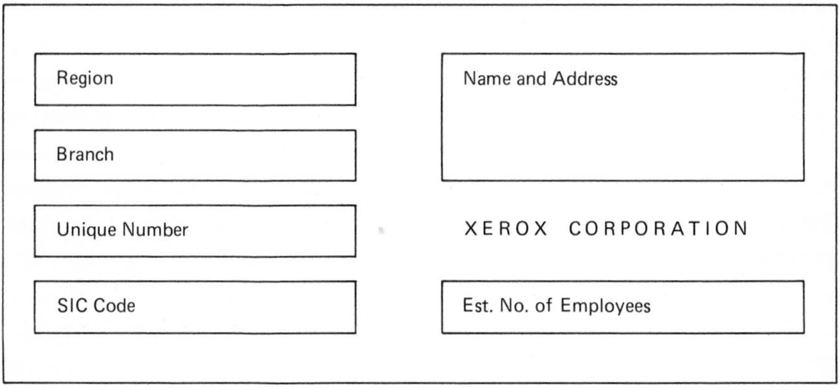

Region		Name and Address
Branch		
Unique Number		XEROX CORPORATION
SIC Code		Est. No. of Employees

Xerox's experience has shown that the cost of coding is approximately seven cents per name. This is based upon a girl's coding 350 names per day and earning $125 per week.

Perhaps the value of ARTS in relationship to the expenditures identified is put in better perspective by a description of the size of Xerox's typical mailing and the average response rate. Though some mailings do go far higher, the normal mailing is in the 12,000 to 20,000 range, usually being limited to a specific geographic area or a specific SIC category. In those cases where the mailing attempts to elicit a response, a 7 to 8 percent response is normal.

Clearly, there are economics of scale. If a company's mailings are larger, then the benefits to be gained from using an ARTS system are greater. Although Xerox has not attempted to identify the breakeven point, a company could probably prove the value of an ARTS system for significantly smaller mailings.

Another consideration is, of course, the market price of the products and whether the prospective user will be renting or selling the product. Xerox direct mail deals with the rental of products ranging from $30 to $500 per month and the sale of supplies, sometimes sold by the carload. If Xerox were dealing solely in the sale of single units that went for less than a dollar apiece, ARTS might not be a very attractive investment—unless the potential market were broad enough.

In other words, if a company is considering an ARTS system, it will have to do a cost-effectiveness analysis to determine its practical value. Although the system is thought to have utility even for a small advertiser, this is an issue for empirical analysis, not idle speculation.

The Sizzle

One of the favorite clichés of the advertising world is, "Sell the sizzle, not the steak!" This chapter has, so far, been concentrating on the steak. Now let's turn to the sizzle. What can you do to increase the effectiveness of direct mail advertising once you have instituted one of the measurement procedures described?

It is impossible, at this time, to buttress descriptions of how ARTS should be used with empirical data. The system is still being put into effect, and many studies are still on the drawing board.

The ARTS approach is relevant for products which cannot be sold by direct mail per se. There is no real need for ARTS if products can be sold by mail directly. ARTS becomes of value in those situations where direct mail can be used only to identify and motivate prospects and where the actual closing of the sale must be done in person.

First, by following the procedure used at Xerox, a company can decide to whom it wishes to advertise directly by mail. It doesn't take much imagination to see that other marketing efforts can be similarly guided by these opportunity analyses.

A company can compare the impact of mailings to samples from alternative SIC groups or geographic areas prior to doing more extensive mailings. For example, it might select two SIC categories and at random pick a thousand names within each. When the reply cards were received, it would put numbers on these prospects and, then, on all new customers. Subsequently, the new customer file with its numbers up should be run against the responders' file in order to determine how many responders had been converted to customers. A comparison would reveal which mailing list yielded the higher conversion rate. The company would then have the basis for deciding to do the larger mailing, perhaps involving tens of thousands of names, to the group that yielded the best response.

The implication is that a company can do its direct mail advertising on a regional or even branch basis with an ARTS system. No longer is it restricted to operating out of the home office on an all-or-nothing basis. One doesn't have to be in the position of the advertiser on a national TV program who found himself beaming snow-tire commercials to the Miami market. Rather, the regional manager can control the direct mail advertising as part of his total marketing effort. He can tailor the audience, the frequency, or whatever to his specific requirements. The acceleration of activity aimed at localizing marketing in order to be more sensitive to regional differences may turn out to be one of the most significant reasons for developing an ARTS system.

With this approach, a manager can determine the effects of different numbers of mailings per customer. That is, there may be a critical threshold below which direct mail advertising—and perhaps any form of advertising—doesn't work. For example, perhaps three mailings per prospect in a month may produce no more sales than one mailing, which, in turn, may not result in many more sales than zero mailings. But more than four mailings per month may cause a sharp increase in the new customers. For example, one major advertiser received a better than twofold jump in revenue by identifying the threshold level for his consumer product advertising.

To avoid oversimplification, it is important to note that creative content may interact significantly with frequency. With a mediocre message, there may be no frequency sufficient to produce positive results. With a highly effective message, the number of mailings required to produce a significant sales effect may be quite small. In essence, it would be dangerous to generalize regarding frequency across all campaigns. Each needs to be tested separately, at least until we build up a body of knowledge on which to base a general rule regarding frequency.

Flights of direct mail advertising can be compared to even spacing of the mailings. Do you get better results by sending one mailing every week for three months, or would you be better off if you sent four mailings in one week, then waited a month, then sent four more mailings in a single week? Although there is a degree of risk involved, one can even generalize to mass media advertising from the direct mail results. If flights of mail work better than evenly spaced mail for brand X, it is not necessarily true that flights of TV spots would be better than evenly spaced spots, but, lacking other data, it is a reasonable working hypothesis. Here again, the caveat regarding the interaction of timing with content should be heeded. Each campaign should be tested until we develop a body of knowledge that says, for example, flights of four mailings a month apart are better than the same number of mailings evenly spaced.

The effects of alternate creative treatments can be determined. Does one type of direct mail copy lead to a greater sales response than another type of copy? At the 13th Annual Conference of the Advertising Research Foundation, Dr. Irwin Gross reported that the selling power of a great idea has been found to exceed the selling power of an ordinary idea by as much as ten to one. Assuming these figures apply to direct mail as well, the value of this application is obvious.

One can even determine the interaction between direct mail and personal selling. Do salesmen require fewer personal calls to close an order when the prospect has received one, two, three, or some greater number of pieces of direct mail advertising for the product? One might, for example, select four panels of 1,000 prospects each. A number would be given to each prospect, and cards for each would be printed and sent to the field as leads for the sales force. One panel would then receive a single mailing, a second, two mailings, and so on. The sales force would be asked to report each time they made a call on one of these prospects via the use of a card that had the corresponding number on it. Then, by running the new customer list up against the four prospect lists and the frequency of sales calls made, one could determine if there were any interactions. Is there an optimum number of calls in relationship to a given number of mailings to close a sale?

The ARTS concept can readily be extended to trade shows if a spokesman simply asks people stopping in the booth to fill out a card and puts a number on the prospect and on all subsequent new customers. This technique makes it possible to compare the relative sales effectiveness of participating in alternative trade shows. Since setting up a booth, manning it, and moving equipment in and out can be an extremely expensive undertaking, this may be one of the more efficient uses of the ARTS system.

*   *   *

At this point, in order to close the loop, a précis on ARTS seems in order.

Essentially, what we have is a *feedback loop* that enables the assessment of direct mail effectiveness. Are we reaching the prospects who have a high potential for becoming customers? Which ways of using direct mail are more effective? Most important, can we assess effectiveness in terms of revenue when the feedback loop includes a link to our billing system?

The key first step in the ARTS system is the application of a number to each establishment. This numbering system provides a means of sorting establishments into customers versus prospects and then into groups of comparable size, geography, SIC, and, in the case of current customers, comparable machine mixes.

Xerox expectations are that the efficiencies of the ARTS approach are such that it easily will have covered the time, effort, and cost required by the increased effectiveness of direct mail. Since Xerox is a relatively moderate user of direct mail, heavy users will certainly find an even greater payoff from building an ARTS system.

25

Some Challenges
and Many Opportunities

Evelyn Konrad

So far in this book, we have discussed a range of relatively sophisticated areas in which the capabilities of the computer and the talents of knowledgeable operations research men can combine to add science to management judgment. We have inevitably also covered the considerable impact of the sheer computational capabilities of the computer when harnessed to the avalanche of data produced throughout the marketing function.

The title of this section might lead readers to believe that we will now discuss the opportunities marketing management may have in some distant future from possibly more esoteric and mind-stretching applications. Those, however, are not the biggest opportunities at all. Strangely enough, the most staggering reservoir of untapped opportunities for turning meaningless and available data into highly useful and accessible marketing information exists today and is nearly entirely unexploited within the communications system of the sales function and in nearly every company in virtually every industry.

In the very area, selling, in which the computer spends the most time—admittedly in customer billing and accounting recordkeeping—the computer stands simultaneously totally neglected as a potential processor of undigested raw data into valuable marketing information.

Some examples may dramatize this comment. The credit cards of oil companies and department stores—to use two examples in mass-consumer marketing areas—already contain a wealth of data without the addition of any new classification and categories. Using only the facts continuously recorded at the point of the sale by the gas station attendant on the one hand and the individual sales clerk on the other, the oil company or department store management respectively could learn a great deal about the product-purchase cycle of credit card customers from meaningful demographic or life-cycle breaks, and the productivity of individual retail outlets, whether these be gas stations or specific departments within the store, analyzed according to geography, dollar volume, location, or any other meaningful criteria. By using only the information that is generated by the current credit card billing records, marketing management could gain insights into patterns and characteristics of the heavy user of diverse products, whether these be oil or gasoline in the one instance or shoes in the other. In short, the data that are part of the daily sales process lend themselves to consumer profile analyses or analyses of purchasing patterns and other reviews that could turn the raw facts into truly valuable marketing guidelines. This is only one simple illustration of a particularly easy processing chore that could be assigned to existing computers using elementary and available programs and working on continuously updated flows of facts.

Is it being done? Usually not. Why not? The answer to this question is a good deal more difficult to perceive. Perhaps management simply still suffers from the excess of departmentalization and functional divisions discussed on a broad level in earlier chapters. Perhaps no one person on a level to implement such an across-department use of files tends to initiate an inquiry into the potential value of these records.

The absurdity of the dilemma becomes even more evident when one considers the sizable marketing research budgets assigned to independent research organizations and to a variety of field studies when the potentially valuable information in the firm's own archives goes unnoticed, undigested, and ignored. It may not be an excessive generalization to say that, with the exception of competitive information, there are few if any insights into customer-purchase behavior and expressed product demand that could not be answered through either intelligent use of existing sales records or a minor modification of these records to add a small fact or a new classification.

Where the sales function is concerned, the computer today addresses itself quite meaningfully to problems of sales controls that parallel, in many ways, the accounting or inventory control function. It addresses itself to routing salesmen, servicing customers according to optimum schedules, and other questions of logistics that parallel the use of computer programs in physical distribution. One or two examples of these are covered in this section, and literally hundreds of them exist throughout the business community. These applications are neither trivial nor minor nor insignificant in terms of the increased efficiency of manpower and in terms of customer servicing advantages that derive from better allocation of salesmen's time.

However, we would not be fulfilling the missionary function of this book —to open a dialogue between those expert in management sciences and EDP and marketing men—if we did not provoke and stimulate management to question the internal environment of the firm. These are some of the questions we suggest for starters.

Is there any one individual or group within the firm and outside the domain of marketing who communicates regularly with the customers of the firm, its suppliers, or any other special outside group with direct impact on the profitability of the firm?

If so, do these regular communications lend themselves to some form of fact-finding without disrupting the prime purpose of these communications?

If they do, do the facts generated through these communications relate in some manner to the responsibilities of marketing management?

Or can they, by simply combining with other information or analyzing them from another viewpoint, shed new light on old questions?

Undoubtedly, there are many other questions that marketing management could ask by taking a new view at overlooked opportunities on their own doorstep. Many of these will come into focus when marketing management begins to understand that the difference between computer-generated data and computer-generated information is often lodged within the question that the initiator of the program originally asked.

One of the great stimulations that can be derived from reading the chapter by Jonathan Bayliss is the fact that he takes a view of the marketing function that is not only broad but compassionate and understanding of the burdensome complexities implicit in it in real life. The information system he describes does indeed incorporate a good deal of intelligence from the field sales force and recognizes the value of their continuing contact with customers. In brief, his approach is based on asking many a probing question.

In writing about linear programming, George R. Dantzig commented: "The final test of a theory is its capacity to solve the problems which originated it." To paraphrase this quotation, the final test of the validity of a marketing question asked may well be the relevance of the material produced in answer to it.

26

Using the Computer
to Plan Marketing

Jonathan Bayliss

THE MARKETING CONCEPT has been gaining general acceptance in con-
sumer-goods industries for nearly a generation, until now most companies
speak of themselves as marketing-oriented. The idea of combining research,
advertising, selling, and physical distribution has established a unifying
tendency within the firm, breaking down many of the walls between departments and filling in the moats that have made islands of particular functions.
General management has begun to recognize the final damage to profits that
can stem from the suboptimization of particular operations at the expense of
the whole. And the need to coordinate various efforts into single "tasks" performed by teams of diverse specialists, perhaps under the influence of
organizational developments and operations research in World War II, has
become well understood.

The Planning Objective

But at the same time we are confronted with an opposing tendency toward multiplicity. Diversification of product lines, acquisition of new logisti-

cal organizations, and new service-level demands have made marketing management more complex. This complexity is reflected in the need for "product management," which is an attempt to regain some of the advantages of specialized effort without losing the comprehensive "ten-fingered grasp of reality" that comes from knowledge of the whole.

Under these conditions it has been difficult for the general manager and the director of marketing to know what is going on—still less to control it. Control is largely a matter of comparing actual performance with expectation. Effective control under complex conditions requires that this expectation be set forth at the same level of operating detail at which day-by-day decisions are actually made. Generalized plans are of little use in measuring achievement for the purposes of taking corrective action. Therefore the marketing plan, which must blend in a mutually responsive manner the plans of supplementary marketing functions, should be nearly as specific as the multifarious analyses of actual marketing performance.

Though many firms have changed their organizational structures to the extent that single executives are responsible for the synergy of activities that stimulate demand, procure orders, and deliver products, the practical difficulty of mastering the innumerable external and internal relations of a large company operating in a dynamic situation has usually prevented any systematic approach to fully integrated planning more than once a year. Yet plans, if they are to be usable by operating people, must be periodically revised.

In ordinary practice, these revisions, if they are formally undertaken at all, are accomplished at the expense of integration. Usually the hard-won unity of the annual budget is lost in the splintering necessity of providing for each separate department a "practical" guide for reacting to its part of the marketing problem, and often these revisions must be made by departmental managers without much knowledge of what the other departments are planning. The chief executive in marketing, like the general management, ordinarily must refer to an inflexible plan that is, on the average, six months old (like the last annual report), without much hope that it can guide him in directing the current efforts of his departmental managers, who have long since escaped the influence of that original idea of what the world was going to be like this year. Perhaps the sales manager has been revising his sales objectives every quarter, as far as national totals are concerned, and surely the distribution manager has been changing his monthly forecasts for inventory planning purposes (maybe using some mathematical technique for extrapolating movement out of his base stock at major warehousing points). In any case, the projections which determine the outlays to be made in advertising are likely to be completely out of phase with those used by regional sales managers and distribution executives. They will be locked together again only at the end of the year.

The computer makes it possible to do better—if it is devoted almost as much to planning as to recording and analyzing actual history. A planning system—as distinguished from independent programs used for particular forecasts but incorporating these forecasts in its total flow of information—considers most of the operating functions of the company.

These familiar ideas are all outgrowths of the marketing concept. They are reviewed here only to point out that in the design of computer systems they are usually either forgotten or given up. The complexity and volume of integrated planning information in most cases cannot be handled by conventional computer techniques. Nor can the problem be solved by the classic methods of operations research. The overwhelming burden of unifying the marketing effort has been left, for the most part, to the largely unaided brain of a single executive—if the responsibility has been accepted at all. If the computer may rightly be called a giant brain, it is surely to this kind of comprehensive use that it should be put. (It may continue to serve particular applications of more restricted scope.)

At any rate, some such thinking underlies the operations planning system being installed at the Gorton Corporation. The following pages cover an actual case now being implemented as a major phase of computer-based management practice. For purposes of clarity and in the interest of communicating basic principles rather than solutions of difficulties peculiar to one company, the operations planning system is presented in generalized form without particular application to Gorton. Comments here are confined to the immediate value of the system for field sales management, sales service, and physical distribution, but further elaboration of the procedures and usages described would clearly assist in advertising, territory planning, market research, pricing, salesman performance evaluation, profitable control of product mix by market, and sales cost accounting.

Fundamental planning requirements, when formally analyzed, probably do not differ substantially from company to company within broad classes of industry. Most of the differences seem to involve varying requirements of production and procurement. In Gorton's business both supply and demand are seasonally variable. The world commodity market from which raw materials are purchased is often uncertain as to particular items. On the other hand, the consumer market for the full line, taken as a whole (seafood and related food products), is relatively stable.

Logistics are complicated by the fact that several sales forces handle products produced under different labels by common processing plants or vendors and by the fact that many markets have especially high service requirements under extremely competitive conditions. Furthermore, most of the producing plants are devoted to specific segments of the product line. For these reasons, the logistical system requires a network of base, distribution, and field warehouses, most of which are public, and must be stocked with a great variety of stockkeeping units in relation to total volume. The planning sequence can be truncated or simplified for companies whose raw material supply is readily available with a certain lead time. Operations planning is undoubtedly easier with fewer products, fewer markets, or fewer inventory locations; but most marketing-oriented enterprises have the same essential problem in systems design.

Let us assume that the job of the computer-based administrative system is to issue new operating and financial plans every period on a moving one-year time horizon, and to do so for 1,000 products divided among three selling divisions, making use of 50 logistical points (warehouses, plants, and receiving points) and 50 vendors of finished products or basic raw materials. Let us say that 3,000 customers buy from one or more of the sales divisions. But the marketing model, shown in most generalized form by Exhibit 26–1, is not limited by particular numbers; its sole constraints are the storage and processing capacity of the computer.

Two other points must be made in further definition of the planning requirements, one related to time and the other to money. The general purpose is to estimate *where, when,* and *how much of* each individual product should be made available to customers, and it takes great detail to furnish figures that indicate how to meet expected demand in a reasonably profitable way.

First, there is the planning time-unit. Sales may well be estimated by the period (a four- or five-week month), but production orders and warehouse replenishment requisitions are issued by the week. Transactions are closed once a week. But, above all, if investment in inventory is to be kept as low as possible consistent with service requirements, warehouse stocks must be maintained in terms of weeks, particularly for items with steady demand. (Daily intervals would be even better, but the expense of daily control is still prohibitive for most firms.) In short, it is necessary to project inventory movements and balances week by week for purposes of sales service and financial control. The week becomes the least common denominator of the system with respect to time, and all plans must be expressed in this unit.

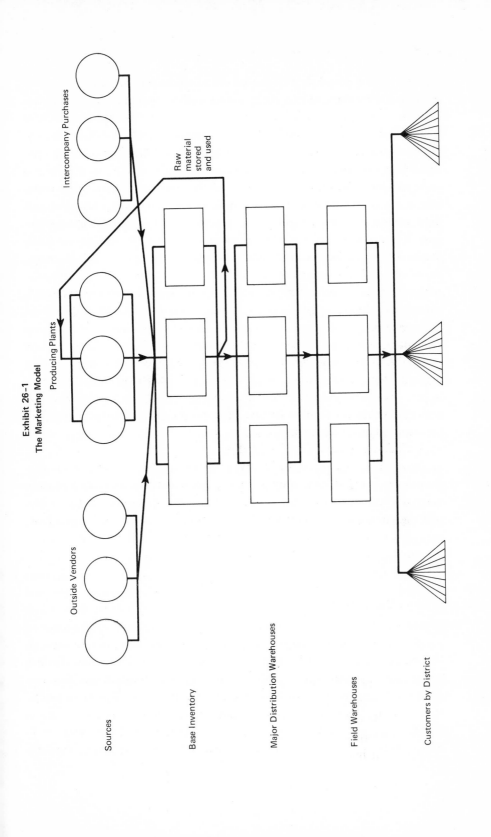

Exhibit 26-1
The Marketing Model

Intercompany Purchases

Producing Plants

Raw material stored and used

Outside Vendors

Sources

Base Inventory

Major Distribution Warehouses

Field Warehouses

Customers by District

Second, it is insufficient to project sales and distribution requirements in physical units alone. Money is the least common denominator of quantity. It is only in terms of dollars that relative success can be measured; and it is only in dollars that a comparison between input and output (that is, profit) can be expressed. Physical units are indispensable for the purpose of calculating storage and freight costs, to be sure, but only money can state investment, carrying costs, distribution expenses, and "netback" in individual markets. Therefore, the system calls for income projections (based on unit price for each product in each market), standard unit cost of goods sold, gross profit in each case, and several factors of distribution cost, all as coefficients or products of the basic estimates in physical quantities.

The planning system must provide most of the variables that go into pro-forma financial statements for marketing in the year ahead. In effect, it constitutes a flexible budgeting method. The fixed budget for the fiscal year is retained and used for purposes of financial management, sales performance evaluation, and fixed overhead computations, but the variable operating plan (12 successive revisions of the original budget, each projected one period further into the future) is the basis of daily decisions. When the year's cycle is complete, therefore, the latest operating plan may be frozen and preserved as the next annual budget. Thus a snapshot is taken of every 12th operating plan for budgeting purposes, and the budget is practically ready-made when the beginning of the fiscal year rolls around.

Budgeting becomes easier every year because the moving forecast is sharpening itself all year long through continual corrections. The greatest workload falls during the first few start-up periods, when the basic structure of the planning system is put together, but gradually a forecast-by-exception technique dominates the proceedings, as the need for mass assembly of input data diminishes.

The Systems Context

A fully developed management system may be conceived as a pair of subsystems played against each other to produce crucial information in effective form. These two hemispheres of the global system construct and measure, respectively, *expected* performance and *actual* performance. The master architecture for the computerized administrative system of a marketing company should be determined by this essential need to compare and analyze the variance between hopes and results. This need is the essential justification for all budgeting and forecasting. Taking for granted the practical value of planning, since the present intention is to speak of means rather than ends, it is not possible to outline the operations planning system (more precisely, the subsystem) without sketching its functional relationship to its counterpart, the system that records and analyzes past and current history.

Exhibit 26–2 represents in stylized fashion the scope of the continuous management system that forms the environment of the planning portion now under discussion. Each zone of the system is symbolized by the conventional figure of a disk file, but, of course, in most instances, several files are represented, inasmuch as the volume of data and the complexity of data handling are too great for this ideal of simplification.

The left side of the wheel stands for the interrelated programs and storage files applied to business documentation, reporting, and analysis, most of which is directly or indirectly related to marketing.

The right side shows two sectors devoted to planning proper. The center line dividing the circle vertically connects the two sectors that are common to the semicircles of performance and planning. Of the two, the bottom subsystem is the more important for present purposes and it is described separately in the last section of this chapter.

The point to be stressed is that throughout the system there is a dynamic interplay among the information elements of plans and actualities.

The Planning Model

At the center of the planning system (again, really a subsystem) lie a pair of files chained to each other in such a way that together they constitute a network of records containing the entire sales and logistical plan.

The master file contains constant, semiconstant, and completely variable data (that is, estimates) pertaining to an individual item in a particular market, warehouse, plant, or source of supply. The market may be an individual customer; the source may be an individual vendor. Master records correspond to the nodes in network diagrams.

The structure file contains records which connect or regulate the data in the master records, like the branches in networks. These relationships are usually variable. In effect, they assign a customer to a warehouse, a field warehouse to a base warehouse, and a warehouse to a plant or vendor—for each product. They also show the flow of product between the two points they each connect and indicate the freight rates.

Exhibit 26-2
Architectural Concept of the Gorton System

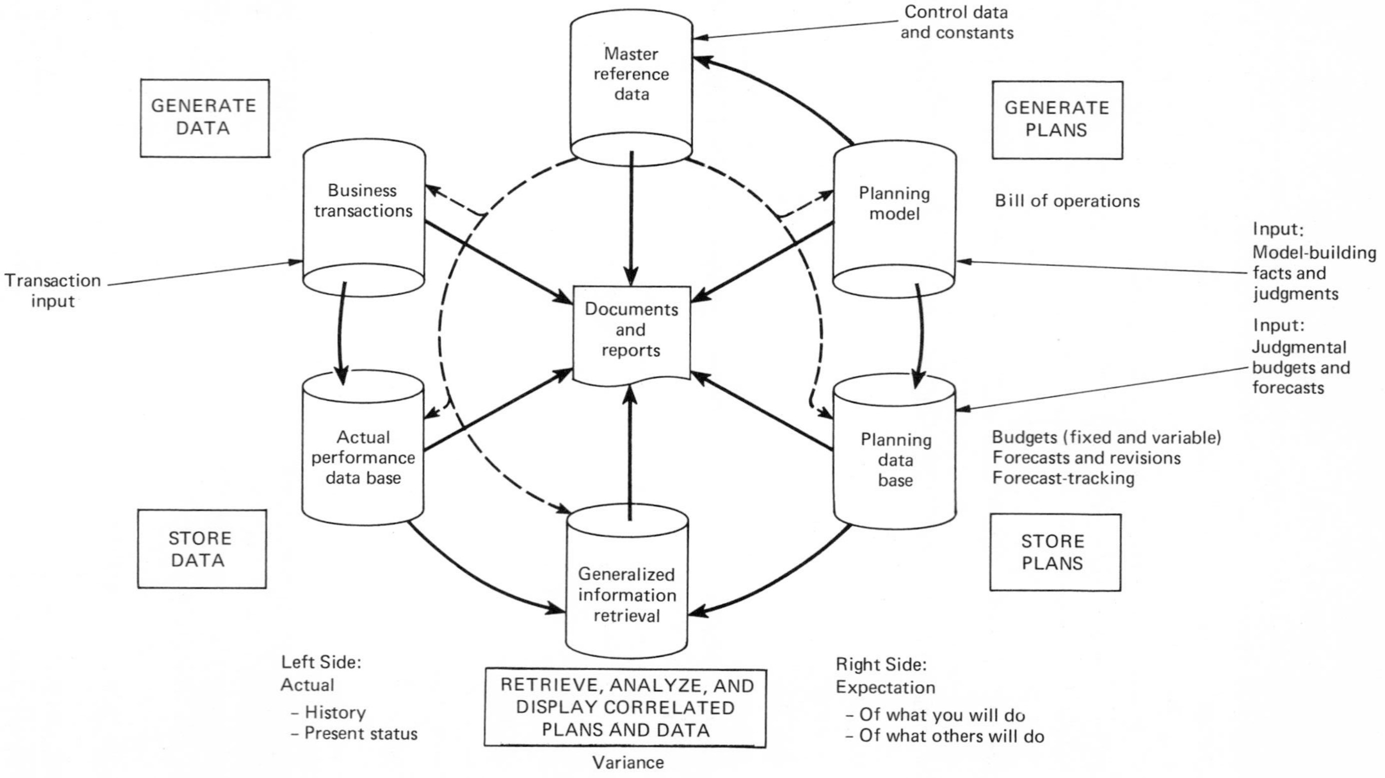

GENERATE PLANS

Input: Model-building facts and judgments

Input: Judgmental budgets and forecasts

Bill of operations

Control data and constants

Budgets (fixed and variable)
Forecasts and revisions
Forecast-tracking

STORE PLANS

Planning model

Planning data base

Master reference data

Documents and reports

Generalized information retrieval

RETRIEVE, ANALYZE, AND DISPLAY CORRELATED PLANS AND DATA

Right Side:
Expectation
- Of what you will do
- Of what others will do

Variance

Left Side:
Actual
- History
- Present status

Business transactions

Actual performance data base

GENERATE DATA

Transaction input

STORE DATA

Linking master records and structure records, therefore, like the circles and sticks of Tinker Toys, one can construct an image of the physical marketing flow and can trace the paths by which the supply from each source is drafted by various warehouses and markets. It is also possible to project the paths and quantities by which this demand will be met, including safety stock and that part of inventory which absorbs seasonal pulses of over-supply. The difference between the negative figures representing draft on inventory at every point and the positive figures representing supply, when cumulated, represents projected inventory balances. Thus key elements of income, expense, and investment appear together in the model. (See Exhibit 26–3.)

The concept is simple enough. The difficulty lies in packing a vast variety of detail into single records. For we are interested in physical quantity, sales dollars, gross margin, storage costs, and freight expense—for *each week* of the year ahead, of the current fiscal year (both that part of it which is past and that part which remains), and of as much as six months' lead time for commodities that must be ordered overseas before any given year begins. Though the success of the system depends upon the solution of such technical problems, space permits no more than the briefest conceptual account of some of the special features of the system.

Consider first a two-year time series consisting of a pair of 52-week spreads. There is not enough space in anyone's computer to store the figures for each week separately. A shorthand is required. If a single figure is stored for each year's total, with a formula for distributing that total over the year by weeks, the amount of information that must be preserved can be abbreviated. But that formula itself may be too long. Furthermore, there is no need to repeat that long formula every time it is called for. Therefore, let us simply *refer to* a formula, kept in a separate file, when the need arises to encode or decode a stored record. The reference is in fact a *pattern number,* and the reference file contains a mathematical description of the pattern by which the annual total can be spread. The amount of each individual week, or of any span of time, can be calculated as required.

Standard capsules of forecast data are called *compendiums.* A compendium contains two annual amounts, their pattern numbers, and a small field indicating "phase."

Phase expresses the number of weeks shift from the current fiscal year at which the two years of data begins. This shift represents lead or lag, which accumulates as a case of product moves hypothetically through its particular path in the logistical network. Transit times require, for example, that product X to be sold in market A must be available from plant 1 four weeks before the time of final release, whereas product Y may be produced two weeks later because its path to the market is more direct.

It is a prime function of the structure records (which connect master records) to introduce the transit time for each leg of the journey from source to market. If changes in transit time are tentatively projected, their effect upon the logistical system can be examined in advance. Perhaps it will be found that expensive reductions of transit time (due to alternate modes of transportation) will have relatively little effect upon overall service; or, conversely, that improved shipping time between two heavily used warehousing points greatly increases the total response.

The structure records also contain compendiums showing freight rates projected over the two-year period. Every flow of product through a segment of its path (represented by the structure record) causes the freight costs for

Exhibit 26–3
Network Model

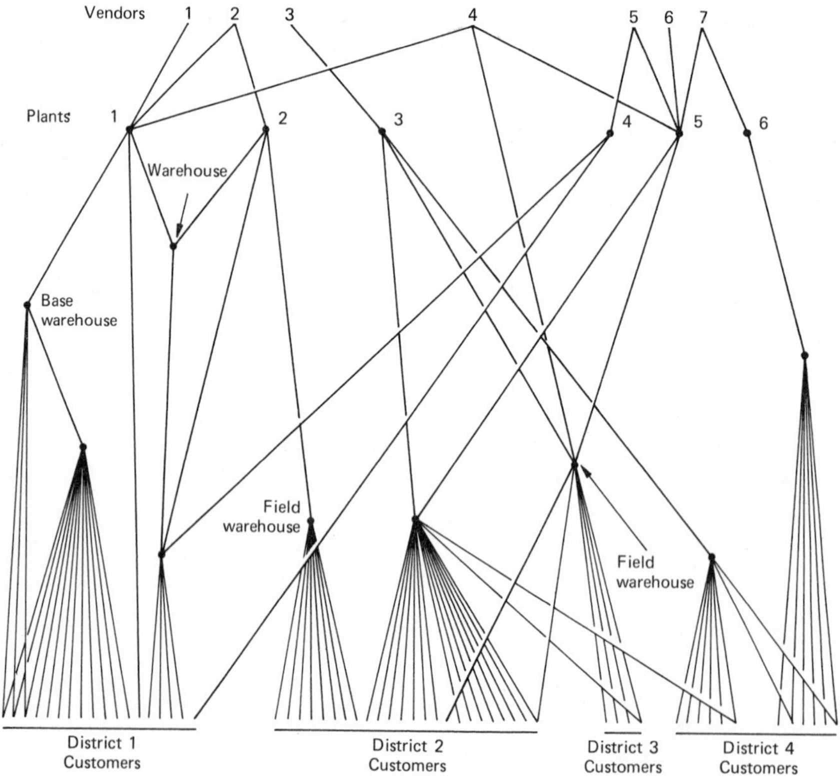

each week to be calculated and stored—again encoded in compendious form —in a master record. Thus total freight costs are built up in stages like mileage on a road map.

Exhibit 26–4 shows all the compendiums used in both master and structure records, as well as other fields. The most important in the master record are those of the sales draft (the basic forecast of demand as reflected at every level) expressed in quantity, unit price, and unit cost. From this sales draft are calculated (week by week, according to expected fluctuations of selling price and standard costs) weight, revenue, cost of goods sold, and gross profit. The most important field in the structure record is the "logistical path coefficient," which is a ratio designating the part of a market or a warehouse (for the particular product) that is supplied from the logistical point to which it is connected by the structure record itself.

By use of these fields alone (except for the indicative codes, which identify product, location, and organizational unit), the entire sales forecast pyramid can be constructed. It is this initial and basic usage of the model that is emphasized henceforth.

The greatest practical problem in forecasting has been to translate demand expressed in terms of the sales organization into demand expressed in terms of physical distribution. The former is identified by district, region, and division; the latter, by trading area, warehouse, and plant. Each customer (or aggregated group of customers) at the lowest level of the pyramid is associated both with the sales organization and with the logistical organization. And so the forecast, which is made at this local level initially, may be built up for either of two purposes—either for sales management or for physical distribution management.

The problem of using a single model for these two purposes is solved by using the customer master records two different ways. As well as being used as the lowest level of the distribution network file, they are taken collectively into a sequential file where they can be freely collated, selected, and, above all, sorted, in order to combine or recombine their contents in ways that will be useful for sales control, salesman goal setting, and other purposes related to profit-responsibility planning. This is called the "colligation" technique because it ties together, through the coding of the master records, elements of the marketing model that are scattered and intermixed throughout the image of the marketing system at the low level.

But that image—the structural organization of the files that abstractly anticipate the real world's marketing operations—reflects the logistical rather than the sales anatomy. The Tinker Toys are put together to show custom-

Exhibit 26-4
Master and Structure Records

Field No.

A	
B	
C	
D	
1	
2	
3	
4	
5	
6	
E	

Master Record

Item No:
Warehouse No.
Account Code
Division and District
Sale Quantity
Storage Cost/Unit
Holding Cost/Unit
Supply Quantity
Cost of Goods Sold/Unit
Work Area
Safety Factor Code

Structure Record

Logistical Code
Forecast Code
Linkage
Work Area
Work Area
Inventory Cost
Storage and Handling

Warehouse A

A	B	C	D	1	2	3	4	5	6	E

Compendiums

B	A	1	2	3	4	C

Market A

A	B	C	D	1	2	3	4	5	6	E

Compendiums

Plant No. 1   Plant No. 2   Plant No. 3

Warehouse A   Warehouse B

Market A   Market B   Market C

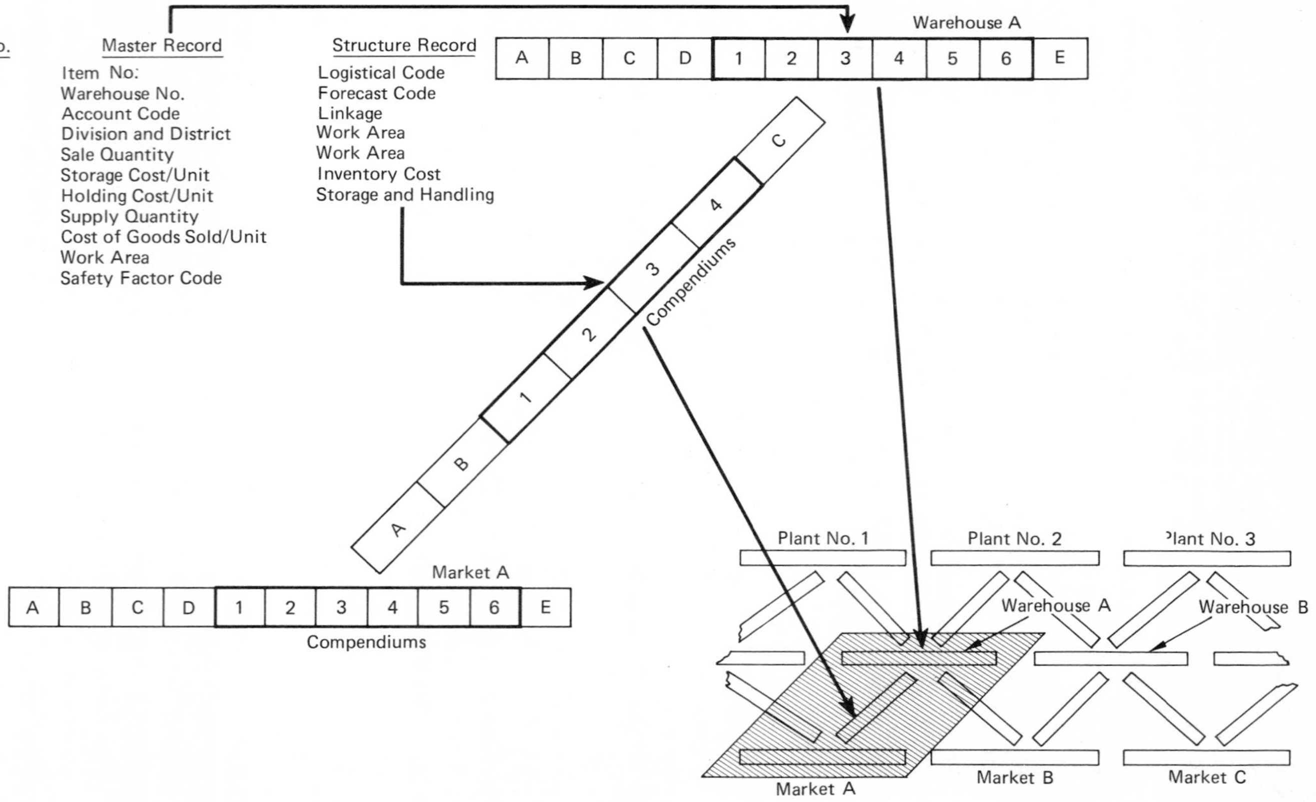

ers, warehouses, and plants, rather than customers, districts, and regions, because the function of the model is to show the flow of materials instead of the flow of orders.

Hence we are able to solve another problem commonly encountered in attempts to compile sales forecasts that are useful for operating purposes (and to avoid the typical situation in which inventory replenishments are managed according to plant forecasts independent of each other and unrelated to the plans of sales and advertising). By using a logistically structured model of the marketing process, it is possible to compile plant and warehouse forecasts, suitably shifted for lead times, as by-products of plans made for demand-creating (sales and advertising) purposes. The same operating forecast (as distinguished from sales goals and budgets) is used by all departments. The products sold in a given market often originate from different manufacturing divisions at various locations, though they may be delivered on the same orders from the same sales warehouse. In practice, without a structural model, it is very difficult to assemble, and then revise, detailed sales forecasts by source of supply.

For the logistical path of a product changes, too, not just the quantity and timing at the marketplace. Products are shifted from plant to plant in order to balance loads or to take advantage of temporarily favorable conditions (or, on the other hand, to meet emergencies). Changes in transportation economics may also dictate the reassignment of a product to a different delivery warehouse, perhaps combining shipments that were formerly split or rerouting the orders of large-volume customers from delivery through mixing warehouses to direct shipment from one or more plant warehouses. In other words, *the model should always be changing.* It is this need that distinguishes administrative systems design from that of most operations research, where investigations are of a special project nature, seldom updated and often insufficiently detailed for the requirements of line managers.

Such changes in the model—or, as data processing people say, file maintenances—are easy and economical with network files, where structure records (branches) may be changed as readily as master records (nodes), the effect of these changes being automatically projected throughout the relevant elements of the network. (In principle, matrices can be used to build structural models of this kind. But when the relationships are very complex and changes are frequent, they seem to be generally less convenient than networks, which are usually known as "bill of material processors.")

Now, the common objection to unified interdepartmental forecasting that comes from production-oriented people—and the reason that many companies prefer to construct production forecasts independently, often on a purely statistical basis—is based on the vague feeling that sales personnel are inefficient, antimathematical, and fundamentally indifferent to the problem of keeping inventory low. Indeed, sales managers themselves sometimes foster this feeling deliberately when they have no incentive, or at least mandate, to consider seriously the *total* cost of doing business. It is a pain in the neck, counterproductive from the sales point of view, to participate in forecasting at all. Sometimes sales executives would rather be regarded as irrational and volatile than be held responsible for tasks that drain their time without (as it seems) the slightest contribution to sales or to sales margin.

There is no simple answer to the question of reconciling the divergent drives of men who are specialists of necessity, for the sake of improving corporate success—especially when the company is already making an adequate return on investment. But there are at least two policies that can be adopted to mitigate the difficulty.

First, forecasting can be made an integral phase of marketing, and sales managers, even field salesmen, held responsible for the accuracy of their forecasts. Naturally, the incentives for good forecasting must be lower than the incentives for making profitable sales that may exceed forecast. However, continual education by the distribution manager will imbue sales people with the understanding that sales service quality is directly proportional to good forecasting.

Second, all distribution expense, including the financial cost of carrying inventory, as well as transportation and storage and order processing, can be charged to marketing. This practice, along with organizational arrangements by which the physical distribution manager reports to the executive who is responsible for other phases of marketing, establishes—at least in the highest reaches of sales and advertising—the *will* to forecast for composite efficiency. Both the balance sheet and the profit and loss statement exhibit the consequences of good forecasting.

But perhaps the most important way out of the psychological phase of the forecasting dilemma lies in the administrative procedure and computer technique for communication, feedback, and display. This aspect of the solution will be treated separately in the last section of this chapter. It is in the interchange of information with the human mind that this genie, the computer, surpasses any battery of clerks that have ever lived if it is programmed to accept in free form the data that a man chooses to offer. Our technical ability to develop such man–machine systems in a business environment is still primitive, but there are great possibilities of exploitation even without on-line, real-time hardware. The conversational mode can be employed on rather small computers in a crude but effective manner, if the conversation is organized to take place over sufficient time.

For the moment, let us return to the question of unified interdepartmental forecasting—that is, to integrated planning. Although we can overcome the psychological objection to operating plans based upon input from "irresponsible" salesmen, perhaps, by gradually improving methods of self-correction and patiently evolving administrative techniques to stimulate general participation in forecasting, it remains true that this kind of mid-range planning (operational planning as distinguished from long-range planning) does not and cannot produce the specific instructions that constitute daily production or transfer orders. Still less, of course, can planning provide us with the actual customer orders that deplete inventory. It goes without saying that all business transactions are full of statistical "noise." Neither plans nor most records show all the fluctuations that occur every day. When we replenish a field warehouse, we want to know the exact inventory position this week and the sales we expect next week in particular—not simply the rough average forecast that was made three or four weeks ago before the weather turned unseasonably hot. This week's production schedule must be modified to compensate for downtime last week. The bread-and-butter decisions of the workweek are guided by the period operating plan, especially in anticipating purchases of materials, equipment, manpower, and such services as advertising, but final decisions on how to use *today's* men, materials, and machines, today's money, today's inventory, are always open until the latest facts are in.

These hard, stubborn facts of life have urged the development of decision-making techniques for each separate function of business as its manager faces the problem of service and efficiency. He cannot have a daily overview of the entire enterprise and its environment. Even the president can't. Determinations must be made on the basis of what a man sees before him and past experience in his own department. The part of the operating plan that applies to his function will prevent him from exceeding relative limits or from otherwise affecting corporate efficiency adversely. Still, the plan won't go far in helping him to cope with the problem of balancing the product mix of his next truckload to the Dallas warehouse if there was an unexplained run on product A last week, although products C, T, and X for some reason didn't move at all. The computer has been used very successfully to help this man do a better job, to reduce inventories, and to diminish the number of emergencies in production and purchasing. But it remains true that the efficiency of a warehouse may militate against the efficiency of the plants that supply it, and, in general, the success of the whole is not the sum of the successes of individual elements. Yet none of the established mathematical techniques of forecasting can deal with the system as a whole. They must be used on a parochial level.

The operations planning model reconciles these requirements for "intrinsic" forecasting with the need for man-machine prediction on a farther and broader horizon. Only the man in the field can know the big customer he's going to lose or the product that isn't going to sell in his territory because of a local competitive specialist; but only an exponentially smoothed projection of last week's experience in Atlanta can specify what to put on the truck from Gloucester tomorrow, whether or not the replenishment manager has any inkling that the Atlanta demand pattern will change a month from now. There are times when the aggregate demand at these plants (as calculated from the market forecasts) may conflict with intrinsic statistical extrapolations of demand at major source points. Which figures are more reliable? Do the salesmen know what they are talking about, or are they getting imprudently optimistic again? Is the exponential smoothing formula detecting a downward trend that no one else sees (because it is obscured by new-product euphoria), or is it simply not recognizing future market conditions that do not yet appear in actual orders?

There is no need to take either side. Sometimes one may be right, sometimes the other—especially in the first few years of the system. No one yet knows how accurate the field sales forecasts can become. It will certainly be a long time before the machine part of the man–machine planning cycle can be fitted with projection formulas suitable to each market or major customer, and therefore we can only gradually begin to help the salesman through mathematical techniques more advanced than simple trend analysis. And even in the end—who knows?—it may be demonstrated that intrinsic forecasting (by machine only) is inherently superior to forecasting that attempts to introduce conjectural elements not foreshadowed by past experience.

But in any case, the operations planning model of the logistical system will continue to be used. Whether the forecast data are introduced at the low level on an intuitive basis, on the top level by management (statistically, intuitively, or otherwise), or on an intermediate level (by exponential smoothing of demand at a major warehouse), the model projects them throughout the system—either by "implosion" or "explosion" or both, upward and downward in an hourglass pattern. Since the model serves as a simulator as well as an administrative reporting and recording mechanism, implications of various forecasts can be compared with each other and with actual performance to evaluate the success of alternate methods. The model should prove useful to couple the intrinsic forecasting programs with the mainline planning system by acting as a governor to the operating plan, checking and approving it at critical points in the network. At the same time the operations planning framework should provide the intrinsic forecasting modules with statistically acceptable adjustments to basic usage rates (thus speeding up the reaction to changed conditions without oversensitizing the smoothed projection to random noise), especially those partially controlled by advertising and promotional efforts.

The Planning Sequence

The full planning sequence is complicated by the requirements of production and procurement, and for that reason it will not be elaborated here. (A bill of operations network file is used to control and explode the manufacture and purchase of the finished product specified by the output of the operations planning program.) But an outline of the whole procedure will help to illustrate the marketing orientation of the entire computer system.

The following steps are listed in normal sequence, but any of them may be repeated individually or by group in the manner of simulation. In fact, the essential process is one of trial-test-revision, heuristic rather than deterministic, inasmuch as the hundreds of thousands of variables dealt with in the model cannot be handled by any fully mathematical method. The consequences of any one projection of sales (perhaps generated mathematically, but normally a blend of statistics and human surmise) are combined by computation with the consequences of any one set of supply plans. The result is tested quantitatively for feasibility, physically and financially. Any part of either the sales or the supply plan can be altered without starting all over again. Informal sensitivity analysis of this kind makes it possible to narrow down logistical difficulties rather quickly. Then, through the trial-and-error of fine tuning, a company can adopt an operating plan that is suitable in all its ramifications, that seems to approach maximum profitability as a whole (though of course one cannot test *all* possible combinations), and that can soon change again in the light of actual events—provided the computer system analyzes results thoroughly.

1. Send to the field salesman computer-printed worksheets listing every product sold in his markets, one set for each district or for some individual customers. He will have the original budgeted sales projection by period (unless this is the first time around), the latest previous revision (if any), this year's actual sales so far in the year, and last year's sales. A computer-calculated projection of this year's sales is also shown, and these figures (perhaps periodic as well as cumulative) constitute the suggested forecast that the salesman is asked to consider. If he disagrees with the figure for any period —or, more important, with the annual total—he blue-pencils his estimate.

After the first period of a fiscal year the time span is increased in graduated steps, until at the end of a cycle, two years are shown: the current fiscal year and the fully "moved" year ahead.

2. These figures are loaded into the computer, together with any actual or anticipated changes in the structure of the supply network. The output is a set of reports showing the projected effect of this draft upon each warehouse and plant in the system.

3. These requirements (reflecting lead-time considerations) are used to construct, either manually or mechanically, a purchasing or production schedule. This supply plan, resulting from the production planning subsystem, is intended to meet demand, while at the same time reflecting the need for purchasing economy, production efficiency, economical transportation, and minimum justifiable inventory. The next two steps test the success of this supply plan.

4. The supply plan, having been loaded, is exploded down through the expanding network, again allowing for transit time. This makes available a week-by-week comparison of supply and demand at each warehouse. Naturally, the supply will not equal the demand every week in the year, since supply comes in pulses, some items must be seasonally stockpiled, and some warehouses are used for current stock only while others are used to accumulate reserves or to absorb purchased items when prices are most favorable. But at this stage it is vital to test total capacity for the year ahead, check the total manufacturing assignments of each plant by product, and examine the possibilities of revising logistical paths at once or later in the year. At this stage, it may be necessary to bounce the basketball several times before you decide to walk off the floor with it.

5. Once a supply plan is established that looks good from the point of view of production, purchasing, and traffic, it must be tested from the viewpoint of inventory. The computer now calculates *balances*—by item, by week, by warehouse—issuing from the marriage of supply and demand pro-

jections. Formulas imbedded in the program make allowances for safety stock. If the balance in any week drops below zero, the plan will have to be changed to meet the out-of-stock situation. Or if irreconcilable periods of shortage are displayed, the sales forecast itself will have to be altered to reflect reality (thereby establishing the incentive to plan the promotion of alternate products).

6. When planners are provisionally satisfied on all these points, they have a *quantity* sales forecast that can be lived with. The model is now used to project sales at various selling-price levels, based on anticipated standard costs (which will vary, because of raw materials, during the year ahead). Costs are standard, however prices vary by region (assuming that freight costs are absorbed). Without this model, it is nearly impossible to calculate the composite revenue of a particular product–price mix, much less the gross margin. At this point, then, it is important to test the financial forecast (or budget) and at the same time translate all market projections into profit and loss terms.

7. Finally (in this much simplified account of the planning process) the computer calculates the freight and storage costs entailed in the plan—nationally and by individual sales district as organizational entities as well as by warehouse and path-segment. (The rates are of course loaded in advance.) If you use public warehouses, or if you have alternate methods of transportation, you are still free to alter your network model and recalculate distribution expenses (and netback remaining from gross margin).

8. The final plan, if it results in the revision of sales forecasts, is republished throughout the organization, and each salesman sees the effect that any shortage or forced-draft promotional plans will have upon his own markets. Thus, as necessary, there is a push-pull effect; management is able to scale up or down the original forecasts made by field men, just as the salesman himself is able to register his thoughts from the firing line.

9. And so the process is repeated continuously, gradually getting easier and more accurate (if there are no radical changes of condition). Every year, when the fiscal plan is captured and frozen, there is one period of full elaboration, but between times the procedure is routine and need occupy little of top management's attention.

It will be seen from the foregoing discussion that this operations planning approach to forecasting may be contrasted to most of the advanced mathematical methods as, in the field of stockmarket investment, fundamentalists are contrasted to technicians (or "chartists"). Although we use the technical approach to determine buy or sell orders at the proper moment, basic selections are made only after bringing to bear all the knowledge that is available about the firm which issues the security. Fundamentalists and technicians mutually benefit from the system and from each other, as critics and judges. In the final analysis, it is more important to be only roughly accurate about the whole operation of the company than to be mathematically valid on a piecemeal basis. In other words, to use philosophical terms, it is possible to trace and (through managerial free will) influence causes. The tools of probability analysis (that is, intrinsic forecasting) can be used closer to the noise of the machinery and the shouts of the people.

Data Display: The Administrative Key

In a sense, everything that has been said so far is merely prologue to this last section. Marketing deals with the human universe, particularly in the selling function: employees who are under less supervision than others, perhaps brokers who are free agents, customers (over whom we have no authority except to collect accounts receivable), and prospects who may be downright hostile. Yet these people make up the sensory nervous system for most of marketing intelligence, at least as far as forecasting for present products is concerned. It is for salesmen that computers must take in and put forth knowledge of the company's relations with the outside world.

Salesmen are the greatest potential source of mid-term and short-term extrinsic forecast data. The administrative problem is to gather the data, convert them into true *information,* and return them to the salesman in such a way that he will find it useful for his own purposes. Most sales departments, despite lip-service to the principle of administrative simplicity, burden their field men with a variety of paperwork and special inquiries from the head office. Indeed, some reporting and communication in general are essential (if they work both ways). Forecasting would seem to be an added burden. But forecasting, properly used, contributes in a major way to the success of the salesman as well as to the success of the company.

There are at least three ways to mitigate this general problem of field sales administration. The first is to employ a unified and systematic reporting procedure whereby all qualitative and quantitative sales reports are integrated into a continuous nonredundant flow (requiring a minimum of handwriting) which is correlated with actual performance in sales analysis reports. Special surveys should be eliminated, in favor of using the forecast worksheet as a vehicle for the transmission of most marketing intelligence. The second way to help solve the problem has been touched upon in earlier sections—to enlist the willing support of the salesmen by *using* their forecasts in the conduct of the business. They will then be more motivated toward the resourceful use of the statistical reports which are sent to them to help them manage their territories. But the third way to assist forecasting administration in a field sales environment lies in *computer* technique.

By fully exploiting in one program the computer's power to store, retrieve, calculate, and print, it is possible to convert data to information very efficiently—efficiently in terms of communicative value as well as in terms of time and cost. The solution to the problem is also a solution to the general problem of the retrieval and display of information—that is to say, of data arranged and processed into meaningful form. Not many companies can afford direct on-line connections from their computers to salesmen in the field, and even when they can, it will be only for the transmission of transactions or other preformatted inquiry-and-reply traffic. After all, even the most advanced airline reservation system permits only a limited number of fixed-type displays or printouts. The effort here has been to develop a retrieval technology suitable for batch processing (though the batches may be very small and the processing may take only a few minutes) and the U.S. mail service.

In Exhibit 26–1, this retrieval subsystem is shown in the six o'clock position. The first functional specification of the program was that it should be able to extract and make use of *any* records in the historical data base and *any* records in the planning data base—any detail of any budget, operating forecast, sales goal, or other plan, whether presently in force or superseded. It is important to preserve old forecasts for the purpose of tracking variations statistically, thereby evaluating the relative success of different formulas or different human forecasters. Extraction is accomplished by a procedure of sorting and selection from a sequential disk file that can be arranged for the occasion in any of a large number of different orders (unlike the chained network files which are used as a business model to *generate* the planning data base).

The second specification for the generalized retrieval program was that it should be able to perform *any* calculation or manipulation of numbers without writing new programs. A few hours' or even a day's delay can be tolerated if it takes that long to introduce a radically new application, but new formulas should be at our disposal almost immediately. This objective is accomplished through modular programming, in which formulas may be inserted into the existing program as cutting tools are inserted into a turret lathe. Every formula is kept in the turret, once fixed there, for future use on demand. Thus a magazine of formulas is gradually built up that meets more and more needs without any delay at all.

Finally, one requires the ability to print in practically any desired way the retrieved and manipulated information. This capability was provided, in fact, by the same formula-writing technique. The formula controls spacing co-ordinates of words and numbers as well as their content. Accordingly, in a very inexpensive way, though not instantly, the single printer in the computer room acts almost as if it were a cathode ray display tube with control knobs for the user to set each row or column where he wants it. In the future, ob-viously, as on-line hardware gets more powerful and less costly, the speed and convenience of this retrieval program can be greatly improved. Perhaps every manager and salesman will be able to use it in his own office. But for most applications, the printed page is superior to a fleeting image, for we expect people to study for a time the figures before them and make penciled entries of their own or notes to the analyst. A printed report of many pages, if reduced to 8½- by 11-inch size in the reproduction process, may be carried around without inconvenience in an ordinary briefcase.

The retrieval program was intended in most cases, especially when used for salesmen in the field, to display *all* pertinent information on the same page or, at least, within the same set of pages. Most people who are not equipped with well-organized offices find it difficult and confusing and per-haps physically prohibitive to study and analyze more than one statistical re-port at a time. Frequently, it is hard enough just to *find* the ones you are look-ing for! Furthermore, analysis under the best of conditions is manifestly facilitated by the collation of comparative figures, notably the simultaneous display of historical and current data in time series. The salesman can return or throw away all past reports if pertinent history is repeated and updated with every new issue. Administrative simplification, which encourages active participation in forecasting, is fully as important as statistical computation, which is left to the computer.

Sales people may take as little or as much interest as they like in the mathematics. See the last line for each product on the forecast worksheet re-produced in Exhibit 26–5. The projection made by the computer is always open to criticism. Not only are the salesmen expected to challenge and amend specific figures for the future, but anyone who is interested may suggest bet-ter formulas—or better concepts upon which to base the formulas—for mak-ing the projections in the first place. In the course of time, increasingly subtle reasoning will be brought to bear, the computer's figures will be changed

Exhibit 26-5
District Forecast Worksheet

10-03-69	Dist 752		Div. 10		SA.19.WO		Per 04		Fisc Yr 69		
	Per 1	Per 2	Per 3	Per 4	Per 5	Per 6	Per 7	Per 8	Per 9	Per 10	Per 11	Per 12

1477-00* 10 oz Rainbow Trout

	Per 1	Per 2	Per 3	Per 4	Per 5	Per 6	Per 7	Per 8	Per 9	Per 10	Per 11	Per 12
LY Per Qty	150	69	104	145	127	126	144	111	195	257	139	133
TY Per Qty	184	110	138	168								
Fct Per Qty	184	110	138	190	156	160	146	148	1220	244	158	156
Bud Cum Qty	166	304	440	624	800	948	1106	1106	1422	1682	1828	2000
Fct Cum Qty	184	294	432	622	778	938	1084	1232	1442	1686	1844	2000
TY Cum Qty	184	294	432	600								
LY Cum Qty	150	219	323	468	595	721	865	976	1171	1428	1567	1700
Projection	184	294	432	600	750	904	1045	1188	1390	1626	1778	1929

1480-00* 12 oz Scallops

	Per 1	Per 2	Per 3	Per 4	Per 5	Per 6	Per 7	Per 8	Per 9	Per 10	Per 11	Per 12
LY Per Qty	34	18	30	21	29	23	26	20	20	39	22	18
TY Per Qty	33	21	20	29								
Fct Per Qty	33	21	20	29	22	24	25	21	26	32	24	23
Bud Cum Qty	29	53	77	109	140	166	194	214	249	294	320	350
Fct Cum Qty	33	54	74	103	125	149	174	195	221	253	277	300
TY Cum Qty	33	54	74	103								
LY Cum Qty	34	52	82	103	132	155	181	201	221	260	282	300
Projection	33	54	74	103	125	149	174	195	221	253	277	300

1492-00* 12 oz Salmon Steak

	Per 1	Per 2	Per 3	Per 4	Per 5	Per 6	Per 7	Per 8	Per 9	Per 10	Per 11	Per 12
LY Per Qty	38	28	49	27	50	36	42	36	56	63	38	37
TY Per Qty	53	44	55	50								
Fct Per Qty	53	44	55	50	60	60	43	37	46	67	44	41
Bud Cum Qty	42	76	110	156	200	237	277	305	356	421	457	500
Fct Cum Qty	53	97	152	202	262	322	365	402	448	515	559	600
TY Cum Qty	53	97	152	202								
LY Cum Qty	38	66	115	142	192	228	270	306	362	425	463	500
Projection	53	97	152	202	262	322	365	402	448	515	559	600

1494-00* 12 oz Swordfish Steak

	Per 1	Per 2	Per 3	Per 4	Per 5	Per 6	Per 7	Per 8	Per 9	Per 10	Per 11	Per 12
LY Per Qty	86	181	96	93	108	110	85	78	146	243	147	127
TY Per Qty	122	105	106	147								
Fct Per Qty	122	105	106	143	115	120	108	111	155	181	117	117
Bud Cum Qty	108	198	286	406	520	616	719	793	924	1093	1188	1300
Fct Cum Qty	122	227	333	476	591	711	819	930	1085	1266	1383	1500
TY Cum Qty	122	227	333	480								
LY Cum Qty	86	267	363	456	564	674	759	837	983	1226	1373	1500
Projection	122	227	333	480	595	716	825	937	1094	1276	1394	1512

14 **Group Total

	Per 1	Per 2	Per 3	Per 4	Per 5	Per 6	Per 7	Per 8	Per 9	Per 10	Per 11	Per 12
LY Per Qty	6180	5611	5054	7827	6522	6438	6356	5349	8450	11874	7202	6737
TY Per Qty	7483	6153	5486	7976								
Fct Per Qty	7483	6153	5486	8681	7765	7264	7993	6350	8008	10931	7059	7427
Bud Cum Qty	6871	12634	18314	26026	33720	40148	46601	51908	60143	71553	77496	84730
Fct Cum Qty	7483	13636	19122	27803	35568	42832	50825	57175	65183	76114	83173	90600
TY Cum Qty	7483	13636	19122	27098								
LY Cum Qty	6180	11791	16845	24672	31194	37632	43988	49337	57787	69661	76863	83600
Projection	7483	13636	19122	27098	34663	41742	49531	55721	63525	74177	81057	88296

more seldom, and the administrative burden will fade out as a practical issue.

It should be pointed out that the forecast worksheet will always continue to serve as a sales analysis report. It can be produced for each customer if necessary. The amounts shown in Exhibit 26–5 are physical quantities, but the same facts can be expressed in dollars, with margins and percentages of gross profit, or in weight. Or any combination of lines, in any sequence, can be displayed. Thus, as the learning curve for the forecasting procedure begins to flatten out, we can alter the worksheets to meet new conditions.

For example, the actual plus or minus deviations from budget could be printed along one line, periodically or cumulatively. This sort of feature is already being used when the program is applied to other aspects of the business—raw material price variances, for instance. Or a whole series of past forecasts can be printed under each other to show the "hunting" effect when we may have overreacted to temporary fluctuations of sales. The analysis of forecasts themselves will become nearly as important as the analysis of sales. As a result of such analysis, mathematical methods can be introduced to filter out random noise, and some of the means of intrinsic forecasting—especially those used for smoothing—can be used within the deterministic apparatus of the operations planning system.

With reference to Exhibit 26–5, let us take a look at the actual procedure for revising in mid-year the sales forecast, which constitutes an individual district's input to the company operating plan. (Compare the annual planning sequence more broadly treated in the previous section.) It is assumed that the operating forecasts are in a state of relative equilibrium after many repetitions of the planning cycle and that no new products are being introduced.

Let us say that it is the end of the first week of the new period. It cannot be sooner because the computer is still too loaded with previous-period work. The planning coordinator orders out the forecast worksheets, with projections based on a formula that takes into consideration the cumulative variance to date and the previously established pattern of sales over the remaining periods of the year. To keep this illustration simple the discussion is confined to the current fiscal year. The salesman receives his sheets, showing the latest complete period, on the second Monday.

He has a week to go over his figures, item by item. The procedure obliges him, for forecasting purposes, to analyze the performance of his district, even if he has few significant changes to make in his estimates. He has before him his original budget (line 4), the fixed bench mark against which he will in part be judged. But he also has in front of him (lines 2 and 6) the actual results that are in, and he knows that the latest forecast (lines 3 and 5) must be altered only in a way that will square with the facts: Any undue pessimism or exaggeration will come back to haunt him four weeks later, again and again. The psychological tension of the budget figure helps motivate his sales efforts. We may soon add a sales goal, higher than budget, for incentive purposes, which would then be displayed on this sheet in lieu of budget figures. But the fact that he is also being judged on his realistic knowledge of the progress of events, as well as the indirect effect that oversupply, based on wildly optimistic forecasts, will have on the regional profit and loss statement for which he is responsible, keeps him conscious of the need for reasonable accuracy.

Using the spaces left on the right side of line 2 or 6 (whichever he prefers to work with), he (*a*) checks column 12 to indicate that he wants to stay with the previous forecast, or (*b*) writes in an annual total revision in column 12 of line 6, or (*c*) writes a cumulative total at any earlier period (signifying to the marketing analyst that he thinks he will end up the year as previously estimated but that he expects the periodic pattern to change, perhaps because of a recently scheduled promotion), or (*d*) writes one or more period figures in line 2, most likely the current and immediately following period, again to show a change in spread rather than a revision of the total.

In most cases, the salesman can move rapidly down the sheet with check marks, lingering only over items with significant variances or those of particularly critical volume.

The sheets are returned then to the sales analyst, who edits all sales forecasts before they are passed to the planning coordinator for use in the operating plan. The latter examines the changes for unusual characteristics and quickly passes them on to the keypunching department. A computer program extrapolates a full annual time-series from the figures given. When these changes have been reentered into the computer, the retrieval program is run again to compile product *group totals* for each district represented and group totals for regions and divisions. (Note that the forecast has not yet been entered into the operations planning system.) The analyst studies these aggregations and discusses them with various product managers and other marketing executives, including the general sales manager, to see if the individual detailed forecasts make good sense when merged into a bulk forecast. If not, changes may be made at the top level and (again with the same program) distributed proportionally among the districts. Or the analyst may call up one of the salesmen to negotiate a consensus for change or to satisfy himself and the managers that the salesman's change was reasonable. Such manipulation of data may occupy the third week of the period.

The final forecast sheets, with all figures now printed, go to the planning coordinator for review in the light of what he knows about the logistical side of the picture. If raw material or production shortages are going to have to cut the sales of certain products, he will negotiate further revisions with the sales analyst (if those difficulties have not already been anticipated by the sales department). In any case, the coordinator enters the forecast into the operations planning model and causes the logistical ramifications to be printed out.

The logistical demand—that is, the drafts to be made on all warehouses and sources—is displayed on an operations planning report used by inventory analysts, production planners, buyers, and the computer itself, to prepare revised schedules before the ensuing period begins. This phase of the planning procedure will not be pursued here, for it is a large subject in itself. The important point is that operating decisions will now be made in full consonance with marketing's leadership and that distribution and field warehouses will be stocked according to forecasts made specifically for the particular areas they serve.

*　　*　　*

The thesis of this chapter has been that the nub of the planning problem is administrative technique and that the computer is fully as useful in this respect as it is in statistical projections or special studies. With the proper man-machine procedure, the computer can be instrumental in eliciting forecasts from field salesmen, in tempering their expectations with those of management, in modifying them for the exigencies of procurement conditions, and in presenting all aspects of the unified plan to every level of operating management.

The crucial usefulness of the program that displays the consequences of hypothetical facts at every stage of the way has here been emphasized. The success of the system depends largely upon the flexibility and power of this seemingly inessential device. It is typical of the computer, as of the human brain, that it is used best when it combines a broad grasp of the total environment with the small skills of sending and receiving communications.

27

COSMOS: An Application of Management Science Techniques to Marketing Decision Making

Thomas C. Jones

THOUGHTFUL MARKETING EXECUTIVES are constantly searching for methods to improve profits and control operations under their scope. Today, the growth of technology and communications is providing exciting new opportunities to do this.

The COSMOS system was developed to assist the retail food store operator. (The acronym COSMOS describes the ultimate goal of this program—that is, computer optimization and simulation modeling for operating supermarkets. In Webster's Dictionary, "Cosmos" is defined as "an orderly, harmonious, systematic universe.") Since there is a close similarity between food store, department store, variety store, other retail operators, the principles used to develop the system can be transferred with some modification to these environments. However, this chapter is intended to provide insight for marketing executives, irrespective of industry, into the assistance they can expect from the computer in improving the profitability of marketing decisions.

In addition to a description of the COSMOS system, what follows includes a summary of the types of problems which can be solved by techniques similar to those used in COSMOS and the basic executive guidelines for obtaining superior results from the computer.

CLASSES OF PROBLEMS TO WHICH THE COSMOS APPROACH IS APPLICABLE

Regardless of the industry, the approach to problem solution utilized in COSMOS is applicable for certain types of problems. Some examples of the types of problems which can be solved with similar techniques are:

- *Product profit review with recommended course of action.* The specific techniques used in COSMOS have applications beyond retailing. A bidding program to recommend prices based on historical and probable future conditions is an example.
- *Allocation of resources to a number of competing uses.* Allocation of shelf space in COSMOS is an example. However, the resource allocation could be salesmen to accounts, vehicles to customers, or men to machines.
- *Balancing of inventory costs with service requirements.* Men, money, and products are examples of resources which are maintained to meet anticipated demand. The cost of idle resources is balanced against the cost of lost sales.
- *Scheduling the sequence in which jobs should be accomplished.* The routing of delivery trucks, assignment of jobs to appliance service men, the delivery of merchandise to customers are examples of scheduling problems.
- *Providing timely, accurate information for decision making.* What information is needed to make *this* decision? The storage, retrieval, synthesis, and display of relevant information are critical to COSMOS and most other management decision-making systems.
- *Simulating the results expected if a particular course of action is followed.* What will happen to sales and profits if we reduce price by 5 percent on product A? A late stage in the total COSMOS proj-

ect will be concerned with small-scale simulators for well-defined, critical management problems.

This list is far from exhaustive. It is intended to suggest the kinds of problems that should be kept in mind while considering the basic approach to problem solution employed in COSMOS.

BASIC COMPUTER GUIDELINES FOR MARKETING MANAGERS

During the development of COSMOS and other profit-making management systems, a set of management guidelines has evolved. These rules have enabled decision makers to obtain superior results from the computer:

1. Experiment with new approaches to the solution of fundamental problems.
2. Search for fundamental management problems which, skillfully resolved, will have a significant impact on profits.
3. Do not delegate the responsibility for the development of practical and profitable computer systems. The executive must get involved in the conception and set up objectives and controls to insure implementation of the system.
4. Invest sufficient time, effort, and resources in the training programs essential to successful implementation.

Experiment with new approaches. The history of the COSMOS project is a story of responsible management searching for and experimenting with improved management methods. Studies started nearly four decades ago provided a theoretical framework for the project. In the summer of 1967, the management of one leading supermarket chain agreed to participate in the preliminary study which led to the design of the first version of the COSMOS I program.

Two systems have been designed to date. The first was operated in four stores for approximately six months. As a result of the operating experience, significant improvements were incorporated into the system.

Without the speculative participation of leading practical operators, willing to test, evaluate, and criticize, the COSMOS system could not have been developed. The basic criteria of "simple, practical, and profitable" require experimentation.

Search for fundamental management problems. Some of the fundamental problems defined jointly by a panel of supermarket executives and the Case and Company research team are as follows. Which of the thousands of available products should be handled in the available store space? How much shelf space should be given to each of these products? Where in the store should each product be displayed? Which products should be promoted? At what price should each of the products be sold? How should *each* of these choices be combined to maximize the net profit of the individual store?

The executive must get involved. The general need for deeper involvement by executives in their computer operations is illustrated by the following quotation taken from a recent Case and Company survey of 800 executives in a cross-section of the business community:

> The major obstacle to effective computer information systems is a lack of understanding by operating executives of computer capabilities as well as insufficient appreciation by computer executives of the operating executives' needs and wants.

The more successful companies have one common characteristic. At least one senior executive has taken a personal interest in fostering the development of the management information system. It is widely believed that the job can be turned over to a technical staff group. However, the better approach is to combine executive judgment with staff technical expertise.

How to get involved. The question is frequently asked: What executive involvement is required for successful systems development? There are three key operations that the executive must perform.

1. Set priorities in order that the scarce technical resources will be focused in directions which will yield the largest payoff for the company.
2. When priority is set, define objectives of each project.
3. Periodically review cost estimates, schedules, and actual progress.

Set priorities. After the fundamental problems of the business have been defined, the next step is to list the problems in priority order and to devise a sequential plan for attacking the problems.

The stages of development of COSMOS are shown in Exhibit 27–1.

The executive panel and the research team decided to limit the scope of

Exhibit 27-1
Project COSMOS: Sequence of Stages of Development

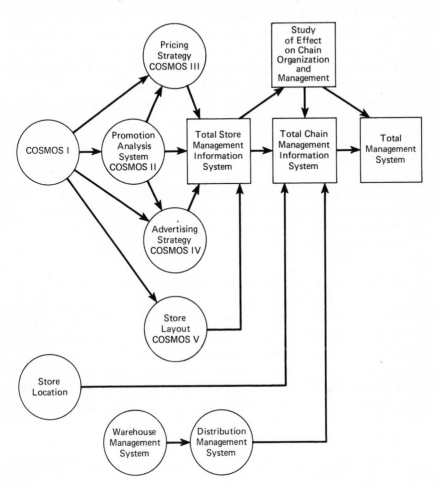

the project. In the beginning, attention was focused on the development of a system to optimize the utilization of available shelf space with profit improvement as the prime criterion. Later this was broadened to include pricing and location based on the results of the research. The research team also concentrated on the dry grocery department within the market.

In the judgment of the research team and the executive panel, it was necessary to limit the scope of the project in this way because:

- A logical theory was available that appeared to have a good chance to significantly improve profits.
- Much of the basic information needed for the system was already available in the regular store order-billing computer systems in use by many chains.
- The data base collected in developing the COSMOS I system would be invaluable in designing COSMOS II through V.
- The problem was manageable with available technical resources.

Define the objectives of each project. The research team debated such questions as:

- What information is needed for this decision?
- How can the necessary information be obtained?
- Are current management science techniques applicable?
- Is management willing to trust the results if these techniques are used?
- Can the proposed system be economically justified?

Following these discussions, the research team set objectives for the project and reviewed them with leading executives in the industry. The recommended actions encompass the following:

- The allocation of shelf space to individual products in each store. This includes not only the physical amount of space, but also the relative location of the item in its display area.
- The direction of potentially profitable product pricing changes.
- The promotion of products because of present or potential high profit returns.
- The review of individual products used to promote customer traffic and the chain's image.
- The deletion of products in order to free shelf space for new offerings from suppliers.

Training programs. Essential to the COSMOS concept is the idea that the decision maker must be thoroughly trained to understand when—and when not—to implement the recommendations provided by the computer. The decision maker is trained to know that most critical factors bearing on sales volume, customer traffic, space utilization, and profitability have been recorded and analyzed. They are trained to devote their attention to those decisions which require human judgment, that are beyond the scope of any computer today.

Frequent training sessions are required to insure that the managers are using the system correctly and to its best advantage. COSMOS represents a new way of thinking to the middle manager in the supermarket industry.

In COSMOS, the following provisions are deemed necessary to insure adequate training for operating personnel:

- Initial orientation meetings with key functional management groups in the chain:
  - Senior management.
  - Merchandising staff.
  - Store operations personnel.
  - Data processing personnel.
- Assignment of key personnel to an installations task force, responsible in part for:
  - Writing training and procedures manuals.
  - Conducting training sessions.
- Intense review and follow-up with merchandising and operating personnel after the first reports are issued.
- Periodic follow-up meetings and spot checks of in-store conditions thereafter.

In order to assist chains to properly and efficiently install COSMOS a detailed training manual has been published. The manual describes not only what to do and how to do it but why each step is important and how it fits into the total installation.

In addition to the manual, training schools and seminars are planned. They will be available at the time of general release of the COSMOS I programs to the food industry.

THE COSMOS SYSTEM

The supermarket industry has suffered profit declines and lower returns on investment in recent years. (COSMOS was begun in 1967). During the years from 1961 to 1967, before-tax earnings as a percentage of sales dropped from 2.5 to 2.2 percent. Similarly, return on owners' investment declined sub-

Exhibit 27–2
Typical Supermarket

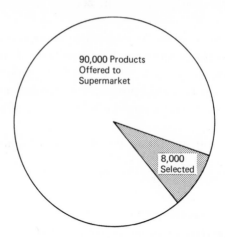

90,000 Products
Offered to
Supermarket

8,000
Selected

stantially—very persuasive reasons to seek new solutions to the industry's problems.

The supermarket business is complex in the sense that each store in a chain carries about 8,000 different products. The three sizes of a brand of soap or cereal are each considered a product in COSMOS. These 8,000 products are selected from the 90,000 products currently available from suppliers. The problem of keeping track of these 8,000 products is further complicated by the need to consider some 6,000 new products each year. Typically, some 400 to 500 new items are added each year, and some 200 to 300 items are dropped from the chain. The result is a net increase of some 200 items in each store each year. Exhibit 27–2 illustrates the complexity of the problem.

The final measure of complexity is the nature of the marketing area served by each store. Because neighborhoods vary, the sales volume and competitive situation are different for each store in the chain. Therefore, the total number of product situations which need to be monitored are not 8,000 but rather 8,000 times the number of stores in the chain. For a 100-store chain, there are 800,000 product situations in need of monitoring.

Facing this dynamic and complex marketing situation is a buying and merchandising staff which typically numbers seven. Using the information and management techniques employed until recently, only 300 to 400 products could be followed closely. Using pre-COSMOS techniques, thousands of items with major impact on chain profits were lost in the sense that they did not get adequate attention.

New solutions were developed to these common management problems because industry leaders recognized the availability of the following new techniques and were willing to experiment with them.

- A method for routinely calculating the net profit contributed by each product sold.
- The mathematical procedures of the management scientist.
- The rapid data processing capabilities of the third generation computer.

The COSMOS System—Its Ultimate Goal

As initially reported at the National Association of Food Chains Annual Convention in October 1968, the ultimate goal of the COSMOS system is to provide supermarkets with an integrated management information and decision-making system which is both profitable and practical. The system is designed for use by all operating elements of a supermarket chain. Selective reports, processed by the computer and tailor-made for specific functions in an organization, recommend profit-improving actions and evaluate the consequences of past decisions. The underlying purpose of these recommendations and analyses is to recognize changes in consumer needs and wants and to respond quickly and efficiently to these demands.

The development of the complete COSMOS system will take many years of research. However, in order to provide chain management with meaningful new information prior to the final design of the entire system, COSMOS has been subdivided into a series of building block systems. (See Exhibit 27–1.) COSMOS I is the first building block of the system and is presently installed and operating in major food chains.

Highlights of the System

In today's competitive marketing environment, chain store operating personnel are confronted, on the one hand, by an ever increasing number of product offerings by suppliers and, on the other hand, by an ever shifting demand for products by the consumer. The COSMOS I system has been designed to manage the complexities of dealing effectively on these two broad fronts. As a consequence, it deals directly with the problems of product mix, product pricing, and in-store allocation of display space.

The integration of man and the computer is the technique for achieving success in solving these complex operating problems. In this regard, the computer calculates the direct product profit (DPP) of each item in the store.

Retail price	29¢
Less cost of merchandise	26¢
Gross margin	3¢

Less: warehouse handling costs ⎫
     trucking costs to each store ⎬ 2¢
     in-store handling and checkout costs ⎭	

Direct Product Profit	1¢

This calculation provides a meaningful new index for measuring the net profit of individual product items. Specifically, direct product profits are computed by subtracting from each product's gross margin those measurable standard handling costs which are directly related to that product item. These costs consist of both direct labor and interest charges. The calculation of the handling costs was possible because Case and Company has accumulated an extensive library of standards as a result of client assignments.

In addition to computing direct product profits, the computer is further used to monitor the sales volume and in-store space of each item in the store. Then, combining pertinent economic data, it recommends specific actions to be taken on both an individual store and chainwide basis. As previously stated, the recommended actions encompass the following:

- The allocation of shelf space to individual products in each store. This includes not only the physical amount of space, but also the relative location of the item in its display area.
- The direction of potentially profitable product pricing changes.
- The promotion of products because of present or potential high profit returns.
- The review of individual products used to promote customer traffic and the chain's image.
- The deletion of products in order to free shelf space for new offerings from suppliers.

While only the computer can process and analyze the quantities of data for individual items economically and simultaneously, its recommendations will only reflect quantifiable factors, such as profits or sales. Operating personnel must supply the qualitative judgments to insure that these recommendations are both practical and in accordance with competitive market conditions. In this manner, management people play an extremely important role in the COSMOS I system.

Through this integration of man and computer and the development of profit information on individual products, the COSMOS I system adds a new dimension to the achievement of increasing profits within the chain. Traditionally, supermarket managements have increased profits by raising volume and decreasing expenses. COSMOS I augments these actions by influencing the mix of items sold. COSMOS I recommends that the most profitable items within a product family be given an increasing share of the preferred space on a store's shelves. Conversely, it restricts the space allocated to unprofitable products, while at the same time providing protection against undue stockouts. As a result, the consumers' attention and ultimately sales dollars are transferred to the most profitable products.

How COSMOS Works

The COSMOS I system has been developed as a result of more than a year of pilot operating experience. During this period, the COSMOS research team has received many valuable suggestions from chain operating personnel concerning improvements in the pilot system. These improvements have been incorporated into the present COSMOS I programs and add to their power and flexibility.

The overall design of the system is presented in diagrammatic form in Exhibit 27–3. This diagram depicts the overall information and processing flow from the development of the basic source data to the ultimate implementation of recommended actions by operating personnel.

Certain basic source data are required to operate COSMOS I. These data must be collected by the chains prior to implementation of the operating system and include the following:

- Handling costs directly attributable to the product. These include warehouse and in-store handling and processing costs. An automatic

Exhibit 27-3
System Diagram—COSMOS 1

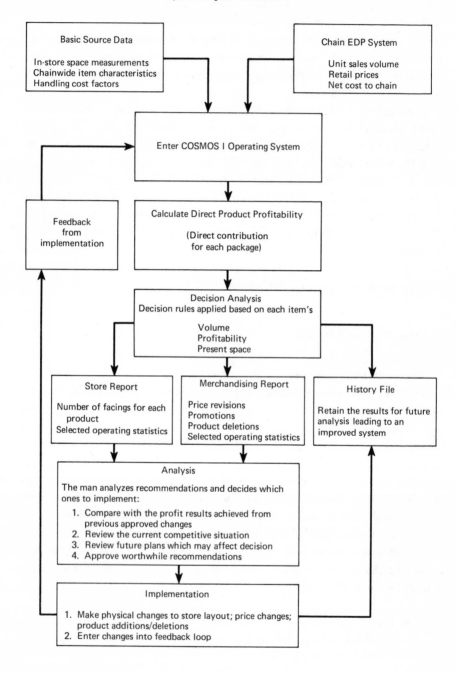

Basic Source Data

In-store space measurements
Chainwide item characteristics
Handling cost factors

Chain EDP System

Unit sales volume
Retail prices
Net cost to chain

Enter COSMOS I Operating System

Feedback
from
implementation

Calculate Direct Product Profitability

(Direct contribution
for each package)

Decision Analysis
Decision rules applied based on each item's

Volume
Profitability
Present space

Store Report

Number of facings for each
product
Selected operating statistics

Merchandising Report

Price revisions
Promotions
Product deletions
Selected operating statistics

History File

Retain the results for future
analysis leading to an
improved system

Analysis

The man analyzes recommendations and decides which
ones to implement:

1. Compare with the profit results achieved from
   previous approved changes
2. Review the current competitive situation
3. Review future plans which may affect decision
4. Approve worthwhile recommendations

Implementation

1. Make physical changes to store layout; price changes;
   product additions/deletions
2. Enter changes into feedback loop

computer system has been designed to compute, from standard time elements, total direct costs for each product.

- Specific in-store data on space assigned to each product. For each store monitored by the system, shelf dimensions and the number of facings normally assigned to each product must be collected.
- Dimensions and weight of each product.

Significantly, these source data must be collected only one time and can be used until basic changes are made that influence the operating costs of individual products. Following this initial collection process, chain data collection is largely limited to reporting information on the shelf space allotted to new products and the changes in space for existing products.

COSMOS I obtains additional product information by tying directly into the chain's existing EDP system. This data entry procedure helps to insure the practicality of operating the system and provides the following required information for each product.

- Retail prices and average chainwide purchase costs.
- Product shipments. Chains have the capability for providing accurate warehouse shipment information for individual stores as a by-product of their computerized store order and billing system.

With these data, direct product profits for each item in each monitored store are calculated. Computerized programs then recommend action for each product item by comparing its performance with all other products in a functionally related group. This related group is best defined as a product subcommodity group. For example, in the "dog food" commodity group of a store, "semimoist dog food" is a subcommodity group.

These COSMOS I recommendations are designed primarily to affect the big profit makers and losers within each commodity group. If a product item is very profitable, the action recommended may be to increase the number of store shelf facings as well as to assign it to the best position in the section. On the other hand, highly unprofitable items may be recommended for deletion, price revision, or space reduction.

Selective Management Reporting

To adequately reflect the different information requirements of the various levels and functional groups within the chain, selected recommendations and statistical information appear on two separate management reports—the store report (Exhibit 27–4) and the merchandising report (Exhibit 27–5). This reporting procedure insures that chain personnel in various operating capacities are not overburdened with data irrelevant to their separate operating needs. The general content of these reports follows.

Store report. A separate report is issued for each store utilizing the COSMOS I system. It is primarily designed for use by in-store operating management. Recommendations are limited to those which store management personnel normally implement for specific items—changes in the physical amount and relative location of space on the shelves. Each report analyzes an entire commodity group, and only products which require action are reported. These analyses are prepared on a predetermined cycling basis so that each commodity group is normally reviewed once every three to six months. This structuring restricts each store report to two or three pages a week in order to accommodate the busy schedules of personnel who review and implement recommendations.

Merchandising report. This report is designed for operating personnel who make centralized decisions on product items—pricing, promotions, additions, and deletions of products. In-store operating results are summarized by price zone to facilitate chainwide recommendations on the raising or reducing of prices, promotions of profitable products, and review of high-volume "traffic builders." Summaries by warehouses are presented to assist in such decisions as whether to continue to stock the product. Also, section summaries can be made, if desired, on a small group of stores to analyze socioeconomic factors.

In addition to these reports, the chain can generate control reports to accomodate other decision-making levels, such as top-echelon operating and financial management. Utilizing the COSMOS I system, it is possible to analyze specific aspects of store operating performance and generate selective reports from these analyses. For example, as illustrated in Table 27–1, a report can be generated showing relevant statistics on in-store sales and direct product profits compared to forecast or to historical results. Another complementary report shown in Table 27–2 features a comparison of actual store operating expenses against COSMOS I standard costs to produce an operating variance report. Further, as Table 27–3 shows, reports detailing the cost and profit statistics of the various suppliers of the chain can also be prepared. The ability to produce these and additional management reports should benefit the users of the COSMOS I system.

Exhibit 27-4

COMOS 1 – Store Recommended Action Report

Zone 011	Section 01	Store 01581F	COSMOS I Store Recommended Action Report	Date 8-02-69

Item No.	Item Description	Size	Case Pack	Current		Face	Average/Week		Direct Product Profit			Recommend			Spec Stk
				Retail	Cost		Vol	$ Sales	Per Week	Unit	Cu Ft	Loc	Face	Now	Rec
270001	Ritzy meat dog food	24 oz.	12	$0.610	$0.519	2	47	$28.67	$2.209	$0.047	$1.884	SPC	+1	Yes	
270006	Prime beef dog food	1 lb	24	$0.410	$0.365	2	35	$14.35	$0.860	$0.024	$0.840				
280019	Whole meal dog food	1 lb	48	$0.305	$0.268	3	61	$18.60	$0.671	$0.011	$0.411	UNF			
280106	Zesty beef/w gravy	15 oz	24	$0.280	$0.272	2	21	$ 5.90	-$0.693	-$0.033	-$0.693				

Cat	Sub Cat	Description	Items		Total/Week			Total Space (feet)		
			Tot	Loss	Sales	DPP/Wk	DPP/ Ft 3	Now	Rec	Change
02	01	Dog food ration wet	4	1	$ 67.52	$3.03	$0.63	2.4	2.6	+0.2
02	02	Dog food semi-moist	15	1	$223.18	$9.28	$1.50	7.8	8.5	+0.7
02	03	Dog food dry	7	3	$105.91	-$0.49	-$0.08	5.1	4.2	-0.9
02		Dog food	26	5	$396.61	$11.82	$1.10	15.3	15.3	0.0

Exhibit 27-5
COSMOS 1 – Merchandising Report

Item 270001		Desc/Size			24 oz	Case Pack 12	Cat 02	Subcat 01	

COSMOS I Merchandising Report — Date 9-01-69
Ritzy Meat Dog Food

Ident Code			Average/Unit			Total/Week			Number Stores				Promotions			COSMOS	Vol
Sec	Zone	Whse	Retail	Cost	DPP	Sales	DPP	Unit Vol	Tot	With Prd	Hvl	Lvl	No.	Date Code	Type Code	Recommends	w/del
01	011	02	$0.610	$0.519	$0.040	$ 98	$ 6	161	3	3	2	0				Promote	161
02	011	02	$0.610	$0.519	$0.040	$129	$ 8	211	6	5	2	0					211
03	011	02	$0.610	$0.519	$0.040	$ 59	$ 4	97	2	2	2	0				Promote	97
Zone	011	02	$0.610	$0.519	$0.040	$286	$18	469	11	10	6	0	2	5	1	Promote	469
01	015	02	$0.600	$0.519	$0.010	$124	$ 2	207	4	4	1	1					207
03	015	02	$0.600	$0.519	$0.010	$166	$ 3	277	5	5	2	0					277
Zone	015	02	$0.600	$0.519	$0.010	$290	$ 5	484	9	9	3	1	2	5	1		484
Whse		02	$0.605	$0.519	$0.025	$576	$23	953	20	19	9	1	2	5	1		953

Cat	Sub	Description	Sales/Wk	DPP/Week	Number Stores			No. Items
					Tot	Profit	Loss	Prom
02	01	Dog food ration wet	$1,350	$ 43	20	3	0	1
Cat	02	Dog food	$8,276	$237	Last report 12 weeks ago			3

TABLE 27–1
SPACE EFFICIENCY REPORT

Product Group Number	Sales	Percent of Sales	DPP	Percent of DPP	Cubic Feet of Space	Percent of Space
10	$980	2.30	$45	1.20	150	5.00
14	$ 70	.16	$ 7	0.19	3	.10

TABLE 27–2
MANPOWER EFFICIENCY REPORT

Store Number	DPP Actual	DPP Percent of Sales	Labor Cost Actual	Labor Cost Standard	Efficiency Index	Historical Index for Comparison
0034	$2,800	4.00	$ 7,500	$ 7,600	0.99	1.02
0036	2,110	3.50	7,200	6,800	1.06	1.06
Total	$4,910	3.76	$14,700	$14,400	1.02	1.04

TABLE 27–3
SUPPLIER ANALYSIS REPORT

Supplier: XYZ	Four-week period ending 11/1 Sales	Purchase Cost	Ware-house Cost	Trans-porta-tion Cost	In-Store Cost	DPP
Products:						
AAA	$1,000	$ 850	$ 20	$ 30	$ 75	$ 35
BBB	500	425	10	11	30	24
CCC	6,000	5,500	140	160	480	—280
Category Total	$7,500	$6,775	$170	$201	$585	$—221
Promotional allowances						300
Other allowances						06
Supplier Total	$7,500	$6,775	$170	$201	$585	$— 85

Results to Date

The first system, COSMOS I, is operating in 25 stores in three major chains. The results of more than a year's operating experience continue to be encouraging. Preliminary tests indicated potential net profit improvement of 10 to 15 percent in each store on the system.

Harry Beckner, president of Jewel Food Stores, at the 1969 National Association of Food Chains Annual Meeting, said:

> The managers seem to be enthusiastic about the direct-product-profit information supplied by the COSMOS printout. They feel that this information in itself will enable them to operate more intelligently in managing their stores.
>
> Jewel is continuing diligently to test this program, on the conviction that we cannot afford to overlook any new profit possibilities in the supermarket business. We believe that the scientific management of space and prices is perhaps the greatest single opportunity available to the industry today.

*   *   *

The COSMOS project is a demonstration of the value of the management sciences and computer sciences to the practicing marketing executive. When carefully planned and executed, with a liberal dosage of executive time and attention, the computer can assist in improving the profitability of marketing decisions.

The development of simple, practical marketing systems in any company or industry is a major research and development project. With the leading competitors constantly searching for better ways to manage, few companies can afford not to pursue such a goal.

28

Using Computers—A Look Ahead

Robert A. Hammond

W E ARE ALL AWARE of our changing environment. Not only are we confronted with normal political and business changes, but currently we are experiencing new changes in the value systems on which our politics, business, and social relationships are based. Many of these changes in our value systems have been brought about by scientific and technological developments and a rebellion against established institutions, organizations, and social codes. And it is in this environment that management is expected to plan!

Clearly, we need new planning approaches and new tools to allow us to evaluate change, understand its implications, and redirect our efforts toward our objectives. One way of evaluating change and uncertainty and determining the likely impact of decisions is to use models. Engineering models have been used for years, and management scientists using computers have provided some inroads into certain types of problems for which quantitative data are available. Now a new era is beginning. With the aid of easily programmed time-sharing computers and bold new efforts of planners and line executives to model business economics, the planning tools we need to cope with rapid change are beginning to emerge. It is these new approaches and tools that are discussed here.

Accordingly, let us first briefly mention some of the changes that typically occur in the business environment and their impact on planning needs and then discuss the recent evolution of computer tools and new applications. Finally, examples are provided of a family of planning models being developed by some companies and suggestions are made as to how management should improve its use of computers.

Needs in a Changing Environment

If we review the significance of planning and information systems during a period of changing conditions, we find that these systems are often completely unable to identify or analyze the impact of dynamic changes in the market and the business. For example, a consumer products company found itself suddenly having to react to a major change in competition and pricing. But planning was tied to an annual process, and changes left the plans almost useless for the remainder of the budgeted year. Management realized that a process was needed for reevaluating plans to take account of major changes as they occurred, and it took steps to develop an adaptive planning (variable budgeting) process.

Key activities for managers are identifying problems, analyzing them, and determining corrective courses of action. However, information systems rarely provide the kind of data a manager needs to identify or analyze problems, and all too often these systems show results only well after corrective action should have been taken. For example, some of the crises that occur when the economics of a business or the marketing factors that affect the business change show the weakness of the information systems. They often give only partial results and do not show the costs or effectiveness of activities or departments. The systems are therefore unable to help in the evaluation of change as it occurs.

We know very well that the computer is still rarely used in planning and top management problem solving. And unfortunately, many of the integrated and large-scale management information systems that have been developed have not derived the payoff that was expected of them. The concept of an integrated management information system is that it allows many kinds of information to be obtained from basic data sources such as sales and billing information. However, technical and economic difficulties in the past and widely differing needs of departments and managers have created roadblocks, and many companies have reverted to a segmented approach and systems that provide more immediate payback than the broader, longer-range data-bank concept.

In the past, computers have been most useful for processing data periodically and developing management information rather than for providing analyses for problem solving or planning. Changes now occurring in computer tools are to a large extent overcoming these old weaknesses.

Changes in Computer Tools

Almost everybody agrees that changes in computer tools over the next few years will be evolutionary rather than revolutionary. For example, the massive reprogramming that took place during the introduction of the third-generation computers will not again be necessary. Yet slight changes in tools may lead to revolutionary change in management use of and significance of computers.

What are some of the changes that are taking place in computer tools? Certainly, technical advances continue to improve performance (which has doubled every two and a half years since the first generation). The emphasis is now more on current data and immediate processing (real-time) than on periodic batch processing as in the past. This means a much greater use of communications in systems to link geographical locations of a corporation to common computers. And, of course, we see more technical improvements that are characterized by such words as multiprogramming, multiprocessing, and multitasking.

Probably more important than the technical advances is the fact that computers are becoming easier to use. A major emphasis of computer manufacturers recently has been to take steps to reduce the rapidly increasing costs of systems and programming work relative to computer costs. This means that they are designing equipment that will eliminate many of the software steps. Also, current improvements in application packages will lead to increased use of these packages, especially by individual divisions and small companies that do not have the capacity to design their own programs. And finally, computers will be easier to use in the future because they will accept both batch processing and time sharing from remote locations.

The most important change is a greater and more profitable use of time sharing. The key characteristic of time sharing is the use of a number of remote terminals that are tied to a computer and can be used simultaneously for direct program development or problem analysis. This, of course, means that the computer is set up for multiprogramming (a number of jobs done concurrently) and has immediate access from each of the terminal locations. Time sharing is not merely a convenience in the use of a computer; it has been shown to have very significant benefits when used by management for solving problems or analyzing important alternatives facing a corporation. In fact, time sharing helps in the creative process of management. During the next few years, we will see the rapid growth of time-sharing service companies and, more significantly, an increase in use of time-sharing installations in companies.

A typical use of a time-sharing facility would be the merger–acquisition model described in Exhibit 28–1. This model might be developed for a cor-

Exhibit 28–1
Merger–Acquisition Model

Financial Data of Parent Company

• Profit and loss records
• Capital structure
  – Common stock
  – Preferred stock
• Market price
• Dividend policy

Acquisition Opportunities
• Projections on sales and earnings • Capital structure • Market price

Combined Operations
• Sales and earnings • Dividends

Combined Capital Structure

• Stock purchase
  – Common
  – Preferred
  – Convertible
• Cash purchase

Detailed Analysis
• Earnings per share projections • Stock conversion • P/E projections • Ranking opportunities

immediate effectiveness of his program. In addition, the marketing manager might use this system to immediately identify problems in the progress of sales of new items in specific types of distribution areas or geographical locations. Therefore, the characteristics of these systems are (1) on-line communication with the end-user locations; (2) preprogrammed analysis and sorting of the data files; (3) a breakdown of information appropriate for problem identification and analysis; and (4) outputs that can be either periodic, further inputs for control systems, or on-call reports.

The most important additions to planning and control activities are the computer planning models. These models typically have three characteristics: They will deal with key management problems and alternatives, incorporate managerial judgments, and be flexible, easily usable models on time-sharing computers. In addition, most models focus on key economic features of a company and provide top management with a tool for analysis of major corporate and divisional policies and strategies as they are developed. They are significantly different, therefore, from most models that have been built in the past, for which the focus has typically been on recurring down-the-line planning situations in production scheduling, inventory control, or distribution analysis. These operational models will also be needed in the future, but they generally require considerably more data, often are better suited to a researchable project approach, and do not generally require time-sharing facilities. Top management planning models will deal with aggregate numbers rather than with detailed data and be simple enough so that top management can analyze broad policy and strategic questions with easy access to the computer.

Exhibit 28–3 is a diagram of a family of such planning models developed for a consumer products company. Management handles the normal facilities and logistics questions by using models that are designed to analyze investments, major alternatives in distribution channels, and production and inventory planning. Three additional models allowing analysis of growth strategy, financial policy, and marketing decisions, respectively, complete the family. Because the company is considering strategic alternatives involving merger and acquisition, it plans to use a model for the analysis of this strategy. Financial policy related to debt, acquisition financing, and investment criteria is important; therefore, an overall financial analysis model is planned to allow top management to evaluate major policy alternatives. Finally, because the company's success depends on good overall marketing planning, they have started to develop a model to analyze questions related to improving the allocation of marketing resources in promotion, advertising, merchandising, and sales effort.

Management might wish to start a family of planning models, with an overall aggregate model in each of these three areas—strategy, financial policy, and marketing—and then plan to develop more detailed models as planning needs require, for the analysis of specific issues such as pricing strategy or new product introduction. The important feature of this planning approach is that these models would become a family of tools to assist both staff and line managers in creatively developing new alternatives and strategies supported by sound economic and financial analysis.

The exact family of models clearly depends on the characteristics of the corporation or division, and possibly a corporation would have two or three sets of families of models based on its economic and industrial characteristics. For example, the corporate group could center around two models dealing with financial policy analysis and investment analysis. They might, for example, develop the picture of profit and loss and earnings per share under a number of assumptions about criteria for selecting investments or about the portfolio of investment projects.

Exhibit 28-3
A Family of Planning Models

Financial Policy
- Debt/equity
- Acquisition financing
- Stock mix
- Investment criteria

Growth Strategy
- Strategic alternatives
- Merger/acquisition
- Internal growth opportunities

Marketing
- New products
- Market analysis
- Promotion
- Pricing

Facilities
- Investment analysis
- Plant expansion

Logistics
- Warehouse system
- Distribution channels
- Production/inventory planning
- Purchasing

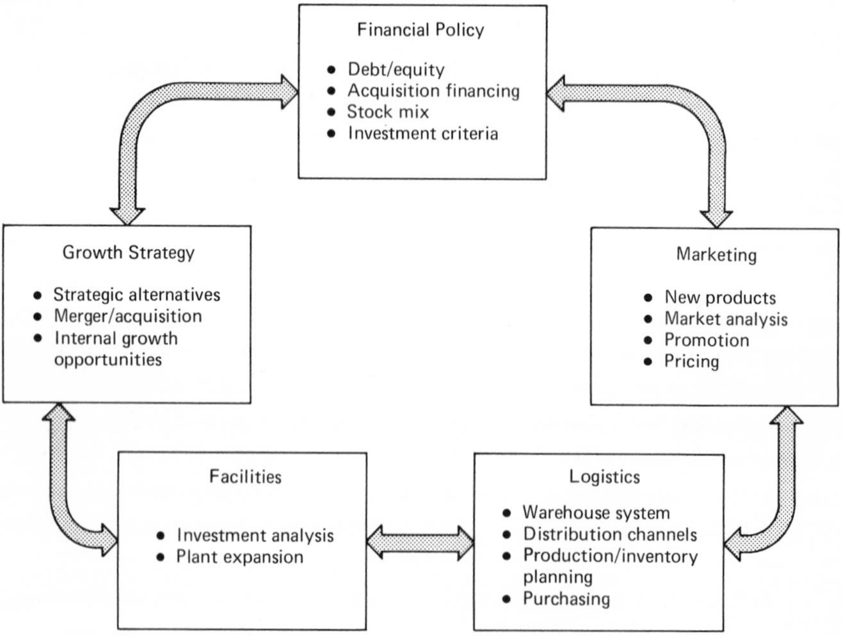

A company in the industrial products area has begun its family of models with just two—one dealing with the logistics area (facilities, production, and inventory planning) and the second dealing with the analysis of the marketing distribution channels. This company began its development of a family of models with a basic economic analysis of the industry and the company's role in that industry. This enabled them to (1) focus on the key factors that influenced the profit picture of each business in the corporation and (2) identify the major issues, alternatives, and problems that they faced.

A consumer products company (for example, in the beer or soft drinks industry) would have to place more emphasis on developing an effective model (or set of models) in marketing than on logistics and finance. The important decision for this company would be the allocation of marketing resources.

In what amount, where, and how should resources be used in advertising, merchandising, promotion, and selling? More specifically, what should the advertising budget be? Where should the money be spent? Should the sales force be increased or allocated to focus on new areas? Each of these areas is usually studied by separate groups—product managers, marketing research and advertising departments. Providing an overall analysis of marketing strategies and profitability is difficult because we have neither sound measures of effectiveness nor a mechanism for testing alternatives.

Developing a strategic marketing planning model is one way to overcome these weaknesses. It is clearly a difficult task, because it requires estimation of the marginal contributions of changes in the allocation of resources and estimation of their interrelationships. But managers have to make decisions, and a step toward understanding the economics and dynamics of change is obviously valuable.

One model being developed includes the features illustrated in Exhibit 28–4 is unique in that it

- Focuses on top-management decisions in marketing; specifically those dealing with the marketing mix of advertising, merchandising, promotion, and selling.
- Uses judgmental inputs where there is uncertainty regarding the factors affecting decisions (including judgments on the marginal effectiveness of marketing allocations).
- Presents results of the model in a format that managers can easily understand, as profit contribution and profit and loss projections.

Exhibit 28-4

Strategic Marketing Planning Model

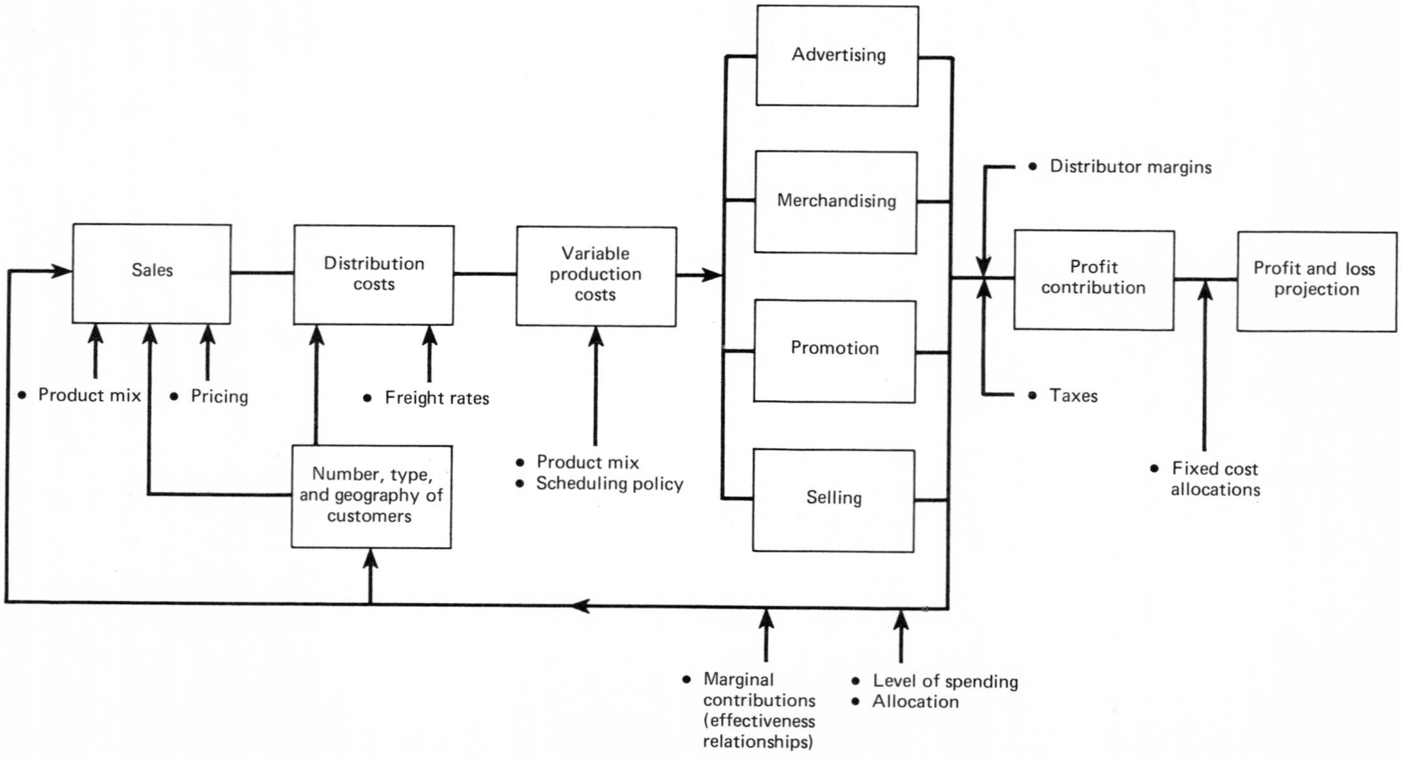

The model can easily be updated as factors change—product mix, scheduling policy, distribution costs—but at any time plans can be evaluated for different estimates and assumptions regarding sales and profitability.

Although many of the computer tools and applications described here are still being developed, management can begin to improve the planning and control activities and the supporting management information systems by taking some immediate steps.

Steps Management Should Take

To improve its approach to selecting and setting priority for computer systems and modeling design, management should insure that, in addition to determining information needs, it uses cost–benefit analyses and identifies key problem areas and opportunities. For example, management might consider how information and control systems can improve (1) problem identification and analysis, (2) analysis of opportunities and strategic alternatives, and (3) allocation of resources. The end result of such a top-level analysis of needs might lead to both moving ahead with basic control systems of the type currently underway and refocusing on developing new planning approaches and models.

It is clearly a mistake for a corporation to wait until all basic systems are installed before it starts using computers for planning and problem solving. Delay might cause it to miss the most effective use of the computer. At the same time, management should be improving its information systems to make them more effective for planning and control in a dynamic environment. And because marketing is often the most dynamic ongoing activity in a company, the computer support for it must have the same flexible, dynamic characteristics.

The manager might ask: Are my systems helpful in analyzing key changes that may occur during the next few months in the areas of competition, market share, price, and government or labor policy? Can a computer system be developed to help in the replanning process when sudden changes or problems occur?

Management should appraise the organization of support activities in marketing, systems design, and EDP to encourage use of new concepts and tools that are emerging in the computer area. For example, it should ask questions such as these: Are new planning skills needed to effectively use computer modeling approaches? Are the systems staff being used in the most important profit-improvement problem areas? Is new organization strength in the corporate staff needed to effectively analyze major financial policy and alternatives? Can corporate guidance in the use of application packages and on-call information systems be provided to divisions?

With adequate expertise and support from the computer, systems and staff departments, it is then the responsibility of marketing managers to seek computer benefits. They should demand a well-planned series of programs to provide basic current data on changing marketing characteristics with flexible access, problem-solving objectives, and benefits that they can obtain (not the systems men). And for planning, management should select key top-management problems and decision areas, work with model builders to develop—with relatively short (two to four months) intensive projects—models of the economics of the business that allow marketing judgments to be evaluated and alternative strategies and allocations of resources to be tested.

29

The Future of
the Computer in Marketing*

Philip Kotler

THE WORDS "mathematics" and "computer" continue to have an alien ring
in the ears of many marketing executives. Those who spend their days firing
up a sales force, planning advertising campaigns, servicing and placating
dealers, and trying to outmaneuver competitors believe that much of marketing defies classification and analysis. They develop a natural suspicion
about statements that mathematics and the scientific method might make a
significant contribution to the understanding and solution of marketing problems. In fact, there is no question that many facets of the marketing process
will not submit to scientific tidiness, particularly facets that rely heavily on
creativity, human relations, and the like. But there are other facets of marketing that have responded well to systematic observation, analysis, and procedures, and here there is a golden opportunity for the marketing executive
willing to adopt an innovative attitude toward the new knowledge.

* Adapted from the author's article in the *Journal of Marketing,* January 1970, pp.
11–14.

Although mathematical models and computers are relative latecomers in marketing, they have already shown payoff in such areas as new product development and strategy, advertising media selection, and product pricing. A growing number of marketing executives are testifying to the various benefits of formal models and computers. According to one executive in an automobile company, the new models have been instrumental in increasing marketing's self-respect and the respect shown by other company departments toward marketing. He has made the point thus:

> Formerly, finance and production would go into the board meeting armed with their carefully documented plans spelled out in dollars and cents. Marketing would go into the same meeting with a lot of vague assertions, guesses, and hot air. We've spent the last couple of years learning and using decision theory, regression analysis, and simulation in our marketing work, and now at the board meetings, our estimates and plans command considerable confidence.

Trends and Major Developments

The character of future marketing management is already adumbrated in today's practices in some of the larger American market-oriented companies. Discussions with marketing executives in a number of these companies confirm that a major revolution is taking place in the information and analytical capabilities of marketing management. Here the more striking developments that are occurring in the areas of information technology and analytical tools are highlighted.

Information Technology

Marketing executives derive their information about the marketplace through marketing intelligence, formal marketing research, and company accounting information. The alert marketing executive recognizes that each of these areas has a potentiality for considerable improvement. Marketing intelligence activity describes the continuous efforts of executives to keep informed about current developments among customers, dealers, competitors, and the marketing environment. Three key trends in the area of marketing intelligence are these:

1. Companies are giving better training and motivation to their salesmen and are now regarding them as "information officers" of the firm.
2. Some companies are assigning full-time personnel to the task of gathering marketing intelligence through field work and continuous scanning of published information.
3. Companies are seeking to build central information files on dealers, customers, and competitors so that their executives will have finger-tip information.

One large company recently appointed an ex-military intelligence officer to take over, design, and manage a marketing intelligence service for the executives in the company.

Marketing research connotes more formal, project-oriented research that usually begins with a company problem or opportunity and ends with a management report. Three important trends in marketing research are:

1. Executives are increasingly recognizing that good marketing research is more than fact-gathering. Much more effort is being put into defining the real problem and the manager's decision alternatives as a basis for collecting action-relevant information.
2. Market experimentation is becoming an increasingly significant information-gathering technique, particularly for learning the response of sales to different types and levels of marketing inputs. A vice-president of a large company predicts that marketing experiments will be budgeted into marketing plans as a routine matter in the seventies. He maintains that some small part of every budget should always be assigned to finding out how to improve the spending of the big part.
3. Marketing executives are increasingly asked to quantify their feelings about sizes of markets, effects of marketing expenditures, and the probabilities surrounding critical marketing events. Their subjective estimates are essential inputs for the more advanced marketing models. The challenge to quantify sharpens the quality of marketing discussion and analysis.

The company accounting system serves the purpose of generating summaries of current sales and costs. Companies are investing heavily in improving their internal reporting systems, the following developments being of great interest to marketers.

1. There is an increased interest in storing sales and marketing cost data on a disaggregative basis to permit executives to retrieve special configurations of information. In one company, an executive can retrieve current and past sales and inventory figures for any brand and package size for each of 400 distributors. Or he can request the computer to list all distributors whose sales fall below a certain figure. In another company, marketing researchers can seek to measure the effects of specific marketing inputs on specific sales results by geographical area.

2. Companies are attempting to reduce the length of time it takes for executives to learn of latest sales. The fast-changing marketing scene means that line executives should be posted continuously on important sales developments. A few consumer goods companies are now able to provide executives with data on shipments that took place yesterday. Grocery goods companies are trying to figure out how they can learn of retail shelf-sales movement as it takes place. Some companies in the airline and motel industries have managed to develop real-time information—that is, they know sales and product availabilities as of the latest second.

3. Companies are finding new uses for their computers as a sales tool in the servicing of customer needs. Salesmen in one large paper company can dial the company computer while in a customer's office and learn in a matter of seconds whether a certain grade of paper is in stock and could be shipped to the customer in time to meet a target date. A large fertilizer company helps farmers decide on next year's best crops—and fertilizer—through a specially designed computer program. Several insurance companies use the computer to prepare long-range insurance programs for clients.

Analytical Models and Tools

The future marketing executive increasingly will rely on sophisticated tools and models to help analyze his information. His familiarity with the new tools will come about through MBA programs, executive development seminars, and exposure to computer time sharing, which will probably be the most potent force in dramatizing the new tools to the marketing executives. Time sharing refers to a setup in which several remote teletype terminals are linked to a central computer, and an executive can sit down at any one, dial the computer center number, type in his user number, and have access to all the power of the computer. An increasing number of computer programs will be available on a conversational basis—that is, the typewriter will type out a description of the requested program and then instruct the executive as to how he should type in his data. After the computer has received the data, it types a solution in a matter of seconds.

The potentialities of this tool can be dramatized by realizing that each of the following programs is already available in one or another company today for their marketing executives to use.

1. A new product manager can sit down at a terminal, dial a new product computer program called SPRINTER 1, and supply such estimates as the estimated size of the target group, recent product trial rates and repeat-purchase rates, the promotional budget, size of investment, target rate of return, product price, and gross profit margin. The computer will digest this information and print out a monthly forecast for the next few years of the total number of buyers, company market share, period profits, and discounted cumulative profits. The new product manager can alter various input estimates and readily ascertain the effect of the altered data on sales and profits.

2. An advertising manager can dial a media selection computer program called MEDIAC and type in information on the size of his advertising budget, the number and size of important market segments, media exposure and cost data, ad size and color data, sales seasonality, and other information. The computer will return a media schedule that is calculated to achieve maximum exposure and sales impact in the customer segments.

3. A sales manager can dial a sales redistricting program, type in data on the workload or sales potential of various counties, their distance from each other, and the number of sales territories he wants to create. The computer will digest this information and assign various counties to make up new sales territories in such a way that (a) the sales territories are approximately equal in workload or sales potential, and (b) they are compact in shape, thus cutting down travel costs.

4. A marketing executive can dial a dealer site-location program, type in a proposed location and size for a new dealership in a large city, and receive a forecast of sales and market share for the new dealership and the loss of sales to other dealerships, including his own.

5. A salesman can dial a sales prospect evaluation program, type in information about a list of prospects, including the estimated value of their annual business, the maximum probability of conversion, and the estimated

number of years they will remain customers and receive a table suggesting the optimal number of calls to make on each prospect and how the prospects rank in order of attractiveness.

6. The marketing controller can dial a dealer size-evaluation program, type in data on annual sales of each dealer, servicing costs, and the behavior of unit production costs with scale of production. The computer program will suggest the minimum-size dealer to retain.

These computer programs represent only the beginning of marketing models tailored to the problems and needs of various industries and executives. They utilize a variety of mathematical and heuristical techniques, the basic principles of which can be conveyed to the executive-user. In fact, most of these models will be formal codifications of how the executives tend to think about these problems, with the additional advantages offered by the computer of logical analysis, computational power, and sensitivity testing.

The two major modeling techniques that will be standard equipment of marketing executives in the 1970s are decision theory and simulation. *Decision theory* is an organized approach for evaluating alternative strategies in the presence of risk or uncertainty. It calls for clarifying (1) the decision alternatives, (2) uncertain events, (3) their probabilities, and (4) the payoffs of every possible outcome. The decision maker can proceed to derive an expected payoff for each course of action and act accordingly. Decision theory has been applied by marketing executives to dozens of real marketing problems, and most of its users testify to its value as a way of organizing their attack on a problem.

The other technique, *simulation,* describes models which are developed to imitate the essential behavior of a process or system. A simulation model is usually complex and probabilistic and its properties are comprehended only by running it under different conditions and studying the output. It is hoped that experimentation on the simulation model will yield insight and meaningful forecasts of the behavior of the real system. One of the most exciting applications of the idea of simulation is in the creation of complex computer models that imitate the behavior of real markets and which can be used by the firm to test and plan marketing strategies. Computer models of markets have already been developed in such industries as petroleum, copying machines, flashbulbs, shoes, beer, and drugs, and they are under development in a number of other industries.

In addition to these modeling techniques, the marketing executive will also have access on a time-sharing basis to various statistical tools for analyzing complex relationships in multivariate data, such tools as regression and correlation analysis, discriminant analysis, factor analysis, cluster analysis, and multidimensional scaling. All told, the marketing executive of the future is headed toward a brave new world of instant information and instant decision logics. These developments will lean the future marketing executive toward a more analytical frame of mind with a heavier emphasis on planning rather than doing and profits rather than sales. If, at the same time, he maintains a creative and innovative temperament and an empathic disposition, he cannot help but be extremely effective in the marketplace.

Index

Abbott Laboratories, 16
Ackoff, Russell L., 25 n.
Ad/Mar Research Company, 142
Advanced Computer Techniques Corporation, 142
Advertising: computer in, 239ff., 367; direct mail, 295–303; economic growth and, 281; goals in, 245; industrial growth and, 281; media models in, 247–256; media problem elements in, 246–247; media selection in, 23, 243–247; research in, 281; SCANS model in, 251–256; timing in, 22–23; *see also* Advertising media models
Advertising Age, 23
Advertising agencies, 11, 17, 23, 269, 272
Advertising budget, 36
Advertising decisions, operations research and, 21–24
Advertising media models, 241–270; alternative media plan in, 293; ARTS system in, 295–303; CAM model, 273; COMPASS model, 273; demographic and marketing characteristics in, 253–254; demographic distribution in, 275; discount rate in, 293; FAST

model, 259–261; heuristic models, 269–270; history of, 272–273; linear programming in, 259–260, 264–269, 273; major types of, 247–250; Media Selection and Program Schedule in, 271–294; random outcomes in, 256–258; SCANS-FAST case history, 261–263; simulation in, 248–250, 252, 255–256, 273–274; *see also* MSPS
Advertising Reporting Test System, *see* ARTS
Advertising Research Foundation, 302
Agostini, Inc., 281
Airlines, computer services in, 133–135
Alderson, Wroe, 181
Almon, Clopper, Jr., 145
American Research Bureau, 141–142
AMS (Applied Management Sciences, Limited), 189–190
Anheuser-Busch, Inc., 11
APEX Corporation, pricing case history of, 210–235
Applied Management Sciences, Limited (AMS), 189, 193–194, 196, 201
Arcata National Corporation, 142
ARTS (Advertising Reporting Test System), 295–303; feedback loop in,

371

About the Authors

ROMAN R. ANDRUS is head of the Department of Marketing at the University of Oregon. He earned his Ph.D. at Columbia University in 1965. Dr. Andrus has served as a faculty member of the Caravan Seminar, "Computers in Marketing: Their Role and Application," of the American Marketing Association and has coordinated such business conferences as "Marketing Perspectives" and "Marketing and the Computer." He has published in several professional journals, including the *Journal of Marketing,* and his article on computer creativity has been reprinted widely. Formerly a member of the faculties of the University of Iowa, Brigham Young University, and Columbia University, Dr. Andrus has also served as assistant director of the Columbia Executive Training Program.

JOEL N. AXELROD is at present a program manager for the Business Products Group of the Xerox Corporation. He served previously as manager of business development, manager of market research and development, and corporate planning manager of the Group. Dr. Axelrod received his A.B. from Brown University and his Ph.D. from the University of Rochester. His articles have been published in the *Journal of Marketing,* the *Journal of Advertising Research, Printers' Ink,* and *Industrial Management.* He is a member of the American Marketing Association, the American Psychological Association, the Association of Public Opinion Research, the NICB Council on Marketing Research, and Sigma Xi.

JONATHAN BAYLISS came to The Gorton Corporation in 1960, serving successively as administrative consultant, distribution analyst, controller, and director of management services. He has directed the integrated development of computer systems, data processing, operations research, and administrative services. His early experience was concentrated in various phases of marketing, as a retail store manager, as an assistant industrial sales manager, and as a marketing analyst. For several years he was a sales analyst at the Carter's Ink Company and later a freelance consultant in marketing controls, sales analysis, and other aspects of administrative management.

LOUIS COHEN is vice-president in charge of research at Motivational Programmers, Inc. (MPI), a marketing research company. He is also on the faculty of Fairleigh Dickinson University. Dr. Cohen received an M.A. in psychology from the City College of New York and completed his Ph.D. in psychology at New York University. One of his major interests is the integration of quantitative and qualitative marketing research techniques. His articles on the research techniques he has developed have appeared in such publications as the *Journal of Marketing Research,* the *Journal of Advertising Research,* and the *Journal of Computer Applications* and he is the co-author of a chapter on motivation research in *Marketing Research: A Management Overview* (American Management Association, 1966). Dr. Cohen holds membership in the American Psychological Association, the American Statistical Association, and the American Marketing Association.

E. J. SANDON COX is president of Applied Management Sciences, Limited, a product development company located in Toronto, Canada. He has a B.A. in science studies from McMaster University and graduate diplomas from the business schools of the University of Toronto and McGill University. Mr. Cox has worked in technical R&D at Dofasco, Canada's second-largest steel producer, and in manufacturing management and industrial sales management at Lever Brothers Limited. He has also served as new products coordinator for Avon Products, Limited, and as senior marketing executive with a subsidiary of MacLaren Advertising. For the past four years, Mr. Cox has been a consultant specializing in the application of computers to the marketing development of existing and new products. In addition to his work as a consultant, Mr. Cox has been a guest lecturer at the American Marketing Association and at the McGill University graduate business school program.

ROBERT D. DAHLE is manager, analytical support, systems analysis at the Xerox Corporation. In this capacity he is responsible for providing analytical support in the areas of technology forecasting, resource analysis, and analytical techniques development. Previously he served as manager of Corporate Management Science where he was involved in providing analytical support for the operating divisions of the Xerox Corporation with special emphasis on the use and development of new analytic techniques. Prior to joining the Xerox Corporation, Dr. Dahle was responsible for the development of the management training program for agricultural industries in North Carolina. Dr. Dahle holds a Ph.D. in economics from North Carolina State University and has published widely in the field of new product development and analysis techniques for use in industrial development decisions.

HERBERT W. DAVIS is currently a director of Drake Sheahan/Stewart Dougall Inc. He holds an M.E. and an M.S. in industrial engineering from the Stevens Institute of Technology and has done additional graduate work in industrial management at Rutgers University. Mr. Davis has specialized in the application of computer systems and mathematical techniques to the solution of the distribution problems of a wide range of industries. At DS/SD he has been responsible for the development of the firm's library of resident computer programs for engineering and physical distribution applications. Mr. Davis is the author of numerous technical papers dealing with the use of computers and mathematical techniques in transportation, distribution, and warehousing.

EMANUEL H. DEMBY is president of Motivational Programmers, Inc. (MPI) and director of research of Fairleigh Dickinson University's College of Business Administration. Since 1947, Dr. Demby has participated in more than 1,000 studies in motivational research in the United States and abroad and was probably the first motivation researcher to turn to large-scale quantification of psychological findings. In 1967, Dr. Demby served as chairman of both the panel on Popular Culture at the American Association for Public Opinion Research Conference and of the panel on Media Research at the Vienna Conference of the World Association for Public Opinion Research. He has presented a number of papers to the Market Research Section of the American Marketing Association, the most recent describing a technique for market segmentation called psychographics, which employs "life style" variables to locate early new-product and premium-brand purchasers.

FRANZ EDELMAN joined RCA in 1950 and has been corporate director of operations research since 1950. His specialties are in the fields of applied mathematics in physical science, engineering, and business research; numerical analysis; computer usage and programming; and operations research and management science. He holds a bachelor's degree from McGill University, where he was also a teaching fellow in mathematics, and both master's and doctoral degrees in applied mathematics from Brown University. Dr. Edelman is a member of the Society of Industrial and Applied Mathematics, the Operations Research Society of America, and The Institute of Management Sciences.

JOHN W. GAROFALO, a member of the GAF Corporation's information systems staff, received his B.S. degree in mathematics from St. Bonaventure University in 1953. He entered the computer field upon graduation and has worked in all phases of computer applications covering commercial, scientific, real-time, and operations research. Formerly manager of the GAF Corporate Systems Department, Mr. Garofalo has worked on projects related to atomic submarines, Polaris missiles, Apollo projects, and sales analysis; he is currently developing a computerized mathematical forecasting system utilizing operations research techniques.

PETER J. GRAY is director of market development at Scan-Optics, Inc. where he is responsible for marketing planning, applications development, and systems and sales support. He was previously manager of market development at Xerox Corporation and served in marketing and engineering positions at IBM. He has been involved in the development and application of a variety of marketing models to the problems of forecasting, market analysis, sales optimization, competition, pricing, and other areas of marketing.

ROBERT A. HAMMOND is principal of McKinsey & Company, Inc. His background and experience in engineering management and consulting consist of the following: radar officer, Royal Navy, 1945–57; five years in research, development, and production in electronics industry at British Telecommunications Research and Marconi Company; systems management and engineering, R.C.A. International Division, 1953–57; marketing, technical planning, and administration of large communications systems in North and South America; consultant for engineering economic studies, 1957; project manager, missile systems at Sylvania Electric, 1958; management consultant at McKinsey & Company, Inc., working on problems in planning and control, manufacturing, and marketing, 1960 to present. His area of specialty is the application of computers to top management decision making and problem solving. Mr. Hammond received a B.S. in physics (with honors) from Birmingham University and an M.S. in mathematics from London University.

LESLIE M. HARRIS is the executive vice-president of AMIC, Automated Management Information Concepts, Inc., which provides data processing services to the media and marketing departments of a number of major advertising agencies. AMIC markets MSPS to the advertising community. He was formerly professor of marketing at Long Island University and was also associated with the Bureau of Business Research. He has also served as a consultant in industry on statistical computer applications.

THOMAS C. JONES is a management consultant with Case and Company Inc. and was responsible for the initial development and installation of COSMOS in retail food stores. His experience covers a wide range of management consulting practice including pricing, sales force management, marketing, and manufacturing feasibility studies. Before joining his present company, Mr. Jones was a product manager with a manufacturer of industrial machinery. He was awarded a Bachelor of Science degree in mechanical engineering by Brown University and a Master of Business Administration degree from Harvard Business School.

EVELYN KONRAD heads the marketing consulting firm that bears her name— Evelyn Konrad Associates. The firm's particular strength is in the conception and development of R&D systems for service industry. The firm also has a long record of success in corporate and financial public relations. Evelyn Konrad's articles on diverse marketing subjects have appeared in leading business and marketing publications. Her book *Marketing Research: A Management Overview* was published by the American Management Association in 1966. She earned her B.A. and M.A. at Stanford University and is a Ph.D. candidate in economics, finance, and marketing at the Graduate School of Business of New York University.

PHILIP KOTLER is A. Montgomery Ward Professor of Marketing at the Graduate School of Management of Northwestern University and advisory editor of the Holt, Rinehart and Winston Marketing Series. He earned his doctorate at Massachusetts Institute of Technology. An active consultant to many companies on marketing planning and information systems, Professor Kotler is the author of *Marketing Management: Analysis, Planning and Control* (Prentice-Hall, Inc., 1967) and *Quantitative Marketing Analysis* (Holt, Rinehart and Winston, 1970). He has also served as chairman of the College of Marketing of The Institute of Management Sciences.

A. R. "HAP" SOLOMON is manager of strategy planning and simulation for the Business Products Group of the Xerox Corporation. He has also held managerial positions in the fields of market statistics, product pricing, distribution, and national service. Prior to joining Xerox in 1963, he was with Western Electric and Columbia University. Mr. Solomon received both a B.S. and an M.S. in industrial engineering from Columbia University as well as an M.B.A. in finance and marketing. He is a member of the American Society of Mechanical Engineers, The Institute of Management Science, the American Institute of Industrial Engineers, the Association for Computing Machinery, and the American Finance Association.

ARTHUR B. TOAN, JR. joined Price Waterhouse & Co. in September 1936. He was admitted to partnership in 1953 and became senior management advisory services partner in 1959. Mr. Toan received his B.A. degree, magna cum laude, Phi Beta Kappa, from Dartmouth College in 1936. He has served as a member of the American Management Association's Planning Council, on the Management Services Committee and as chairman of the ad hoc committee on Computers of the American Institute of Certified Public Accountants, and as consulting editor of *Management Services*. Mr. Toan has published about 50 articles and books on various management-oriented subjects.

ALLAN VESLEY, The Sperry and Hutchinson Company's director of information systems, has been a pioneer in the use and development of computer applications to management operational and decision problems. He originally plunged The Sperry and Hutchinson Company into its first computer project in 1956, investigated the potential of electronics, and. installed the first in-house computer for the company in 1958. From that time on, he began to encourage the development of a large data communications system, then directed the design of applications for inventory control and demand forecasting, turning marketing data into marketing information and management accounting and control. In 1965, he organized the firm's own operations research department. He has taught programming, computer system design, and other management science courses at the American Management Association, at the National Association of Accountants, and at New York University. He is a graduate of Cornell and has an M.B.A. degree from the Graduate School of Business Administration of New York University.

ART YOUMANS, JR. is the assistant to the president of Gernsback Publications, Inc. He is the founder and former president of The Society of Arts, Inc., a New York marketing research firm specializing in finding new uses for "old" products and services. Formerly, Mr. Youmans was a senior management consultant, performing marketing research studies for domestic and international clients. Prior to this, he founded and was president of The International Arts Advertising Agency. Mr. Youmans is active as a guest lecturer at local universities. He has contributed to an article in *Sales Management* and is the author of three articles in *Marketing Review*.

LAWRENCE F. YOUNG is director of Marketing and Management Sciences Division of Dataplan, Inc., a computer service and consulting company specializing in marketing applications. In this position and in his prior position as vice-president in charge of operations research for Interpublic's MIDAS component, Mr. Young has been responsible for the development of many of the media models described in his chapter. He has been applying mathematics and the computer to marketing and advertising problems since 1960 when he joined Interpublic, Inc. Prior to that, Mr. Young was a consulting analyst with the Service Bureau Corporation and a computer systems analyst with the Western Electric Company. He lectured on decision theory and operations research in the graduate division of Baruch College, City University. He holds a master's degree in operations research and a bachelor's degree in industrial engineering from New York University.

TOM TENG-PIN YU is the president of Innovation Research Corporation, a leading technical consulting company specializing in the development of a number of complex mathematical models. His experience has included positions with the National Bureau of Economic Research and working as research manager for the Systems Programming Group of the Univac Division of the Sperry Rand Corporation.

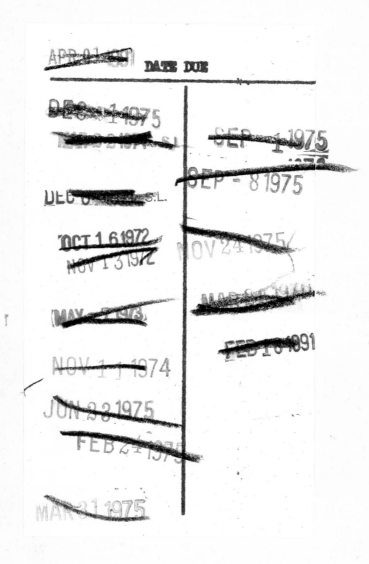